# A HISTORY OF JEWISH LITERATURE
## VOLUME II

A VOLUME IN THE
CWRU PRESS TRANSLATIONS

## Israel Zinberg's *History of Jewish Literature*

| | | |
|---|---|---|
| Vol. I | *Part One:* | The Arabic-Spanish Period |
| Vol. II | *Part Two:* | French and German Jewry in the Early Middle Ages |
| | *Part Three:* | The Jewish Community of Medieval Italy |
| Vol. III | *Part Four:* | The Struggle of Mysticism and Tradition Against Philosophical Rationalism |
| Vol. IV | *Part Five:* | Italian Jewry in the Renaissance Era |
| Vol. V | *Part Six:* | The Jewish Center of Culture in the Ottoman Empire |
| Vol. VI | *Part Seven:* | The German-Polish Cultural Center |
| Vol. VII | *Part Eight:* | Old Yiddish Literature from Its Origins to the Haskalah Period |
| Vol. VIII | *Part Nine:* | The Berlin Haskalah |
| Vol. IX | *Part Ten:* | Hasidism and Enlightenment (1780–1820) |
| Vol. X | *Part Eleven:* | The Science of Judaism and Galician Haskalah |
| Vol. XI | *Part Twelve:* | The Haskalah Movement in Russia |
| Vol. XII | *Part Thirteen:* | Haskalah at Its Zenith (published posthumously, 1966) |

An Analytic Index to the *History of Jewish Literature* will appear in Vol. XII.

*Israel Zinberg*

# A HISTORY OF JEWISH LITERATURE

TRANSLATED AND EDITED BY BERNARD MARTIN

## *French and German Jewry in the Early Middle Ages*

## *The Jewish Community of Medieval Italy*

THE PRESS OF
CASE WESTERN RESERVE UNIVERSITY
CLEVELAND & LONDON
1972

The full translation into English of Israel Zinberg's HISTORY OF JEWISH LITERATURE, comprising twelve volumes, is being brought to publication by the generous and continuing support of the Memorial Foundation for Jewish Culture.


Printed in the United States of America.

**Library of Congress Cataloging in Publication Data**

Zinberg, Israel, 1873–1938.
A history of Jewish literature.

Translation of Di geshikhte fun der literatur bay Yidn.
Includes bibliographical references.
CONTENTS: v. 1. The Arabic-Spanish period.—v. 2. French and German Jewry in the early Middle Ages. The Jewish community of medieval Italy.
1. Jewish literature—History and criticisms.
I. Title.
PJ5008.Z5313 809'.889'24 72-183310
ISBN 0-8295-0230-0 (v. 2)

# Contents

A note on Israel Zinberg / ix

Acknowledgments / xi

Transliteration of Hebrew Terms / xiii

Abbreviations / xv

**PART II: FRENCH AND GERMAN JEWRY IN THE EARLY MIDDLE AGES**

*Chapter One:* BIBLICAL EXEGESIS IN FRANCE; RASHI AND THE TOSAFISTS / 3

The cultural situation of the Franco-German community — The vernacular and the language of culture — The cultural role of the Kalonymos family — Rabbenu Gershom, Meor Ha-Golah — The Bible commentators of France — Menaḥem bar Ḥelbo and Joseph Kara — Rashi and his significance; his influence on Christian scholars and theologians — The Tosafists — Rashi's grandchildren: Rashbam and Rabbenu Tam.

*Chapter Two:* SUPPLICATIONS AND LAMENTATIONS IN THE PERIOD OF THE CRUSADES / 23

The terrors of the Crusades and their echoes in Hebrew literature — Supplications and laments — Memorial books and chronicles of that era.

*Chapter Three:* THE *SEFER ḤASIDIM* / 35

Books of ethical instruction — The *Sefer Ḥasidim* and its authors — The horrors of the Middle Ages — Generations of darkness and cruelty — The ethical foundations of the *Sefer Ḥasidim* —

The *Sefer Ḥasidim* as a popular book and mirror of Jewish life — The significance of the *Sefer Ḥasidim* as a source for Jewish folklore.

*Chapter Four:* JEWISH MYSTICISM; ELEAZAR OF WORMS / 57

The first mystical tendencies among Jews — The *Sefer Yetzirah* and the Yordei Merkavah — Their doctrine and world outlook — The mystical doctrine is transported from the Orient into the Rhine region — Persecutions and troubles strengthen mystical tendencies — Jehudah Ḥasid as a mystic — Eleazar of Worms and his work.

*Chapter Five:* THE KIMḤIS, TIBBONIDES, AND OTHER PROVENÇAL SCHOLARS / 77

Provence and its cultural role — The description of Benjamin the Traveller — Abraham bar Ḥiyya — The cultural and enlightening role of the Kimḥis — The polemic work of Jacob ben Reuben — Joseph Kimḥi as grammarian and polemicist — The brothers Moses and David Kimḥi — Jehudah Ibn Tibbon as translator; his *Tzevaah* (Testament) — The influence of Maimonides on the scholars of Provence — The translators of Maimonides' *Moreh Nevuchim* (Guide for the Perplexed) — The Jewish poets in Provence: Joseph Ezobi, Abraham Bedersi, and Isaac Gorni — The Talmudists Zeraḥyah Ha-Levi, the author of *Ha-Maor,* and Rabbi Abraham ben David (Ravad) of Posquières, the author of *Ha-Hassagot.*

*Chapter Six:* THE BEGINNING OF THE WAR AGAINST RATIONALISM / 103

The attack of Rabbi Abraham ben David, the author of *Ha-Hassagot,* and of Meir Abulafia — The reply of the scholars of Provence — Averroes and his influence on Judaism — Allegorical interpretation of the Bible — The influence of the Christian theologians — Samuel Ibn Tibbon and his *Yikkavu Ha-Mayyim* — The Jewish allegorists — The preacher Moses of Coucy — The attack of Solomon of Montpellier and his collaborators, Jonah Gerondi and David ben Saul — The poet Meshullam ben Solomon

Dapiera — The Maimunists against the rabbis of France — The open letters of Naḥmanides and Meir Abulafia; polemical literature in letter form — Solomon of Montpellier under the ban — David Kimḥi and his propaganda journey — Joseph ben Todros Ha-Levi and Jehudah Alfachar — Epigrams as weapons of struggle — Solomon's denunciation — Maimonides' work on the pyre; the tragic end.

**PART III: THE JEWISH COMMUNITY OF MEDIEVAL ITALY**

*Chapter One:* THE FOUR ELDERS; SHABBETAI DONNOLO; *JOSIPPON* / 135

The role of Italy as culture mediator — The legend about the four elders — Shabbetai Donnolo and his work — The Catholic saint Nilus and the Christian clergy — *Josippon* and its versions — The Alexander romances in world literature — The literary significance of *Josippon.*

*Chapter Two:* THE BEGINNINGS OF LITURGICAL POETRY IN ITALY; THE *SEFER YUḤASIN* / 151

The first religious poets in Italy — The *paytan* Shephatyah, his son Amittai, and Solomon Ha-Bavli — The Midrashim literature — *Tanna De-Be Eliahu* — The *Sefer Zerubbabel* and the hope for the coming of the Messiah — The legend of Armilus — Aḥimaaz' *Sefer Yuḥasin* and its literary-historical value.

*Chapter Three:* ITALIAN JEWRY COMES OF AGE; ANATOLI'S *MALMAD HA-TALMIDIM* / 165

The slight scientific knowledge of the Italian Jews in the eleventh century — Nathan bar Yeḥiel and his *Aruch* — The enlightenment role of Abraham Ibn Ezra and Solomon Parḥon in Italy — The cultural significance of the Crusades — Christian Europe and the Oriental world — The scientific centers in south Italy and the role of Jewish scholars — The Emperor Frederick II as freethinker and his friendship with Jewish scholars — Jacob Anatoli and his *Malmad Ha-Talmidim* — Anatoli as Maimunist — Anatoli's intellectual aristocratism.

*Chapter Four:* SCHOLARS AND POETS IN ITALY / 181

Anatoli's school — Moses of Salerno and the Latin translation of *A Guide for the Perplexed* — Jewish scholars and their significance for Italian culture in the Middle Ages — The cultural role of the Roman community — The brothers Zedekiah ben Abraham and Benjamin ben Abraham — Benjamin's satire *Massa Ge Ḥizzayon* — Yeḥiel ben Yekutiel and his book of ethical instruction *Maalot Ha-Middot* — Patrons and manuscript copyists — The rationalist Zeraḥyah Ḥen and his literary work — A controversy between two Maimunists — Hillel of Verona as a personality; his philosophical-ethical work.

*Chapter Five:* IMMANUEL OF ROME / 201

The first rays of the Renaissance — The rise of Italian national poetry and its influence on Jewish literature — Immanuel of Rome and Dante's circle — Immanuel as freethinker and harbinger of the coming Renaissance — Immanuel and Petrarch — Immanuel as "master of love and passion" — Humor and satire in Immanuel's work — Immanuel's poem *Ha-Tofet Veha-Eden.*

*Chapter Six:* THE ROMAN POETS; KALONYMOS BAR KALONYMOS / 219

The Roman Poets — Jehudah Siciliano and Joab; the poet Naḥum and his work — Kalonymos bar Kalonymos as translator; his parody *Masechat Purim* and satire *Even Boḥan* — The epic *Iggeret Baalei Ḥayyim* — Jehudah Romano as culture bearer and enlightener.

Bibliographical Notes / 233

Glossary of Hebrew Terms / 245

Index / 249

# *A Note on Israel Zinberg*

DR. ISRAEL ZINBERG is widely regarded as one of the foremost historians of Jewish literature. Born in Russia in 1873 and educated at various universities in Germany and Switzerland, he devoted more than twenty years to the writing, in Yiddish, of his monumental *Die Geshichte fun der Literatur bei Yidn* (History of Jewish Literature). This work, published in eight volumes in Vilna, 1929–1937, is a comprehensive and authoritative study of Jewish literary creativity in Europe from its beginnings in tenth-century Spain to the end of the Haskalah period in nineteenth-century Russia. Based on a meticulous study of all the relevant primary source material and provided with full documentation, Zinberg's *History* is a notable exemplar of the tradition of modern Jewish scholarship known as *die Wissenschaft des Judentums* (the Science of Judaism).

In addition to his *magnum opus*, Zinberg, who earned his living as a chemical engineer, wrote numerous other valuable monographs and articles on Jewish history and literature in Russian, Hebrew, and Yiddish. In 1938, during the Stalinist purges, he was arrested by the Soviet police and sentenced to exile in Siberia. He died in a concentration camp hospital in Vladivostok in that same year.

The reader who wishes a fuller introduction is invited to consult the Translator's Introduction to Volume I of Zinberg's *History of Jewish Literature.*

# *Acknowledgments*

The generous support of the Memorial Foundation for Jewish Culture, New York City, and of Mr. Leonard Ratner and the Ratner family, Cleveland, is gratefully acknowledged by publisher and translator alike. Without this generosity it would not have been possible for Israel Zinberg's monumental work to reach the new audience that it is hoped a translation into English will afford. The editor and translator wishes to express his appreciation to his friend Dr. Arthur J. Lelyveld, Rabbi of the Fairmount Temple of Cleveland and President (1966–72) of the American Jewish Congress, for his aid in securing a grant from the Memorial Foundation for Jewish Culture for the publication of this work. Finally, the editor and translator desires to acknowledge his gratitude to the staff of the Press of Case Western Reserve University for their kind helpfulness at every stage in the publication of this work.

# *Transliteration of Hebrew Terms*

| | | | |
|---|---|---|---|
| א is not transliterated | ו = v (where not a vowel) | ל = l | פ = f |
| | | מ = m | צ = tz |
| בּ = b | ז = z | נ = n | ק = k |
| ב = v | ח = ḥ | ס = s | ר = r |
| ג, גּ = g | ט = t | ע is not transliterated | שׁ = sh |
| ד, דּ = d | י = y | | שׂ = s |
| ה = h | כּ = k | פּ = p | ת, תּ = t |
| | כ = ch | | |

| | |
|---|---|
| ◌ָ = a | ◌ֶ = e |
| ◌ַ = a | ◌ִ = i |
| וֹ, ◌ֹ = o | ◌ֵ = ei |
| וּ, ◌ֻ = u | ◌ֱ = e |
| short ◌ָ = o | ◌ֳ = o |
| ◌ֵי = ei | ◌ֲ = a |

vocal *sheva* = e

silent *sheva* is not transliterated

# *Abbreviations*

| | |
|---|---|
| *JQR* | *Jewish Quarterly Review* |
| *JQR*, n.s. | *Jewish Quarterly Review*, new series |
| *MGWJ* | *Monatsschrift für die Geschichte und Wissenschaft des Judentums* |
| *PAAJR* | *Proceedings of the American Academy for Jewish Research* |
| *REJ* | *Revue des Études Juives* |
| *ZHB* | *Zeitschrift für hebräische Bibliographie* |

# FRENCH AND GERMAN JEWRY IN THE EARLY MIDDLE AGES

# CHAPTER ONE

## *Biblical Exegesis in France;* RASHI AND THE TOSAFISTS

S THE peoples of the world behave, so also is the way in most places among the Jews."[1] The validity of this generalization, expressed by the authors of the most popular Jewish book of ethical instruction in the Middle Ages, becomes obvious when one compares the cultural situation of the Spanish Jews at the beginning of the second millennium of the Christian era with that of their Franco-German brethren.

We speak of Franco-German Jewry as *one* community because in that period there was as yet no noticeable cultural distinction between the Jews of northern France and those of Germany. The Jewish community of both lands was identical, sharing the same way of life. The influence of the era of the powerful emperor Charlemagne and his heirs, when the lands on both sides of the Rhine remained politically united, was still powerfully felt. Beyond this, it must be borne in mind that the majority of German Jewry at that time consisted of the communities of the Rhine region, the closest neighbor of the French provinces. The Jews who settled in the Rhineland migrated from the Roman states and their

1. *Sefer Ḥasidim,* No. 1107.

route passed through France.[2] It is also quite probable that they brought with them from there the Romance vernacular. Even considerably later, in the twelfth and the first half of the thirteenth centuries, when the Jews of Germany had already adopted the German dialects, they still spoke fluent French as well, owing to their close bonds with their French co-religionists and the intensive commerce they carried on with France.[3]

The largest Jewish communities developed in the so-called episcopal cities, such as Mainz, Metz, Trier, Worms, Cologne, and Regensburg. In the high Middle Ages, when the feudal order was still in full sway and the Christian urban populace did not as yet play a role of any significance, the Jews formed the middle class, the class of merchants and middlemen. At that time the Jews were the major international traders; almost the entire wholesale trade was in their hands. Jewish merchants dispatched their own freight vessels from Cologne to England and the principal ports of France and Italy, as well as to the great mercantile centers of the Oriental countries. The spiritual princes of that era, the bishops, who as practical men of affairs wanted urban life to develop as quickly and strongly as possible, understood how to make use of such an important mercantile element as the Jews. The relationship between the bishops and the Jewish populace is clearly expressed in the first sentence with which the bishop Rüdiger of Speyer begins his famous *privilegia*, with which he endowed the Jews in the year 1084: "Since I wish to make a city out of the town of

2. See Stobbe, *Die Juden in Deutschland während des Mittelalters*, p. 18: "*Das sie (die Juden) in grösserer Zahl nur in der südlichen Hälfte von Deutschland und in den Westen, dagegen bis in das Ende des XIII Jahrhunderts . . . so gut wie gar nicht in den an der Ost und Nordsee gelegenen Städten und in den nördlichen Marken vorkommen. Dieser Umstand rechtfertigt die Annahme, dass sie gröstenteils von Italien und Frankreich nach Deutschland eingewandert sind.*"

3. Very interesting in this respect is the abovementioned book of ethical instruction, the *Sefer Ḥasidim*, produced in the course of the twelfth and first half of the thirteenth centuries. In it numerous words are accompanied either by a German or a French translation, and sometimes both. See for example Nos. 3, 15, 18, 44, 205, 244, 893, and 1143. Another thirteenth-century resident of the Rhine region, the compiler of the small *Aruch* of which the well-known Christian scholar Buxtorf made use, also translated most of the words of his dictionary in both languages, German and French (see Kaufmann's article in *MGWJ*, 1885, p. 232). We observe a similar phenomenon among the early Bible exegetes of northern France—Menaḥem bar Ḥelbo, Joseph Kara, and Rashi. These translate many Biblical words not only into French but also into German (see M. Littmann's monograph *Joseph Kara*, p. 20, and A. Geiger, *Parschandatha*, p. 33).

Speyer, I have invited the Jews to enter." In the same document the bishop further declares: "I think I will increase the honor of our city a thousandfold if I invite Jews into its gates" (*putavi milies amplificare honorem loci nostri et sei*).

Until the end of the eleventh century, i.e., until the period of the Crusades, the Jews lived in tranquillity under the protection of the emperor and the bishops and exercised an important function in the economic life of western Germany. They took a large part in the commerce of Mainz with the cities on the Rhine and the Main. Like the Jews of Mainz, the Jews of Worms were also famed as merchants. They dealt in wine, dyes, salt, meat, and medicaments. Jewish traders used to purchase furs from the Russians and slaves in other Slavic lands and sell these to French Jewish merchants, who would transport the merchandise on to Spain.[4]

As merchants, both the German and French Jews came into close contact with Christians. The result of this intercourse, however, was altogether different than in Arabic Spain with its advanced civilization. The Christian populace in Germany and northern France at that time was still at a rather low level of culture. The only persons of knowledge at the time were the higher clergy, and even their knowledge was extremely one-sided, confined to the realm of Christian doctrine. Even this limited subject matter was studied in the only cultural language of Christian Europe, Latin. But the Jews looked upon Latin as the language of their fiercest enemy, the Catholic Church. This, for them, was the "Christian language," the "language of the priests." As far as the other strata of the Christian populace are concerned, literate persons were to be found among these only with the greatest infrequency. It is sufficient to note that even the brilliant twelfth-century German poet Wolfram of Eschenbach, who was of the nobility, could neither read nor write.[5]

Thus it is readily understandable that the Franco-German Jews, living in such an uncultured environment, had very slight knowledge of the sciences and philosophical matters. Intellectually isolated, they devoted their mental powers exclusively to religious questions connected with Jewish faith and law. According to an ancient tradition, the first disseminators of Jewish knowledge in the Rhine provinces came from Italy. "Rabbi Moses bar Kalony-

4. Interesting details about the economic situation and the commerce of the Jews in the Rhine provinces is to be found in *Teshuvot Ḥachmei Tzarefat Ve-Lutir*.

5. He himself relates this with frank simplicity:

*Swar an den Buochen stet gerschrieben*
*Den bin ich künstelos beliben*

mos of Lucca," Rabbi Eleazar of Worms[6] relates, "was the first who came here from Lombardy [north Italy], he with his two sons Kalonymos and Yekutiel, his relative Rabbi Yekutiel, and a few other distinguished men. The emperor Charles brought all these with him from Lombardy and settled them in Mainz."[7]

For a long time it was difficult to determine which emperor Charles this was, Charles the Great (Charlemagne) or his grandson Charles the Bald.[8] Thanks only to the discovery and publication of the *Sefer Yuḥasin* of Aḥimaaz ben Paltiel, which we shall discuss later, it has been established that Moses bar Kalonymos' teacher in matters of Kabbalah, Abu Aharon, lived in Italy in the sixties of the ninth century. Thus it is clear that the migration of the Kalonymos family to Germany took place in the time of Charles the Bald.

It was these Jewish scholars from Italy who began to build a center of Torah in the Rhine provinces. The first significant scholar who emerged there is Rabbi Jehudah ben Meir Ha-Kohen of Mainz, better known by the name Sir Leontin. He was the teacher of the famous Rabbenu Gershom Meor Ha-Golah (the Light of the Exile), with whose activity a new era in the cultural history of the Franco-German Jewish community is inaugurated.

Very few details of the life and activity of this extremely important figure have come down to us. Only the year of his birth, 960, has been definitely established, but on the year of his death there are differences of scholarly opinion. According to certain sources,[9] Rabbenu Gershom died in the year 1028. Others,[10] how-

6. On Rabbi Eleazar, see *infra.* Moses bar Kalonymos is the author of the well-known liturgical poem *Emat Norotecha.*
7. See *Letterbode,* X, 112–13; *Matzref Le-Ḥochmah,* first edition, p. 146.
8. According to an old register in a parchment manuscript of the *Maḥzor,* this event is supposed to have occurred in the year 787 (see Carmoly, *Annalen* [1839], p. 222). According to the report of another anonymous author, the settlement of the Italian scholars in Germany took place not earlier than the year 810 (see L. Zunz, *Literaturgeschichte,* p. 625). The well-known historian Joseph Ha-Kohen declares explicitly in his *Emek Ha-Bacha* that it occurred in the time of Charlemagne. A later historian (Ghirondi, in his *Toledot Gedolei Yisrael*) asserts that it took place "in the days of King Charles the Second who was called Calvo." The famous Talmudist Rabbi Solomon Luria, in his *Responsa* (No. 29), gives a still later date, the year 849 after the destruction of the Second Temple, i.e., the year 918–19, at which time both Charlemagne and Charles the Second had long been dead.
9. See *Kerem Ḥemed,* V, 108; *ibid.,* VIII, 107; Neubauer, *Catalogue of the Hebrew Manuscripts in the Bodleian Library,* p. 775.
10. *Sheelot U-Teshuvot Rashal,* No. 29; Zunz, *op. cit.,* p. 238; I. H. Weiss, *Dor Dor Ve-Doreshav,* IV, 279.

ever, believe that he died in 1040. His birthplace has also not been determined. Some point to Metz, others to France; still others believe that he was born on the banks of the Rhine. In any case, his major activity was carried on in the city in which his teacher lived, Mainz. There he founded his famous *yeshivah* or Talmudic academy, to which hundreds of students from the cities of the Rhine and France flocked. To establish the study of the Talmud on solid foundations Rabbenu Gershom considered it necessary, first of all, to determine the correct text of the Talmudic tractates, to compare various manuscripts and, in this way, to rectify the errors that copyists had made. After much effort, a more or less accurate text, which Gershom attempted to explain and make comprehensible through his commentary,[11] finally appeared.

It is not, however, to be imagined that this first and oldest commentary to the Talmud was called forth by purely religious factors. Proficiency in the Talmud, in its laws and statutes, was desired not for the sake of the commandments and piety alone; it was also a matter of practical necessity. The Talmud, which originated under other social conditions and in an altogether different environment, was, nevertheless, for the Jewish communities of central Europe the authoritative *corpus juris*, the accepted code of law. However, this code was not only written in a little-understood language but also required adaptation to the new demands of life. In this respect Rabbenu Gershom played a tremendous reforming role. A man of iron will and great moral strength, he became even in his lifetime the foremost authority in the Jewish world, not only in Germany and France but even in Italy.[12] Jews applied to him from all countries with questions about religious and juridical matters. Taking account of the requirements of actual life, Rabbenu Gershom employed his vast authority to regulate the social exigencies of his brethren through special "ordinances" (*takkanot*) which were quickly accepted by all of European Jewry as inviolable statutes.[13] Among these ordinances, for ex-

11. Some historians believe that Rabbenu Gershom wrote a commentary on the entire Talmud, but this commentary was eventually lost. A medieval scholar, Menaḥem ben Zeraḥ, who saw the commentary, indicates that it was extremely long. See the introduction to *Tzedah La-Derech*.

12. Rashi speaks in one of his *responsa* of the great reverence with which all the Jews of Europe regarded him: "Rabbenu Gershom . . . who enlightens the eyes of the exile, and from whose mouth all of us live, and the pupils of whose pupils are all the Jews of Germany, France, and Italy." See *Otzar Neḥmad*, II, 115; *Teshuvot Ḥachmei Tzarefat Ve-Lutir*, No. 21.

13. To be sure, several modern scholars have shown that some of the

ample, are that forbidding polygamy and another to the effect that a divorce is valid only when both parties consent to it. He also lightened considerably the stringency of the laws concerning proselytes and apostates who changed their minds and wished to return to Judaism. To this day also the "ban of Rabbenu Gershom" which forbids anyone to read a letter addressed to another without the latter's permission remains in effect.

To be sure, it is quite possible that not all the *takkanot* bearing Rabbenu Gershom's name were actually enacted by him. The fact, however, that so many important ordinances were attributed to him demonstrates how powerfully he was inscribed in the minds of the people as a reformer and legislator. Thus, Rabbenu Gershom's significance consists not only in the fact that the Talmudic academies founded by him and his method of studying and interpreting the Talmud became models for later generations. He was also one of the first and greatest of the figures who laid the foundations of culture for the Franco-German Jewish community. Not without reason did he remain in the memory of later times as the Meor Ha-Golah, the bright star of the exiled people.

Like Moses bar Kalonymos, Rabbenu Gershom was a liturgical poet.[14] He was not, however, endowed with genuine literary talent, and his poems and hymns have slight poetic value. Only his well-known supplication "Zechor Berit Avraham Ve-Akedat Yitzḥak" moves one with its pathos:

> . . . the Holy City and all its environs have become a mockery and a scorn, all its treasures robbed and lost. One thing alone has remained to us—the sacred Torah. . . . The covenant which Thou hast sealed with our fathers, Thy great mercy and grace from of old—let these be remembered for us who are oppressed and persecuted, who are every day slaughtered for Thy name's sake.[15]

At the same time that the *yeshivot* which Rabbenu Gershom founded in the Rhine provinces became centers of Talmudic knowledge, there began to develop in northern France a school of exegetes whose aim was to investigate and interpret the text of the Bible. This school of commentators separated into two tendencies or movements. One movement proceeded on the way of

---

*takkanot* which bear Rabbenu Gershom's name were issued no earlier than the twelfth and thirteenth centuries. On the question of the extent to which the "*takkanot* of Rabbenu Gershom" really are his, see L. Finkelstein and F. Baer in *MGWJ*, 1930, pp. 23–34.

14. On this see Landshuth, *Ammudei Ha-Avodah*.
15. The prayer is recited on the eve of Rosh Hashanah.

*derush*, which had been laid down by the creators of the Midrashim, the preachers of the Talmudic and Geonic period, for whom the "verse," the Bible text, was only a kind of introduction to their ingenious elaboration of legends and moral teaching. The second movement set for itself a completely different task: to understand and explain the plain or literal meaning of the text.

The founders of this exegetical school, with its two tendencies, were the brothers Shimeon Kara and Menaḥem bar Ḥelbo. The former is believed to be the compiler of the popular collection of Midrashim entitled *Yalkut Shimeoni*,[16] in which all the legends of the Midrash based on the Biblical text are assembled in very ingenious fashion. Of an entirely different sort was the activity of Menaḥem bar Ḥelbo. Of his biography we know almost nothing. On the basis of his surname, Kara, we can assume that he may have been a reader of the Torah in synagogues and houses of study and a commentator who explained the meaning of the text for the young. It is possible that it was precisely this occupation that suggested to Menaḥem bar Ḥelbo the idea of devoting himself especially to explication of the Bible and becoming a Bible exegete.[17] Of all his explanations (*pitronim*) and commentaries to various Biblical books, only a few fragments, quoted in the writings of later French commentators, have come down to us.[18] Even these fragments, however, give us a clear picture of bar Ḥelbo's method. He was a man of sober, lucid intellect who set himself the task of expounding the Biblical text, not seeking in it symbolic allusions or relying on various legends, but clarifying the meaning of each word and investigating the material in a lexicographical fashion. This task was, under the circumstances, an extremely difficult one. The Jewish Bible commentators of Arabic Spain were in a more advantageous position. They had before themselves classical mod-

16. See Solomon Judah Rapoport (Shir) in *Kerem Ḥemed*, VII, 4–12. To be sure, Rapoport's view that the compiler of the *Yalkut Shimeoni* was Menaḥem bar Ḥelbo's brother has numerous opponents. The most prominent of these is A. Epstein (see his work *Rabbi Shimeon Kara Veha-Yalkut Shimeoni* [1891]), who believes, with Zunz, that the *Yalkut Shimeoni* was produced in the thirteenth century. It is more probable, however, that the *Yalkut* was composed in the time of Menaḥem bar Ḥelbo but that in later times numerous changes were made in it and many passages added.
17. See A. Geiger, *Parschandatha;* Einstein, "Josef Kara und sein Kommentar zu Koheleth," *Magazin*, 1886, p. 219; E. M. Lipschütz, *Rabbi Shelomoh Yitzḥaki* (Warsaw, 1912), pp. 154–57.
18. A complete collection of the *pitronim* of bar Ḥelbo that have been preserved is given by S. Poznanski in *Sefer Ha-Yovel Le-Naḥum Sokolow*, pp. 402–39. See also Dukes, *Literaturblatt des Orients*, 1847, pp. 344–48.

els: first, the Arabic school of grammarians who had raised scientific philology to a very high level, and second, the work of the great Jewish philologists, such as Ḥayyuj, Jannaḥ, and Samuel Ha-Nagid. Bar Ḥelbo's mother tongue, however, was the still undeveloped French dialect, and of the Jewish grammarians of the Spanish school only the works of Menaḥem Ibn Saruk and Dunash ben Labrat were known to him, since these alone were written in Hebrew. Despite the very limited scientific instruments of which bar Ḥelbo could make use, he succeeded, as a result of his philological and critical sense, in accomplishing a great deal in accurately explaining the literal meaning of the Biblical text.

Menaḥem bar Ḥelbo created an entire school. The most important of his followers was his pupil and nephew, Joseph ben Shimeon Kara, and it is due to him and his commentaries that some fragments of Menaḥem's *pitronim* have come down to us. On Joseph Kara's life also we have very little information.[19] It is known only that he lived in Rashi's birthplace, Troyes, and was in fact one of Rashi's intimates. As a Bible commentator, Joseph Kara remained faithful to the principles that his teacher Menaḥem had established, and sought to show how greatly in error are those who, in their exposition of the text, confuse the way of simple, literal explanation (*peshat*) with the way of homiletic explanation (*derush*) and do not even realize that these are two altogether different systems. "You must know," he writes in his commentary to the Book of Samuel,

> that Holy Scripture is written clearly and precisely, without allusions at which one must guess, and it is not necessary to make use of proofs and arguments from the Midrash. The Midrash is a separate study, which our sages ordained in order to beautify and adorn the Torah. He, however, who does not understand the literal meaning of the Torah and endeavors to grasp its content with the aid of the Midrash is like a man who is carried along by a powerful sea and struggles with the waves, trying to catch hold of anything that he touches with his hands. One who wishes seriously to investigate God's word must, first of all, endeavor to understand the plain meaning of each individual word.[20]

Joseph Kara practiced what he preached. In all his commentaries he is loyal to the requirements established by himself and his uncle, and interprets the text exclusively in terms of its plain meaning. An interesting point is worth mentioning here. Like Menaḥem bar

19. See Einstein, *op. cit.*, pp. 206–61.
20. See *ibid.*, p. 250.

Ḥelbo, Joseph Kara was distinguished by his large measure of common sense. But the austere and acute mind of this man of the eleventh century was combined with an integrity thanks to which he frequently expressed in his commentaries ideas which doubtless foreshadow the free scientific criticism of later times. For that era this was plainly heresy, but Kara himself, with his simple world outlook, never even suspected such a thing. For example, he notes the sentence in the First Book of Samuel (9:9), "He who is nowadays called a prophet [*navi*] was formerly called a seer [*roeh*]," and remarks: "From this it follows that at the time the Book of Samuel was written, the man who was once called *roeh* was now called *navi;* this shows that the book was composed long after the prophet Samuel."[21] Kara's remark is, indeed, very just. In the entire Bible a prophet is nowhere called by the term *roeh* except in the place noted, where Samuel's generation is considered as belonging to "former times." But since in the entire Pentateuch, too, a prophet is never referred to by the term *roeh,* one must conclude that the Pentateuch also was edited not only after the death of Moses but even long after the generation of Samuel. Naturally, such a heretical idea could not even occur to the pious Joseph Kara.[22]

In the city in which Joseph Kara spent his life the towering figure who excelled all the other Franco-German commentators and interpreters of the Bible and the Talmud also grew up. We speak, of course, of Rabbi Shelomoh ben Yitzḥak, universally known among Jews as Rashi. This greatest of medieval Talmud commentators and most popular of Bible exegetes was born in 1040 in Troyes, then the major city of the Champagne province, and died in the same place in 1105. As a boy Rashi crossed the Rhine to study Torah in the *yeshivot* located there. As we have noted, the academies which Rabbenu Gershom founded in the Rhine cities, Mainz, Worms, and Speyer, were major centers of Talmudic knowledge. These academies attracted hundreds of students from the east and west, and "the scholars of Lutir"[23] were everywhere recognized as the foremost authorities in Jewish knowledge. From these academies came many outstanding German rabbis and scholars, and it was in them that Rashi spent his youth.

21. See *ibid.;* Geiger, *op. cit.*, pp. 32–33.
22. For a more extended discussion of Joseph Kara see Einstein, *op. cit.*, and S. D. Luzzatto, *Kerem Ḥemed*, VII, 56–57.
23. The name Lutir (Lotharingia) was then used to designate the entire territory lying on both sides of the Rhine.

Rashi's first teacher was Rabbenu Gershom's disciple Rabbi Jacob ben Yakir,[24] the *rosh yeshivah* or head of the academy in Worms. After the latter's death, he proceeded to Mainz to study Torah with the *rosh yeshivah* there, Rabbi Isaac ben Jehudah. He also spent some time in Speyer and then returned in 1065 to his birthplace, where he established his own academy which eventually became an important center of Talmudic scholarship.

While still a student in the academies of the scholars of Lutir, Rashi began to assemble, with great diligence and devotion, the materials for the monumental undertaking which became the goal of his life: to make the Babylonian Talmud, with its difficult and little-understood language, accessible to all, so that no one would any longer need to consult experts in order to understand the meaning of a page of the Gemara. To this end Rashi had, first of all, to continue and complete the work which Rabbenu Gershom had begun, i.e., to arrive at the correct text of the Talmud and remove from it all the errors and distortions that ignorant copyists had perpetrated. Rashi's immense scholarship and keen critical sense helped him accomplish this difficult task with great success. For his own commentary Rashi skillfully employed the commentaries of his predecessors, the explanations and interpretations of the heads of the academies which their pupils used to jot down in their notebooks (*kuntrasim*). Out of this vast and varied material he understood how to select the essential and most important, and to make of it an integral entity, an organically whole and perfect thing.

Rashi never forgets that his central purpose is to make the strange and complicated text comprehensible; hence, he does not allow himself to enter into profound speculations or to set forth subtle, tortuous hypotheses. He never for a moment overlooks that he is merely a clarifier and interpreter, who must express the thought of the author precisely and not allow himself any superfluous comments not pertinent to the subject matter and having no direct relationship to the literal meaning of the text. An incomparable master of lucid style, Rashi understands how to render his explanations in the most clear and universally understandable fashion. In addition, Rashi is not at all verbose; he knows the "secret of condensation." With him every word is counted and measured, every expression pointed and polished. Throughout his life he never tired of editing and reediting his commentary on the Talmud and making it simpler and more comprehensible.[25] The

24. Rashi mentions him as *mori ha-zaken* (my old teacher). See, e.g., his commentary to *Sukkah* 38b.

25. Rashi's commentary on the Talmud has come down to us in three editions.

most obscure passages are quite frequently explained by Rashi in two or three words which at the same time clarify the entire subject under discussion and resolve all difficulties and questions.[26]

In order, however, to be able to render clearly the thought of each of the teachers of the Talmud, Rashi had to reckon with another difficulty. In the Talmud itself there is great confusion on the matter of chronology. The well-known dictum "There is no earlier and later in the Torah" manifests itself in the Talmud in a very odd way: its authors generally had no concern with fixed dates, with "earlier" and "later," and persons of very different periods are not infrequently treated as contemporaries. But clearly to understand a given ordinance established by a Talmudic teacher, it is often essential to know precisely at what time and under what circumstances this individual lived. Here Rashi displayed his remarkably acute historical sense. He so immersed himself in the world of the Talmud and so familiarized himself with all the details concerning the life and environment of each Tanna and Amora that he largely succeeded in avoiding the anachronisms and confusion of dates and generations commonly found in Talmudic literature. In this way Rashi was able to explain the Talmudic laws, ordinances, and decisions according to their historical order. In those cases, however, where he could not, with all his brilliance, arrive at the meaning of some obscure Talmudic statement, he candidly admits, "I do not understand"; "I do not know"; "It is not clear to me."[27]

Rashi's commentary to the Talmud was at once accepted throughout the Jewish world. All the *kuntrasim* formerly used in the academies were rendered obsolete in the face of this one and only *kuntras*,[28] and Rashi himself was crowned with the title Parshandata, the one, peerless commentator and expositor.

Rashi became famous, however, not only as an interpreter of the Talmud. He acquired no lesser a reputation with his commentaries on the Bible, mainly that on the Pentateuch. This commentary, however, is of a very different nature from the Talmudic. To be sure, here also Rashi's great virtues—his simplicity, his talent for clarifying every subject in a few lucid words—are evident. Despite the fact that he was unfamiliar with the studies in Arabic by the great Jewish philologists, Ḥayyuj, Jannaḥ, and others, he managed to penetrate deeply into the spirit of the Biblical language in his

26. This remarkable quality of Rashi's was already noted by a scholar of the fourteenth century, Isaac Lattes, in his *Shaarei Tziyyon*, p. 38.
27. See I. H. Weiss, *Dor Dor Ve-Doreshav*, IV, 288; *Bet Talmud*, II, 135.
28. In medieval literature Rashi's commentary to the Talmud is called simply *Kuntras*.

exposition of the meaning of the text. But in his commentary on the Pentateuch Rashi appears in an altogether new image. In the commentary on the Talmud we have before us the austere and objective man of logic, the clarifier who counts each word. In the commentary on the Torah, however, we see, above all, the pious believer with a tender, sensitive soul, for whom the stories and legends of the Talmud and Midrashim are actual, living events.[29] In his simplicity and complete lack of religious doubt this medieval genius blurred the distinction between *peshat* (literal meaning) and *derush* (homiletical explanation). His clear and precise explanations of the text are frequently interwoven with poetic legends,[30] and this is done with such childlike naivete that it gives the entire work a special charm and irradiates it with the light of inner beauty. It was not without reason that this work became the most popular and beloved book among the Jewish people. For centuries Rashi's commentary was welded in the consciousness of the people with the Torah of Moses; *Ḥumosh mit Rashi*, the Pentateuch with Rashi, became a single entity, and every word of the commentary was analyzed and studied with almost no less diligence than the word of the Bible itself.[31] It is also quite understandable that Rashi's commentary, on which so many generations of Jews were nurtured, was the first Hebrew book to be printed.[32]

In a short time Rashi's commentary displaced those of all the commentators who preceded him or who lived in his day. The names of Menaḥem bar Ḥelbo, Joseph Kara, and others were for-

29. On Rashi's use of the Midrashim see Weiss, *Bet Talmud*, II, 226.
30. The very perceptive Abraham Ibn Ezra, who generally regarded Rashi with great respect, already indicated this in the twelfth century. "Rabbi Shelomoh," Ibn Ezra writes, "expounded the Bible by way of homiletic interpretation but believed that he was not departing from the way of literal interpretation" (see *Safah Berurah*, p. 5). Also extremely characteristic of Rashi's fundamental stance is his attitude toward ancient customs. "A custom," he used to say, "may not be nullified"; "a custom is of no lesser importance than a law"; "a custom is a Torah"; "every custom is based on a firm foundation." "So the people have been accustomed to do" was for Rashi the strongest argument. In his *Pardes* there are many such utterances, e.g., the following: "Israel in exile, if they are not prophets, are the sons of prophets, and they abide by customs that are beneficial and appropriate; and customs are not to be changed." "Listen, my son, to the instruction of your father . . . it is pleasant . . . to act according to the good custom . . . for men were not accustomed to do so for no reason, but because they saw that it is a good custom." "A custom of the later authorities is Torah, and it is to this that the Biblical verse 'And do not forsake the teaching of thy mother' refers."
31. On commentaries to Rashi see Toledano, *Apiryon* (1905).
32. In the Italian city of Reggio in 1475.

gotten, and only in relatively recent times, as a result of the efforts of assiduous scholars, has a "resurrection" of these dead occurred and their lost names have become known again. Even the Spanish Jews, who gloried in their high culture and extensive knowledge, were extremely respectful toward the French commentator on the Bible and Talmud. Ravad (Rabbi Abraham Ibn Daud) speaks in his *Sefer Ha-Kabbalah* with great enthusiasm of the master of Troyes and calls him "the great light who dazzles eyes,"[33] and the celebrated Abraham Ibn Ezra wrote poems of praise in honor of Rashi, the "star risen in France" by whose light "even the blind have become seeing."

In the Christian world, too, Rashi's commentary was deeply influential. The foremost Christian exegete of the Middle Ages, Nicholas De Lyra, is greatly indebted to Rashi; he makes extensive use of his commentary, often copying it word for word. Thanks to De Lyra's work, Martin Luther became familiar with Rashi's explanations and employed them to a considerable degree in his German Bible translation.[34]

As a man Rashi made a profound impression on his generation. His modesty, kindness, and simplicity, his gentle converse with men, gave his personality an extraordinary attractiveness, irradiated with spiritual beauty and grace.[35] It is therefore not surprising that he soon became one of the most beloved spiritual heroes of the Jewish people, and around his name popular imagination began to weave a tapestry of legends. One of these recounts his friendship with Godfrey of Bouillon, who played a significant role in the First Crusade. Before Godfrey set out for Palestine, Rashi predicted to him—so the legend goes—that at first he would be victorious in battle but afterwards suffer a dreadful defeat and return to France with only three horses. This prophecy enraged Godfrey, who promised that he would settle accounts with Rashi as soon as he returned home, even if it were only with one horse more than had been foretold. Rashi's words were fulfilled. Godfrey suffered a defeat and his entire army perished, but he returned to France

33. See *Sefer Ha-Kabbalah* (Neubauer's edition), p. 84: "And in France a great light, the like of which was never before seen, appeared. This is the great and pious Rabbi Shelomoh bar Yitzḥak of Troyes. . . . And if, God forbid, the Torah were forgotten in Israel, he would restore it; and he made it not to be forgotten."
34. On this matter, see K. Siegfried, *Rashis Einfluss auf Nicolaus de Lyra und Luther;* A Geiger, *Gesammelte Schriften,* II, 175–76.
35. These qualities of Rashi's character appear very clearly in his *responsa.* See *Otzar Neḥmad,* II, 178; *Ḥofes Matmonim,* p. 8; and esp. A. Berliner, "Zur Charakteristik Rashis," in *Kaufmann-Gedenkbuch,* pp. 260–78; also Lipschütz, *Rabbi Shelomoh Yitzḥaki,* pp. 22–38.

with three riders besides the horse on which he himself rode—thus, altogether with four horses. He proceeded with his knights toward Rashi's house to punish the Jewish scholar who had not predicted the event precisely. But at the gate of the city, the horse under one of the riders fell dead, and Godfrey entered the city with only three horses. With bowed head he rode humbly to the house of the godly man but there learned that Rashi was already dead.[36]

In point of fact this legend is inconsistent with the historical data. Godfrey actually died three years before Rashi, and that in Palestine, not in Troyes. The only truth in it is that the First Crusade, which was accompanied by horrible massacres in all the Franco-German Jewish communities, produced a powerful impression on the aged Rashi. He responded to the catastrophe with a series of heartfelt supplications and elegies. "Since the Temple was destroyed," he laments in one of these,[37]

> our troubles have increased without number and without measure. Every day brings new sorrows and oppression; our terror grows constantly greater, and our splendor lies in dust and shame. . . . We are like broken shards; stripped and naked are we now. Silent is the prophet's word. There is no consolation, no redemption. We stumble like blind men on all paths, and every day we ask, When will the end come? Better death than such a life, where at every step lurk terror and fear. . . . Because of our sins we have become a shame and a reproach. We are trodden down by all, despised, covered with gall and vomit. Strangers rule over us; we perish, we are lost. O God, Almighty One, redeem us from slavery, send Thy help speedily . . .

Rashi had managed to raise the Talmudic academies in France almost to the same high level which the famous academies of Babylonia once occupied. After the First Crusade, in which the Jewish communities of the Rhine cities of Metz, Worms, Cologne, Mainz, and Speyer suffered most, the importance of the academies which "the scholars of Lutir" had founded declined greatly, and their place was gradually taken by the academies which Rashi's disciples and sons-in-law[38] founded in various cities of France—

36. See *Maasei Nissim,* No. 17.
37. The prayer "U-mishe*ḥ*arav Bet Ha-Mikdash," recited in the Musaf service of Yom Kippur.
38. Rashi had no sons, only three daughters who married three of his pupils. In numerous sources it is indicated that one of Rashi's daughters was so deeply versed in rabbinical literature that she filled the office of secretary for her father and wrote his *responsa.* This, however, has been shown to be nothing more than a legend, traceable to a corrupted

Ramerupt, Dampierre, Sens, and Paris. These new academies, however, were not of the same character as those of the Rhine provinces. There the students, under the guidance of skillful teachers, had endeavored to arrive at the plain meaning of the obscure and difficult Talmudic text. But the great Rabbi Shelomoh Yitzḥaki, the master of simplicity and clarity who possessed the talent of illuminating every dark corner and making comprehensible the most difficult and profound subject matter, had already done his work. All by himself, he had completed what two generations (from Rabbenu Gershom to himself) had not been able to accomplish: to make the Talmud something "alike for every person," and its text accessible to all. Rashi's disciples and followers therefore had to set themselves different goals and attempt to break new paths. But these men, the majority of them very talented, lived in a restricted circle of ideas; their entire scholarship was limited to Jewish religious problems and questions relating to ritual and law. Of all sciences and disciplines they recognized only their own. For them the only possible and only important science was the Talmud. To it they devoted their extensive intellectual powers, their sharply honed minds and keen dialectic. After the work of their celebrated teacher, the incomparable Rashi, they deemed it superfluous once again to interpret and expound the Talmudic text. They therefore set themselves a new task: to explore it critically. After the great exegete came the "investigators," the Tosafists,[39] who began to analyze the text of the Gemara according to the same system by which the Amoraim had in their day reflected on the text of the Mishnah. The Tosafists undertook the task of penetrating into all the hidden corners of Talmudic jurisprudence, exploring in a critical and analytic fashion every section of the Talmud, comparing and contrasting all the theories and decisions that have some relationship and analogy to each other, and in this way illuminating the extremely confusing process by which the sages of the Talmud finally arrived at their conclusions.

There is no doubt, however, that the remarkably subtle analysis and the amazingly keen mental activity of the Tosafists in exploring the complicated and entangled sections of the Talmud were not merely the result of their desire to discover and determine the

---

text of one of Rashi's *responsa* (see Zunz, *Zur Geschichte und Literatur;* S. Buber, *Shibbolei Ha-Leket*, Preface; A. Berliner, *MGWJ*, 1872, p. 288).

39. These investigations of Rashi's disciples and followers were written down by the students of the *yeshivot* as notes and "additions" or "supplements" (*tosafot*) to the Talmud, and the name Tosafot was preserved in later generations.

value and the course of development of its individual laws. The Tosafists also cultivated for their own sake the hairsplitting dialectic, the playing with flashes of thought, the dazzling with clever inventions, the showing-off of the brilliance of steel-sharp minds and the wealth of intellectual ability, just as the knights of that era endeavored to display in tournaments their strength and love of battle.

The earliest representatives of the Tosafists were Rashi's pupil Rabbi Isaac ben Asher[40] and his son-in-law Rabbi Meir ben Samuel of Ramerupt. But the school first attained genuine eminence in Rabbi Meir ben Samuel's children, Rabbi Samuel (known as Rashbam) and Rabbi Jacob (or Rabbenu Tam).

Rashi's oldest grandson, Rabbi Samuel ben Meir or Rashbam,[41] was the most gifted successor of his grandfather in the realm of Biblical exegesis. However, he distinguished himself very sharply from Rashi by being a categorical opponent of the method of *derush*, i.e., employing stories and popular legends in expounding the text. He himself indicates in his commentary to the Pentateuch that he used to carry on long arguments with Rashi on this score, in order to prove to him how essential it is to keep strictly to the literal meaning of the Biblical text and not mingle extraneous homilies and legends with it. "I, Samuel, the son of his son-in-law Meir," relates Rashbam, "long wrangled with him on this subject. And he finally admitted that if only he had sufficient leisure, he would make a new commentary to the Pentateuch following exclusively the method of *peshat*."[42]

Holding fast to the system of Menaḥem bar Ḥelbo and Joseph Kara, Rashbam set forth as his basic principle the well-known dictum of the Gemara: "One must be faithful to the simple meaning of the verse." No other commentator of the French school can be compared with Rashbam as an interpreter of the plain meaning of the Bible. Yet even Rashbam's commentary could not compete with the commentary of his grandfather. Rashi's touching style, and the legends and stories of the Midrash so ingeniously woven into his commentary, were far more appealing to hearts saddened and terrified by the atrocities of the Crusades than the intellectually

40. Known by the acronym Riba. For a discussion of him, see I. H. Weiss, *Dor Dor Ve-Doreshav*, IV, 298–99, and A. Epstein in *MGWJ*, XLI, 470, and XLV, 47.

41. Born c. 1085, died c. 1174. For more about him, see D. Rosin, *Rabbi Samuel ben Meir als Schrifterklärer* (1880). For a good characterization of Rashbam, see D. Kaufmann, *Magazin*, 1886, pp. 129–31.

42. Commentary to Genesis 37:2.

lucid but arid discussions of Rashbam. Despite the fact that Rashbam achieved renown as one of the major Tosafists,[43] his commentary to the Torah was completely forgotten. Not until the eighteenth century was a single, error-filled manuscript copy found and published for the first time.[44] Then only did the learned world discover that Rashbam must occupy an honored place among the best of the medieval Jewish Bible commentators.[45]

Revered as Rashbam's name was among the Tosafists, he was excelled by his younger brother Jacob, better known as Rabbenu Tam.[46] Jacob is the true glory of the period, the most celebrated name after Rashi's in the entire Franco-German Jewish community of the Middle Ages. "From the close of the Talmud on," declares one of the foremost rabbinic authorities,[47] "Rabbenu Jacob has no peer in the realm of *pilpul* [dialectic]." Rabbenu Tam himself proudly declared: "If the most contradictory opinions anyone could imagine should be expressed in the Gemara on the same subject, it would not be difficult for me so to explain them that they harmonize extremely well with one another." He could carry out the most difficult intellectual activity with deft lightness, as if it were a simple game to while away the time. The hard and brittle Talmudic material became, in the hands of this master, pliable as wax, and he kneaded it and poured out of it the most novel and astonishing forms. None of his predecessors manifested such scholarship or such dialectical skill. Rabbenu Tam succeeded in developing to the ultimate degree the critical investigation of the Talmudic text by skillful comparison and collation of various sections, by disclosing in an analytic fashion their hidden contradictions and then logically reconciling them. Thanks to him, the subject of Tosafot became a complete system, a kind of architec-

43. A complete list of the Tosafists is given by Zunz in his *Zur Geschichte und Literatur*, pp. 29–60.
44. In 1705. A critical and corrected edition was published by Rosin in 1881.
45. The same fate befell Rashbam's pupil Joseph ben Isaac Bechor Shor, the last important exegete of the school of northern France. His excellent commentary on the Bible, in which one not infrequently encounters the ideas and conceptions of the most modern scientific Bible critics, was entirely forgotten and was rediscovered only in modern times. For a discussion of him, see N. Walter, *Josef Bechor Shor, der letzter nordfranzösischer Bibel-Exeget* (1890); N. Porges, *Josef Bechor Shor* (1908).
46. *Tam* derives from the Biblical expression: "And Jacob was a plain man [*ish tam*]."
47. Rabbi Isaac bar Sheshet (Ribash) *Responsa*, No. 294.

ture in which the possibility was achieved of expanding the structure of Talmudic law, of developing and grounding new principles and laws for communal and religious life.[48] It is therefore not surprising that Rabbenu Tam was regarded by medieval Franco-German Jewry as the chief authority in all questions relating to religious ritual practice.[49] While he was still alive his fame resounded in all lands. His contemporary, Rabbi Abraham Ibn Daud, indicates in his *Sefer Ha-Kabbalah* that from France, Germany, and Provence hundreds of pupils come to Ramerupt to study Torah and listen to God's word from the celebrated scholar Rabbi Jacob.[50]

Rabbenu Tam was also the first among the French Talmudic scholars who manifested a certain interest in the literary activity of the Spanish-Arabic Jews. He composed a philological work, *Sefer Ha-Hachraah*, in which he endeavors to demonstrate that Dunash ben Labrat was mistaken in his controversy with Menaḥem Ibn Saruk. However, the famous Tosafist showed himself to be a rather weak grammarian, and his work[51] has very limited scientific value. Rabbenu Tam also wrote poems according to the principles of Arabic meter. This greatly astonished the perpetual wanderer Abraham Ibn Ezra. To the latter it seemed extremely odd that a French Talmudist should attempt to master Arabic meter, and he therefore sent Rabbenu Tam a sharp epigram in which he proudly asks, "Who brought the Frenchman into the temple of poetic art? How does a stranger undertake to penetrate into the sanctuary?" Rabbenu Tam replied with great modesty in a poem: "I am Abraham's slave who bows before his master." Such a reply from the foremost Talmudic scholar greatly moved Abraham Ibn Ezra, and in a later poem he humbly begged forgiveness from Rabbenu Tam. "It is not meet," he wrote, "that the greatest leader of the chosen people should abase himself before a simple wanderer. How should God's elect bow before a man of no consequence?"

One further aspect of Rabbenu Tam's activity must be mentioned. By reason of the tremendous reputation which he acquired, he succeeded in laying the foundations of Jewish central self-

48. A considerable part of Rabbenu Tam's *tosafot*, *novellae*, and *responsa* were gathered together in *Sefer Ha-Yashar*. The book itself, which Rabbenu Tam worked up in two versions, was lost. We have only the imprecise and erroneous reports assembled by one of his pupils.
49. In this connection there is an interesting folk legend which relates how Moses himself carried on a debate on a difficult point of law with the famous Tosafist and Rabbenu Tam triumphed over him (see *Shalshelet Ha-Kabbalah*, *Maaseh Shel Shemuel Ha-Navi*).
50. See *Sefer Ha-Kabbalah* (Neubauer's edition).
51. Published by Filipowski (1855), together with Dunash's *Teshuvot.*

government. Under his leadership there occurred in the year 1160 in Troyes the first rabbinic conference, at which new ordinances were worked out and new decisions, called forth by the demands of practical life, were adopted. Such rabbinic conferences took place periodically from that time on.

CHAPTER TWO

# *Supplications and Lamentations in the Period of the Crusades*

JEWS IN Germany and France at the middle of the twelfth century saw increasingly darkening horizons. Fifty years after the First Crusade came the Second (1147), and the atrocities against Jews were repeated. Rabbenu Tam saved his life then only, as it were, through a miracle. A band of men entered his room, wrecked everything, dragged him away to a field, and left him to be tortured and killed in revenge for the death of Jesus. "You," they said, "are a great man in Israel, and so we shall avenge upon you the sufferings which our crucified savior endured." Rabbenu Tam lay with five wounds in his head when, by chance, a knight who knew him rode by. The knight saved his life and, as a reward for his aid, demanded of the Jewish scholar an expensive horse.[1] Rabbenu Tam afterwards settled in Troyes and in the last year of his life had to witness the new tragedy which befell French Jewry: the first blood libel, or ritual murder charge, then took place in France, and in the neighboring city of Blois thirty-one Jews were burned at the stake as martyrs on the twentieth of Sivan 1171.[2]

Sadder still was the situation of the Jews in Germany. Persecuted by the pious but rapacious Crusaders, the Jews sought aid and protection from the secular power, above all from the Holy Roman Emperor. The Emperor and his associates quickly perceived that

1. See the memoirs of Ephraim ben Jacob in *Hebräische Berichte über die Judenverfolgungen während der Kreuzzüge*, II, 64.
2. Details concerning this blood libel are provided in the letter which the community of Orleans sent to Rabbenu Tam. This letter is given in two sources (see *Hebräische Berichte*, pp. 32–34 and 66–68).

this could be a source of great revenue, and for the help which the Jews at times received they had to pay very dearly. In a relatively brief time, the previously free Jewish populace became *servi camerae*, servants of the Holy Roman crown and the property of the Emperor.[3]

But the Jews did not turn to the secular power alone in their need. Men of strong faith and profound religious sentiment, they also appealed in their time of trouble to the highest tribunal, the most powerful authority, the master of the universe and God of their fathers. From Him, the constant and omnipotent helper, they begged aid. From Him, the true judge, they demanded judgment for the horrible injustices perpetrated against them. And these prayers and protests, these laments and supplications which burst from pained souls and lips frozen by terror, occupy a special place in Hebrew religious poetry. Leopold Zunz, in comparing the religious poetry of the Spanish and the Franco-German Jews, makes the following observation:

> Notwithstanding the fact that the conceptions and national motifs are almost identical, it is easy to note one quality that is to be encountered almost exclusively among the Spanish Jews, namely, poetic skill. In France and Germany the mother of the *seliḥah* [supplication or penitential poem] was misery alone, and very rarely did genuine talent also have a part in its creation. In Spain, especially in the time of cultural flowering, the *paytanim* or liturgical poets were, above all, gifted writers, and precisely because they were true poets they also wrote religious poetry. In other lands, however, . . . it was the Muses of terror and misfortune that inspired lamentations and religious poems.[4]

The German and French Jews adopted the forms for their religious poems from the Kalonymos family which had come from Italy and settled in the Rhine provinces. But they did not wish to employ the Arabic meter that was so alien to them.[5] Furthermore, they made no use of the philological investigations of the Spanish Jewish grammarians who had so greatly advanced the

3. The completed and established process of instituting the *Kammerknecht* status is disclosed very clearly in the *privilegia* of both Fredericks. In the *privilegia* of Frederick I (in 1182) Jews are declared as "belonging to the imperial *camera*" and in the *privilegia* of Frederick II the German Jews are already *servi camerae nostrae*.
4. See Zunz, *Die synagogale Poesie des Mittelalters*, pp. 332–33.
5. Characteristic in this matter is the remark of the popular *Sefer Ḥasidim:* "When the Jews went into exile, the lawless ones [*ha-peritizim*] there sang lovely songs put together according to the meter of the gentiles. The Jews learned from them and also produced such songs."

development of Hebrew language and style. The ancient *paytan* Eleazar Kallir remained for them the chief authority and peerless master,[6] and in their lamentations and religious poems his influence and style, with his strange expressions that know nothing of grammatical principles, are strongly discernible. And yet the inspiration of "the Muses of terror and misfortune" at times attained literally shattering power. Not without reason did later generations piously collect these "human documents" bearing the marks of tears and blood and read them aloud with trembling hearts and broken spirits on days of fasting and sorrow. To give the reader some notion of the unique style of these medieval cries of anguish, we shall present several of them here.

The *paytan* David ben Meshullam, who himself lived through the terrors of the First Crusade, implores the master of the universe:

God Almighty, let not my blood that has been shed be silenced! Forget not my murderers, demand it from my destroyers! Let not the earth cover the blood of my children. Let it run and spurt and seethe before Thine eyes—the blood of those who have perished, slaughtered like sheep! . . . Venomous as serpents, they determined to wipe out our name from the world. But the children of Thy people remained faithful to Thee. "Our God is our pride," they sang, "He is our hope, our joy and our praise!" Women and children offered themselves as a sacrifice to Thee, on burning pyres gave up their lives. Thou only and powerful One, for Thy name's sake are we slaughtered and killed. Little chicks, little lambs, beg their mothers to forget compassion, to steel their hearts: "We are demanded, demanded as a sacrifice by the heavens above!" They swim in blood. They embrace and kiss one another, and kissing and embracing, quickly slay each other. A great altar has been built for Thee, O God! It is full and crowded all around with Thy burned and slaughtered child sacrifices. On all paths and in all corners they lie naked, dismembered, dishonored, and burned to ashes. Priests and God's chosen servants sanctified with the death of martyrs both men and women; the slaughterers and the slaughtered fell together in cries of lamentation; the blood of children flowed together with the blood of their elders; and loudly there resounded the "Hear, O Israel" of the victims. How is it to be believed, how is such a terrible thing to be seen—that tender, loving mothers should joyously lead their own children to the slaughter as if to the marriage canopy? . . . Faithful Jewish daughters were stripped naked in broad daylight, dragged out and slaughtered. Unborn children were ripped

6. Moses Taku, the author of *Ketav Tamim,* who lived at the beginning of the thirteenth century, calls Kallir "an angel of God" (see *Otzar Neḥmad,* III, 85).

from their mothers' wombs. And dost Thou behold this and remain silent, O Thou great and mighty One, Thou God of vengeance?[7]

This twofold motif—how the God of justice can look calmly on such horrible deeds, and the bitter, anguished cry for vengeance and justice—echo powerfully in many supplications and laments of that bloody era. "See," calls out the *paytan* Kalonymos ben Jehudah,

> how my slaughtered ones, slain by the sword, roll around stripped naked. On their bodies wild beasts and birds feed. Little children and old men, youths and maidens—all has the enemy destroyed, covered with shame and mockery. "Where is their God," they arrogantly demanded, "their helper and protector? Let him show himself and raise the slaughtered to life again." Almighty God, great, truly, is Thy patience, who can compare with Thy spirit? But how canst Thou now remain silent and not break out in wrath when these mock and laugh: "If He is God, let Him manifest His power!"[8]

"Who is like unto Thee among the speechless, O God, who can be compared with Thee in Thy silence?" cries another *paytan* of the twelfth century.[9]

> Thou wast silent when Thy temple was destroyed, remained silent when vile men trod Thy children underfoot, and looked on calmly when Thy people were sold for a farthing. We were thrown into deep abysses, burned in flaming fire, stoned with rocks, hung on gibbets, oppressed and degraded; and we always praised Thy name, for strong as death is love. . . . We were cast into Hell while yet alive—there we perish, we are all lost. . . . Thou art the avenger—where, then, is Thy vengeance?

The greatest anguish was aroused in the heart of the people by two things—the slaughter of innocent little children and the desecration of the sacred Torah scrolls. And the passionate protest of their enraged consciousness finds a sharp echo in many elegies of that time. "Into the dirt," cries the *paytan* Isaac ben Shalom, "they cast Thy holy Torah and the Talmud of Rabina and Rav Ashi—and wilt Thou look on and remain silent?"[10] "A delicate little

7. The well-known *seliḥah* "Elohim Al Dami Le-Dami."
8. The well-known *kinah* "Mi Yiten Roshi Mayyim," which is read on the Ninth of Av.
9. Menaḥem ben Jacob, in his *kinah* "Allelai Li," published in *Kovetz Al Yad,* III, 5–9.
10. In the *yotzer* for the first Sabbath after Passover, *En Kamocha Ba-Illemim.*

flower," complains another lamentation,[11] "was choked in its mother's lap, the child destroyed with the mother. Repay them for their cruelty, repay them manyfold! . . . Thou God Almighty, wilt Thou not have compassion on the blood of Thy children that has been shed? Behold, Thy sacred Torah is trodden in the dust underfoot, and they mock and laugh: 'Where is He, their royal helper and redeemer?' " "King of all worlds, mighty and fearful, Thou omnipotent Lord, repay them speedily, speedily send them ruin, overthrow them like Sodom and Gomorrah!"

The innocent victims of the blood libel in Blois are mourned by another poet of that period, Hillel ben Jacob,[12] in his passionate "Emunei Shelumei Yisrael," of which we here quote several lines:

The best and noblest of Thy people Israel, pure as crystal, hast Thou, O God, forsaken, handed over to the enemy. . . . It was spring,[13] the trees were in bloom, and these, the finest children of Thy people, were taken captive. But all decided to die for their faith. The flowers were odorous, and the fate of the captives was already determined. They were locked in a high tower to break their will with horrible tortures. But not one of them surrendered. Like a bride going to the marriage canopy, they joyously ascended the pyre, and all together, both men and women,[14] triumphantly cried out, "Hear, O Israel!"

Not of God himself but of His servants, the ministering angels, does a poet of the end of the eleventh century, Samuel Ha-Kohen, beg mercy and help:

Compassionate angels, ye servants of the Most High, beseech God with heartfelt words. Perhaps He will have mercy on the unfortunate people. Perhaps He will have compassion on the last remnant of Joseph's children who are everywhere persecuted and oppressed, stripped naked, sold for a farthing, made a mockery and a scorn. Yet they utter their prayers and cry to God, their helper. Perhaps He will have compassion on those who languish in chains, who starve in solitude and misery, who are the object of awe of all the peoples and are mocked and spat upon by all of them. . . . Perhaps He will have compassion on those whose sufferings are numberless and measureless, who in dens

11. The *kinah* "Amarer Ba-Bechi" (reprinted in Bernfeld's *Sefer Ha-Demaot,* I, 250–54).
12. Hillel's brother, Ephraim ben Jacob, also wrote two *kinot* or lamentations in memory of those who perished as a result of the blood libel at Blois: "Asiḥah Be-Mar Nafshi" and "Lemi Oi U-Lemi Avoi."
13. The libel took place on the twenty-third of Sivan.
14. Among the thirty-one who died were seventeen women. The names of all who perished are listed in the third volume of *Quellen zur Geschichte der Juden in Deutschland,* pp. 135–36.

of lions and in lairs of snakes still do not forget the holy word, God's eternal script. Perhaps He will have compassion on those who silently endure all sufferings and shame; they are silent and hope—for His help and mercy. Perhaps He will have compassion, listen to the cries, break the chains, free from slavery, heal the wounds, and quickly send the day of redemption.

One of the prominent *paytanim* of Germany, Ephraim bar Isaac of Regensburg,[15] complains in his well-known supplication "Avotai Ki Bateḥu," which is recited on the fast day of Asarah Be-Tevet:

How wide have my enemies opened their mouths against me; all my possessions and fortune have they swallowed. They have vanquished me and greedily drink my blood. From all sides hostile peoples surround me, oppress and persecute my brethren. Esau's children cry out, "Destroy them, annihilate them." "Come," they call, "let us root them out, wipe out their memory!" . . . O God, Thou God of vengeance, repay them for their deeds, frustrate their hopes, break their support. Let their ruin be immense! . . . All my wounds are open, and unbearable is the pain. My eyes are dimmed from long waiting for the redeemer, for the tender friend. . . . Is the terrible wrath not yet stilled? Will it endure forever? Why? Wherefore? For what sins? Have compassion, O God, forsake us not forever! How fearfully long are the days of my sorrow, how great the pain of my grieved heart. Turn, O my God, into my tent, end the days of my sorrow, come to my help, take away from me the garments of sadness, and gird me with rays of joy. The darkness of my night illumine Thou with Thy brightness, Thou, my only hope, my only light.

The horrible events which occurred in the era of the Crusades also called forth another type of literature, memorial books and chronicles. Those who survived and had witnessed with their own eyes the catastrophe that had befallen the Jewish communities had one desire—to inscribe in the memory of future ages all that their fathers had lived through in the days of terror, to have written down in the book of the people the names of the martyrs who had sacrificed their lives for the sanctification of God's name. The events, however, were of such vast tragedy, and so uniquely interwoven in one dramatic fabric were the most extreme qualities of the human soul—the highest degree of self-sacrifice and spiritual devotion, on the one side, and bestial thirst for blood, on the other—that even the protocol-like accounts of the plain chroniclers are

15. On him and his work see Zunz, *Literaturgeschichte*, pp. 274–79; Landshuth, *Ammudei Ha-Avodah*, pp. 4 and 48.

deeply moving. The tragedy of the events themselves affected the chroniclers so greatly that their pen received an extraordinary power of description, and pages arose, images and scenes came forth, that can never be forgotten.

To provide some notion of the character of this literature, we shall dwell on four examples. Three of these relate events that occurred in the time of the First Crusade, and the fourth describes events of the Second Crusade.[16] One of the first three was composed by the scholar Rabbi Eleazar bar Nathan (Raban)[17] of Mainz, the author of *Even Ha-Ezer*, who in his youth lived through the First Crusade. The second chronicle was put together in 1140 by one Solomon ben Samson.[18] The author of the third chronicle[19] is unknown, but because it is conjectured that he was a resident of Mainz he is called "the anonymous one of Mainz." The fourth chronicle was written by the talented poet Ephraim ben Jacob of Bonne,[20] who, as a thirteen-year-old boy, experienced the terrors of the Second Crusade.

The "anonymous one of Mainz" begins his chronicle with the following description:

It was in the year 1028 after the destruction of the Temple [1098] that the tragedy befell us Jews. The nobles, knights, and common people first rose in France. They conceived an idea and determined to rise like eagles and, with weaponry in hand, to beat a path to Jerusalem, the holy city, where the sepulchre of the crucified one, the trampled corpse, who can be of help to no one because he is himself corrupt and waste, is located. And they said to one another: "Look, we are setting out to distant lands, going to wage war against the kings who reign there, risking our lives to destroy and subdue the kingdoms that do not believe in him who was hanged. Surely we ought to settle accounts with the Jews who killed and hanged him." Thus everywhere, in all corners, they incited men against us. And they declared that either we Jews must accept their faith or they would annihilate us, not sparing even the suckling children. And they sewed the evil symbol, the cross, on their garments, both the knights and the plain

16. All four are printed in *Hebräische Berichte über die Judenverfolgungen während der Kreuzzüge*, issued by A. Neubauer and Stern (Berlin, 1892).
17. Raban also composed some laments and supplications on the same theme, "Elohim Zedim Kamu," "Elohim Be-Oznenu," etc. (see Zunz, *Literaturgeschichte*, p. 261).
18. His name and the date are given in the chronicle itself.
19. Of this work there is only one manuscript, which is located in the library at Darmstadt.
20. See Zunz, *Literaturgeschichte*, pp. 288–93; Landshuth, *op. cit.*, pp. 47–48.

folk, and put metal helmets on their heads. When the Jewish communities in France heard of all this, they were seized with terror. They then did what their ancestors used to do: they at once wrote letters and dispatched them with messengers to all the communities on the Rhine, requesting that they decree fasting and beseech compassion for them from the Almighty, that He might have mercy on them and deliver them from the enemy's hand. And when these letters reached the great and holy men who live in Mainz, these immediately wrote a reply to France. And here is what they wrote: "All the communities have decreed fasting. We have done ours. May the master of the universe help us and all of you out of every trouble and peril. We are in great dread for you, but for ourselves we have nothing to fear. Here everything is calm. Nothing is heard of any decree or danger that might hang over our heads."

When the deluded ones [i.e., the Crusaders] began to appear in our land, they demanded money from us to buy bread. We fulfilled their request, as is written in Scripture, "Serve the king of Babylon and live." All this, however, was of no avail. Our sins brought it about that in all the cities to which the deluded ones came, the people residing there rose up against us and all of them together determined to destroy the entire vineyard [i.e., the people Israel], along with the roots, on their way to Jerusalem. And when the deluded ones began to come, band after band, numerous as Sennacherib's host, some of the local nobles said, "Why do we sit here in our places? Let us go with them. For everyone who will set out on the way and manage, after all difficulties, to arrive at the sepulchre of the crucified one will thereafter be certain of entering Heaven." And the deluded ones gathered, along with those who joined them in every land and region, into a tremendously large camp, numerous as the sand of the sea, both of the nobility and of the commons. And a proclamation[21] was issued that whosoever shall kill a Jew, his sins will be forgiven him. There also was one among the nobles named Ditmar, who declared that he would not leave the land until he had killed at least one Jew; only then would he set out on his way. As soon as the holy community of Mainz heard this, it immediately decreed fasting, addressed prayers to God, and called to Him loudly and strongly. Day and night were spent in fasting, day and night lamentations and supplications were recited by both old and young. But God in His wrath had turned away from us. And the deluded ones approached our houses with their flags and ensigns, and as soon as they saw one of us they pursued him and ran him through with a spear. We were therefore terrified of going outside.[22]

The Jews of Mainz attempted to resist with weapons. But they were unable to drive away the great hordes of the Crusaders.

21. In the text is written *beranki,* from the Old French word *franchise,* i.e., charter.

22. *Hebräische Berichte,* pp. 47–48.

When the enemy had surrounded them on all sides, they locked themselves in a large courtyard. Another chronicler, Solomon ben Samson, describes the last act of the tragic drama:

The enemy broke into the house on Tuesday the third of Sivan, a day of darkness, of curse and of horror—let the memory of it be blotted out, let no light illuminate it; on it our great tragedy took place. O you stars, why did you not blot out your light? Is not Israel likened to the stars, and Jacob's twelve tribes to the planets? Wherefore, then, did you not hide your light so as not to illuminate the enemies who determined to erase the name Israel? . . . When the children of the holy covenant saw that the evil decree was already determined, that the enemy had prevailed and was breaking through into the courtyard, they, all of them—old and young, maidens and children, manservants and maidservants—began to cry to the Father in heaven, lamented and wept for themselves and their lives. They accepted the justice of the judgment that had been passed on them and said to each other, "Let us strengthen ourselves and faithfully bear the yoke of the fear of Heaven. Of the four kinds of execution, death through the sword of our enemies is the easiest, and this death is only temporary, for through the merit of it our souls will enjoy eternal life in the radiance of Paradise. . . . Happy are we that we fulfill the will of His beloved name, happy are we who sacrifice ourselves for His holy name." . . . Afterwards all as one man cried out in a loud voice: "To resist further makes no sense. The enemy has reached us. Let us anticipate them and offer ourselves speedily as a sacrifice to God. Whoever has a knife, let him quickly examine it to see that it has no defect, and let him slaughter us for the sanctification of the name of Him who lives eternally, and thereafter let him, with the same knife, cut his own throat or thrust it into his belly." . . . And when the enemies broke into the courtyard, they found there several pious men with the great scholar Rabbi Isaac bar Moses, "the uprooter of mountains." He quietly stretched out his neck and was the first whose head they cut off. The others remained wrapped in their prayer shawls. They wished to fulfill as quickly as possible the will of their Creator, and so they did not run to hide in the chambers and lovingly accepted the decree of Heaven. The enemies hurled arrows and stones at them, but none of them moved from their places or tried to run away, until all were slain and not one was left. When those who had locked themselves in the chambers saw what the enemies had done with the holy men in the courtyard they cried out, "Better that we ourselves should offer ourselves as a sacrifice!" Women then girded up their loins and slew their sons and daughters, and afterwards themselves. Also many men strengthened themselves and killed their wives and children. Gentle, tender mothers killed their dearly beloved children. All of them rose, both men and women, and sacrificed one another. And young girls, brides, and grooms, looked through the windows and cried with a terrible cry: "See, O master of the universe, see what we do for Thy name's sake, only not to exchange Thee for him who was hanged and crucified, for the vile, dirty, despised bastard, the offspring of lewdness." . . . Pious, righteous women stretched out their necks to one another and sacrificed themselves for the One and only One. A man his son and his brother, a brother his sister, a woman her son and daughter, a neighbor his friend, a groom his bride—one was the sacrificer, the other the sacrificed. Blood mingled with blood—the blood of men with women, of parents with children, of brothers with sisters, of rabbis with pupils, of grooms with brides, of precentors with scribes, of suckling children with their mothers. All were slaughtered for the sake of His, the eternal and omnipotent One's, name.[23]

"Has it ever been seen or heard," asks the chronicler further,

that men should hasten to each other with the fervent request, "I wish to be the first to die for the sanctification of the name of the King of the kings of kings, the Holy One, blessed be He!"? The pious women threw gold and silver to the enemies through their windows, in order to keep them back for a while and gain time to slaughter their own sons and daughters and fulfill the will of the Creator. And when the enemies broke down the doors and entered the chambers, they found there only men drowning in their own blood and struggling in their death agonies. They took all objects of value, stripped everyone naked. Whosoever was still alive they killed, leaving no one. Thus they did in every chamber, wherever Jews were hidden. Only one room with solid doors remained, and the enemies could not break these down until evening. When the holy ones who were in that room realized that the enemy had prevailed and that it was no longer possible to resist, they determined to anticipate them. First the men and women slaughtered all the children. Then the righteous women began to throw stones through the windows at the enemy. The latter responded with stones, but the women remained calm under the hail of stones. Their heads and bodies became nothing but swellings and abscesses, yet they remained standing at the windows and mocked the deluded ones, laughed at and blasphemed the dirty hanged one, the son of lewdness. . . . "In whom do you trust," they shrieked, "in a stinking corpse?" Then the deluded ones began to break in the door. . . .

Who has ever seen, who has ever heard such a thing as the young righteous woman, Rachel bat Isaac ben Asher, the wife of Rabbi Jehudah, did? She said to her friends, "I have four children. Have no mercy on them. Otherwise, these uncircumcized ones will come and capture them alive and lead them into their false faith. Therefore, sanctify God's name with my children!" So one of her friends took up the knife to slaughter her son. As soon as the mother saw the knife, she uttered a bitter shriek, struck herself in the face and breasts, and

23. *Ibid.*, pp. 6–8.

cried, "God in heaven, where is Thy mercy?" The miserable mother in her anguish said to her friends, "Do not slay my son Isaac before his brother Aaron, that the latter may not see how his brother is killed." Aaron ran away and hid himself. So the woman took the younger and slaughtered him, the little one who was so small and beautiful. . . . The mother stretched out her palms and gathered the blood of her child in the skirt of her dress, a whole vessel of blood. When the little Aaron saw how his brother had been slaughtered, he began to shriek, "Mother, do not kill me!" and hid himself under a chest. The mother had two daughters, Beila and Madruna, lovely girls, the daughters of her husband Jehudah. The girls themselves took the knife and sharpened it, so that there should be no defect in it. The mother stretched out their necks and sacrificed both of them before the Lord of hosts, who has commanded us to hold fast to His pure faith and to remain faithful to Him, as it is written, "Thou shalt be perfect with the Lord thy God" [Deuteronomy 18:13]. After the righteous woman had slain her three children, she began to call aloud, "Aaron, Aaron, where are you? I will not have compassion on you either!" And she dragged him by the foot from under the chest where he lay hidden and sacrificed him also in the name of the great and exalted God. And then she took all of her slaughtered children, two on each side, and cradled them to her bosom, while the children were still throbbing in their death agony. When the enemies broke into the room as she was sitting and weeping for her children, they cried, "Show us the money you have hidden in your bosom." But when they saw the slaughtered children, they killed her also, and her soul expired. And concerning her was fulfilled that which is written, "And the mother is pierced through together with the children . . ."![24]

The same terrible scenes were enacted in all the cities of the Rhine. The chronicler recounts the bloody end of another community, not far from Cologne:

On Friday, the fourth day of Tammuz, the enemy surrounded the community of Altenar [Ilna] and determined to force its members through horrible tortures to accept their black faith. When the pious community learned of this, they confessed their sins before God and chose five men, God-fearing and courageous persons, to slaughter all the rest. There were also about three hundred fine people there who had fled from the communities around Cologne. All these were slain as well. Not one of them was left. All sacrificed themselves for the sanctification of God's name. . . . Women also sacrificed themselves in multitudes in the sight of all. Among them was a young girl, a bride by the name of Sarit. She was wondrously beautiful and full of grace in the eyes of all. When she saw that the women were slaughtering each other with knives and swords, she wanted to run away through a

24. *Ibid.*, pp. 9–10.

window out of great terror. Her prospective father-in-law, the pious Jehudah bar Abraham, saw this and said to her, "My daughter, I have not been privileged to live to see my son Abraham take you as his bride, but I will not allow you to fall into the hands of the Christians." And he seized her, took her down from the window, kissed her on the lips, and together they both began to weep and lament bitterly. He turned to all around him and said, "Behold, all of you, how I today lead my daughter, my bride, to the marriage canopy." Hearing this, all of them began to shriek and lament with a terrible cry of anguish. And the pious Rabbi Jehudah said, "My daughter, come and rest in the bosom of Father Abraham. In one hour you will obtain the world of eternity and will be in the same place as all the righteous and the pious." And he took her, set her down on the knee of her groom Abraham, severed her with a sword, and then killed his son.[25]

But the petrified heart of the chronicler does not hold out. He suddenly interrupts the description of the horrible events, and from his breast anguished cries of hatred and vengeance are torn:

Let Him who by His word created the world take vengeance for the blood of His faithful strvants that has been shed! Let Him take vengeance upon those who said, "We will destroy them from among the peoples, and we will blot out the name of Israel!" God is the Lord of vengeance. Show Thyself, then, O God of vengeance! See how they kill us for Thy name's sake! Repay them, O God of justice, for all their deeds! Pour out Thy wrath upon them! Demand of them the blood of Thy slain servants! Let not the earth cover our blood that has been shed! Let the hollow of the world be filled with our cries of woe!

25. *Ibid.*, pp. 20–21.

# CHAPTER THREE

# The *Sefer Ḥasidim*

WE MAY consider the twelfth century a boundary separating two eras in Jewish life in medieval Europe. Until that century the Jews lived more or less in tranquillity and occupied a definite and important place in economic life. With the first two Crusades, however, a bloody period of oppression and massacre at the hands of the surrounding populace began for the Jews. "Until that time," correctly notes the historian Heinrich Graetz, "persecutions of Jews occurred only sporadically. But after 1146 (i.e., after the Second Crusade) these persecutions became ever more frequent, ever more severe and inhuman." History, however, can relate not only the cruelty of the Christian mobs, of the Crusader bands whom Rabbi Eleazar bar Nathan compares to the "wolves of the desert"; the chronicles,[1] as well as numerous supplications and laments written at that time,[2] also tell of remarkable devotion, of entire Jewish communities willingly surrendering their lives for their faith.

1. See Zunz, *Die synagogale Poesie des Mittelalters*, p. 20; *Quellen zur Geschichte der Juden in Deutschland*, Vols. II and III.
2. For example the *kinot* or lamentations "Elohim Al Dami Le-Dami"; "Ha-Et Ha-Kol Kol Yaakov"; "Mi Yiten Roshi Mayyim"; "Shelumei Emunei Yistrael"; and many others. Many of these lamentations and supplications were published by S. Bernfeld in his *Sefer Ha-Demaot*, Vol. I.

We have observed in the preceding chapter how many Jews in the era of the Crusades preferred to die at the hands of those near and dear to them rather than fall into the hands of the beasts in the form of men. They chose to burn themselves in their own houses or to slaughter each other. In Worms 800 Jews perished in this way, for example, and in Mainz 1,300 sacrificed themselves as martyrs. Apostates who saved their lives through conversion were very rare, and of these, legends about how they quickly regretted their act are told.[3] Every Jew was prepared to give up his life for his sanctuary, the heritage of his fathers, with all the passion of the true believer. With his simple faith, he knew neither of doubts nor of compromises, and in the struggle for his religion could not and would not yield on the least point. Every member of the community, even the common and unlearned man, in that horrible era had to have tremendous moral strength and be ready at any moment to become a hero, a "saint," a martyr.

Naturally the ingenious dialectics of the Tosafists, their *novellae*, their clever theories and subtleties, could not arouse and confirm such moral power in Jews or kindle the flame of devotion in their hearts. It was not sharply pointed, clever words that were now required, but fervent words speaking not so much to the mind as to the emotions, penetrating to the depths of the soul, awakening the most intimate dreams and hopes. These requirements were perfectly fulfilled by the so-called books of *musar* (ethical instruction) which burgeoned within Franco-German Jewry in the twelfth and thirteenth centuries.

To give the reader a notion of this literature we shall dwell at length on the most important and popular book of ethical instruction of that era, the *Sefer Ḥasidim,* which is not the work of a single individual but of an entire group and was compiled in the course of several generations.

The *Sefer Ḥasidim* has come down to us in two versions. One, the later version, consisting of 1,178 paragraphs, was first published in Bologna in 1538 and thereafter many times reprinted.[4] The second, much older version remained in manuscript in the library of Parma.[5] The value of the older version consists not only in the

3. One of these legends was employed by the poet Saul Tschernichowsky in his poem *Baruch Mi-Magentzah* (1902).
4. In the second edition, which appeared in Basel at the end of 1580, only 1,172 paragraphs are reprinted. The other six were eliminated by the censor.
5. *Cod. de Rossi,* No. 1133; first published in Berlin in 1891–93 by the Mekitzei Nirdamin Society under the direction of Jehudah Wistinetzki.

fact that it is approximately one and a half times larger[6] than the one known before; more important is the fact that only through it, since it was written many years earlier, can we obtain some understanding of how this collective book was produced. In the later edition these signs are no longer evident, and it is therefore impossible to recognize in it the seams uniting the separate parts that were composed and put together in the course of three generations. The scholars who knew only the later version offered, in their day, various theories about the authorship of the *Sefer Ḥasidim.* Güdemann, for example, in his well-known work,[7] endeavored to show that the book was composed by Rabbi Jehudah Ḥasid but that in the *yeshivot* of his disciples (Rabbi Eleazar of Worms and others) it was passed along from hand to hand in three versions and, following these three versions, the text published in Bologna was put together. The Parma version, however, refutes all such theories.

In the Bologna edition the second paragraph speaks of the author of the book in the third person and indicates, incidentally, that the same author also composed various notebooks on "matters of piety," on "humility" and "reverence." Completely different is the beginning of the *Sefer Ḥasidim* according to the Parma version published by Wistinetzki. At the beginning of the book is written in large letters the name Samuel, and immediately thereafter comes the phrase *Sod Yirei Elohim*, whose numerical value is equivalent in *gematria* to the name Samuel (377). After this begins, in the name of the author himself, the text of the first of the three notebooks or *kuntrasim* (*Sefer Ha-Yirah*) of which the Bologna edition speaks. Immediately following the first *kuntras* is the second, *Sefer Ḥasidim* II.[8] There is now no longer any doubt that the first twenty-six paragraphs of the Parma manuscript are the oldest part of the *Sefer Ḥasidim*, which Rabbi Jehudah Ḥasid's

6. In the manuscript of Parma there are 1,983 paragraphs. Even the paragraphs that are included in both versions are to be found not only in a different order but are also edited in different ways. Not infrequently a certain paragraph from one version is found in fragments in various paragraphs of the other version.
7. *Geschichte die Erziehungswesen und der Kultur der abendländischen Juden*, Vol. I, *Beilage* IV–VI.
8. The *Sefer Ha-Yirah* occupies the first thirteen paragraphs. At the beginning of the fourteenth paragraph is written: "*Sefer Ḥasidim bet* [II]." The twelve following paragraphs (15–26) are a separate *kuntras* dealing exclusively with repentance. Of the first thirteen paragraphs only ten appear in the Bologna edition, and this in various places. Also only a part of the *Sefer Teshuvah* appears there.

father, Rabbi Samuel ben Kalonymos,[9] a scion of a prominent family in Mainz, composed in the form of two separate *kuntrasim.*

Of Samuel's life we have only a few details. We know merely that he was left an orphan early in life,[10] that most of his years he was a wanderer,[11] and that from his youth on he separated himself from the world and lived under a regimen of strict asceticism. He was therefore, out of great respect, called "the holy," "the pious," and even "the prophet." He was also, as we shall see later, a Kabbalist, one of the first and most important Kabbalists among the Franco-German Jews. For the moment, however, we shall consider him only as the composer of the first and oldest parts of the *Sefer Ḥasidim.* To the *kuntrasim* of Samuel ben Kalonymos his son Rabbi Jehudah Ḥasid added many of his own words of instruction, and later Jehudah Ḥasid's disciple, Rabbi Eleazar of Worms, supplemented the work with numerous new sayings. These three ethical preachers and Kabbalists must be considered the authors of the most important parts of the *Sefer Ḥasidim.* Later on, copyists changed in places the individual *kuntrasim* of the three authors, made certain additions and notes,[12] and also inserted sayings and fragments of earlier authors.[13] In this way copies of the *Sefer Ḥasidim* in various versions were produced, and later editors attempted to combine these and make of them a complete and

9. On Samuel ben Kalonymos see Abraham Epstein's article in *Ha-Goren,* IV, 92–95, and in *MGWJ,* XXXIX, 448. There is an interesting report by the author of *Shalshelet Ha-Kabbalah* that he himself saw a small ethical book with the title *Sefer Ḥasidim* in which it was explicitly indicated that the author was Rabbi Jehudah Ḥasid's father, Samuel Ha-Navi.

10. His father, Kalonymos, fled at the time of the First Crusade from Mainz to Speyer and died there in 1126. Samuel was then no more than ten years old. See *Letterbode,* X, 112, which gives the report of Rabbi Jehudah Ḥasid's disciple Rabbi Eleazar of Worms, who indicates that "when the elder Rabbi Kalonymos died, his son Samuel Ḥasid was still a boy."

11. For the legend of how Samuel ben Kalonymos met Rabbenu Tam see Brüll, *Jahrebücher fur jüdische Geschichte und Literatur,* IX, 26. Interesting also is the "story of Rabbenu Samuel Ḥasid," included in the *Shalshelet Ha-Kabbalah,* in which there is an account of Rabbenu Tam's debate with Moses in Rabbi Samuel's schoolroom.

12. In the version of the Parma manuscript we see in places very clearly how new additions were made to the basic text. Near No. 430, in the margin, is written the word *tosafah* (addition), and as "addition" a fantastic story of Rabbi Jehudah Ḥasid is introduced. Later there is another addition, and it is even indicated who is responsible for it: "I, Isaac ben Moses, wrote this."

13. For example, from Rabbenu Nissim ben Jacob's *Megillat Setarim,* from Saadiah's *Sefer Teshuvah,* and from Shabbetai Donnolo's *Hakemani.*

corrected text.[14] This explains why, in the many times reprinted Bologna edition, the same paragraph is not infrequently repeated several times in various places.[15] Occasionally one paragraph even contradicts another.[16]

Properly to appreciate this book, one must take into account the circumstances and the milieu in which its creators lived. For this purpose, however, it is unnecessary to turn to the historians who have studied that era. The *Sefer Ḥasidim* itself provides us enough material to obtain a very clear picture of that dark and terrible time. It suffices merely to pay attention to events that had become common and everyday and of which the *Sefer Ḥasidim* speaks in a calm, matter-of-fact tone.

In No. 197, for example, a community about which it was decreed that either it would convert or be killed is spoken of. The rabbi of this community did not have the required endurance and advocated a compromise, namely, to convert externally and later return to the faith of Israel. Elsewhere (No. 212), there is an account of a community in which there were rich men who, because of their wealth, became arrogant and concerned themselves little with Torah. An old man who was a great scholar lived there, and he warned: "Know, if you do not repent and occupy yourselves with the study of Torah, I am afraid that the community will suffer destruction." And so it was. After the old man died, the enemy came and destroyed the entire community.

We read in another place (No. 222) that

> many Jews perished in the time of the evil decree [i.e., the period of the Crusades]; many others, however, were prepared to die but were saved. A certain Jew named Shabbetai saw in a dream one of those who had perished who was also named Shabbetai. The Shabbetai who had been slain said: "All who were ready to sacrifice themselves to sanctify God's name have a place with us in Paradise prepared for them."

In one city, the *Sefer Ḥasidim* relates, the gentiles killed all the Jews because they refused to surrender their faith. Only two young men, students in the Talmudic academy, were saved. They managed to hide themselves, and the gentiles did not know about

14. In the Bologna edition it is indicated before No. 1136, "this is taken from another *Sefer Ḥasidim*." A similar remark appears in the Parma version before No. 721: "I found this in another book."
15. For example, Nos. 14 and 300; 69 and the end of 207; 97 and 911; 129 and 275; 422 and 704; 255 and 639; 588 and 785.
16. For example, Nos. 679 and 701.

them. At night in the dark the two young men were able to run away. One then said to the other, "I will come out of my hiding place so that they may slay me for the sanctification of God's name; I wish to die such a death as Rabbi Ḥananiah ben Teradyon,[17] who was burned at the stake." His comrade replied: "No, if they come to us, I am prepared to sacrifice myself, but I will not of my own free will hand myself over to them. For Rabbi Ḥananiah ben Teradyon was burned *together with the scroll of the Torah*."[18] It was not his own young life that he grieved for, but it seemed a pity to him that with him, the student of the *yeshivah*, the Torah should perish.

The prince of a certain city, the *Sefer Ḥasidim* further relates,[19] was very cruel toward the Jews residing there, and so they determined to run away. The prince learned of this, stopped them, and forced them to swear that they would not flee again. Later the Jews of the community were in doubt whether they might violate the oath that had been given under duress. Finally they came to the conclusion that the oath must not be violated, that there must be no "desecration of God's name," for Jews would no longer be believed when they swore an oath.

Such cruel "princes" apparently were very numerous. Immediately afterwards, in the next section, is the story of another prince who was extremely wicked and wished to convert all the Jews. Hence they fled. The neighboring communities then wanted to decree a ban to the effect that no Jew should ever again live in that city. But a certain scholar said to them, "Why make difficulties for future generations? It is sufficient that you decree that no one may dwell there as long as this wicked man is alive."

The horrible circumstances of that tragic and dark era placed on the agenda many ethical problems which had to be resolved practically in daily life. For example, the following rule is stated in the *Sefer Ḥasidim* (No. 699): in case the enemies declare, "Give us one of your number and we will kill him; if not, we will kill all of you," they must all be slain; it is not permitted to hand over a single soul of Israel. If the enemies say, "Give us one of your daughters and we will violate her; if not, we will degrade all your women," let them rape all of them, but one must not hand over a single Jewish woman, even one who is not married, to lewdness.

The practical demands of daily life also required that the following kinds of questions be answered: What, for example, is the law

17. One of the *asarah harugei malchut*, the ten martyrs of the Hadrianic persecution in the second century C.E.

18. Parma version, No. 251.

19. *Ibid.*, No. 423.

when, many years later, a knife is found in the grave of persons who perished for the sake of God's name?[20] The decision was that the knife must be replaced where it was found and may not be used. The *Sefer Ḥasidim* further rules[21] that in a house where martyrs were slain for the sanctification of God's name and their blood spattered the stones and walls, the owner, when whitewashing his house, must not scrape off the blood stains nor cover them, for it is written, "Let the earth not cover my blood."

Despite the fact that the Torah forbids women to wear men's clothing, the *Sefer Ḥasidim* declares that in a time of oppression, when the enemy besieges a city, or when Jews are travelling and there is a danger that the enemy may attack and rape the women, the latter should disguise themselves as men (No. 200). Immediately thereafter in the next paragraph is related the story of a beautiful woman who while travelling put on a beard and was thereby saved. The *Sefer Ḥasidim* warns, however, that one may not put on a cross or any garment of the Christian clergy; one may also not display in his windows holy images (icons), even when he is certain that only in this way can he be saved from death (No. 221). "Only Jews," proudly declare the authors of the *Sefer Ḥasidim*, "are commanded to sacrifice themselves for the sanctification of God's name, but not the other peoples of the world."

The massacres and persecutions which the Jews had to endure are related by the *Sefer Ḥasidim* in an altogether calm, epic tone. Only rarely, and then when to massacre are added falsehood and vileness, does a feeling of wrath also manifest itself. "Their mouths are full of lies, their hand is the hand of falsehood," the *Sefer Ḥasidim* cries out. In proof of this it relates the following story which occurred in the time of the Crusades:

> It was once decreed against the Jews that they must forsake the God of their fathers and adopt the alien faith. The Jews determined to flee from their places. Many of them had acquaintances among the princes, and these pretended to be their friends and dissuaded them, saying, "Come to us; we will protect you from your enemies." But when the Jews came to them, they killed them. [No. 697]

The era in which the *Sefer Ḥasidim* was produced was not only steeped in blood, rapine, and massacre; it was also a time of ignorance and stupidity, when bizarre superstitions, crude fairy tales, and fantastic legends dominated men's minds. In central Europe Jews lived among a populace which was still at a very low level of

20. Ordinary edition, No. 1113.
21. *Ibid.*, No. 449.

culture. The ability to read and write was extremely rare. Among the Christian inhabitants the rule of the old pagan conceptions, of the terrible fears and dark dread that stem from the primal home—the thickly overgrown forests—was still powerful. The teaching of the medieval church on "original sin," and on the two dominions, the kingdom of heaven and the kingdom of Satan, the exalted angels and the demons of the "other side," increased the fear and melancholy of the common people, confirmed their dread of their mysterious surroundings, of the unknown and hidden lurking on all sides. The benighted man of the Middle Ages, downtrodden as he was and filled with terror because of his sinfulness, felt himself solitary and forsaken. He sought to appease and bribe with prayers and supplications, with incantations and amulets, the evil spirits lying in wait for him, so that they might have mercy on him and aid him in time of trouble. The atmosphere of the Middle Ages was filled with millions of destroyers, demons, and evil spirits; the world swarmed with hosts of scoffers, witches, angels of destruction, and evil ones; and all these whirled and danced, conducted feasts, stuck out their tongues, deafened men with their diabolic laughter.

The *Sefer Ḥasidim*, which was produced in such a suffocating and unnatural environment, could not liberate itself from this enchanted and fantastic world. Many pages of the book are filled with bizarre tales and superstitions. To be sure, the *Sefer Ḥasidim* complains strongly of those who deal in whispering magic and incantations, for they thereby violate a negative commandment of the Torah, and it warns that they will have a bad end because of this (Nos. 59, 205, and 206). "A son of Israel," it insists, "must address his prayers and requests only to the Almighty, the God of mercy, not to the 'other side,' to the princes of darkness and angels of detruction." But the princes of darkness and angels of destruction were, in the eyes of its authors, actual, living powers. They, along with their Christian neighbors, firmly believed in witches who could change a man into the form of a wolf or a cat. "Only the eyes remain the same in all metamorphoses" (No. 1166). The *Sefer Ḥasidim* also relates at length the tricks perpetrated by the various kinds of witches, who are listed by name: Ashtriyah,[22] Maresh,[23] Varvelsh.[24] It declares that Ashtriyah, before flying into the air, lets down her hair. The hairs fall on a person while he sleeps and suck out his blood (Nos. 464 and 680). These witches can also disguise themselves as cats. If such a cat receives a blow from a

22. From the Old French word *Estrie.*
23. From the word *maren.*
24. From the word *werwolf.*

person, it must die unless it manages to get bread and salt from the person who struck it (No. 465). The witches can also carry a disease from one child to another (No. 681), work magic on a woman so that she will remain barren (Nos. 391, 447, and 476) or on a man so that he will die of love (Nos. 172 and 175). "When a maidservant or a manservant," the *Sefer Ḥasidim* naively warns, "demands of his master that he free him, otherwise he will work magic upon him, let the owner not be stubborn but liberate him."[25]

The *Sefer Ḥasidim* also knows definitely that witches can harm only when they are on earth but not when flying in the air.[26] Demons, when in the air, frequently carry on warfare and hurl arrows at each other (Nos. 443 and 469). Among the demons, the most noxious are of the kind called *dragon*. A *dragon* cannot be harmed even by a sword. He can be overcome only by a man born of a woman who has lived with the *dragon* himself (No. 469). Demons, as well as the wild men who dwell in the forest, the *Sefer Ḥasidim* tells us, usually gather in groups, nine to a group. Hence, anyone who has been harmed by them must recite an exorcism nine times, "as is done in Germany," or hang on his neck nine little sticks called *stiletti*, and these sticks must be taken from nine draw-bridges that hang before nine gates (No. 1153). If someone is afraid that a demon may attack him while he is asleep, the best remedy to insure that the demon will have no power over him is firmly to bend the thumb.[27] The *Sefer Ḥasidim* also provides precise information concerning the appearance of the demons. The males are over-grown with hair. Among the females, however, the head is entirely bald (Nos. 1155 and 1162). The *Sefer Ḥasidim* further relates, as if it were a well-known fact, that when one traces a thief's form on a wall and strikes a blow on the place where the eye is traced, the thief will immediately feel a sharp pain in his eye.[28]

The *Sefer Ḥasidim* also provides the most precise information about the dead and their behavior. The dead can speak, but speaking is very difficult for them. However, they can read as easily as living persons. "Among them books lie on their tables," and the person who was accustomed to study in life does so after death also. "It once happened," we are told, "that some gentiles passed by a cemetery Friday evening, and they saw a dead Jew sitting with a

25. Parma version, No. 381.
26. Ordinary edition, No. 478.
27. *Ibid.*, No. 236. For a comparison of the legends and formulas in the *Sefer Ḥasidim* with similar legends among the surrounding Christian populace, see Güdemann, *Geschichte die Erziehungswesen*, I, Chapter 6.
28. Ordinary edition, No. 1172. On similar superstitions or beliefs among other people see Potebnya, *Iz Lyektsii Po Teorii Slovyesnosti*, p. 105.

book at a table" (Nos. 455–56). On certain nights, e.g., the night of Hoshannah Rabbah, the dead come out of their graves to pray. The *Sefer Ḥasidim* relates that two young men once hid themselves in a cemetery and overheard one dead person saying to another, "Let us go out and pray together." All the dead then left their graves and prayed for the living that the latter be preserved from death and that those concerning whom it had already been decreed that they must leave the world might repent before death and die an easy death. The young men returned to the town and related what they saw and heard. The next year the young men again hid themselves on the night of Hoshannah Rabbah in the cemetery and once more all the dead left their graves, except a maiden who had died just before the Sabbath. She explained that her father, who had once been a wealthy man, had become so impoverished that he had no money for shrouds and she had, therefore, been buried naked. The young men also heard how several of the dead spoke among each other: "We must no longer pray as a group. People have overheard and reported this among the living. Let every man now pray by himself in his grave." When the young men related all this, the community was extremely angry with the maiden's father. Shrouds were immediately obtained and her body was clothed in them.[29]

But the dead do not pray only at the cemetery. The *Sefer Ḥasidim* relates that a man once fell asleep at night in the synagogue. The sexton did not notice him and locked the synagogue. At midnight the man awoke and saw the entire synagogue filled with dead men wrapped in prayer shawls, and among them were also two living persons. In a short time these two died (No. 711).

The dead are eager to have their graves visited frequently. Once, relates the *Sefer Ḥasidim*, a community wished to leave its town and settle in a new place. One of the dead came in a dream to a member of the community and warned him, "Do not leave us. We have great pleasure when you come to the cemetery. Know that as soon as you leave us, you will be killed." The community paid no attention, and all of them were slain (No. 709). The dead are also displeased with bad neighbors. It once happened that a learned and righteous man was buried near a disreputable person. The righteous man came in a dream to members of the community and complained, "Why did you lay me in such an unclean place? The stench

29. Ordinary edition, No. 452. Here it is also related that whoever sees his shadow without a head on Hoshannah Rabbah will die during the coming year. "However, it happened that a certain man saw his shadow without a head that night; but he fasted and gave large sums to charity, so he lived many more years."

of it is not to be endured." A wall of stones was then erected between the graves, and the righteous man ceased to appear in dreams (No. 705).

The dead are also easily angered at the least disrespect and avenge themselves mightily for it. The *Sefer Ḥasidim* has a story about this—how once, when a coffin was made for a dead man, one of the boards was left over. A certain person decided to carve himself a fiddle out of it. The dead man then appeared to that person in a dream and admonished him not to do so. The latter did not listen and proceeded to make the fiddle. The dead person then came to him again in a dream and said: "If you do not break the fiddle, you are in grave danger." The man, in fact, soon became seriously ill. His son then took the fiddle, carried it to the grave of the dead person, broke it, and left the pieces there. Thereupon the sick man promptly recovered (No. 724).

We could cite many more such tales from the *Sefer Ḥasidim*, but those we have already given provide a sufficiently clear picture of the superstitious and backward milieu in which its authors lived. Against this dark background of cruelty and spiritual and intellectual barbarism, however, is unveiled before us the remarkably exalted moral teaching of the pious men who gave their people the famous book of ethical instruction.

We have noted how Maimonides and those who followed his philosophical system declared that the chief obligation of man is to *understand* God, to comprehend through reason the great wisdom of His works.[30] The creators of the *Sefer Ḥasidim*, however, held that the greatest and most important goal is *love* of God—a fervent, burning love that is stronger than death, stronger even than the desire for life.

"Mightier than all else," declares the *Sefer Ḥasidim*,

> must be the love of God. With great and radiant joy must it illuminate the soul. And this love of God must be free of any external motives—not out of fear of punishment and not for the sake of any reward, but out of genuine devotion to God the Creator, because He is the highest level of truth, the most perfect essence of goodness and graciousness. . . . One must love God with passionate love. One must be sick of love, as a man is sick of love for a woman; he cannot forget his beloved for a moment and thinks of her, whether sitting or standing, coming or going, when he eats and when he drinks, and he cannot sleep because of love. Much more powerfully must the love for God burn in man's heart. [No. 14]

30. See *Moreh Nevuchim*, III:54.

"Corresponding to the eighteen benedictions in the *Shemoneh Esreh*," the *Sefer Ḥasidim* emphasizes, "the word love is mentioned eighteen times in the Song of Songs."[31] All the pleasures of the world lose their value before the joy which a man has when he feels in himself the flame of love for God. There is no greater bliss than to sacrifice oneself out of love for the Creator of the world.[32]

In that dark era of blood and terror, when even an ordinary Jew was presumed to be a "saint" and had to be prepared at every moment to sacrifice himself for his faith, the *Sefer Ḥasidim*, which was produced not by an individual but, in a sense, by the community, endeavored to arouse in the hearts of the people the fervor and mystical ecstasy of self-sacrifice and martyrdom. It is therefore quite natural that its authors, who regarded study of the Torah as the chief commandment, adopted an attitude of definite coldness, at times even of indignation, toward the hairsplitting Talmudic dialectic of the Tosafists. The chief authors[33] of the *Sefer Ḥasidim* were, in fact, personally quite close to the Tosafists, but as men of emotion and enthusiasm they could not be casual toward the clever but cold system of oversophisticated mentality and ingenuity which could give so little to the grieved heart of the common people with their longing for consolation. A protest against Talmudic hairsplitting is already clearly discernible in the introduction to the oldest part of the *Sefer Ḥasidim*, Rabbi Samuel Ha-Navi's *Sefer Ha-Yirah*.

"For men who fear God and revere His holy name," the author of the *Sefer Ha-Yirah* begins,

> I write this book as a memorial. Let them and their children learn from it how one must fear God. I do not undertake this because I am the cleverest of our generation. I know how small I am in good deeds and in Torah; in my generation there are surely many greater than I in Torah, knowledge, good deeds, and fear of heaven. But they occupy themselves, out of much knowledge, with hairsplitting in the Talmud, the wisdom of which is inexhaustible.[34]

However, adds the author, not all God-fearers are men of Torah and good scholars. There are many whose "hearts burn with desire

31. Parma version, No. 389.
32. Bologna edition, No. 300.
33. Samuel Ha-Navi, Jehudah Ḥasid, and Eleazar of Worms.
34. *Sefer Ḥasidim*, Parma version, No. 1. See also the Bologna edition, No. 51. Nos. 292 and 599 also are directed against *pilpul* or hairsplitting dialectic.

to obey the will of the Creator, but they do not know how to fulfill the longing of their hearts." For these simple, sincere people, who are not well versed in the difficult sections of the Gemara but whose hearts "burn" with love for God's will, the pious Samuel ben Kalonymos wrote his book.

To such plain people the *Sefer Ḥasidim* explains that a pious man is worthier than a scholar,[35] and that the greatest joy of the soul is prayer—the prayer that comes out of the depths of the heart, not the cold, mechanically repeated one. The *Sefer Ḥasidim* teaches,

> If a Jew who understands no Hebrew but is a fearer of God comes to you and wishes to pray with devotion, or if a Jewess, who certainly does not understand Hebrew, comes to you, you must tell them to pray in the language they understand, for prayer is the petition of the heart, and if the heart does not understand what the lips say, how can such a prayer be of any avail? Therefore, it is better that every man should pray in the language he understands.[36]

The *Sefer Ḥasidim*, in this connection, introduces a lovely story which moves one with its very simplicity. But there is also discernible in it a hidden, mocking smile at the "scholars" who carry on hair-splitting discussions about the Law. It is the story of a young Jewish cowherd who was so ignorant that he could not even pray. Every morning he would simply say, "Master of the universe, you know that if You had cows and gave them to me to watch, while from others I receive payment for this, for You I would watch them free of charge, so strong is my love for You." Once a scholar passed by and heard how the boy prayed. He said to him, "Fool, do not dare to pray thus!" The boy asked: "How should I pray?" The scholar rehearsed with him the order of the benedictions, the recital of "Hear, O Israel" and other prayers, and urged him no longer to say his own ignorant prayer. The scholar then went his way, but the boy promptly forgot all the prayers he had rehearsed with him. He was afraid, however, to continue to say his customary prayer to God, and so he ceased praying altogether. The scholar then heard a voice speaking to him in a dream at night: "Know that if you do not go to the cowherd and explain to him that he may say his customary prayer which he used to offer before you came to him, you will have a bad end, for you have robbed the next world of one of My true servants." The scholar immediately went and asked the boy, "What prayer do you

35. Parma version, No. 36.
36. Ordinary edition, Nos. 588 and 785.

say?" The boy answered, "I do not pray at all now because the prayers that you taught me I have forgotten, and the prayer about the cows you forbade me to say." The scholar then told him of his dream and ordered him again to say his customary prayer. "God sees," adds the *Sefer Ḥasidim,* "that here was neither Torah nor good deeds but the simple wish to do good, and this is accounted a very important thing, for God requires the heart above all."[37]

"A pure heart, a right spirit, and truth on the lips" (No. 51)—this is the ideal of the authors of the *Sefer Ḥasidim.* "Great is the joy that stems from heartfelt prayer," the *Sefer Ḥasidim* asserts, "but only when not merely one's own pain and desires but the sorrows and longings of those near to him are poured out in the prayer—as is written in Scripture, 'And thou shalt love thy neighbor as thyself.' " "Thou shalt love thy neighbor as thyself"—this is the chief principle of morality, the true and only criterion by which, according to the *Sefer Ḥasidim,* one must evaluate all deeds, all of human life.[38]

How should a man who has power over other men conduct himself? Let such a man, the *Sefer Ḥasidim* teaches, consider how he would wish to be treated if he were in the other's power, and then let him so conduct himself with his slaves and servants (No. 668). "A man shall not pray for his own benefit for such things as may bring injury to others, but he who has in mind the general good even before he thinks of his own, with him it will also be well."[39] A man must not place himself before others. He must not say, "I and you" but "you and I."[40]

The authors of the *Sefer Ḥasidim* teach their oppressed and persecuted brethren that "of all the virtues, the best is humility."[41] "Do not reply to another man's insults; if another curses you, be silent" (No. 650). "There is a story of a certain pious man," the *Sefer Ḥasidim* relates, "who was unusually long-lived. When he was asked, 'How did you merit such length of days?,' he replied, 'All my life I have never responded to anyone's insults or curses but have always immediately forgiven the one who offended me' " (No. 649). "There is a story of another pious man," the *Sefer Ḥasidim* further relates,

37. Parma version, Nos. 5–6. For parallel stories among other peoples see *Hebrew Union College Annual,* 1927, pp. 370–74.
38. See Nos. 218, 247, 349, 470, 932, 967, 982, and others.
39. Parma version, No. 478.
40. Ordinary edition, No. 15.
41. *Ibid.,* No. 53.

whom someone had the arrogance to shame and greatly revile. The community was indignant and decided that such a person must be excommunicated. The pious man said to them, "Do this not." The others argued, "He must be punished so that he will not again permit himself to do thus." But the pious man answered, "Learn from me and do likewise. I reply to insult with silence, and I do not wish you to carry on a controversy for my sake. And do further as I do. If vile men mock you, if they revile and shame you, take no account of their words." [No. 182]

Not to take account of words of mockery and scorn—this is the root of piety (No. 7). And the greatest sin is to shame someone publicly (No. 54). If someone openly shames or offends another, it is as if he had slain him. One must guard himself not to shame another, even unwittingly. In the presence of a slave or the son of a slave, one must not speak contemptuously of slaves.[42] In the presence of one who is blind in one eye, one must not speak of one-eyed creatures.[43] If one hears a teacher make an error in instructing his pupils, one must not openly say, "You interpret incorrectly." If it is possible to make him take note of his error and not shame him in the process, it is well. If not, give the task to someone close to him, and let him explain things to him so as not to shame him (No. 310). From a guest one must not ask words of Torah so long as one is not certain that he is in a position to comply (No. 312). One must not shame publicly either servants or slaves (No. 665), and it is a great sin to cause pain to any creature whatsoever or to place on a beast a greater burden than it can carry.[44] It is not permitted to cut off an extremity of an animal, because it is pained thereby and cannot drive away the flies from itself (No. 589). "You may hate," teaches the *Sefer Ḥasidim*, "only that which God, blessed be He, hates."[45]

In many of the maxims and proverbs of the *Sefer Ḥasidim* is heard the authentic perspicacity of the common folk, with its simple world outlook. "Do not envy him who is greater than you, and do not despise him who is smaller than you" (No. 282). "Silence is the best wisdom. If I have spoken, I may later regret it; if I do not speak, I have nothing to regret. As long as the word

42. Parma version, No. 96.
43. *Ibid.*, No. 635.
44. Ordinary edition, No. 666. In the Parma version an interesting story about a donkey is introduced in this connection (No. 144).
45. Ordinary edition, No. 973.

has not come forth from my mouth, I rule over it; once I have brought it out, the word rules over me."[46]

"Our world compared to the other world is like a dream compared to the waking state," we read in the *Sefer Ḥasidim* (No. 15). The authors of this work, however, have little use for self-mortification. They declare that "he who afflicts himself is a sinner." Man is obliged to preserve his health so that he may have the strength to serve the Creator (Nos. 127 and 617). He must, however, guard himself greatly against the "evil inclination." Especially must he take care not to stumble through lust for the beauty of women, for this lust often leads one away from the path of righteousness and brings him into the power of sin. "See how great is the power of love for women," warns the *Sefer Ḥasidim;* "Samson was the mightiest of all the mighty, David the most pious of the pious, and Solomon the wisest among all the wise, yet all three stumbled because of women. . . . That is how great the temptation of women is" (No. 619). Hence, the book admonishes, one must keep far away from women and look them in the face as little as possible. Young men should not go around with young girls. Let girls dance separately, and let the young men associate with the old. Even children should not play together, but girls and boys separately (No. 168).

The *Sefer Ḥasidim* places great emphasis on the purity of family life and is very precise in every detail concerning the intimate life of man and wife. "Let a man not say," warns the *Sefer Ḥasidim,* " 'I am so poor; how can I take a wife? I will not have the wherewithal to support her.' " He who thinks thus is one of those who lack faith. He, too, who has bread only for the present day and worries about what he will live on tomorrow is of those who lack faith (No. 519). "If a young man wishes to take to wife a much older woman, then the man who fears sin must remove himself and take no part in the match" (No. 379). "One may not marry his daughter to an old man," warns the *Sefer Ḥasidim,*

> except if she herself wishes him and no other man. It is written in the Torah, "You may not hand your daughter over to unchastity." This means: do not marry her to an old man or to one whom she does not love. . . . It is written, "And you shall love your neighbor as yourself"; just as you would not wish to take a woman who is hateful to you, so you must not compel your daughter to do such a thing. [*Ibid.*]

Again, an old man who takes a virgin commits a sin. The *Sefer Ḥasidim* relates a tale about this:

46. *Ibid.*, No. 86.

It once happened that people wanted to match an old man with a virgin. The old man refused because he was afraid of committing a sin. They said to him, "But she wishes only you." The old man then went to the girl, bared his head, and said, "See how old I am; my head is entirely gray. I am bowed with age. You should not say that you did not know of this." She answered, "My lord, I am ready to wash your feet so long as I can bear your name." And so they married, and had honorable children. [*Ibid.*]

"An old man was once told, 'In such and such a place lives a beautiful woman who wishes to have you. Follow our advice. Go there, but first dye your hair black so that she will think you are not old.' The man answered, 'God forbid! I will not mislead her. Let her see that I am, indeed, already old' " (*ibid.*).

The *Sefer Ḥasidim* also dwells much on child-rearing. Typical are the following statements. If you see that a boy finds study of the Bible easy but the Talmud is difficult for him, you should not press the issue and demand of him that he now study the Gemara. Let him learn what he understands; he will study the Gemara when he reaches the age of fifteen. But if at that age the Gemara is still too difficult for him, let him study the *Halachot Gedolot* and Midrash (No. 308). Every father is obligated to study Torah with his daughters also, to familiarize them with the laws and commandments. When the Gemara says, "If one teaches a woman Torah, it is as if he taught her unseemliness," this refers only to the profundities of the difficult sections of the Talmud and to the hidden secrets of the Torah. However, the *Sefer Ḥasidim* adds, naturally no young man should teach the girls, but the father himself should study with his daughters and his wife (No. 313).

Certain passages move one with their sensitivity and compassion. "A father," the *Sefer Ḥasidim* admonishes, "must not kiss his child in the synagogue, for there are people there who have no children and who may suffer pain from this" (Nos. 255 and 639).

Very interesting also is the attitude of the authors of the *Sefer Ḥasidim* to the book. One must bear in mind that at that time there was still no cheap paper or printing press. A manuscript book was extremely rare and expensive, a luxury, and not everyone was in a position to buy it. We shall observe later that even famous rabbinic scholars never in their lives saw certain tractates of the Talmud (not to speak of other books), because it was very difficult to obtain them. Hence the *Sefer Ḥasidim* frequently emphasizes what a great religious duty it is to lend books. "If a man has two sons," it declares, "one of whom gladly lends his books and the other does not, the father should leave all his books to the one who gladly lends. It will be well with his soul" (No. 870). "There was a man," the *Sefer Ḥasidim* further relates,

> who used to lend his books so that people could study them, and he said to his children, "Remember, even if you are on bad terms with someone, you must not, on that account, refuse to lend him books. If you are afraid that he will not return the books to you, take a pledge from him, but you must lend them. . . . Know that if you sometimes see books being burned, this is a punishment for the fact that people did not wish to lend them so that others might learn from them." [No. 871]

If someone has books to sell and there are two persons eager to purchase them, his own brother of whom it is known that he lends to no one and a complete stranger who willingly lends his books, he should sell them to the stranger and not to his miserly brother (No. 931). "There is a story of a certain man," the *Sefer Ḥasidim* further relates,

> who died and left many books. His heirs then sold all of them. Certain persons were saddened that the heirs had to sell the father's legacy. A wise man living there said, "You have nothing to weep over in this case. I know what sins brought it about that the books should not remain in the hands of the heirs: their father would never lend a book to anyone." [No. 869]

The *Sefer Ḥasidim* goes on to relate that a certain righteous man was exhumed from the grave and his body mistreated. Thereafter he came to someone in a dream and said, "This happened to me as a punishment because I did not give proper care to books. I used to see books torn and spoiled, and did not mend them" (No. 911). The *Sefer Ḥasidim* also cites a whole series of tales of an intimate character which portray the great love that the medieval Jewish woman had for the holy book.[47]

But no matter how precious and beloved were books, more precious than everything else, the *Sefer Ḥasidim* insists, is the quality of compassion for living persons. The *Sefer Ḥasidim* teaches,

> If someone says to you, "I can now give away some money, but tell me what is better—shall I give it to a scribe so that he may write a scroll of the Law, or should I give it to some decent poor people who

47. *Ibid.*, Nos. 873–75. These stories and tales have a significant ethnographic value.

have no clothes?," you shall say to him, "Isaiah the prophet commanded, If thou seest the naked, thou shalt cover him." [No. 1036]

Elsewhere the *Sefer Ḥasidim* declares, "It is better to associate with an ignoramus who is generous and gladly gives alms than with a scholar who is a miser" (No. 323).

The *Sefer Ḥasidim* is even harsher toward men who take interest on loans and those who rub gold from coins and thereby diminish their value. "He who has business with interest-takers, with those who shave gold coins, and their like, will become impoverished," it angrily declares (No. 1073). "Whoever lends money at interest," further says the *Sefer Ḥasidim*,

whoever shaves coins, whoever falsifies weights and measures, or does similar evil things—all these will have a like end: they will become poor and their children will be scattered abroad and have to beg others for help. The same end will those who do business with them also have. [No. 1076]

Among the most interesting pages of the *Sefer Ḥasidim* are those dealing with the relationship of its authors to their Christian neighbors. We have noted that precisely at that time, in that era of terrible persecutions, the isolation of the Jewish community from the surrounding populace increased sharply. The authors of the *Sefer Ḥasidim* endeavor, in fact, to intensify this separation as much as possible. They wish the Jews to be a "people which dwelleth alone," a nation keeping apart from the world and shunning foreign customs. Characteristic in this respect are these warnings: "You may not mention the names of strange gods. You may not even cause gentiles to mention them, aside from not bringing them to your own lips. You may not tell your gentile maidservant that she should lull your crying child with songs if you know that she will sing religious songs."[48]

This hostility, however, is manifested by the *Sefer Ḥasidim* only to "alien customs" and "alien gods." Altogether different is its attitude toward the Christian neighbors themselves. The authors of the *Sefer Ḥasidim* personally suffered a great deal from the Crusades. But they regarded their tormentors as merely blind instruments of the divine will, the rod of punishment for the sins which Jews had committed against God and His commandments.

48. Parma version, Nos. 346 and 389. The *Sefer Ḥasidim* also forbids lulling a child to sleep with Jewish religious melodies. See ordinary edition, No. 238.

"Every time the nations of the world do us injury," the *Sefer Ḥasidim* insists, "this is punishment for the evil that Jews themselves have committed against one another or because they have despised the Torah."[49] "When you see a king or the prince of a city placing a heavy burden of taxation on the community, you must realize this is because the community did not properly support the poor, who were compelled to leave their households and wander about gathering alms" (No. 211). "One may not cheat anyone, either a Jew or a gentile"; "one may not do any kind of wickedness to a gentile"—utterances such as these abound in the *Sefer Ḥasidim.*[50] "If a gentile makes a mistake, you must not exploit it for your benefit, so that God's name not be desecrated through you. If a man is poor, better that he beg alms and not run off with gentile money and God's name be thereby desecrated, for the gentiles will say of the Jews, 'They are thieves, cheaters and liars' " (No. 1080). "One may not benefit from the mistake of a gentile who observes the 'seven commandments of the sons of Noah,' for profit from the mistake of such a one is forbidden. If he has lost something, you must return it to him. You must not conduct yourself toward him contemptuously, but hold him more in honor than a Jew who refuses to occupy himself with the Torah" (No. 358). "When a gentile comes to a strange city and beforehand asks a Jewish acquaintance who of the Jews residing there is an honest man, so that one may do business with him, and who is not, the Jew is obliged to speak the truth and to warn the gentile that with such and such a person he should not do business" (No. 1086). "When a Jew is walking on a path and on both sides of the path there is a swamp and someone laden with a burden comes toward him, even if that person be a gentile, he must step aside, as is written in Scripture, 'So shalt thou find grace and good favor in the sight of God and man' [Proverbs 3: 4]. It is better that another should push you aside than that you should push him aside" (No. 551). "There is a story of a certain Jew," relates the *Sefer Ḥasidim,*

> who had many sons and daughters all of whom died immediately after their weddings. This was punishment for the fact that he had committed injustice and cheated the gentile with whom he had done business, for God, blessed be He, is a righteous judge. He takes up the cause of those who have been robbed, whether they be Jews or non-Jews. [No. 661]

49. *Ibid.*, No. 209.
50. See, for example, Nos. 7, 51, 1074, and many others.

"One may pray to God for a gentile who does good, even for an apostate who does favors for Jews" (No. 793). "If a Jew mentions a decent person who has died, whether it be a Jew or a gentile, he may say of him, 'His memory be for blessing' " (No. 982). Characteristic is the following passage of the *Sefer Ḥasidim:* "If a Jew sees that another Jew wishes to kill a gentile who bears no evil toward that Jew, then he must come to the aid of the gentile" (No. 1018). But, then, shortly afterwards, comes another statement which suddenly casts, like a flash of lightning in a stormy night, a blinding light on the horrible and bloody circumstances under which Jews then lived. "When," says the *Sefer Ḥasidim,*

> Jews are attacked on the way by robbers, and they have decided to overcome and kill the robbers but are observed by other gentiles, and the Jews are afraid that these will go and tell the robbers' relatives and friends, who will later take revenge on them, then the Jews have the right to slay these other gentiles who were merely witnesses. [No. 1021]

We have observed that the *Sefer Ḥasidim* was produced not by an individual but by a community in the course of several generations. It was produced not only *for* the people but, in a certain sense, *by* the people. Like a sponge, it absorbed the hopes, attitudes, beliefs, and superstitions of the broad masses. It thereby becomes one of the most important sources of Jewish folklore in the Middle Ages. Even the style of the book is characteristic in this respect. Religious laws and ethical maxims are interwoven in it with naive folk legends and fantastic stories, and its pages are filled with expressions that became typical in later popular Jewish literature—"a story of a certain sage"; "a story of a woman"; "a story of a pious man"; "a story of an old woman"; "a story of a gentile"; etc. Most of the ethical maxims and homilies are also interwoven with anecdotes. When, for instance, the *Sefer Ḥasidim* indicates that on the eve of the Sabbath it is a religious duty to concern oneself exclusively with "the needs of the Sabbath," it immediately introduces in this connection a story,

> the story of a certain Jewess who used to occupy herself on the eve of the Sabbath with spinning flax and did not devote herself properly to "the needs of the Sabbath." After her death someone saw in a dream how the eyes and hands of this Jewess were being burned on bundles of flax. He asked, "Why does she deserve this?," and was told, "Because she used to spin flax on the eve of Sabbath and devoted herself little to preparing for the Sabbath." [No. 122]

Again, when the *Sefer Ḥasidim* warns that young men must not dance with girls, immediately, "to add authority," a very typical folk tale is introduced,

> the story of a certain man who was riding alone at night in the wilderness by the light of the moon. Suddenly he saw a great camp with many wagons. The wagons were occupied by men and were also pulled by men. . . . When he came closer he saw that they were all dead. He asked them, "Why do you pull these wagons the whole night?" They answered, "This is punishment for our sins, that in life we used to play and dance with girls and women." [No. 169]

The *Sefer Ḥasidim* warns strongly against stumbling through the evil inclination toward women, and in this connection also a story is immediately given. "Learn from the pious men of the nations of the world," says the *Sefer Ḥasidim.*

> There was a prince in whose city a great fair was held each year. . . . Many harlots used to come together there, and a certain woman was their chief. The prince commanded his servant to go to this woman and promise to pay her and all the harlots more than they expected to earn in the course of the entire fair. He ordered his servant to rent a house for the harlots, provide each of them with a bed, clean clothing, and good food, and support them with everything. . . . So the prince did at each fair. [No. 179]

"A man," the *Sefer Ḥasidim* teaches, "must not be irascible or quick-tempered." Immediately, in connection with this, is introduced the story of one whose father had told him before his death that whenever he became angry, he should "wait over one night" and only in the morning do what he had in mind to do in his hour of wrath. The son promised to fulfill the testament of his father. The *Sefer Ḥasidim* then relates how this man once suspected his wife of infidelity. In the moment of anger he almost killed both his innocent wife and his own son, but he remembered his father's commandment. In the morning everything became clear to him. The man became convinced that he had been in error, and "all of them rejoiced greatly" (No. 655).

# CHAPTER FOUR

# *Jewish Mysticism;* ELEAZAR OF WORMS

THE *Sefer Ḥasidim* is closely associated with the name of Rabbi Jehudah Ḥasid. In the memory of the people he was the only author of the beloved book, and popular imagination surrounded his name with a colorful garland of legends. An ancient tale relates that even before he was born miracles were performed for his sake. Once, when his mother was pregnant with him, she passed the women's synagogue in Worms. Suddenly a heavily loaded wagon drove into the narrow alley, and the pregnant woman pressed herself against the wall. A miracle then occurred: a hollow was formed in the wall, and the woman was saved.[1] According to folk legend, Rabbi Jehudah Ḥasid as a youth was a wild ignoramus.[2] He did not even know how to pray and ran around all day with bow and arrow. Once Rabbi Sam-

1. *Maaseh Nissim* of Juspa Shamash, Section 8. The same legend, but in a different version, is given in the well-known *Shalshelet Ha-Kabbalah:* "And I received as a tradition from the sages of the generation that when Rabbi Jehudah Ḥasid was going to the synagogue a wagon passed behind the synagogue while he was there, and the wagon pressed very strongly against him; but a miracle took place and the wall opened and received him, and thus he was saved. The sign is still to be seen to the present day."
2. The same legend is told of many other great figures, e.g., Maimonides.

uel Ḥasid, Jehudah's father, was sitting and studying with his pupils. Suddenly Jehudah ran in and began throwing arrows. The pupils were angered and said to the rabbi, "You are a great and holy man and a scholar, your ancestors were also great scholars, and your son is such an ignoramus and occupies himself with the work of robbers!" Rabbi Samuel was intensely grieved and said to his son, "Do you wish to study?" He answered, "Yes." Rabbi Samuel then went with his son to the house of study and sat him down near his elder son Abraham. Rabbi Samuel then uttered a holy "name," and the entire house of study was filled with a blinding light, so that Abraham had to cover his face, but Jehudah remained calmly seated. Rabbi Samuel then spoke another "name." Abraham could not endure it and covered himself with his father's mantle, but Jehudah merely bowed his head. Rabbi Samuel then called out, "Abraham, my son, the constellation of this hour shines especially for your brother Jehudah. Know, my son, that you will be a great scholar and the head of a *yeshivah*. For your brother, however, all the hidden secrets of the esoteric wisdom will be open, and everything that occurs in the heavens and on the earth will be revealed to him."[3]

Very few factual data about Rabbi Jehudah's life are available. We know only that for his Talmudic knowledge he was indebted to his teacher, Rabbenu Tam's disciple, Rabbi Isaac bar Samuel,[4] and that in the year 1195 he founded his famous *yeshivah* in Regensburg. In this academy blossomed the unique mystical doctrine (*torat ha-nistar*) which Rabbi Samuel first planted in Germany. Already in the time of his son, and especially in the generation of his son's disciples, it dominated Jewish minds and occupied an important place in Jewish cultural life.

The origins of this doctrine must be sought in antiquity. There is no doubt that the ideas of the *torat ha-nistar* first appeared in the East, in Babylonia and Palestine. Evidence of this is discernible in the Babylonian and Jerusalem Talmuds, in the remnants of the literature which the Essenes[5] produced, and also in the numerous books of wonders and mystical writings which arose in Babylonia in the era of the Geonim. As early as the period of the Second Temple there was much concern in the schools of the Essenes and Gnostics with interpreting certain sections of the Book of Ezekiel[6]

3. See *Maaseh-Buch*, p. 48, Rödelsheim edition (quoted according to Grünbaum, *Jüdisch-deutsche Chrestomathie*), pp. 418–19; *Sefer Maasiot*, Brüll's *Jahrbücher für jüdische Geschichte und Literatur*, XI, 32.
4. See Weiss, *Dor Dor Ve-Doreshav* (edition of 1904), IV, 310.
5. An ascetic sect which played a certain role in the Jewish world of ideas in the last two centuries of the period of the Second Temple.
6. Chapters 1, 10, and 43.

in which God's chariot or throne is described in allegorical imagery (*maaseh merkavah*). Men here sought profound mysteries and allusions to exalted matters. They found numerous hidden names of "the heavenly family," as well as veiled divine names with the aid of which one could fathom the secret of the "work of creation" (*maaseh bereshit*). The Talmud frequently mentions commentaries on *maaseh merkaveh*. There is also much discussion in it of the mysteries concealed in various combinations of words and numbers, and of the miracles that can be wrought through "combinations of letters" (*tzerufei otiot*), through joining the letters of God's names, for God Himself brought the heavens and the earth into being through the power of the creative word.[7]

There is no doubt that two hundred years before the destruction of the Second Temple there were already among the Jewish Gnostics certain mystical writings with definite principles and instructions on how to fathom the deep mysteries of "combinations of letters" and make use of the power inherent in the letters of God's name. The oldest Hebrew book we have in which philosophical-mystical problems, together with questions concerning *maaseh bereshit*, the secret of world-creation, are dealt with is the *Sefer Yetzirah*.

This celebrated work, which had a tremendous influence on the subsequent development of Jewish religious-philosophical thought, was, like the *Sefer Ḥasidim*, preserved in two versions.[8] Both of them, however, are strongly corrupted, and this makes the text of the work, which is written in a difficult, mystical language and is full of allusions and secrets, even harder to understand. But, in fact, the difficult and obscure language only increased the importance ascribed to the book.[9] It was believed that it derived from

7. See *Sanhedrin* 65b and 67b; *Berachot* 55b; etc. In these mystical conceptions the influence of Greek and Egyptian elements, as well as the influence of Babylonia, may be discerned. Among the Tannaim, for example, the statement "With ten sayings [*memrot*] was the world created" is often repeated. In the term *memra* (word or saying) we have almost the same symbolic concept as in the Greek word *Logos* that occupies such an important place in the religious-philosophical system of Philo of Alexandria.
8. Both versions, one a shorter and the other a longer, are to be found in manuscript in Mantua. From both of them derive the texts of the printed editions of the *Sefer Yetzirah* (see A. Epstein in *MGWJ*, XXXVII, 226; XXXIX, pp. 16 and 135; Shemtov Ibn Shemtov, *Sefer Emunot*, 39b; A. Jellinek, *Beiträge* 15; M. Lambert, *Commentaire sur le Sefer Jezira Iner*, IV–VI).
9. According to Abraham Epstein's theory (*Ha-Ḥoker*, II, 1–5), there was still a third, later version which the German mystics of Rabbi Jehudah Ḥasid's school used extensively.

very ancient times, and the patriarch Abraham himself was considered its author.[10] Many great Jewish figures throughout the centuries had an attitude of deep reverence for the *Sefer Yetzirah*. Men of various world outlooks, the compromise-seeker Saadiah Gaon, the neo-Platonist Solomon Ibn Gabirol, the eclectic Shabbetai Donnolo, mystics of various periods from Rabbi Eleazar of Worms and Naḥmanides to the Gaon of Vilna, Rabbi Elijah—all wrote commentaries on this book and relied on it as on the greatest authority.

The *Sefer Yetzirah* is not an integral work with a unitary style. Interwoven in it are three different themes: (1) the idea of divine influence, out of which later developed the doctrine of emanation (*atzilut*), of which we shall speak at length further on; (2) the doctrine of the "great world" (macrocosm) of stars and planets and its connection with the "little world" (microcosm), the structure of the human body; and (3) the mystical doctrine concerning the vast creative power that inheres in "combinations of letters."

According to the *Sefer Yetzirah*, the foundation of the entire work of creation is God's spirit, out of which, without any external aid, ten *sefirot*[11] radiated or emanated. "Their end is connected with the beginning, like the flame with the coal."[12] The ten *sefirot* are considered the space of the world, the element of extension, through which the possibility that things and creatures may co-exist, i.e., simultaneously occupy a place, each by itself, is created. Aside from the six "depths" connected with the six[13] directions "which have no end and no beginning," the *Sefer Yetzirah* also lists another four "depths": the depth of beginning and of end, and the depth of good and of evil. Over these ten "depths" the "only Lord"[14] rules eternally.

The *Sefer Yetzirah* gives a further commentary on the nature and meaning of the *sefirot*. The first *sefirah* is the holy spirit, the "spirit of the living God," which reveals itself "through voice,

10. See, e.g., Jehudah Halevi, *Sefer Ha-Kuzari*, IV:25. The legend derives from the fact that in the last *mishnah* of the *Sefer Yetzirah* it is, in fact, indicated that this mystical doctrine was revealed by God to the patriarch Abraham.
11. On the origin of the word *sefirah* there are differences of opinion. Some think that it derives from the verb *safor* (to count). Others, again, conclude that it derives from the Latin word *sphaera*. A Kabbalist of the thirteenth century, the author of *Maarechet Elohim*, even thinks that it derives from the word *sappir* (sapphire).
12. *Sefer Yetzirah*, Chapter 1, Mishnah 7.
13. Two in each direction: length, breadth, and height.
14. *Sefer Yetzirah*, Chapter 1, Mishnah 5.

spirit and word."[15] From the first *sefirah* emanates "spirit," i.e., the "air," out of which the twenty-two letters of the Torah, as well as the element of water, were created. Out of water, earth and fire were formed. Air, water, and fire are the primal elements, the first substances, from which everything that exists arose. The symbols and sign images of the three primal elements are the three basic letters, the three "mothers" of the Hebrew alphabet: *alef*, *mem*, and *shin*. The silent *mem* with which the Hebrew word *mayyim* (water) begins is the symbol of the water in which the silent fish live; the hissing *shin*, which is the basic letter of the Hebrew word *esh* (fire), is reminiscent of the hissing fire; and the not-to-be-enclosed *alef*, the first letter of the word *avir* (air), is the symbol of the not-to-be-enclosed air.[16]

The remaining letters of the Hebrew alphabet are associated by the *Sefer Yetzirah* not with the terrestrial elements but with the stars and planets. The seven doubled letters correspond to the seven planets, the seven days of the week, and the seven orifices of the human body. With the aid of the twelve plain letters, the twelve constellations[17] were created. To be sure, from the obscure text of the *Sefer Yetzirah* it is not altogether clear what relationship the twenty-two letters of the Torah have to the *sefirot* and what role each of them played at the time of the work of creation (*maaseh bereshit*) when, from the simple elements, from lifeless and formless chaos, living forms permeated with order and regularity emerged. In any case, however, one thing is obvious, that according to the philosophy of the *Sefer Yetzirah*, the letters and numbers, the elements and building materials of God's creative word, are not merely symbols but the basic forms of everything that exists. On the very first page of the *Sefer Yetzirah* the "thirty-two wondrous ways of wisdom, which the Lord God of hosts established,"[18] are spoken of. And in the penultimate two sections there is an account of the great mystery of how God's holy names, with whose power "He constructed His entire world, formed all creatures, and everything that will yet be born,"[19] are put together out of the twenty-two letters.

15. *Ibid.*, Chapter 2, Mishnah 6.
16. *Ibid.*, Chapter 3, Mishnah 1.
17. *Ibid.*, Chapter 5, Mishnah 3.
18. *Ibid.*, Chapter 1, Mishnah 1. The ten numbers, together with the twenty-two letters of the Hebrew alphabet, are the thirty-two ways of wisdom, and they are all united in their single source—God.
19. *Ibid.*, Chapter 6, Mishnah 14. Besides the *Sefer Yetzirah*, a series of other mystical works in which the letters are considered as symbols

We shall have opportunity later to dwell on the very interesting phenomenon in the history of civilization that among various peoples belief in the mystical power and significance of the word, of the letters out of which arise the name, the concept, the symbol, has been extremely powerful. In the meantime, we shall here merely note the unique coloration which the belief in the mysterious power of the letters out of which God's names are constructed acquired among a little-known but very interesting group of Jewish mystics who lived in Babylonia in the time of the Geonim. We have only slight information about this group, which was organized in a kind of order and bore the characteristic name Yordei Merkavah (those who descend to God's chariot). However, we have as a legacy from them a literary memorial which had a profound influence on the religious-mystical conceptions of the European Jewish community. This is the Midrashic work *Hechalot Rabbati*, which is also known by many other names.[20]

*Hechalot Rabbati* is written in a fervent, mystical-poetic, but very uneven style. Stormy effusions of the soul, heartfelt prayers filled with emotion and flaming pathos, are braided together in it with obscure and incomprehensible incantations, with a chaos of sounds and syllables, out of which the difficult and strange names of hosts of angels surrounding the divine chariot are put together. Characteristic of the style of this work is its great fondness for epithets. When, for example, heavenly riders who traverse the heavens on fiery steeds are mentioned, *Hechalot Rabbati* does not weary of listing the kind of horses these were: "Their horses were horses of darkness, horses of deathly terror, horses of black night, horses of fire, horses of blood, horses of storm, horses of iron, horses of horror."

To be accepted as a member of the community of the Yordei Merkavah, the novice has to undergo extremely severe ordeals; to sit in solitude twelve days in succession in one place without eating and drinking, his eyes turned to a certain point, and recite prayers without cease. Thereby the novice arrives at ever greater ecstasy and gradually begins to weave into his prayers special incantations filled with names of whole groups of angels. When a

---

and the basic material of everything that exists were written in Palestine and Babylonia, e.g., *Midrash Alfa Beta De-Rabbi Akiba* (or *Otiot De-Rabbi Akiba*) and others.

20. The other names of this Midrash are *Sefer Hechalot*, *Baraita De-Rabbi Ishmael*, *Perek Merkavah*, *Maaseh Merkavah*, and *Sefer Ha-Merkavah*. The work was published in Jellinek's *Bet Ha-Midrash*, III, 83–108 and 161–63.

new member of the community attains this high level, the great mystery, "the mystery of the Torah," which has lain hidden in God's treasuries from the "days of creation on" and for which the world yearns as for its loveliest ornament and most precious crown, is disclosed to him.[21]

"Rejoice, My servants, for whom the secret of My hidden treasures has been revealed! From you comes salvation for the whole world, and great and limitless is your power" (p. 105). For the opened eyes of the Yordei Merkavah there are no longer any mysteries. To each member of the community everything that takes place before the Throne of Glory, and that will and must take place, is known. All human deeds, open or hidden, good or bad, lie revealed before him (p. 83). Whoever raises a hand against a member of the Yordei Merkavah or speaks gossip about him is lost forever. Great is the power of one who has the privilege of seeing the "chariot" itself, for whom all that occurs in the heavenly halls is disclosed.

The Yordei Merkavah nullify decrees, annul oaths, assuage wrath, turn aside jealousy, and remind their King of the great love of the patriarch Abraham. When they see that the heavenly Father is angry with His children, what do they do? — They throw off their crowns, ungird their loins, strike themselves on the head and fall on their faces and cry: "Indulge, indulge, Thou creator of the world! Forgive, forgive, Thou help of Jacob! Pardon, pardon, Thou holy One of Israel, Thou great and mighty king!"[22]

Among the ordinances of the community of the Yordei Merkavah the most important place was held by prayer. In it they saw the foundation, the preservation of the world.

Well it is with Israel, whose children are more beloved of God than the ministering angels. When the angels wish to be the first to recite songs of praise before God, rivers of fire and streams of flame surround the Throne of Glory, and God says to them, "Be silent, all you angels, seraphim, and ophanim that I have created. I desire to hear the song and praise of Israel first."

And all the families of the angels stand and wait; they withhold their song until the children of Israel begin praying. As soon as

21. *Bet Ha-Midrash,* III, 106–7. The incantations must be repeated 112 times. On Persian influence, see Jellinek's preface, p. xxi.
22. *Hechalot Rabbati,* Chapter 12, p. 92.

the cry from the houses of study, "Holy, Holy, Holy," is heard, the song of the angels and the heavenly princes is raised; in one sacred and powerful melody all the voices and tones are merged. "And through all the heavenly gates flow and rise rivers of sweet, luminous joy, rivers of happiness, rivers of love, rivers of peace, rivers of friendship; and all these rise and flow and stream ever higher around the Throne of Glory."[23]

There is no power comparable to that of God's true servants, the Yordei Merkavah, when they recite their songs and praises three times a day. When they utter God's holy name, all the worlds are filled with blinding rays of light that shine and glisten more than all the precious stones in the world; for great and indescribable is the mystery hidden in the name by which heaven and earth were created.[24]

God's voice is heard, saying:

> Blessed are you in heaven and on earth, you Yordei Merkavah, when you recite before Me what I do at the hours of the morning, afternoon, and evening service, every day and every hour, when Jews pray and cry, "Holy, Holy, Holy!" Teach them and say to them, "In your houses of study raise your eyes to the heavens when you say before Me, 'Holy, Holy, Holy!' " For in the whole world that I have created, I have no joy as great as that when, at the time you recite your prayers, your eyes are raised to Mine and My eyes are turned to yours. . . . Tell all of them, give testimony about what I do in the hour of prayer with the features of your father Jacob's face that are inscribed on My Throne of Glory. Three times a day, when you cry to Me, "Holy, Holy, Holy," I turn to his image and embrace and kiss it.[25]

That this unique literary memorial of the Yordei Merkavah had a great influence on the mystical moods of European Jewry in the twelfth century is attested by a younger contemporary of Jehudah Ḥasid, the Kabbalist Isaiah ben Joseph, who in the year 1127 wrote a commentary (*Otzar Ha-Ḥochmah*, the fifth part of his composition *Ḥayyei Ha-Nefesh*) on the *Sefer Hechalot*. In it he asserts that this work is the source of all wisdom and that whoever studies it attains not only the character of a "true sage" but also merits having the spirit of prophecy rest upon him.

The mystical belief in the great force inherent in prayer and in the tremendous effect of prayer on all the worlds, the intense faith in the secret power hidden in the combination of the letters of

23. *Bet Ha-Midrash*, III, 90.
24. *Ibid.*, pp. 90–91.
25. *Ibid.*, p. 90.

God's name and the names of the angels—all this was transported from Babylonia and neighboring lands to the Jewish communities of the Rhine. We know quite definitely how these notions, which for generations were guarded in secret in narrow circles, finally became generally familiar in the distant lands of Germany. The disciple of Rabbi Jehudah Ḥasid, Rabbi Eleazar of Worms, gives us clear information about this in his mystical work, *Sod Sechel*, which is concerned with the mysteries in the prayers and in the letters of which the words of the prayers consist. Rabbi Eleazar relates:

> I, Eleazar, received the secrets hidden in the prayers from my father, Rabbi Jehudah bar Kalonymos . . . and from my master, Rabbi Jehudah Ḥasid, to whom these were given by his father, Rabbi Samuel. . . . The secrets were transmitted from mouth to mouth, from generation to generation, and from scholar to scholar, back to Rabbi Moses bar Kalonymos who, together with his sons, was taken by King Charles from the city of Lucca in Lombardy to Germany. To Rabbi Moses, again, they had been given by Abu Aharon, the son of Samuel Ha-Nasi of Babylonia. There, in Babylonia, the mysteries had been transmitted from mouth to mouth from Rabbi Simeon Ha-Pakoli on, and he had received them as a tradition from the elders and the prophets. Previous generations kept this knowledge secret, revealing it only to a few chosen persons. So it was until the generation of my master, Rabbi Jehudah Ḥasid. He transmitted all these mysteries to me and commanded me to reveal them to the pious of our generation.[26]

In the same work Rabbi Eleazar again touches upon this matter and indicates that Abu Aharon ben Samuel Ha-Nasi migrated from Babylonia to Lombardy (i.e., north Italy) and there, in the city of Lucca, became acquainted with Rabbi Moses bar Kalonymos and "handed over to him all his secrets." Rabbi Moses ben Kalonymos thereafter moved at the command of King Charles to Mainz, where he familiarized certain chosen persons with the mysteries. Thus they were transmitted from generation to generation until Rabbi Jehudah Ḥasid.[27] "Through him personally," Rabbi Eleazar adds,

26. See *Matzref Le-Ḥochmah* (Warsaw edition, 1890), p. 65. Rabbi Eleazar's interesting report was printed in its entirety by Neubauer in *Letterbode*, X, 111–13.
27. Rabbi Solomon Luria (sixteenth century) relates in his *Responsa* (No. 29) that in the home of Rabbi Jehudah Ḥasid a whole chest of *kuntrasim* or notebooks in which holy mysteries were written down was hidden.

"I learned the mysteries hidden in the prayers, as well as many other mysteries."[28]

Another Kabbalist who lived a generation later than Eleazar of Worms, the Spaniard Isaac ben Jacob, testifies that the oldest books of the Kabbalah (for example, the *Sefer Ha-Bahir*) came from Palestine "to the ancient pious men, the sages of Germany, the Kabbalists" and from there were brought "to some of the ancient scholars, the rabbis of Provence."[29] Rabbi Isaac further relates that when he was in the city of Arles in Provence, the "sages of the Kabbalah" showed him a very old *kuntras* or notebook filled with secrets of the Kabbalah, and this *kuntras* was written by the scholar Rabbi Matzliaḥ of Jerusalem and brought to Provence by Rabbi Gershom of Damascus.[30]

From Rabbi Eleazar's account it appears that it was Rabbi Jehudah Ḥasid who decided to "reveal" to broader circles the mystical secrets which the Kalonymos family brought from Italy to Germany. This "decision" taken by Rabbi Jehudah Ḥasid was, however, the effect of numerous causes. We shall dwell later on one of a general character, namely, the strengthening of mystical tendencies at the beginning of the thirteenth century in Christian Europe as well. For the moment we mention only the following point: at the same time that Rabbi Jehudah Ḥasid and Rabbi Eleazar of Worms lived, there lived also the famous Francis of Assisi (1182–1226), the first "true Christian" of the entire Middle Ages, who considered Christianity a doctrine of love and wished to see in it the faith of mystical, tender kindness and asceticism. The factor which mainly produced the intensification of mystical tendencies in the Jewish community of Germany, however, was the alteration in the social and legal condition of the Jews which occurred at that time.

In the twelfth century the situation of the Jews in central Europe deteriorated greatly. The massacres the Jews suffered at the time of the first Crusades were merely the initial link in a long

28. The well-known fifteenth-century mystic Shemtov Ibn Shemtov tells of "a great scholar Rabbi Keshisha," who left the famous Talmudic academy of Sura and came to Apulia in south Italy. There, Shemtov relates, he composed for his pupil Rabbi Jehudah Ḥasid a work in which he taught him the hidden mysteries of Kabbalist wisdom; and Rabbi Jehudah, for his part, familiarized his pupil Rabbi Eleazar of Worms with them (see *Sefer Ha-Emunot*, Part IV, Chapter 14). There is also an account of this in an old manuscript in the Royal Library of Berlin (see Steinschneider, *Verzeichnis der hebräischen Handschriften der königlichen Bibliothek zu Berlin*, II, 135).
29. *Sefer Ha-Emunot*, p. 92b.
30. *Maddaei Ha-Yahadut*, II, 248–49.

chain of oppressions. Gradually, and more and more as time went on, the process of restricting Jews in their economic activity, of driving them out of most branches of commerce and other occupations that until that time had been the source of their livelihood, was intensified. The urban Christian populace, the merchants and artisans who first began to play a prominent role in the period of the Crusades, considered the Jews their most serious competitors. They carried on an obdurate struggle against "the crucifiers of Christ" until they managed to expel the Jews from both wholesale trade and the crafts and left them only petty trade and money-lending. This process of economic degradation went hand in hand with persecutions and massacres, all against the background of the great struggle between two hostile worlds—Christendom and Islam—which took place in the land of the patriarchs, at the ruins of Zion.

It is therefore hardly surprising that in popular Jewish imagination the struggle around the sepulchre of Jesus became "the war of Gog and Magog." The sufferings of the Jews were the "pangs of the Messiah," the birth agonies following which salvation would come and the redeemer appear in all his splendor.

Just at that time such mystical works as the *Midrash Rabbi Simeon ben Yoḥai*, in which the sorrows and sufferings of the children of Jacob in exile are described, were composed. The hero of popular imagination, Rabbi Simeon ben Yoḥai is the voice of the people's dreams and hopes. In pain and terror he asks in their name: "When will the Messiah the son of David, the redeemer of Israel, come?"[31] To this question an answer *had* to be given, for the sorrows were too great, the wounds too terrible. Yes, the day of great, luminous joy is near! Morning comes and also night! It has become pitch-dark—for soon dawn will break through. In the clamor of war, in the noise of destruction, the Messiah, the savior of Israel and the whole world, will suddenly reveal himself. "O, may the redeemer come speedily and in our day!" With this cry one of the Midrashim of the time ends.[32]

The impatience of the people was so intense that popular messianic movements arose in various Jewish settlements. In Germany and France, in the Byzantine empire, in Yemen and in Africa, the joyous tidings that the Messiah had already appeared at the head of the powerful armies of the "Ten Lost Tribes" living on the other side of the river Sambatyon flared up. Documents found in ancient *genizot* tell of eight messianic movements that broke out

31. *Bet Ha-Midrash,* IV, 118–19.
32. *Ibid.*, III, 82.

in various lands in the hundred years of the first three Crusades.[33] So powerful was the belief of the people that the "end" was near, for great and terrible were the "pangs of the Messiah."

The longer this fearful situation lasted and the darker the exile became, the stronger and more fervent became the hope that the day of salvation was coming, *must* come. As the real world became a vale of sorrow, the miserable people, struggling for its existence, had to create for itself, out of its desire for life, another world, an imaginary world of mystic dreams and golden hopes. There it found its consolation, there it saw realized everything for which its soul yearned so greatly. In real life the Jew was bent and bowed. He was considered merely an object, a possession of the king's *camera*. His personality and his self-respect were trodden underfoot by everyone, spattered with hatred and mockery. Hence, he constructed another world, the secret mystical world. In it the human personality is regarded as the foundation stone of the world. In it the dead are resurrected; even inanimate things receive life, glisten with splendor and beauty. Common words and sounds become living creatures, and even in single, separate letters a great magical power, a profound divine mystery, is disclosed.

The heavier the burden of exile grew and the more bitter life in the ghetto became, the stronger became the faith in the redemption, the more ardent the hope of speedy recompense for the frightful oppressions. The ancient belief in the coming of the Messiah, in the redemption that will supervene "at the end of days," became from the thirteenth century on the only hope and consolation of the Jewish people.

Out of the womb of these popular dreams and hopes, the unique phenomenon of the *ḥochmat ha-nistar*, the Kabbalist doctrine and mystical philosophy, which eventually occupied such an important place in Jewish life, came forth. One must not, however, overlook another factor which should always be taken into account in considering ideological tendencies among Jews, namely, the influence of the environment. In Christian Europe also mysticism became significantly stronger in the thirteenth century as a result of the great social changes which followed in the wake of the Crusades. Acquaintance with an entirely new world, the rich and colorful Oriental world of the Moslem peoples, disturbed the half-slumbering soul of the medieval European. His little-developed mind, terrified and enslaved as it was under the strict supervision of his

33. For a discussion of these messianic movements see Jacob Mann's work *Ha-Tenuot Ha-Meshiḥiot Be-Yemei Massaei Ha-Tzelav Ha-Rishonim* in *Ha-Tekufah*, XXIII (1925), 243–61; XXIV (1928), 335–58.

spiritual overseers, simply could not grasp this whole new world of ideas. Hence, fantasy, hand in hand with superstition, came to the help of the weak intellect; these undertook to conduct medieval man, restless and tormented, over the tangled paths of mystical secrets, incantations, and magical formulas.

Rabbi Jehudah Ḥasid, who founded his famous Talmudic academy in Regensburg in the year 1195, contributed much, as we have noted, to the spread of mystical ideas in broader circles. His mystical and religious-philosophical conceptions were expressed in two works, in his commentary on the prayers and in the *Sefer Ha-Kavod*, which is frequently mentioned in the *Sefer Ḥasidim*.[34] Both of these works were lost. We have only one hymn that bears his name.[35] This is the poem "Anim Zemirot" (also called "Shir Ha-Kavod"), which is recited on every Sabbath and festival at the end of the synagogue service.

Maimonides, with his keen and cold intellect, considered the poets who allow themselves to portray God with positive qualities and attributes as fools and ignoramuses. But men of religious fervor, no matter how high the level of their philosophical thought, had to pour out their love for God in images and symbols. "Sweet songs will I sing," Rabbi Jehudah Ḥasid begins his "Shir Ha-Kavod,"

> because for Thee longs my soul. It yearns to rest under the protection of Thy right hand and to fathom the wonder of Thy mysteries. When I recall the radiance of Thy splendor, my soul longs for Thy love. Therefore my lips praise Thee and I sing love songs to Thy name! I recount Thy praise and glory, even though Thou art hidden from me. The radiance of Thy name do I laud, even though I cannot comprehend Thee. Through Thy prophets, Thy faithful servants, Thou hast

34. *Sefer Ḥasidim*, Nos. 197, 321, 449, 464, and 804. See also *Ketav Tamim*, the work of Jehudah Ḥasid's disciple Moses Taku.
35. See Zunz, *Literaturgeschichte*, p. 300. Rabbi Jehudah Ḥasid's father, Rabbi Samuel, was long considered the author of the other poem, "Shir Ha-Yiḥud," that is also recited at the conclusion of the synagogue service (see Landauer in *Literaturblatt des Orients*, 1845, p. 564). More recent scholars, however, reject this attribution. A. Epstein believes that the "Shir-Ha-Yiḥud" was, in fact, composed by someone named Samuel ben Kalonymos, a *ḥazzan* or precentor in Erfurt who was a contemporary of Rabbi Jehudah Ḥasid. We consider more correct the theory of Jacob Reifmann (*Otzar Tov*, 1885, pp. 20–23) that various parts of the "Shir Ha-Yiḥud" were composed by different persons. We believe that the first three poems were written by a poet more gifted than the authors of the last four, which are stretched out and rendered overly diffuse with excessive rhetoric and flourishes.

revealed the reflection of Thy glory [*Kavod*].[36] According to Thy works and Thy creation have men imaged Thy form. Many are the images, yet only one. They have seen in Thee the old man and the youth, the head crowned with black locks and also one covered with snow—in the day of judgment, a hoary old man; in the day of battle, a champion full of the strength of youth, His radiant armor, the best protection, His holy arm, the surest help. With dew is His head covered, with drops of night His locks watered. He longs for me, I am His joy; He is my crown and my pride. Like fine gold His proud head shines and on His forehead glistens the crown of praise and splendor—the gift of His people, the beloved folk. . . . His beauty is my pride, and I am His ornament. How close He is when I call to Him. . . . Thou whose word of truth resounds eternally, listen to Thy people's prayer, Thy people who call to Thee from generation to generation. Accept my song of praise which resounds before Thee! Let my songs rise to Thee! Let my simple prayer be accepted by Thee, as the Levites' song at the altar. . . . My God, listen to my prayer; full of longing for Thee is my soul.

Since Jehudah Ḥasid's mystical works were lost,[37] we can obtain some notion of his religious-philosophical conceptions only from the writings of his disciple Rabbi Eleazar of Worms. Rabbi Eleazar's personal life was interwoven with the terrors of the era of the Crusades. As a youth he saw the city of his birth, Mainz, where his father Jehudah[38] was the rabbi, attacked in 1187 by bands of Crusaders. He managed to escape and described what he had lived through in his well-known letter, which is an important historical document.[39] About ten years later the Crusaders destroyed his house and his whole family. He relates how on a night late in

36. The word *Kavod* is used by the Kabbalists in a very special sense. *Kavod* is the vesture, the blinding light that radiates from the *En Sof* or Infinite.
37. It is very possible that among the lost works of Jehudah Ḥasid there was also a commentary on the Torah. An allusion to this is found in an old manuscript written not later than in the 1280's. Along with the commentaries of Rashi and David Kimḥi, there are in this manuscript *ḥiddushei Ḥumshei Torah* (*novellae* on the Pentateuch) by an unknown author. In it the following statement appears: "Why are the ox and the ass taken out of all the other beasts? Rabbi Jehudah Ḥasid explained, because the ox chews its cud and the ass does not." (This manuscript is in the Asiatic Museum in Leningrad.)
38. Jehudah ben Kalonymos was also a liturgical poet. See Zunz, *op. cit.*, pp. 280–82.
39. Published in *Quellenschriften*, II, 76–78. He laments the Third Crusade in his *kinah*, *Taavat Aniyyim*.

Ḥeshvan in 1196, while he sat quietly over a manuscript, two Crusaders broke into his dwelling, killed his wife Dolca and their three children, two daughters and one son, before his eyes and severely wounded him.[40] With a broken spirit and a deep wound in his heart, the miserable rabbi immersed himself in the mysterious world of the Kabbalah, with which his teacher, Jehudah Ḥasid, had acquainted him. Barbarism and cruelty had robbed him of the most precious things in life, and he devoted himself entirely to the powerful and sweet elixir of mysterious, world-encompassing love for God.[41]

Most of the moral ideas and principles of conduct in his major work, *Rokeaḥ*, are closely connected with the *Sefer Ḥasidim.* Many maxims and sayings are repeated in both books almost verbatim.[42] This is quite natural, since the author of *Rokeaḥ* was also one of those who contributed most to the composition of the *Sefer Ḥasidim.*

"There is no love," declares Rabbi Eleazar, "stronger than the love for God and no lovelier crown than the crown of humility"; "thirteen times the Sacred Torah repeats that God must be loved with the whole heart and that one must always be prepared to sacrifice himself for the sake of His name"; "love for God must fill the soul entirely. One must serve God not as a slave serves his master, but with enthusiasm and joy, taking no account of any hindrances. One must fulfill the will of the Creator because his soul yearns for this and in his heart burns the flame of the love that prevails over everything in the world"; "you must do everything out of love; if hatred awakens in you, remind yourself of your great love, for he who loves may not hate."

"Humility, to be lowly in one's own estimation," teaches Rabbi Eleazar,

> is the greatest virtue. . . . If someone publicly points out a man's failings, he should thank the Creator, for he will see in this deserved punishment for his sins and obtain the possibility of improving himself and repenting. . . . The humble man forgives one who speaks evil of him. . . . He himself speaks little and softly; he does not desecrate

40. See Landshuth, *Ammudei Ha-Avodah*, p. 25; A. Epstein, *Die Wormser Minhag-bücher* (in Kaufmann's *Gedenkbuch*, p. 295).
41. Eleazar ben Jehudah also wrote numerous liturgical poems. See Landshuth, *Ammudei Ha-Avodah;* Zunz, *op. cit.*, pp. 317–24.
42. Compare, e.g., *Sefer Ḥasidim*, No. 7, with the chapter entitled "Shoresh Rosh Ha-Ḥasidut" in *Rokeaḥ*.

his lips with vulgar talk and never sits among scorners. . . . He never becomes angry, and if he is insulted he keeps silent and pardons the insult, even when he has the opportunity to take revenge. If some disaster befalls him, if he loses his fortune or his children and dear ones, he accepts it all in love and with locked lips bows humbly before the decree of the Creator.[43]

Here Eleazar of Worms is speaking of himself. He from whom barbarism and wickedness took away "his children and dear ones" declares: "If someone has done evil to you, do not think of vengeance. You must recognize that it is a punishment for your sins, and the other person is merely the blind instrument fulfilling God's will."

In the first chapter of *Rokeaḥ*[44] and in the essay *Shaar Ha-Yesod Veha-Yiḥud*,[45] Rabbi Eleazar expounds several important features of the mystical philosophical system which developed in the schools of Regensburg and Worms.[46]

He complains indignantly of those who represent divinity in human form.

Whoever thinks that He who created the world has an image and a form with limbs has no God! . . . Who can understand what God is? Has any eye seen Him? — No, neither angel nor seraph nor prophet. . . . He cannot be compared with any form or appearance, because everything has a limit and end, but the Creator is infinite. . . . He has no beginning or end, neither He nor His wisdom nor His power. Only in His works does He reveal to His people His power and splendor. At the same moment all His creatures call and pray to Him. They pour out before Him the sorrows of their hearts, and He answers each one's cry. He is near to everyone who calls upon Him. . . . But, my son, strive not vainly to understand Him. For all your concepts and analogies, all your images and words, can only tell of what is created and what man's reason can attain. But the human mind cannot grasp God, for there is nothing with which to compare Him. He is the One and Only One. He fills and embraces everything, and He is veiled and hidden from the eyes of His creatures. . . . He, the One and Only One, created the world by His own free will, without any compulsion.

43. *Rokeaḥ*, "Shoresh Anavah."
44. "Hilchot Ḥasidut, Shoresh Kedushat Ha-Yiḥud."
45. Published in *Kochevei Yitzḥak*, XXVII, 15–17.
46. Rabbi Jehudah Ḥasid's disciple Moses Taku, in his *Ketav Tamim*, testifies that not only in Regensburg, where Jehudah lived, but also in Worms there was a mystic religious school in which special theosophical works were produced (*Otzar Neḥmad*, III, 77).

Rabbi Eleazar quotes from the *Sefer Yetzirah* the previously mentioned statement concerning the ten *sefirot* as a concept of place and extension, and adds:

The Creator, however, stands above all space and time, for He is prior to all that came into existence. He permeates and bears in Himself all worlds, and all our concepts, such as light and shadow, image and form, lose their meaning when one speaks of Him. Of His own free will He radiated from Himself the appearance of His Glory [*Mareh Kevodo*].[47] According to His will, His reflection, the Glory [*Kavod*] together with the Creative Word [*Kol Nivra*][48] reveals itself and takes on a specific form, a wondrous, exalted form of brilliance, light and flaming fire. This form is called *Shechinah*. . . . And when the prophet says, "And God revealed Himself to me," he saw only God's Glory [*Kavod*]. . . . Even Moses our master, who saw more than all the prophets and all the angels with Sandalphon at their head, was not able to see God.

We observe how Rabbi Eleazar of Worms repeatedly underscores the idea that man is incapable of grasping with his reason or expressing in words the nature of the Creator, for man can only

47. There is no doubt that the concept of *Kavod* as the first emanation of God occupied the central place in Rabbi Jehudah Ḥasid's *Sefer Ha-Kavod*. Testimony to this is given not only by the title of the work but also by the long quotation from it which Moses Taku gives in his *Ketav Tamim* (see *Otzar Neḥmad*, III, 65, 67). Both Rabbi Jehudah Ḥasid and Rabbi Eleazar apparently derived this concept from the Italian scholar Shabbetai Donnolo, who lived for a long time in the Orient. Rabbi Eleazar himself points this out in his commentary to the *Sefer Yetzirah*. The authors of the *Sefer Ḥasidim* even include in their work a considerable part of the preface to Donnolo's *Ḥakemani* (see the *Sefer Ḥasidim*, Parma version, No. 545). It is also very possible that the doctrine of the *Kevod Elohim*, God's radiance or reflection, developed among the Jewish mystics under the influence of the Karaite religious thinker Benjamin Nahavendi, of whom we read in Jehudah Hadassi: "And Benjamin Nahavendi said that before creation God created the Glory [*Ha-Kavod*] and its Throne . . . and when Scripture says that in the image of God made He man . . . this is the image that He made with the Throne of Glory [*Kisse Ha-Kavod*]" (see Harkavy, *Ḥadashim Gam Yeshanim*, X, 16).

48. The doctrine of the *Kol Nivra*, i.e., the divine Creative Word, which has considerable affinity to the teaching of Philo of Alexandria about the *Logos*, had numerous adherents among Jews in various periods. Moses Taku indicates the source from which the Jewish mystics in the Rhine region drew this doctrine. He tells of a Karaite book in which it is said that it was not God Himself who spoke with Moses but a special voice created for this purpose. He further says that this book "was brought from Babylonia to Russia and from Russia to Regensburg."

grasp and express verbally that which can be compared and is to be found in the order of time and of being. But Eleazar was also one of the founders of the Kabbalah Maasit (Practical Kabbalah). He was one of the first who devoted himself to discovering the secrets hidden in the "combination of letters," the joining at the hour of prayer of the letters of God's name and of certain sentences in the Torah. Thus, the philosophically inclined mystic concerned himself with incantations involving all kinds of *gematria*[49] and *notarikon*[50] and strongly believed that there was vast magical power in these. One may perceive a great contradiction in this, but human life and the human soul are full of contradictions.

There is hardly any doubt that the author of *Rokeaḥ* is also the author of the most important part of the well-known Kabbalist work *Sefer Raziel* or *Sodei Razayya*.[51] The book itself insists that it stems from ancient times. The angel Raziel handed it over to Noah after the deluge, and from him it was transmitted as a legacy from generation to generation. Despite the fact that the book allegedly derives from such distinguished ancestry, it is, in content, a bizarre mixture of all kinds of things. Heartfelt prayers, words of moral instruction, and religious-astrological conceptions[52] are mingled with all sorts of incantations, amulets, and images.

49. In which the letters are considered numbers, e.g., the name Moshe (Moses) is equivalent to the number 345 in *gematria*.

50. In which the letters of a word are considered as the initial letters of other words. For example, the word *mayyim* (water) is the *notarikon* of *Mashiaḥ yavo meherah* (the Messiah will come speedily).

51. There is a copy of Rabbi Eleazar's three works which the well-known Elijah Levita (Elijah Baḥur) made for a prominent Christian scholar. The three works are a commentary to the *Sefer Yetzirah*, *Ḥochmat Ha-Nefesh*, and *Sefer Razayya*. S. D. Luzzatto, who studied this manuscript, discovered that the largest part of the last work, *Sefer Razayya*, is reprinted in all editions of the *Sefer Raziel*. That the *Sefer Razayya* was composed by Rabbi Eleazar of Worms is clearly seen from the following lines: "I received from the mouth of my teacher Jehudah Ḥasid, as he received from his father Rabbenu Samuel Ḥasid, and I also received from the mouth of my father and teacher, Rabbi Jehudah —I, Eleazar the little [*Ha-Katan*]" (see *Iggerot Shadal*, 1891, p. 1021; also *Literaturblatt des Orients*, 1847, p. 341). Incidentally, in the title of the book itself the name of the author is concealed. The terms *Sefer Raziel*, *Sefer Razayya*, and *Eleazar* are all equivalent in *gematria* to the same number—308. Graetz did not notice this and therefore constructed some false theories.

52. These conceptions are closely bound up with the *Sefer Yetzirah* and with Shabbetai Donnolo's work *Ḥakemani*. The author of the *Sefer Raziel* several times refers to the *Sefer Yetzirah* (see, e.g., pp. 13, 215, and 219 in the Medzhibozh edition [1818]). Also included are several quotations from Donnolo's work, e.g., the proof of how earth arises from water (*ibid.*, p. 15).

In the *Sefer Raziel* also much is said of the love of God and, indeed, in almost the same words as in the *Sefer Ḥasidim* and *Rokeaḥ*. Even the comparison of the flaming love for God with erotic desire for a woman is to be found in the *Sefer Raziel* verbatim, as in the *Sefer Ḥasidim*. And just as it was common in the Middle Ages for love of a man or woman to be closely associated with various incantations and formulas, so mystical love for God is braided together in the *Sefer Raziel* with incantations, amulets, and combinations of letters. To be sure, among the incantations are also some that were introduced only later,[53] but the most important segment of them doubtless stems from the author of *Rokeaḥ* himself, who apparently obtained them from his teacher Rabbi Jehudah Ḥasid, together with other "mysteries." This seems at first blush somewhat strange, yet it is psychologically quite explicable. In the medieval love incantations lies great "magic," and in the "adjuration" the ardent wish that what is desired may take place as quickly as possible is expressed. As life in the Jewish ghetto became fearfully dark, it is hardly surprising that the wish to obtain the wondrous "magic" which would give one the capacity to prevail over hostile powers, and to "conjure," so that what is desired might come all the sooner, became ever more fervent.

Thus, in the first half of the thirteenth century, at the very time that the rationalist system of Maimonides and his disciples obtained dominance in Spain, in northern France and in the Rhineland the mystical tendency became increasingly stronger. These were not only two separate but two hostile worlds. At first they could not come into conflict because they were too distant from each other. Too great was the contradiction, too vast the difference in the cultural situation of the Jewish community in Spain and of its brethren on the other side of the Pyrenees. But as soon as one of the German scholars, Rabbi Jehudah Ḥasid's disciple, Moses Taku, became acquainted, even though in altogether slight measure, with the rationalist work of the Spanish-Jewish religious thinkers, he immediately issued his polemic work *Ketav Tamim*,[54] in which he declares all philosophical speculation as such heretical.

53. Such later additions are especially noticeable in the closing part of the *Sefer Raziel*. In one prayer, for example, in the Medzhibozh edition the phrase, "I, David the son of Zlatah," is repeated twice (pp. 3 and 43). In the other editions the phrase "so-and-so, the son of so-and-so" appears there.

54. Several chapters of this work were published for the first time, with numerous errors, in 1798 in *Likkutim Mi-Rav Hai Gaon* (pp. 15–25). These chapters are reprinted with a better text in *Otzar Neḥmad*, III. It has still not been definitely established whether the author of

Moses Taku's attack was merely a prelude to the great controversy which had such vast importance in the history of Jewish literature and social-ideological tendencies. The battleground of the controversy was the country lying between these two very different Jewish communities, the lovely land of Provence.

---

*Ketav Tamim* is the same person as the liturgical poet Moses ben Ḥasdai (see Zunz, *op. cit.*, pp. 316–17). For the differences of opinion on this question see *MGWJ*, 1910, pp. 600–607, and M. Wiener in *Ha-Mazkir*, VI, 44–45. According to the *Responsa* of Rabbi Israel Bruna, the author of *Ketav Tamim* lived in Neustadt near Vienna. See *Responsum* 24: "And I saw in the *responsum* of Rabbi Moses Taku, may his memory be for a blessing, who wrote *Ketav Tamim* and is buried in the city of Neustadt . . ."

CHAPTER FIVE

# *The Kimḥis, Tibbonides, and Other Provençal Scholars*

IN THE wondrously beautiful land lying between the Alps and Pyrenees," the German historian Schlosser begins his chapters on southern France and the war of the Albigenses,

> remnants of the ancient Roman and especially Greek civilizations which had flourished there since the time of the founding of the city of Marseilles still remained. There, as early as the beginning of the Middle Ages, science, art, and technology began to develop, along with urban life. There, where Romance, Latin, and Spanish elements converged with Oriental-Arabic elements, an altogether unique phenomenon—Provençal poetry—appeared. There the "gay art" was born. There a unique kind of court, in which beautiful women were the "arbitrators" and judges in love matters and in questions having to do with songs, nobility, and manners, arose. As in Greece in Homer's time, so in Provence poetry occupied the most important place on all joyous occasions and festivals at which poets and singers sought to demonstrate and perfect their art. These poets were the first sources from which Dante and Petrarch drew nourishment at the beginning of their poetic creativity. Among the sciences, medicine especially flourished in Provence. . . . Besides this, the Jews there founded many scientific institutes.[1]

Outside of northern Italy, southern France was the land in which the remnants of the old Roman civilization were best preserved. Intensive urban life developed in Provence considerably

1. Schlosser, *Weltgeschichte* (Frankfurt-am-Main, 1847), VII, 251–52.

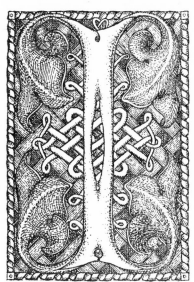

earlier than in all other Christian lands, and commerce and crafts flourished. Because of this, the Provençal cities had already attained a certain independence in the early Middle Ages and enjoyed freedoms such as other Christian lands in Europe did not even dream of. The flourishing cultural situation of Provence in the period from the ninth to the thirteenth centuries was also aided considerably by the fact that there was no strong ruling power. Most of the rulers and noblemen among whom the land was divided[2] were renowned as patrons of poetry, art, and the sciences. Alongside the nobility a strong urban citizenry which stubbornly defended its autonomy emerged. Even in the city of Toulouse, which was under the sovereignty of the powerful Count Raymond, an independent urban government developed.

It was in the Provençal cities also that the first protest against the power of the Catholic Church emerged. Provence was the cradle of the first heretical societies, such as the Albigenses and the Waldenses. Constant intercourse with the Jews and the Moslems of neighboring Spain significantly weakened national and religious prejudices among the populace. The representatives of the ruling nobility, who were connoisseurs of the fine arts and of science, were very tolerant in their attitude toward Jews and frequently entrusted important offices to them. Among the freethinkers of that time, many were especially friendly to Jews, the people of the "Old Testament." In these circles, even the principle that "the Jewish faith is better than the Catholic" was widely accepted.[3]

Under such favorable circumstances, it is not surprising that in the Middle Ages rich and flourishing Jewish communities developed in the old Provençal cities of Narbonne, Marseilles, Lunel, and Montpellier. The famous traveller Benjamin of Tudela, who made his journey over the world in the years 1160 to 1173, gives us a lively portrait in his memoirs of the economic and cultural condition of these communities.[4] On his travels Benjamin visited

2. See Graetz, *Geschichte der Juden*, VI, 209.
3. "Dicunt quod lex Judaeorum melior est quam lex Christianorum" (see Graetz, *op. cit.*, p. 210).
4. These reports of the Jewish traveller, which give extremely interesting information about most of the lands of the then-known world, are one of the most important literary monuments that have come down to us from the Middle Ages. Benjamin is the first European who describes the sect of the Assassins in Syria and Persia, gives information about trade with India, and tells about China and the dangers that travel over the Indian Ocean at that time entailed. In short, he presents information about distant lands which no one before him and for a long time after him was able to provide. Hence, it is not surprising that the travel descriptions of this cultured and perspicacious figure have been translated

the Jewish communities in Provence, and he describes what he saw in the following way:

In three days I arrived at Narbonne. There is an old Jewish community which has been renowned from ancient times for its scholars and is known among many lands as a center of Torah.[5] There I found numerous sages and worthy men. At their head is Rabbi Kalonymos, the son of the great prince [*nasi*] Rabbi Todros, who is descended from the seed of the house of David. Rabbi Kalonymos is the owner of many estates and fields, which the rulers of the land have given him in perpetuity and which no one has the right to take away from him. Then there are Rabbi Abraham, the head of the academy, Rabbi Machir, Rabbi Jehudah, and many other scholars. Altogether about three hundred Jews dwell there. . . . Two days' journey from the city of Bedras [Béziers] is located Har-Gaash, i.e., Montpellier, a very pleasant market town. . . . Merchants from Edom and Ishmael [i.e., Christians and Moslems] come to do business there from various lands —from Alhambria, Lombardy, the old Roman land, Egypt, Palestine, Greece, France, England—in short, merchants from all the peoples and tongues who come to do business with the Pisans and Genoans residing there. In Montpellier, too, many great scholars and prominent people dwell. At their head is Rabbi Reuben bar Todros. . . . Men of great wealth and philanthropists who gladly aid anyone who applies to them also are there. Four miles away is the city of Lunel, where there is a very pious Jewish community and men study Torah day and night. There the celebrated Rabbi Meshullam lived and now his five sons are there: Rabbi Joseph, Rabbi Isaac, Rabbi Jacob, Rabbi Aaron, and the ascetic Rabbi Asher, who has completely withdrawn from the world, pores day and night over his books, fasts, and never eats meat. . . . There dwells also . . . the doctor Rabbi Jehudah Ibn Tibbon of Spain. All the young people who come to Lunel from distant places to study Torah are supported at the expense of the community and provided with everything they need—food, clothing, etc.— throughout the whole period that they study in the Bet Ha-Midrash. True sages, pious and holy men, doers of good deeds who are always ready to come to the aid of their brethren dwell there. . . . Two miles further is situated Posquières, a great city. . . . There is a large Talmudic academy under the supervision of the famous Rabbi Abraham ben David,[6] who has a great reputation as a scholar in the Talmud and

into almost all languages and occupy an honored place in historical literature.

5. Already in the eleventh century Rabbenu Gershom's well known pupil Moses Ha-Darshan, the author of the celebrated Midrash on the Bible, lived in Narbonne. For a discussion of Moses, see A. Epstein, *Moses Ha-Darshan aus Narbonne* (1891).

6. Rabbi Abraham ben David of Posquières (1125–98) is known by the name Ravad Baal Ha-Hassagot, after his famous work *Ha-Hassagot,*

the Bible. To him pupils come from the furthest lands, and all live with him in his house, and the needy among them are provided at his expense with all their needs, for he is a very wealthy man. Three miles from there is located the city of Saint-Gilles. There also is a Jewish community with numerous sages. . . . This is a place to which men come to serve God from the furthest lands and islands. . . . At the head of the community is the prince, Rabbi Abba Mari bar Isaac, who is entrusted with all of Count Raymond's estates and manors. . . . From Arles it is a three days' journey to Marseilles. This also is a place of scholars and sages. The Jewish populace dwelling there is divided into two communities. One lives below, at the shore of the sea, the second somewhat higher, near the fortress. There also a great *yeshivah* is located. At the head of both communities are great scholars: Rabbi Simon bar Anatoli, the wealthy Rabbi Jacob Perpeno, and many others. . . . Marseilles is a large commercial city that lies on the shore of the sea.[7]

The proximity to, and close association with, Arabic Spain contributed significantly to making the influence of the Spanish Jewish community felt ever more strongly in the flourishing communities of Provence. As early as the first half of the twelfth century the versatile Jewish scholar from Spain, Abraham bar Ḥiyya Ha-Nasi (the Prince), who is known in the Christian scholarly world by the names Abraham Judaeus or Savasorda,[8] exercised a considerable cultural and enlightening role in Provence. He not only had a vast reputation in the Arabic learned world but also occupied a very honored place in the science of Christian Europe of the Middle Ages. His astronomical tables were everywhere known, and his treatise on geometry *Ḥibbur Ha-Meshichah Veha-Tishboret*[9] was translated into Latin by his contemporary Plato of Tivoli and served as the major source for Leonardo of Pisa when the latter wrote his famous work *Practicia Geometriae.*

This renowned astronomer and mathematician, however, was not only a scholar but an enlightener. He was convinced that the su-

---

which consists of critical comments on Maimonides' *Mishneh Torah* and other codes of that time.

7. See *Sheloshah Baalei Ha-Massaot* (Margolin's edition [1881]), pp. 4–11.
8. From the Arabic *sahib al shurta* (governor of a city), because Abraham was entrusted by one of the Moorish rulers with the post of city governor. From this derives his Jewish title *Nasi.* Biographical details about this famous scholar are very scanty. It has been established only that he lived for a long time in Barcelona and died after the year 1136. On him see Filipowski, Preface to *Sefer Ha-Ibbur;* Goldenthal in *Kevutzat Ḥachamim* (1861), pp. 8–12; Rapoport and Freimann, Preface to *Hegyon Ha-Nefesh;* see also *Literaturblatt des Orients,* 1850, p. 423.
9. Published by Steinschneider in *Kovetz Al Yad,* XI (1905).

preme duty of man is not merely to accumulate wisdom and knowledge; the important thing is to disseminate these among the people. "Ignorance is darkness," declares Abraham bar Ḥiyya in his ethical work *Sefer Hegyon Ha-Nefesh,*

> and the darkness can be driven away only by the light of knowledge. . . . He who has accumulated much knowledge and keeps it to himself, his wisdom is locked in the darkness with him; he, however, who spreads his knowledge and makes it available to all who seek it, his wisdom shines like the sun at noontime. . . . He strengthens the foundations of the world and creates immortality for himself. For he endows man's soul, which was like a beast's, with eternal life. . . . He who spreads knowledge in his generation is blessed with four great things: he receives payment in the other world, he has honor and glory in this world, his Torah shines like a crown over his disciples, and the source of his wisdom becomes ever fresher and stronger.[10]

In the years Abraham bar Ḥiyya spent in Provence he became quite familiar with the local Jewish community and set himself the task of acquainting his brethren, who did not understand Arabic, with the scientific works that had been written in that language. Modestly he explains in his mathematical-astronomical work *Sefer Ha-Ibbur:*

> Had I found in France a Hebrew work which clearly and comprehensively presented this important subject, I would naturally not have had the presumption to appear before the learned world with my work. If there had at least been a suitable textbook in Arabic, I would simply have translated it into Hebrew. . . . But since I have not found such a book, I had no alternative and myself wrote such a treatise as far as I was able.[11]

In similar terms he explains why he composed his astronomical work *Tzurat Ha-Aretz,* which the Christian scholar Sebastian Muenster published with a Latin translation in Basel in the year 1546.[12]

But it was not only information about the natural sciences that the *nasi* of Barcelona spread among his brethren. He also wrote a popular work on ethics entitled *Sefer Hegyon Ha-Nefesh,* in which he speaks in heartfelt words about ethics and right conduct, about the life of righteousness and piety. The learned natural philosopher speaks in a tender, moving way about the "end of

10. *Hegyon Ha-Nefesh,* pp. 16–18.
11. *Sefer Ha-Ibbur* (Filipowski's edition [1851]), p. 4.
12. See the preface to *Tzurat Ha-Aretz.*

days," when righteousness and truth alone will rule the world. "Then," Abraham bar Ḥiyya declares, "in the days of redemption, the chief foundation of social life will be the maxim 'And thou shalt love thy neighbor as thyself.' All men will love each other as true brothers; jealousy, hatred and lust, which cause murder and wickedness, will be forgotten, and love and holiness alone will govern the world."[13] Abraham bar Ḥiyya was convinced that the Jews are a chosen people.[14] Nevertheless, he constantly insists that one must not think that in the days of the redemption the Jewish people alone will be saved. "I am persuaded that the gates of repentance are open for all men alike, as is written in Scripture, 'Return unto the Lord, and He will have mercy.' God has compassion on anyone who returns to Him, for He is a God of compassion."[15]

This scholar, with his liberal and tolerant outlook, was, however, a son of his generation, a child of the Middle Ages. In order to strengthen in the hearts of his brethren the hope of the redemption that must come at the "end of days," he wrote an essay entitled *Megillat Ha-Megalleh*[16] in which he showed, on the basis of astrological computations and verses from the Book of Daniel, that the Messiah would certainly appear in the year 5118 (1358 C.E.).

Because Abraham bar Ḥiyya was one of the first who wrote scientific works in Hebrew,[17] he had to create new technical terms and expressions. His works are therefore also of importance for the history of Hebrew scientific style. His language, to be sure, is excessively difficult, and many of his terms unclear and imprecise. Soon, however, some Spanish-Jewish scholars who successfully completed what Abraham bar Ḥiyya had begun came to Provence.

We have already noted the respect and gratitude with which the Jewish communities of Provence greeted the enlightening activity of Abraham Ibn Ezra. Ibn Ezra set himself the task of familiarizing them, as well as the Jews of Italy, with the scientific riches which the Spanish-Jewish community had accumulated. In order to arouse interest in scientific philology in the Jewish centers which did not understand Arabic, he translated the classic work of Ḥayyuj into Hebrew and also composed his own grammatical

13. *Hegyon Ha-Nefesh*, p. 42b.
14. *Ibid.*, p. 7b.
15. *Ibid.*, p. 8a (end of Chapter 1).
16. The complete title of the work is *Sefer Megillat Ha-Megalleh, Sod Ha-Geulah, Ḥamishah Shearim.*
17. Abraham bar Ḥiyya also composed a large encyclopedic scientific work. Fragments of it were printed in *Hebräische Bibliographie* (*Ha-Mazkir*), VII, 84–95.

works. Shortly after Ibn Ezra, many other Jewish scholars arrived in Provence. These had fled from Spain because of the persecutions which the Jews had to suffer in the middle of the twelfth century from the fanatical Almohades. The refugees came to the strange land not with empty hands but laden with the most valuable treasures of learning and knowledge. In the dissemination of Spanish-Jewish culture in Provence, two richly endowed families especially distinguished themselves—the Kimḥis and the Tibbonides.

The father of the Kimḥi sons, Joseph ben Isaac Kimḥi, migrated from southern Spain in 1150 and settled in Narbonne. His literary activity was extremely versatile. He wrote grammatical works, composed a commentary on almost the entire Hebrew Bible, translated from Arabic into Hebrew Baḥya's *Ḥovot Ha-Levavot*,[18] and wrote religious poems. But he achieved his reputation mainly with his two philological works, *Sefer Zikkaron* and *Sefer Ha-Galui*.[19] His *piyyutim*[20] are written in lovely language but lack genuine poetic inspiration. Much more important and interesting is his collection of didactic sayings and proverbs, *Shekel Ha-Kodesh*. This work belongs to the "books of wisdom," so popular among the Jews from ancient times, in which in brief proverbs and fine, pointed maxims are given principles and instructions on how one must conduct himself in order to follow the way of righteousness. The classic "book of wisdom" of the Biblical era is the eclectic work the Book of Proverbs, and of the period of the Talmud, *Pirkei Avot*. In the Middle Ages there also appeared similar didactic books, e.g., the *Mivḥar Ha-Peninim* of Solomon Ibn Gabirol and the anonymous *Sefer Ha-Yirah*, which has been published only in modern times.[21] The latter is written in verse, and also in the form of poetry is Kimḥi's *Shekel Ha-Kodesh*.[22] As the major source for his work Kimḥi employed the *Mivḥar Ha-Peninim*,

18. Of the translation only a fragment, which Jellinek published in 1896, has survived.
19. Both works were published by the Mekitzei Nirdamim Society (1887–88). A critical evaluation is given by Blüth in his monograph in Berliner's *Magazin für die Wissenschaft des Judentums*, XVIII and XIX (1890–91). See also A. Geiger in *Otzar Neḥmad*, I, 98–106.
20. See Landshuth, *Ammudei Ha-Avodah*, pp. 90–92.
21. By the Mekitzei Nirdamim Society in 1896. It was reprinted on the basis of another manuscript by H. Gollancz in 1919.
22. Until modern times this work was known to us only from certain fragments published by Dukes in *Tziyyon*, 1841, pp. 97–100, and *Literaturblatt des Orients*, 1846, pp. 728–31, and then by Edelman in *Derech Tovim*, 1852, p. 24. It appeared in complete form only in 1919. On the two versions of the *Shekel Ha-Kodesh* see Alexander Marx's article in

but apparently in the Arabic original, not the Hebrew translation. Kimḥi demonstrated great skill in the technique of versifying, and his *Shekel Ha-Kodesh* deserves an honored place among the "books of wisdom" of the Middle Ages.

Joseph Kimḥi's apologetic work *Sefer Ha-Berit*[23] also has considerable cultural-historical value. From this work one sees clearly how tolerant and liberal attitudes in religious matters in twelfth-century Provence were. In the Middle Ages men were fond of debates on matters of religion, especially between representatives of various faiths, such as Jews and Christians. Until the thirteenth century, before the fanatical Pope Innocent III began to persecute Jews, these religious disputations bore a rather amicable character. The disputations were often initiated on the Jewish side, and Jews would freely criticize the principles of the Christian faith. The Christians realized that it was difficult for them to argue in religious matters with Jewish scholars since the latter were much better versed in the text of Scripture. Hence, they were very eager to put forth on their side converts who, as former Jews, were also well acquainted with Jewish religious literature. Especially in northern Spain, the closest neighbor of Provence, the Church there (which, as we shall see later, was extremely militant) endeavored to employ converts as missionaries, hoping that through their disputations and propaganda successful results would be obtained among the Jews, who would "repent" and adopt Christianity. These apostate missionaries, in their debates with their erstwhile brethren, sought to demonstrate the truth of the Christian faith not only through arguments from the Bible but from the Talmud and the Aggadah. In this missionary activity the convert Moses the Spaniard, who after adopting Christianity took the name Peter Alfonsi, especially distinguished himself. He acquired renown with his famous collection of stories and legends, *Disciplina clericalis*, composed in 1106. Alfonsi also wrote a polemical work, *Dialogi*,[24] in which he attempted to demonstrate that the only true faith is the Christian. At that time the Jews, for their part, also began to concern them-

---

the *Hebrew Union College Annual*, IV, 433–48. Cf. M. Sokolow's work on the Arabic original of the *Mivḥar Ha-Peninim* in the Russian *Bulletin de L'Académie des Sciences de L'URSS*, 1929, pp. 287–300.

23. This work has not come down to us in complete form. Only a part of it was printed in *Milḥemet Ḥovah* (Constantinople, 1710), pp. 18–33.

24. This work consists of twelve discussions or debates between the Jew Moses, and the Christian Peter. A monograph on Alfonsi's *Dialogi* was published by Joseph Oesterreicher in *Fünfter Jahresbericht der deutschen Landes-oberrealschule in Göding* (Moravia), pp. 1–40.

selves with apologetics and wrote handbooks on the art of conducting debates with the Christians.

One of the oldest polemic writings we have from this era is Jacob ben Reuben's *Milḥamot Ha-Shem* (also called *Sefer Ha-Teshuvot*), in twelve arguments or disputations, like Alfonsi's work. Of Jacob ben Reuben we know only that he lived in the second half of the twelfth century and completed his book in the year 1170. Apparently he was born in Spain, because the well-known Karaite scholar Caleb Afendopolo calls him Jacob of Valencia. For some reason he had to leave his fatherland and settle in Gascogne, where he became friendly with a Christian priest, "a great scholar in philosophy and in other branches of wisdom." The two friends would often enter into long religious discussions, and the priest sought to demonstrate with quotations from Jerome, Augustine, and other Christian authorities that Christianity is the only true religion. To this, however, he always added, "If you wish to show that I am in error, you have nothing to fear. You may say frankly and freely what you wish. No one will stop you." And Jacob ben Reuben did, in fact, answer all his arguments in his book, in which a lengthy debate between the Christian *ha-mechaḥed*, the denier of Judaism, and the Jewish *he-meyaḥed*, the believer in the one God, is reported. The first protagonist raises questions and the second replies.[25]

Almost at the same time as Jacob ben Reuben, Joseph Kimḥi wrote his polemic work, in order, as he indicates, to provide a weapon for those who "must conduct debates with apostates from our people, who spread lies and preach falsehood and have the presumption to think that with childish stories and foolish arguments they can overthrow the words of the living God."[26] Kimḥi's book is also written in the form of a debate between a pious Jew, the *maamin*, and a heretic, the *min*. In the theological section of the work he demonstrates his familiarity with the Latin Bible translation of Jerome, and in fact shows with great skill that the great Christian scholar often translated incorrectly because he was not

25. *Milḥamot Ha-Shem,* which polemicizes strongly against Christianity, has not been printed up to the present time. Steinschneider published only a few fragments of Jacob ben Reuben's work in *Otzrot Ḥayyim* (pp. 371–78) and as a supplement to *Vikkuaḥ Ha-Ramban* (1860). We became familiar with *Milḥamot Ha-Shem* through a manuscript copy (written in 1423) which is found in the library in Leningrad of the Society for the Dissemination of Enlightenment Among Jews.

26. *Milḥemet Ḥovah*, 19a.

sufficiently competent in Hebrew. The *maamin*, naturally, is firmly convinced that the only true and divine faith is the Jewish, and this, he argues, can be seen from the clean moral life that Jews lead:

No other nation fulfills so faithfully the commandments of the Decalogue as we Jews. We believe in the one and only God and are faithful to the commandment, "Thou shalt not make any image." Only we fulfill the commandment concerning Sabbath-keeping and do not desecrate this sacred day with any labor. No people in the world fulfills so strictly as we the commandments "Thou shalt not murder" and "Thou shalt not commit adultery." We have no murderers, no adulterers. Murder and robbery are not at all as common among Jews as with you Christians, among whom men are often waylaid on the road, their eyes stabbed out, and they themselves hanged on trees. Do Jews do such things?[27]

"Or does there prevail among you," further asks the *maamin*,

such chastity as among us, in the case of both men and women? Every child is taught Torah from infancy on. . . . The girls are educated in proper conduct. One does not see them going around freely on the streets. There are among us no profligate persons as among you Christians, persons who are met constantly in the marketplaces and at the fairs. And have you the gall to mock our morality and our way of life? Do you consider yourselves people with a higher ethic—you who lead such a life and trample underfoot all the laws of morality and justice?

"Another thing I will tell you," the *maamin* further says;

we know what brotherhood means. If a Jew stops with another Jew, he may stay a day, two days, or even a whole year. For this he will not be charged anything, neither for food nor for lodging. And such is the custom among Jews the whole world over. They gladly welcome travellers because Jews are sons of compassionate fathers and conduct themselves with love towards their brethren. If a Jew sees that another Jew has been taken captive, he immediately ransoms him. If another is naked, he clothes him. . . . And among you Christians it is precisely the opposite.[28]

The *min*, i.e., the Christian, reproaches the Jews for taking interest and making a living from usury. In Provence, however, where commerce flourished, men could not do without credit, without lending money at interest or offering merchandise on pledge with the condition that the profit would afterwards be

27. *Ibid.*, 20b.
28. *Ibid.*, 21a.

divided. All this was essential. Lacking it, trade would have failed, just as an organism dies for lack of blood. Life refused to recognize the prohibition of the Christian church which considered the taking of interest the most grievous sin. And Kimḥi's *maamin* reports, indeed, the interesting fact that many Christians in Provence made allowances for themselves and did lend money at interest. "In the sin of taking interest," indicates the *maamin*, "the Christians are much guiltier than we, because they take high interest both from Jews and Christians. We, however, at least do not take any from our brethren."[29]

When the *maamin* offers the reproach that the life of Christians is filled with sin and vice, the *min* points to the many Christian ascetics who separate themselves from all the pleasures of the world, withdraw to deserts and lonely forests, and there spend their lives in poverty and deprivation. "Yes, that is true," answers the *maamin*, "but your holy men and ascetics are only single individuals. For every holy man among you there are thousands steeped in sin and shame. Even your religious, your priests and cardinals, who ought to lead a pure and honest life—everyone knows how eager they are for unchastity."[30]

Joseph Kimḥi's work was continued by his two sons Moses and David. The elder acquired special renown with his textbook *Mahalach Shevilei Ha-Daat*, the first Hebrew grammar to appear in print.[31] In the period of the Reformation Moses Kimḥi's work was, among Christian scholars, the favorite textbook from which they studied the Hebrew language. The renowned Elijah Levita published Kimḥi's work with numerous critical comments and addenda. Thereafter it was many times reprinted, and in 1531 the Christian scholar Sebastian Muenster translated it into Latin and published it in Basel. Moses Kimḥi also wrote commentaries on several Biblical books—Job,[32] Proverbs, Ezra, and Nehemiah. The last three commentaries had an odd fate. In the Middle Ages they were attributed to Abraham Ibn Ezra, and to this day they are printed in numerous editions of the Hebrew Bible as Ibn Ezra's commentaries.

29. *Ibid.*, 21b.
30. *Ibid.*
31. The bibliographer S. Wiener was the first to point out that the work was initially printed in Soncino in 1488. A copy (a defective one) of this very rare edition is to be found in the Asiatic Museum in Leningrad. In Firkovich's manuscript collection No. 1 (112) there is a copy of this first Soncino edition. The third edition of Kimḥi's grammar (1519) appeared with an interesting preface by Benjamin ben Jehudah.
32. Published by Y. Schwartz in *Tikvat Enosh* (1868).

More important than Moses Kimḥi is his younger brother David, the famous Radak (Rabbi David Kimḥi, born in 1160, died in Narbonne in 1235), of whom in the later literature is often quoted the proverb, *Im en kemaḥ en Torah*, "If there is no flour [for bread], there is no Torah," but meaning here, of course, that without Kimḥi one cannot understand the meaning of the Torah. A remarkable systematizer and brilliant expositor, who had a talent for setting forth the most difficult subject matter in clear and comprehensible form, Radak managed in his two-volume *Michlol* to bring into strict order all the vast grammatical and lexicographical material which the famous philologists of the Spanish school had assembled. In the first part,[33] in which the grammar of the Hebrew language is presented, Radak succeeded in so skillfully employing everything that his predecessors produced in this realm that their work was no longer necessary. They were, in fact, eventually forgotten completely, and only in modern times have they been resurrected. Rabbi David Kimḥi was widely known not only among Jews but also among Christians, and his work was employed by such scholars as Reuchlin and Sebastian Muenster.

Kimḥi's great reputation as a philologist contributed to the fact that his commentaries to the Hebrew Bible[34] were extensively read and studied. These were so popular in the Christian world that they were several times translated into Latin. Kimḥi appears in his commentaries as an ardent follower of Maimonides,[35] and his philosophical-rationalist explanation of "the work of creation" (*maaseh bereshit*) and the "work of the chariot or throne" (*maaseh merkavah*) had, as we shall see later on, the effect of rousing the pious rabbis of northern France against him. When, in his last years, the controversy between the followers of Maimonides and his opponents erupted, the aged Kimḥi at once joined the Maimunists and took a very active part in this struggle, of which we shall speak in the next chapter.[36]

33. The second part, which bears a separate title, *Sefer Ha-Shorashim*, is a Bible dictionary and is printed separately as an independent work.
34. David Kimḥi wrote commentaries to Genesis, the prophets, Psalms, and Chronicles.
35. Kimḥi read Maimonides' *Moreh Nevuchim* in the Hebrew translation of his friend Samuel Ibn Tibbon. A faithful adherent of Maimonides' system, Kimḥi declares that the conversation between the patriarch Abraham and God took place only in a dream. He also explains rationalistically the Biblical account of how the prophet Elijah was taken up to heaven alive.
36. Like his father, David Kimḥi also frequently carried on debates with Christian priests and scholars. His polemical remarks on Christianity in his commentary to the Psalms were removed by the Christian censor.

The chief merit of the Kimḥi brothers lies in their grammatical work. The cultural significance of the second family mentioned above, the Ibn Tibbons or Tibbonides, consists mainly in their activity as translators. Thanks to them, the most important scientific work of the Jewish scholars and investigators in Spain became accessible also to those Jews who did not understand Arabic.

At about the time that Joseph Kimḥi settled in Provence, Jehudah ben Saul Ibn Tibbon (1120–after 1190), who was born in Granada, left Spain and settled in the Provençal city of Lunel, where the head of the Jewish community was the Rabbi Meshullam ben Jacob of whom the traveller Benjamin of Tudela speaks so enthusiastically. A man of broad culture, Meshullam ben Jacob was a connoisseur and patron of science and literature. With great assiduity he collected manuscripts and copies of the major scientific works produced by the Arabic-Jewish civilization. He also decided to employ Jehudah Ibn Tibbon's knowledge of Arabic, and in 1161 commissioned him to produce a Hebrew translation of Baḥya Ibn Pakuda's *Ḥovot Ha-Levavot*.[37] Jehudah at first translated only the first section, *Shaar Ha-Yiḥud*, which deals with philosophical matters; in place of the rest of Ibn Pakuda's work, he rendered from Arabic Solomon Ibn Gabirol's *Tikkun Middot Ha-Nefesh*, in which the ethical "duties of the heart" that are dealt with in *Ḥovot Ha-Levavot* are discussed briefly but clearly. Only after Joseph Kimḥi's translation of *Ḥovot Ha-Levavot* appeared and Jehudah Ibn Tibbon was not pleased with it did he decide to translate the entire work. The translator's introduction, in which he complains of the great difficulties connected with his work, is interesting. "The Arabic language," writes Ibn Tibbon,

> is very rich and extensive. One can easily express in it every subject, every thought with all its nuances, for Arabic has developed to the highest level—not like the Hebrew language, the sum of whose words and expressions is extremely limited. We draw everything from one source, the Bible, but this cannot suffice for all our needs. . . . We are, therefore, in no position to render our thoughts and feelings in as

---

For this reason they were printed separately under the title *Teshuvot La-Notzrim*. He also wrote a special polemic work against Christianity entitled *Vikkuaḥ*, a fragment of which is reprinted in *Milḥemet Ḥovah*. In this fragment Kimḥi relates how he had a debate with a certain Franciscan.

37. Ibn Tibbon himself writes of this in the preface to his translation: "Rabbi Meshullam, the son of the venerable sage Rabbi Jacob, may his memory be for a blessing . . . commanded me to translate this material for him into the Hebrew language."

beautiful a form and as clearly and precisely in Hebrew as we are in the case of Arabic.[38]

The term "beautiful form" is, in fact, hardly appropriate to describe Jehudah Ibn Tibbon's language, which is hard and unpolished. However, Ibn Tibbon is a very faithful and precise translator, one of those diligent and thorough craftsmen who can be relied on. For this reason, his translation quickly displaced Joseph Kimḥi's. After *Ḥovot Ha-Levavot*, Ibn Tibbon translated a whole series of other Arabic-Jewish works. In 1167 he completed his translation of Jehudah Halevi's *Kuzari*. Thereafter he translated Solomon Ibn Gabirol's *Mivḥar Ha-Peninim*, then Jonah Ibn Jannaḥ's works, *Sefer Ha-Rikmah* and *Sefer Ha-Shorashim*, and finally, in his old age,[39] Saadiah Gaon's famous *Sefer Ha-Emunot Veha-Deot*.

Jehudah Ibn Tibbon rightly earned the name "chief of the translators." Despite all his defects, he endeavors to translate word for word, to remain as faithful as possible to the Arabic original, disregarding the fact that the spirit of the Hebrew language suffers considerably thereby and his sentences come out hard and pedantically dry. But Ibn Tibbon was a pointer of the way. With his industrious labor he created a philosophic-scientific terminology in Hebrew. Though crude and unpolished, it was, for those who did not know Arabic, the essential instrument for mastering the realm of philosophic thought. He and his successors, through their translations, preserved rich treasures of Arabic-Jewish culture which would otherwise have been lost, and disseminated and made them available throughout the Jewish world.

Of Jehudah Ibn Tibbon's own work only his *Tzevaah* (Testament), which he wrote when he was seventy for his only son, Samuel Ibn Tibbon, has a cultural-historical interest. "Testaments" or "ethical wills" generally occupy a very honored place in medieval Hebrew literature. We have no contemporary works, as it happens, that portray for us the way of life which then prevailed. It was not understood at that time that describing everyday life could have any significant value. For this reason, the testaments that many Jewish scholars wrote in their old age for their children, in which they give them moral instruction and teach them how to live so as to obtain favor in the eyes of God and man, are extremely

38. See Ibn Tibbon's letter to Meshullam's son Rabbi Asher. We have no doubt that it is against the thought which Ibn Tibbon expresses here that the poet Alḥarizi aimed in his preface to *Taḥkemoni* which we quoted in the first volume of our work.

39. In 1186.

interesting. In these, numerous details of contemporary life, which it is impossible to discover in other sources, are touched upon. In this respect, Jehudah Ibn Tibbon's testament is one of the most interesting. In it we find a great many characteristic features of the cultural life of Spanish Jewry. Typical is his account of how he "refused to take account of the great expense involved and the dangers that stood in his way, and travelled to distant lands to obtain for his son a good teacher in the external branches of wisdom [secular sciences]." "I have done everything," says the aged Ibn Tibbon,

> to gather for you all the books you need, so that you should not have to look for any. You see how others must run around seeking a volume they require and cannot find it. You however, thank God, lend to others and do not have to borrow from anyone. . . . You see how great scholars come from distant places out of the desire to become acquainted with me and my library.[40]

In that era, when books existed only in manuscript, clear and beautiful handwriting played a very significant role. It was actually an important cultural factor, because the fate of the book, in great measure, lay in the extent to which a manuscript was clear and easy to read, and the text correct and without errors. For this reason the aged Ibn Tibbon gives his son the most detailed instructions on copying, emphasizing the care one must take that each letter be clear and prominent. "Writing," he declares, "is an art, like all other arts."[41] "My son," further writes the father,

> let books be your companions and bookshelves your fields and gardens. . . . You should go over your Hebrew books once very month, your Arabic works once every two months, and the bound collections once every three months. Your books should be in good order so that you need not search long for the one you require. . . . Every bookcase should have a complete register of the books shelved in it, and you should replace every book in its case. Be careful of single pages or letters that lie in books, because in these frequently are very important notices that I accumulated and wrote down over a period of time. See to it that not a single book or letter that I leave to you is lost. . . . Hang the cases with beautiful cloths and make sure that no water

40. *Tzevaat Rabbi Yehudah* (Steinschneider's edition [1852]), p. 4.
41. *Ibid.*, p. 8. For the same reason the sages of the Talmud called the work of the scribe or copyist "the work of heaven." When Rabbi Meir, who was a skillful scribe, came to Rabbi Ishmael, the latter admonished him: "My son, be careful in your work, for your work is the work of heaven."

enters them. See also that the books are not spoiled by mice or other destroyers, for they are your best treasure. If you lend someone a book, write down his name in your notebook in his presence; when he returns it to you, cross out the notation.[42]

Jehudah Ibn Tibbon reproaches his son in his Testament for being overly frivolous and not having a sufficiently respectful attitude toward scientific matters. The reproach, however, was not at all deserved by Samuel Ibn Tibbon. He continued his father's cultural-scientific activity and even surpassed him with his broad philosophical equipment and keen, analytic mind. Jehudah Ibn Tibbon's work enlarged the interest of the educated Jews of Provence in philosophical problems. It also contributed greatly to the fact that, already at the beginning of his son's scientific activity, Maimonides was considered the foremost authority and spiritual guide in all the Jewish communities of Provence. Everyone regarded him as the greatest scholar, the "pillar of fire" illuminating the way for the exiled people. "From the sea of ignorance," writes Rabbi Aaron, the son of the previously mentioned Rabbi Meshullam, "did he [Maimonides] lead forth his people, and he inscribed his doctrine in their hearts. . . . Since Rabina's and Rav Ashi's times there has not been anyone comparable to Moses among the Jews."[43] In connection with every significant problem men immediately applied to Maimonides in Egypt. He was the "Urim and Tummim," the final court of appeal. Several Jewish communities turned to Maimonides with the question whether astrology has in fact any scientific value, whether it is really true that the constellations rule man's fate.[44] A number of scholars in

42. *Ibid.*, p. 12.
43. *Taam Zekenim*, p. 67; *Iggerot Kenaot*, p. 11.
44. Maimonides' answer is characteristic. In his letter to the community of Marseilles he very sharply attacks astrology and declares that this "science" in which men believed so strongly up to modern times is false and deceitful. "Know," he writes, "that there are three kinds of truth in which a man may believe: (1) that which can be demonstrated by the arguments and proofs of man's reason, e.g., the principles of mathematics, astronomical calculations, and the like; (2) knowledge which a man obtains through his senses; e.g., through vision man comes to know that this thing is black and that thing is red, etc.; and (3) truths which a man has received through tradition from prophets and righteous men of the generation. . . . And every man of knowledge must always give a clear account to himself as to which kind this or that judgment or opinion is—whether he has obtained it with his own reason, or as a result of his senses, or through tradition. Of him, however, who believes and considers true such things as do not come under any of these three categories, it is said, 'A fool believes everything' " (*Teshuvot Ha-Rambam*, *Iggerot*, Leipzig edition, p. 24).

Lunel, led by Jonathan Ha-Kohen, requested Maimonides in 1194 to explain several obscure passages in his *Mishneh Torah.* When they received word that Maimonides' philosophical work *Moreh Nevuchim* (A Guide for the Perplexed) had appeared, they sent a special emissary to Egypt with the request that the author send them his work in the original or in Hebrew translation. Upon receiving the original of the treatise, they at once requested Samuel Ibn Tibbon to translate the work into Hebrew. *A Guide for the Perplexed* made a tremendous impression on Samuel, and he remained an ardent champion of Maimonides' system throughout his life. Out of his great reverence for the work, Samuel at first declined the commission. "I explained to them [the representatives of the community of Lunel]," he wrote, "that I do not know both languages perfectly. They, however, urged me so long that I finally acquiesced and undertook the translation."

Samuel Ibn Tibbon wished to accomplish his task with perfection. He therefore applied, in 1199, to the author himself for necessary information. Maimonides, who had for a long time been considering translating his Arabic work into Hebrew,[45] was delighted at the news that Ibn Tibbon intended to translate his *Guide.* He replied promptly and gave Ibn Tibbon many important points on how to proceed in his difficult undertaking. He also indicated to him that a translator must constantly hold to the rule that to render the thought correctly is far more important than to translate each word faithfully.[46]

It is difficult to determine whether its action was motivated by the fact that the translation of Ibn Tibbon, who had so much reverence for the *Guide,*[47] took too long,[48] or whether there were other reasons; in any case, the community of Lunel, which wished to familiarize itself as quickly as possible with the philosophical work of the great scholar, applied to Maimonides personally, in 1200, with the request that he favor them by translating the *Moreh*

45. See his letter to Joseph Ibn Gabir of Baghdad, *Taam Zekenim,* p. 73; *Teshuvot Ha-Rambam,* II, 15b.
46. *Teshuvot Ha-Rambam,* II, 27b.
47. He even decided to make a special trip to Egypt to obtain from the author explanations of a number of difficult passages in the text. Maimonides dissuaded him from this but later fulfilled his desire.
48. Ibn Tibbon completed his translation on November 30, 1204, two weeks before Maimonides' death. This date is found in the supplement at the end of the first printed edition of the *Moreh Nevuchim* (Rome, c. 1476). In all other editions this supplement by the translator is missing. On the defects of Ibn Tibbon's translation see Shemtov Falaquera, *Moreh Ha-Moreh,* pp. 148–58.

*Nevuchim* himself. Maimonides replied that he had, indeed, been thinking for a long time of rendering his Arabic works into Hebrew but lacked the time for it. "Among you, however, is the worthy son of the learned Jehudah Ibn Tibbon; he is the man best qualified for this task."[49]

Just at that time the poet Jehudah Alḥarizi came to southern France. An outstanding stylist and a man with a philosophical education, he was very much in demand as a translator. Soon, in fact, the community of Marseilles and Jonathan Ha-Kohen of Lunel requested him to render Maimonides' Arabic work into Hebrew.[50] Alḥarizi agreed and translated Maimonides' commentary to the Mishnah as well as the *Moreh Nevuchim*.[51]

The enlightened Jews of Provence, however, were not content merely with the work of Maimonides. They also wished to familiarize themselves with the world of ideas of Maimonides' contemporary, the Arabic rationalist and freethinker Averroes. So the intelligentsia of Narbonne and Béziers applied to the expert translator Jacob ben Abba Mari Anatoli,[52] to render Averroes' philosophical work into Hebrew.

The communities of Provence, as we see, manifested a strong interest in science and education and eventually became a major cultural center. Here a whole school of first-rate translators was formed. Thanks to these, treasures of culture from the Islamic world were saved, as well as the possibility created for the Christian West to become familiar with them. The Jewish scholars in Provence, however, remained merely talented pupils, excellent middlemen and disseminators of cultural riches that had been produced earlier. The Jews of Provence did not themselves become independent investigators and creators for a long time. Until the end of the thirteenth century they did not yield one outstanding name in the realm of philosophical thought or a single scientific investigator. In this cradle of medieval European poetry, where in the course of the eleventh to the thirteenth centuries the wandering minstrels or troubadours raised the knightly lyric to the level of genuine art, the Jews did not during this period produce a single poet whose name might occupy an honored place in the

49. *Teshuvot Ha-Rambam*, II, 44; *Otzar Neḥmad*, II, 3.
50. See *Taḥkemoni* (Warsaw edition), Preface and p. 410.
51. Alḥarizi's translation is easier to read but less precise than Ibn Tibbon's. For a comparison of the two translations, see D. Kaufmann, *Gesammelte Schriften*, II, 163–66.
52. We shall have more to say about Anatoli and his translations in Part III of our work.

history of Hebrew poetry.[53] In his work *Zur Geshichte und Literatur* the great scholar Leopold Zunz devotes a whole chapter to the Hebrew poets in Provence, but the many scores of "poets" Zunz lists were really only poetasters who more or less skillfully wrote hymns, songs, and praises after the pattern of the famous Spanish poets, but without their talent and without their poetic inspiration.

The best known of the Provençal poets is Joseph Ezobi, who lived in Perpignan in the first half of the thirteenth century. He acquired his reputation with his didactic poem *Kaarat Kesef*,[54] which he sent as a wedding present to his son. This poem was extremely popular, and the celebrated Christian scholar Johannes Reuchlin translated it into Latin. Reuchlin was powerfully affected by Ezobi's poem and calls him "the sweetest of the Hebrew poets" (*Judaeorum poeta dulcissimus*). Nevertheless, *Kaarat Kesef* is hardly a masterpiece. The poem, to be sure, is written in a tender, intimate tone. The loving father concerned for his son is discernible in it, but true poetry is very little in evidence. In contrast to Jehudah Ibn Tibbon, Ezobi teaches his son to strive that his associates and teachers be living men, not books. "Choose the mouth of writers, not the mouth of writings; acquire for yourself a teacher, and do not trust in the book." "My son," writes Ezobi, "buy wisdom, buy knowledge!" But the father also considers it necessary to warn his son not to enter too much into the "wisdom of Greece," i.e., Greek philosophy. "Avoid her vineyards, for her vines are of Sodom and her branches of Gomorrah."[55] On the other hand, he speaks with great enthusiasm of "Moses, the man of

53. To be sure, one must here take into consideration that Provençal poetry, with all its unique beauty, could not have any noticeable influence on Jewish literature. First of all, the inner world of the Christian troubadour was essentially too elementary and primitive for Provençal Jewry, which lived in a complex and rich civilization. Furthermore, knightly poetry very clearly carried the impress of the class from which it largely drew its nourishment; it was closely bound up with the feudal manner of life, which was entirely alien to urban Jewry. In addition, knightly poetry was primarily an *oral* kind of poetry, closely associated with singing. The knight did not read the troubadour's song but listened to it while it was declaimed or sung to the accompaniment of a musical instrument. The Jewish poets of Provence adopted only one thing from their Christian colleagues—poetic tournaments or competitions. The tournaments among the Jewish poets, however, did not take place orally, as among the troubadours, but in writing, through the medium of pen and parchment.

54. Printed for the first time in Constantinople in 1523. Reprinted with some changes in Wolf's *Bibliotheca Hebraea,* IV, 1140–67.

55. Verse 36.

God," the great scholar of Cordova, whose books are "more precious than the most precious stones." Himself a lover of art, he advises his son to devote himself to elegant style and poetry. "Then you will compose songs like your father."

Ezobi's disciple was the famous *melitz* (rhetor) Abraham Bedersi of Béziers.[56] Bedersi was well acquainted with the poetry of the Provençal troubadours. He even adopted from them the custom of engaging in poetic tournaments, and often challenged his comrades to poetry contests. He composed many religious hymns, among them *Elef Alfin*,[57] a poem consisting of a thousand words, each one of them beginning with *alef*, the first letter of the Hebrew alphabet. Bedersi also wrote satires, parodies, and songs of praise to Jewish patrons and officials.[58] All suffer from the same defect: they lack the poetic spark, true inspiration. Nevertheless, Bedersi considered himself the foremost poet of his age. In his poem *Ḥerev Hamithaphechet*[59] he declares proudly: "As the ancient poets were great in their time, so am I in the present generation." Bedersi, who proceeds constantly in his poems as though he were walking on stilts, is convinced that his "tongue is as sharp as an arrow and his songs are filled with magic." Nevertheless, this poem of Bedersi's has a certain historic interest because the author attempts to present in it a brief overview of Hebrew poetry from the time of Jehudah Halevi (the "Urim and Tummim," as he calls him) to his own time. Bedersi complains that in his generation the poetic art has deteriorated greatly: "Of what avail is it that on my harp sweet tones sound in a generation so poor in songs?" "The beautiful songs of the Romance and Provençal poets have become dumb. One no longer hears the sweet song of Folquet[60] and his comrades. Snuffed out are the fragrant sounds of the great Cardenal."[61]

56. For bibliographical details on Bedersi, see Renan-Neubauer, *Les Rabbins français du commencement du quatorzième siècle*, pp. 707–19.
57. The poem is published in *Kerem Ḥemed*, IV.
58. As, for example, to Kalonymos ben Meir of Arles, the well-known Kabbalist and poet Todros Abulafia, etc. See *Ḥotam Tochnit*, Mordecai Tamah's *Maskiyyot Kesef*, pp. 23–26, and *Literaturblatt des Orients*, 1846, p. 563, where the content of Bedersi's collection of poems is given. In 1929 M. Meir published in Berlin Bedersi's *Kinah Al Serefat Ha-Talmud* (Elegy on the Burning of the Talmud).
59. Published in 1865 at the end of his philological work *Ḥotam Tochnit.* The poem consists of 210 verses, all ending with the same syllable, *ri.* This syllable, as well as the title of the poem, *Ḥerev*, are equivalent in *gematria* to the number 210.
60. Folquet de Marseille, an important Provençal troubadour.
61. Peire Cardenal, another prominent Provençal troubadour.

Bedersi complains of his orphaned generation, in which "poets and singers have become dumb," but he could not, out of petty vanity, forgive any of his comrades if one of these had the presumption to be more talented than he. Especially characteristic of Bedersi in this respect is the contempt and hatred that he manifested toward the truly gifted poet of that day, Isaac ben Abraham Gorni.[62] Gorni's was a talented but very unsettled nature. A constant wanderer, he roamed from city to city and loved to spend his time in taverns and hostelries with a full cup.[63] Like Alḥarizi in his day, Gorni also suffered hunger and deprivation. His only fortune was his poetry, but Bedersi is certainly unjustified when he accuses Gorni of wasting his talents and selling his poems for money. With his irascible temperament, Gorni was quite unsuited to be a lackey with bowed back. Toward the rich and powerful he conducted himself without any self-depreciation but rather with a certain pride, and endeavored to show his indifference to them.

He declares in one of his poems,

> I curse the poets who sell their songs . . . who cry "bravo" and fall on their knees before sacks of silver. . . . Proudly I raise my fist against the rich man, even if he be the greatest philanthropist. . . . I know them well and realize that even when they esteem the scholar, he nevertheless remains with a pierced ear [i.e., bears the mark of a slave].[64]

Indeed, through his proud and independent temperament, the poet acquired numerous enemies and had to endure much in his poverty-stricken, wandering life. "What sins, what guilt," he asks in grief,

> do my enemies find in me? Have I violated commandments, have I broken the covenant? They are powerful and rich and enjoy the cup of life, while I am exiled with languishing lips. They bloom like a garden, and I am sick and poor. . . . I am trodden underfoot by the rich officials. My fiddle, my comfort, is drowned in sorrow, and my song is changed into weeping. . . . Where shall I run, where hide? Everywhere the net is spread for my feet. . . . Oh Gorni, for whom

62. *Goren* is the Hebrew word for the name of the poet's birthplace, Aire. On him, see *Les Rabbins français*, pp. 719–23.
63. His love for strong drink is alluded to by the poet's opponent Isaiah ben Samuel Devash (Muel) when he speaks of "those drunk with wine."
64. See *MGWJ*, 1882, p. 516.

is there ruin, for whom mockery and laughter? —All for you, for your prostrate heart.[65]

It was not, however, only the powerful and rich who persecuted Gorni, but also his comrades, the literati and poets. In the city of Aix, the poet Isaiah Devash persecuted him; in Perpignan, Abraham Bedersi. Gorni himself was very fond of Bedersi and considered him "the chief of all the poets" in his generation. While living in Perpignan, he sent Bedersi a song of praise which he had composed in his honor.[66] According to the custom of that era, Bedersi ought to have replied with a poem. But the arrogant Bedersi believed that it was inappropriate for him to put himself on the same footing with some wandering poet and did not respond. Gorni then challenged him to a poetry contest. To this Bedersi replied with the epigram:

> When Alexander declared war against women
> They cleverly said to the mighty man:
> "No great honor is involved in conquering women,
> But how shameful to be conquered by women."

Poetic talent—this is what Bedersi could not forgive in Gorni. He wanted to assure future generations that "Bedersi's songs are sweeter than honey while Gorni's poetry is bitter as salt." Gorni's only comfort was the goddess of song who had befriended him. In his poems he poured out the pain of his heart and the sorrow of his soul. Typical is the poem in which he describes his life in the city of Aix:

> In Aix my soul found no rest,
> No one listens to my words, my prayer.
> All gossip about me and utter false rumors;
> They cry: Gorni is a wretch,
> Great is the sin of the poet!

The poor poet recounts the persecutions and humiliations he had to endure there, not only from the rich men who would not even greet him, but also from his colleague, the poet Isaiah Devash. Nevertheless, Gorni does not fall in his own esteem and proudly declares:

65. *Ibid.*, pp. 513–14.
66. Steinschneider published it in *Ḥotam Tochnit.*

Say not, there is no longer a poet,
As long as Gorni holds his harp in hand!
His song can destroy and create,
Build and bring to ruin.
It rises proudly to the heavens
And with astonishment the spheres receive the sounds.
. . . . . . . . . . . . . . . . . . . . . . . . . . . . . . . .
All you winds of the north, come quickly toward me!
Give me, O sun, your bright rays—
I will still all sorrows with my song.
With new powers is my heart filled,
Fresh spirit revives the tired limbs,
And old and young will gather around me
And, astonished, hear of my great deeds.[67]

The same proud tone resounds in many of Gorni's poems:

Great is the number of Gorni's enemies in Provence;
They also persecute my songs.
But this I know: I am the father of poetry,
In our generation—the only poet.
When my song resounds, the mountains dance round about,
And all the valleys and forests throb for joy.
When I take my harp in hand,
The daughters of Zion happily join the dance circle.
If I call to the bones in graves,
They too will promptly rise from death's sleep;
If I raise my song to the stony rocks,
They will flow like the Jordan.[68]

The poet further indulges his fantasy:

After my death, young maidens daily
Will come to lament for me at my tomb.
In distant lands, for fine gold and precious stones,
Will merchants sell bags of earth from my grave.
Out of the wood of my casket they will make amulets,
The most precious remedies for barren women.
My hair on harps and fiddles
Will be stretched like strings,
And the most tender, beautiful melodies
Will resound on them, touched by no hand.

67. *MGWJ*, 1882, pp. 511–12.
68. *Ibid.*, pp. 521–27.

My clothes, everything that my hand has touched,
Coming generations will revere.
Let my bones be ground quickly into dust;
Otherwise, they will make idols of them.[69]

The poet and wanderer consoled himself: "Coming generations will remember my songs." But this hope was not fulfilled. Persecuted in life, he was also forgotten in later times. Poor and solitary, without a strong character and firm will, he did not properly employ his poetic talent and did not create anything that would prevail over the ravages of time and endure for generations. His name and his songs were forgotten.[70]

We have observed that until the end of the thirteenth century Provençal Jewry did not produce a single prominent name in any field of science and art. To be sure, one exception must here be noted. This is the realm of Talmudic investigation, in which two Provençal scholars acquired great reputations. These two investigators lived in an earlier generation, before the Provençal communities attained the highest level of their cultural development. Both of them lived in the twelfth century. They were Zeraḥyah Ha-Halevi Gerondi and the previously mentioned Ravad, or Rabbi Abraham ben David, the author of *Ha-Hassagot*.

As a youth Gerondi[71] was renowned as a prodigy, and at nineteen had already written his commentary and critical notes to Alfasi. It appears that some of the Talmudists of his native city complained that such a young man should have the presumption to write criticisms of one of the greatest of scholars and mockingly declared that "young must be the wine, seeing that the vessel is still young." Gerondi, who wrote poems quite fluently,[72] replied

69. *Ibid.*, pp. 522–23.
70. Only a certain Jacob Provinciali, a writer of the end of the fifteenth century, mentions Gorni's name favorably and puts him in the same category with Alḥarizi. Of Gorni's literary legacy only a few fragments have been published (by Steinschneider in the preface to *Ḥotam Tochnit* and by Gross in *MGWJ*, 1882, pp. 510–23). Neubauer reports in M. Rabinowich's name (*Les Rabbins français*, p. 721) that Gorni's *diwan* is contained in Firkovich's collection. On this basis, apparently, it is indicated in the *Jewish Encyclopedia*, VI, 619, that Gorni's poetry collection is to be found in St. Petersburg. However, we have become convinced that the report is false and that Gorni's *diwan* is not contained in Firkovich's collections.
71. Born around 1125, died around 1186 in Lunel.
72. Gerondi also wrote numerous liturgical poems which found their way into the Sephardic *Maḥzor* and many secular poems, but all lack the poetic spark. On his religious poems see Zunz, *Zur Geschichte und Literatur*, p. 476; Landshuth, *Ammudei Ha-Avodah*, p. 63.

with a sharp epigram in which the self-esteem of the young scholar and his belief in his own intellectual powers are evident:

*They* are the true spiritual beggars; how petty and vain they are compared to me! Turn away with your fragrant roses from these pointed thorns. They, the wild growth of the desert, say "Young is your wine, seeing that the vessel is still young." They cannot understand that you are young in years and old in knowledge. Like an eagle you will rise ever higher and build your nest among the stars.[73]

Gerondi left his native city and settled in Lunel, where he finished his famous *Sefer Ha-Maor*, which brought him recognition as a first-rate Talmudic scholar.[74]

In close proximity to Lunel, in the city of Posquières, lived at that time the scholarly opponent and rival of Zeraḥyah Ha-Levi, Rabbi Abraham ben David, the author of *Ha-Hassagot.*[75] To this expert in Talmudic knowledge all other realms of knowledge were absolutely alien. Maimonides justifiably emphasized his one-sidedness when he called him "the master of one trade." Abraham ben David was the first harbinger of the historic battle of ideas which soon divided the learned Jewish world into two hostile camps, Maimunists and anti-Maimunists.

With this battle another epoch in the development of Jewish thought began. Jewish culture received a new direction, called forth by new tendencies. To this subject we shall turn in the next chapter.

73. The poem is printed by Jacob Reifmann in his *Zeraḥyah Ha-Levi,* p. 30.
74. As a sequel to the *Sefer Ha-Maor,* Zeraḥyah wrote a second work, *Sefer Ha-Tzava.*
75. For a discussion of Rabbi Abraham ben David of Posquières see the monograph by Gross in *MGWJ,* 1874.

## CHAPTER SIX

# *The Beginning of the War Against Rationalism*

THE rationalist elements in Maimonides' system called forth considerable opposition even in his lifetime. One of the first opponents was Abraham ben David of Posquières, who sharply attacked Maimonides because the latter wished to make Aristotelian philosophy the foundation of religious thought and tried to rationalize the Jewish faith by analyzing it into principles which reason entails and which can be established through logical arguments.[1] The ascetic scholar of Posquières was especially irritated by Maimonides' tendency to smuggle in philosophical ideas under the cloak of sayings of the Talmudic sages. But, more than by anything else, he was angered by Maimonides' attitude toward the question of "the world to come" and resurrection. The fact is that when Maimonides touches upon these matters,[2] he, the clear expositor and excellent stylist, suddenly

1. His *Hassagot* against Maimonides are filled with expressions such as "He has confused everything"; "it is a mistake"; "this never happened"; "childish talk"; "everything he writes is foolishness, vanity, and falsehood"; "he has falsified"; etc. See I. H. Weiss, *Dor Dor Ve-Doreshav,* IV, 266.
2. *Hilchot Teshuvah,* Chapter 8, Section 28 ff.

becomes obscure and incomprehensible. He speaks only half-words, stumbling over himself. This embarrassed even many of his ardent admirers, and Maimonides finally had to issue a special explanation in his *Maamar Teḥiat Ha-Metim*. He here replies in a very irate tone and speaks with great contempt of those who "consider themselves sages in Israel but are in fact the most foolish of men; they stumble around more than beasts, and their mind is filled with crazy old wives' tales."[3] Maimonides finally admits that in his *Mishneh Torah* he discusses the resurrection of the dead at no great length because this subject cannot be grounded philosophically with logical arguments and transcends the order of nature.[4]

Maimonides' explanation, however, satisfied neither "the most foolish of men" nor such genuine scholars as Meir Abulafia of Toledo, the son of the "prince" of Burgos, Todros Abulafia. Even Meir Abulafia's literary rivals speak of him with great respect. Aaron ben Meshullam calls him a "lover of wisdom" and a "great scholar," and Maimonides' devoted follower, the poet Abraham Ibn Ḥasdai, who knew Abulafia personally,[5] speaks of him as "the pride of his generation," the "man of keen intellect."[6]

In 1202 the twenty-two-year-old Meir Abulafia addressed a letter to Maimonides' staunch admirers, the "scholars of Lunel." He expresses his apprehensions about the fact that the author of the *Mishneh Torah*, when speaking of the world to come, is completely silent on the resurrection of the dead.[7] Abulafia's letter greatly irritated the scholars of Lunel and, in their name, Aaron ben Meshullam answered him with an extremely indignant letter.[8] A Spaniard, Sheshet bar Isaac Beneveniste, also attacked Abulafia, replying to his letter with a biting epigram: "My friends ask why he is called Meir [in Hebrew, "one who lights up"], since he walks on dark ways. I answer them, 'Do you not know that night is called light[9] among the sages? This is euphemistic language.' "[10]

3. *Maamar Teḥiat Ha-Metim*, in *Teshuvot Ha-Rambam*, II, 8.
4. *Ibid.*, pp. 10–11.
5. Their personal acquaintanceship is indicated by a passage in Abraham Ibn Ḥasdai's letter (*Iggerot Kenaot*, p. 7).
6. Meir Abulafia obtained a reputation as a Talmudic scholar with his *Yad Ramah*. He also wrote *Masoret Seyag La-Torah*, on the Masoretic text of the Bible.
7. The letter is printed in *Kitab al-Rasa'il* (*Sefer Iggerot*), 1871, pp. 13–16.
8. The letter is printed in *Taam Zekenim*, pp. 66–70, and in *Iggerot Kenaot*, pp. 11–13. A more correct text is printed in Meir Abulafia's *Kitab al-Rasa'il*, pp. 25–40. From this text it appears that Aaron's letter was written while Maimonides was still alive (see pp. 29, 32).
9. This is a reference to the Talmudic word *urta* (evening).
10. Beneveniste's letter to the scholars of Lunel on Meir Abulafia is reprinted, but not in its entirety, in *MGWJ*, 1876, pp. 511–12. Beneveniste

Abulafia did not remain silent. He replied to Aaron ben Meshullam with a long letter and, not waiting for an answer, turned to seven prominent rabbis of France,[11] told them of his controversy with the scholars of Lunel, and requested them, as true "shepherds of Israel" and recognized authorities, to give their opinion. The French rabbis, however, led a very isolated life and had only a slight grasp of the significance of Maimonides. They had little familiarity even with his *Mishneh Torah*.[12] In their name Abulafia was answered by the prominent Tosafist Rabbi Samson of Sens.[13] He agreed with Abulafia, but his reply was not clear. His letter is full of hairsplitting and has little relationship to the issue.

The reply of the French rabbis was written after Maimonides' death.[14] But the rationalistic tendency called forth by the philosopher did not grow weaker after his death; on the contrary, it became stronger. Just at that time the Arabic Aristotelian philosopher Averroes, who went even farther than Maimonides in his rationalism, became extremely popular in Jewish intellectual circles.[15] Averroes regarded Aristotle's logic as the summit of human wisdom. Man's happiness and joy he measured with one yardstick, that of knowledge. Only in understanding, in rational inquiry, Averroes was convinced, lies the source of happiness, and the keener the mind, the greater the possibilities of true bliss. Averroes' doctrine of the sole sovereignty of reason, in fact, denied personal immortality. The only immortal thing in man is thought. When a man dies his soul does not survive by itself; it is only a spark of the universal reason, of the collective, all-human understanding. Maimonides, who was nine years younger than Averroes, read the works of his contemporary after he had completed his *Guide for the Perplexed*. He was delighted with them and urged his disciple, Joseph Ibn Aknin, to study Averroes' commentary to Aristotle.

---

had a fluent pen and wrote many poems. Some of these were published by Kaufmann in *REJ*, XXXIX, 62–75, 215–25. Beneveniste was also a prominent patron, and the poet Joseph Zabara dedicated his *Sefer Shaashuim* to him.

11. *Kitab al-Rasa'il*, pp. 105–51; *ibid.*, p. 4, where all seven rabbis are called by their names.
12. *Ibid.*, p. 113.
13. For a discussion of Rabbi Samson of Sens see the work of Gross, "Étude sur Simson ben Abraham de Sens," in *REJ*, VI (1883), 167–86; VII (1884), 40–77.
14. *Kitab al-Rasa'il*, p. 131, where Rabbi Samson of Sens writes: "And the great lion cannot be brought back; I came after his death."
15. Averroes was born in the same city as Maimonides in 1126 and died in 1198.

In the first decades of the thirteenth century Aristotle's ideas, in Averroes' understanding of them, became widespread among the Jewish intelligentsia in Spain.[16] But the ideas of the Greek philosopher had an unfortunate destiny: they became a thing of fashion and fell into the hands of dilettantes. An Aristotelian school, which employed Maimonides' method but without his profundity and intellectual acumen, was gradually formed. Unskilled hands transformed his ideas into clichés, and philosophy became philosophical play. The allegorical method of interpreting the Bible, which had been so eagerly employed by Maimonides, suffered a strange transformation. Maimonides himself in this respect had been extremely cautious. He had sought an allegorical meaning only in those cases in which it would otherwise be impossible to explain the text rationally, or in which it was a matter of the philosophical grounding of the Biblical conceptions of God or the account of creation. His followers who lived in Christian Spain and especially in Provence, however, went much further. Here, undoubtedly, Christian influence is discernible.

It must be remembered that the allegorical method is very old. Even the ancient Greeks had made use of it. Homer, who is considered the author of the *Iliad* and the *Odyssey*, was regarded by the Greeks not only as a brilliant poet; he, the beloved of the Muses, the man endowed with the holy spirit, the blind seer with open, far-seeing eyes, was also looked upon as the peerless teacher of morality, the true guide who alone can reveal the mystery of existence. Life, however, moved forward. With intellectual development, changes in the moral self-consciousness and the whole world view of the ancient Greek also occurred. The simple concepts and naive faith of the Homeric world could no longer satisfy him. These ancient concepts, however, still survived in the memory of the people; they had grown up with the popular faith. And so, unconsciously, into the classic form and the old concept a new content was introduced. The ancient Homeric text received a new interpretation. Not only dogmatists and teachers of morality based themselves on Homer's poems and sought to demonstrate the truth of their doctrine through verses and lines from the *Iliad* and the *Odyssey*, in which they saw profound, hidden mysteries; even philosophers and scholars endeavored to find in Homer an authority for their scientific laws and theories. "In Homer is everything"—of this no one had any doubt, and the greater the inconsistency between real life and the long-gone Homeric world grew,

16. At the beginning of the thirteenth century, the German scholar Ritter points out (*Göttinger gelehrten Anzeiger*, 1847, p. 46), Averroes' followers came from Jewish circles only.

the more artificial and ingenious the commentaries became. In every sentence and word of Homer secrets, parables, and allusions were sought. Homer's tales concerning the gods and heroes were transformed into parables and intimations. The stern god Zeus is merely an allusion to abstract thought; his daughter Athena is an allegorical symbol of art. The story in which the god Apollo hurls deadly arrows at the camp of hostile warriors is only a parable of how a dreadful plague broke out in the summer heat.

The difficulties which educated Greeks encountered in interpreting the "divine" Homer also confronted the Hellenized Jews of Alexandria, brought up on Greek philosophy, when it came to *their* Homer, the Hebrew Bible. In the Torah, too, they found many conceptions that were in definite contradiction to the doctrines of Greek philosophy. To the Greek Jews in Alexandria the faith of their fathers was still very precious; hence, they had to make peace between the two different worlds, proceeding from the old Talmudic dictum, "These *and* these are the words of the living God." They had no way other than the way of allegory, than to see in the text of the Bible merely a garment for hidden mysteries. On this way the Hellenized Jewish scholar Aristobulus, who lived in the second century before the Christian era, already proceeded. In his allegorical interpretation of the text he saw no contradiction between the Torah and Greek philosophy, and was even convinced that the Greek thinkers had drawn their truths from the Torah of Moses. This allegorical method was greatly developed, as has already been indicated, by Philo of Alexandria.

These methods were employed in even greater measure by Christian theologians and exegetes. Among them, too, this was essential. In the Gospels the words of Jesus in which he asserts that he came not to destroy the Torah but to fulfill it, and that "till heaven and earth pass away, not one jot or tittle of the Law shall pass away, until all be fulfilled," are quoted.[17] The Christian Church, which Paul established, however, soon abrogated most of the commandments and laws of the Mosaic Torah. To reconcile this contradiction, the Christian theologians had no instrument other than Philo's allegorical method.[18] But they went even further. While Philo employed the method only in interpreting the text of the Pentateuch, the Christian scholars used it in relation to the entire Bible. In this way it was easy not only to transform all the commandments and laws into mere allusions and allegories, but

17. Matthew 5:17–18.
18. The well-known Jewish scholar of the fourteenth century, Profiat Duran, already indicates this in his apologetic work *Kelimmat Ha-Goyyim.*

also to show that every incident in the Bible is an allusion to Jesus' life and miracles. Those works which Paul himself wrote, according to Christian tradition, already annul all the ritual laws of the Mosaic Torah by means of allegory, and many other Biblical narratives are explained in them allegorically in such a way that they serve to prove that the Christian faith is superior to the Jewish.[19]

Relying on such a great authority, the great Christian theologian of the third century Origen saw that obviously the patriarch Jacob's wives, Leah and Rachel, were merely an allegorical reference to the two faiths; Leah, the older wife with the weak eyes, is "blind" Judaism which refused to see the light of the true faith. Tertullian saw in the twelve stones set into the high priest Aaron's breastplate an allusion to Jesus' twelve disciples, and the Christian historian Eusebius points out that it is well known that many of the stories of the Old Testament are a symbolic description of Jesus' life. St. Augustine finds in almost every one of the Psalms references to the appearance of Jesus. The Spanish Isidore of Seville even saw in Moses' parents, Amram and Jochebed, an allusion to Christ and the Church. Another Christian scholar discovered in the four rivers that flow around the Garden of Eden an allusion to the four Evangelists. When David kills Goliath, this is an allegorical description of how Christ conquers Satan. Even the famous thinker Abelard, who was suspected of heresy, saw in almost every Biblical verse an allegory.[20] The Christian theologian Bede explains, "We must not imitate the Jews, who content themselves with the plain meaning of the Biblical text." In the twelfth century Abraham Ibn Ezra indicates, in the introduction to his commentary on the Pentateuch, that among the Christians the allegorical method, which consists in "their seeing in the entire Torah only allusions and riddles, whether in the stories of the Book of Genesis or in the commandments and laws," is accepted. "The Christians," says another Jewish Biblical exegete of that time, Joseph Bechor Shor, in amazement, "see in the words of Moses our teacher only allegories and parables and do not interpret a single word with its true meaning."

Soon, however, the allegorical method became extremely popular in certain Jewish quarters as well, especially in the circle of

19. See Galatians 4:21–23, 3:5–10; Romans 4:9–10, 10:4; First Corinthians 9:8–10.

20. For a discussion of this subject see Diestel, *Geschichte des Alten Testaments in die christlichen Kirche;* E. Hatch, *The Influence of Greek Ideas and Usages on the Christian Church;* Eliezer Schulman, *Ha-Peshat Veha-Derash* (*Sefer Ha-Yovel Le-Naḥum Sokolow* [1904], pp. 512–23).

Maimonides' followers. The philosopher's authority served as the stamp of approval for the method, and Christian influence contributed much to its spread among the rationalistically minded intelligentsia. The translator of the *Guide for the Perplexed*, Samuel Ibn Tibbon, who from his youth on was acquainted with Christian scholars, considered it a "scandal" that Jews should content themselves with the literal meaning of the Biblical text and refuse to understand the deeper essence and content. Interesting in this respect are the last pages of his *Yikkavu Ha-Mayyim*,[21] a philosophical commentary on the "work of creation" (*maaseh bereshit*). "Let people not complain of me," he writes in the last (twenty-second) chapter,

> that I have uncovered too much of that which our sages commanded be held secret. God is my witness that I did this only for His honor, because I was persuaded that the mysteries which our prophets and sages in their day considered it necessary not to reveal are now disclosed to the nations of the world, and they explain according to these revealed truths all the profound matters that are concealed in the Torah and in the words of the prophets. In this particular, our people is very backward and has no understanding. Other peoples, therefore, laugh at us and say mockingly that we possess only the shells of the prophets' words, not the true kernel. We have from this enough reproach and shame.[22]

"Only Maimonides saw with his luminous intellect," writes Ibn Tibbon enthusiastically,

> how little understood among us are the symbols in the sacred writings, and he uncovered very profound matters, but unfortunately few among us understood his allusions. Therefore, I, one of the youngest of his disciples, when I saw that the true sciences are much more widespread among the Christian peoples in whose midst I live than in the Moslem lands, deemed it necessary to enlighten the eyes of those who are eager for knowledge and to acquaint them with the little with which God has blessed me.[23]

Samuel Ibn Tibbon had, as we shall see later, numerous followers. Naturally, the Jewish rationalists rejected all Biblical allegories with any Christian coloration, because, as rationalists, they were thoroughgoing opponents of the Christian faith.[24] On the other

21. This work was published in successive parts by M. Biseliches in Pressburg in 1837.
22. *Yikkavu Ha-Mayyim*, p. 173.
23. *Ibid.*, p. 175.
24. The Jewish rationalists from Maimonides to Moses Mendelssohn were all very inimical to the fundamental dogmas of the Christian faith, be-

hand, they eagerly sought in the Bible allusions to philosophical truths. Here they manifested no less acumen than the Christian theologians. The struggle of Moses with Pharaoh is the struggle with the "evil inclination." The sinful city of Samaria is "accursed matter." The sanctuary with its appurtenances is a symbol of man and his organs; the ark is the heart, the tablets the mind, the table the liver, the candelabrum the gall, etc. Leviathan, which the righteous will feast on in the next world, is an allegorical allusion to the "corporeal desires which they must overcome in themselves."[25] The whole Bible became a rationalist-philosophical allegory. In every custom, every commandment and precept, the reason, the intellectual meaning, intended by it was sought; without this, no commandment could have any validity. This, for the Jewish rationalists, was clear as day. It is not surprising, then, that in the wealthy Jewish circles and among the intelligentsia, men ceased to observe the commandments and precepts connected with religious ritual and took no account even of Ezra's prohibition against marrying women of other faiths. That mixed marriages were at that time a very common phenomenon in Spain is attested by such a reliable witness as the French preacher and Talmudic codifier, Jehudah Ḥasid's pupil, Moses ben Jacob of Coucy.[26] A fiery orator,

---

cause these were difficult to explain through simple, sober common sense. Maimonides in his *Mishneh Torah* declares the Christians plain "idolaters," and one of his followers, a Provençal rationalist of the second half of the thirteenth century, Nissan bar Moses of Marseilles, speaks with contempt of the Christian theologians, the "astrologers" (*hovrei shamayim*), who believe in all kinds of foolishness. Sarcastically he relates how Christian scholars reproach him in argument that "everything your teacher Moses says in his Torah is also said and believed by the philosopher." Nissan of Marseilles adds: "They think thereby to denigrate our Torah. They do not understand that, on the contrary, they thereby exalt it, for religion and reason were both given by the same God—not, as the Christians in their great folly think, that the essence and substance of every religion consist precisely in having to believe in bizarre, crude fairy tales which reason must reject" (see *He-Ḥalutz*, VII, 110).

25. See the apochryphal letter of Maimonides to his son (*Kovetz Teshuvot Ha-Rambam*, II, 39). It has long been established that Maimonides did not write this letter; it was written by his followers when the first battle against his system broke out (see *Jeschurun*, I, 3 and 47).

26. Moses of Coucy, the author of the well-known code *Sefer Mitzvot Gadol* (*Semag*) was an interesting personality. Possessed of a deeply religious nature, he once heard while dreaming a decree that he had been appointed to compose a collection of Jewish ritual laws which would be more suited in spirit to the customs and manner of life of the pious French communities than Maimonides' *Mishneh Torah*. The temperament of the preacher and orator is strongly discernible in this

he made a tour of the Spanish communities in 1236, gave sermons in the synagogues and houses of study, provided moral instruction for the people, and demanded that they strictly obey all the commandments of the Torah.[27] "With the help of God," relates Moses of Coucy, "thousands and tens of thousands began, as a result of my sermons, again to put on *tefillin* and fulfill the commandment of *mezuzah* and *tzitzit*. They also separated from their non-Jewish wives."[28]

We have already noted that, in Provence, Aristotelian philosophy had no fewer ardent followers than in neighboring Spain. Maimonides himself pointed out a number of times that he had written his philosophic work only for the elect few, for men of philosophic education, not for wide, even though intelligent, circles.[29] But Samuel Ibn Tibbon's translation, and especially Jehudah Alḥarizi's, which was written in easily comprehensible language, made his *Guide for the Perplexed* accessible also to those who had only slight knowledge of philosophical matters. Indeed, Samuel Ibn Tibbon and the other rationalists, whose fond desire was to disseminate the ideas of their teacher more widely, actually aimed at this result.

Precisely at the time that the rationalist tendency and the attitude of indifference toward religious commandments and customs grew stronger among the Jewish intelligentsia, the social position of the Provençal Jews became radically changed for the worse. After the defeat of the Albigensian movement at the beginning of the thirteenth century, the Catholic clergy in Provence obtained complete authority. The priests skillfully employed the struggle

---

work. It is more a collection of fervent ethical sermons than a code of rules and laws. Moses of Coucy employs every opportunity to admonish the people, to remind them that one must avoid as much as possible the foolish desires of the world which so easily lead one into temptation. Humility, love, and a heart that forgives everyone, this faithful disciple of Rabbi Jehudah Ḥasid teaches, are the best guides in life. The Jewish people, he further says, must be the bearer of the highest morality, so that all nations may recognize that the Jews are, indeed, the chosen people of God. Through evil deeds God's name is desecrated (*Sefer Mitzvot Gadol, Ḥelek Lo Taaseh,* Sections 2, 3, and 16; *Ḥelek Taaseh,* Sections 2, 64, and 170).

27. *Sefer Mitzvot Gadol, Ḥelek Lo Taaseh,* Section 12; *Mitzvot Aseh,* Sections 3 and 23. That the Spanish-Jewish intelligentsia were not fond of ritual laws is attested also by the Christian theologian William of Auvergne (quoted by Graetz, *Geschichte der Juden,* Vol. VII).
28. *Sefer Mitzvot Gadol, Lo Taaseh,* Section 112 (the first Venetian edition of 1546).
29. See the preface to the *Moreh Nevuchim,* as well as Maimonides' letter to Samuel Ibn Tibbon (*Teshuvot Ha-Rambam,* II, 27).

against the heretical sects to take vengeance on their old enemies, the Jews. At the church council in Narbonne in 1227 the decision was taken to enforce in the strictest possible way the limitation of Jewish rights that had been promulgated at the Fourth Lateran Council in Rome.[30] To degrade the Jews further, it was determined again to enforce the old statute forbidding the Jews to appear on the streets during the Christian Holy Week. The Inquisition, led by the Dominicans, was extremely active, rummaged everywhere for secret followers of heretical sects, and persecuted Jews with special intensity. The condition of the Provençal Jews became even worse after 1229, when the freethinking and tolerant Count Raymond of Toulouse was forced to cede sovereignty over part of his land to the mother of Louis IX (Saint Louis), the fanatically pious Blanche of Castile.

A reactionary spirit gradually manifested itself in Jewish circles as well. Frightened by the new decrees, the orthodox elements in the Provençal communities also began to fear heresy. In the rationalists who permitted themselves to violate the commandments ordained by the Torah, they saw "breakers down of the fence" who threatened the very survival of Judaism. Since the name of the author of the *Guide for the Perplexed* was the rationalists' banner, it is not surprising that the battle which erupted between the orthodox and the freethinkers promptly took on the character of a struggle between Maimunists and anti-Maimunists.

In this battle the Maimunists made much more frequent use than their adversaries of lampoons, leaflets, and epigrams. In their polemic literature their opponents are always portrayed with the same material—coal and soot. All who take exception to Maimonides' philosophical ideas are here depicted as ignorant obscurantists who cannot free themselves from the grossest anthropomorphisms. Even such a gentle and restrained man as Maimonides' son Abraham, in his essay *Milḥamot Adonai* (written in 1235), depicts the opponents of his father as a band of "fools with blind hearts and dirty minds"[31] who think only of the reward they will receive in the next world for their piety: stuffing their bellies with fat pieces of Leviathan, eating rolls that grow ready-made on trees, and drinking aged wine.[32] The historical documents and letters, published in part long ago and in part only in modern times,[33] however, require the objective investigator to be somewhat

30. The Fourth Lateran Council took place in 1215.
31. *Iggerot Kenaot*, p. 18b.
32. *Ibid.*
33. Among the latter, particularly important is the packet of letters which S. J. Halberstam published in *Ginzei Nistarot*, III–IV.

suspicious about these black portraits painted by rivals and enemies.

The struggle broke out in the year 1232. Its initiators were the Talmudic scholar Solomon bar Abraham of Montpellier and his two disciples, David ben Saul and Jonah ben Abraham Gerondi, the latter of whom later obtained renown for his books of ethical instruction.[34] They came forth with a strict ban against those who occupy themselves with philosophy, and issued a prohibition forbidding the reading of Maimonides' two books, *A Guide for the Perplexed* and the *Sefer Ha-Madda*,[35] because in them are dangerous ideas that can shake the very foundations of the faith. Preserved from that time is a letter by Solomon of Montpellier which gives us some notion of this figure who called forth such a storm in the most cultured part of the Jewry of that era. The letter is written to a Spaniard, one Samuel ben Isaac. Solomon explains to him the motives which impelled him to rise against the free-thinkers. "Taking into consideration our old friendship," he writes,

> we [i.e., Solomon and his disciples] deem it necessary to acquaint you with the causes through which the controversy has broken out. We who love and revere the Torah that God has commanded us observed how old and young began to spread ideas and opinions of which neither we nor our forefathers had ever heard. We saw that they go in evil ways and, seduced by the new tendencies, wish to destroy everything we have received by way of tradition. They pervert the meaning of the Torah. Everything with them becomes a parable—the work of creation, the story of Cain and Abel; every verse in the Torah becomes for them an allegory, something fabricated. We heard from the very mouth of the translator[36] how he revealed for all that which the master,[37] may his memory be for a blessing, considered it necessary to hide, how he openly explained to everyone that all the stories in the Torah, all the commandments and statutes, are only parables. . . . I heard many times how they mocked the words of the Talmudic sages —and terror fell upon me when I heard all this. I often entered into hot argumentation with them; we would frequently wrangle, but it never came to warfare. But the dark hour arrived, and into our disputations the scholars of Béziers with their pride and arrogance intervened. They rose like enemies who wished to annihilate us. They wanted to make me a shame and mockery in the eyes of all, and they

34. His ethical works *Shaarei Teshuvah* and *Sefer Ha-Yirah* were extremely popular. They were published many times both in Hebrew and in Yiddish translation. The first Yiddish translation of *Sefer Ha-Yirah* appeared as early as 1546.
35. The first, philosophical part of the *Mishneh Torah.*
36. Meaning Samuel Ibn Tibbon.
37. I.e., Maimonides.

accused me of blaspheming in God's holy camp and of derogating the memory of the great scholar who spread Torah in Israel, Rabbi Moses, the son of the teacher and judge, Rabbi Maimon. This they did to make us ridiculous before the whole world and so that all the communities should turn away from us. When we realized in what a difficult situation we were, we determined to turn to the rabbis of France who have long been recognized as disseminators of Torah in Israel. . . . When they received our letter,[38] they also were seized with terror and sent a letter of reproof to these men and their followers. They also dispatched an emissary to investigate on the spot whether the situation was really as I described it to them. At the same time they also received a copy of the *Guide for the Perplexed.* When they read the book their wrath flared up because of the desecration of God's name which they saw in it. They immediately girded up their loins and, as one man, all rose to defend God and His Torah with curses and bans, with strict commands and cries, so that all everywhere, and I among them, were astonished.[39]

We learn from this letter that the controversy was initiated by the "scholars of Béziers," of whom Solomon of Montpellier complains that they devised slanders against him. That Solomon's accusation is correct is confirmed by several letters which Halberstam has published.[40] These letters relate at length how some of the "scholars of Béziers," in order to discredit Solomon's closest collaborator, Jonah Gerondi, fabricated a slander against his whole family.[41] It is therefore not surprising that the offended Gerondi, at the command of Solomon, set out for Paris to agitate against the Maimunists. In Paris at that time lived the chief of the rabbis of France, Yeḥiel ben Joseph, who achieved renown through his dis-

38. According to the report of Maimonides' son, Solomon of Montpellier in his letter to the rabbis of France particularly emphasized the doubts necessarily elicited by Maimonides' views on "the world to come" and the resurrection of the dead, as well as by his rationalist explanations regarding the "reasons for the commandments" (*taamei ha-mitzvot*) in the third part of the *Moreh Nevuchim.*
39. *Ginzei Nistarot,* IV, 10–13.
40. See the letters numbered 9–12 (*Ginzei Nistarot,* IV, 15–36; see also Steinschneider's report, *ibid.*, p. 70).
41. The family "defect" which they fabricated consisted in their nullification of a certain divorce and, on this basis, declaring the subsequent marriage illegal and branding the children born from it as bastards. The Gerondi family was one of the most prominent in the land; from it came a number of famous rabbis and scholars, among them Naḥmanides. Not without reason does Jonah Gerondi emphasize in his *Shaarei Teshuvah,* when he speaks of the grievous son of gossip, "and our sages said that he who gives an evil report in the matter of family defects has no atonement forever" (Warsaw edition [1848]), p. 26a.

putation with the apostate Nicholas Donin.[42] Thus, through the fault of several overly ardent Maimunists, the war of ideas took on, from its very inception, a personal and bitter character.

Solomon of Montpellier soon acquired a talented collaborator in the person of the poet Meshullam ben Solomon Dapiera. Dapiera was not at all a "rebel against the light." Not without reason does he say of himself, "In my heart the Jewish faith burns, but I do not afflict myself with fasts." He loved nature, gladly whiled away time with friends over the cup, and sang of nature and wine in lovely verses.[43] But the rationalist world outlook was alien to his romantic soul. A close friend of Moses ben Naḥman (Naḥmanides) and an ardent admirer of the mystics Ezra and Azriel,[44] Meshullam could not remain an uninvolved spectator of the controversy that had flared up. In his composition "Yehegu Mezimmot"[45] he sharply assails the rationalists and praises Solomon of Montpellier for the courage with which the latter defends the "holy covenant." In his poem "Anshei Minut"[46] he pours out his wrath on Jehudah Al-ḥarizi because the latter, with his translation of Maimonides' *Guide*, "became a stumbling block for the corrupted generation," and he turns to the rabbis of France, asking them "quickly to clothe themselves with armor" and "wrathfully proceed against the men of Béziers." And the rabbis of France did, indeed, promptly "raise their armor." Solomon of Montpellier had written the plain truth in his letter. The orthodox and pious rabbis who spent their entire lives "in the tent of Torah" were horror-stricken when they learned of Maimonides' *Guide*. They immediately addressed to the communities of Provence a proclamation in which they sharply attacked Maimonides and threatened with the severest ban of excommunication anyone undertaking to read such heretical books as his *Guide* and *Sefer Ha-Madda*.[47]

The attack of Solomon ben Abraham and his followers called forth tremendous rage within the intellectual circles of the large Provençal communities of Lunel, Béziers, and Narbonne, for Maimonides, to them, was the supreme authority, the unique and peer-

42. For a discussion of this disputation, see A. Kisch's work, *MGWJ*, 1874.
43. See his poem *Be-Yom Sagrir, Be-Yom Raam Geshamin* in *Ha-Ḥoker*, II, 26.
44. More of these mystics later. In one of his poems the poet says: "The son of Naḥman came to us as a tower of strength . . . Ezra and Azriel. . . . They are my priests, they light up my altar, they are the stars of my soul."
45. Printed in *Divrei Ḥachamim*, pp. 75–77, and also in *Moreh Mekom Ha-Moreh*, pp. 9–12.
46. *Divrei Ḥachamim*, p. 78; *Moreh Mekom Ha-Moreh*, p. 3.
47. See Naḥmanides' letter to the rabbis of France, *Iggerot Kenaot*, p. 8.

less teacher. With great indignation they rose against the "vile men" who opposed his views and summoned all the communities of Provence, Catalonia, and Castile to champion the desecrated honor of the great scholar and teacher, and to excommunicate the "presumptuous blasphemers" (i.e., Solomon ben Abraham and his followers).

One of Maimonides' ardent followers wrote an extremely caustic letter to the rabbis of France. This letter is characteristic of the rationalist circles. It indicates clearly the attitude of these circles toward the rabbis who were versed only in the Talmud and ignorant of the secular sciences.[48] The anonymous author writes to the French rabbis:

> Before you so sharply attacked the great scholar and his books, you should first have thoroughly acquainted yourselves with them. You, however, apparently never actually saw the *Sefer Ha-Madda* or *Guide for the Perplexed;* yet you issued your decision and your unjust judgment. It is clear that you, who have spent all your years only within the four ells of Talmudic hairsplitting, are not able to understand philosophical matters or comprehend the wondrous ways of the sciences. Why, then, did you step outside your bounds and undertake decisions on such high matters which you cannot understand? And how do you have the presumption to declare as heretics us who proceed on the true way of wisdom as our teacher, Rabbi Moses ben Maimon, taught it to us—you, for whom all the stories of the Torah, even all the legends of the Midrashim, are accepted in their literal meaning? You represent God to yourselves in the form of a mortal with the organs of a man. . . . Are there, then, among the nations of the world, with all their barbaric stupidities, such idolaters as you? And you have the gall to accuse us, who defend the purity of the sacred Torah, of heresy and to declare that we deny God's word? I swear by God that there are not among us any seducers, false prophets, or heretics who deny God. You are in error. You have blindly relied on liars and gossip-mongers who have led you astray. You have attacked us with curses and excommunications. You consider yourselves the great scholars of the generation and us petty, worthless men. All this we would forgive you, but of one thing we cannot and may not be silent: you have undertaken to speak with contempt and hatred of our pride and crown, of the great scholar Rabbi Moses ben Maimon who, since the time of Rav Ashi, has had no peer in Torah, against him, the true pointer of the way.

But Solomon of Montpellier and his comrades also were not without support. The first who came to their aid was Moses ben

48 This letter was published by S. J. Rapoport in *Kerem Ḥemed,* V, 9–13. The author of the letter is unknown. The conjecture that it was written by Samuel Saporta has been shown to be incorrect.

Naḥman (Naḥmanides), a close relative of Jonah Gerondi,[49] who felt personally insulted by the libel which the "scholars of Béziers" had issued regarding the Gerondi family. This is discernible in the acid tone with which Naḥmanides attacks the "false testimony" and "gossip-mongers" of Béziers, whom he calls a "group of wicked men" and "the accursed band."[50] In letters to private persons, as well as in his open letter to the Provençal communities "from Narbonne to Marseilles," he summons the "gossip-mongers" to legal proceedings, and as arbitrators proposes either the rabbis of France or Rabbi Meir Abulafia. And when the Maimunists, the "scholars of Béziers" among them, began to agitate for the excommunication of Solomon of Montpellier and his disciples, Naḥmanides addressed a letter to the communities of all three Spanish kingdoms, Navarre, Aragon, and Castile. He warns them that travelling about are "emissaries of sin, with false letters filled with flattery and trickery." Let them not be led astray by the words of these deceitful men who represent themselves as pursuers of peace but are actually stirrers of conflict. The communities must be cautious and not give their consent to the excommunication before they have heard both sides.[51]

The first who replied to the summons of Naḥmanides was Meir Abulafia who, immediately after the conflict broke out, gathered the packet of letters that he had saved from the time he had turned to Marseilles and the rabbis of France and sent these in many copies throughout the Provençal communities.[52] The letter which Abulafia wrote in reply to Naḥmanides' summons is extremely interesting, because in it are revealed in the clearest way the inner motives which impelled the anti-Maimunists to attack their opponents. Sadly Abulafia notes that the number of those "who lop off the living branches of religious laws" and endeavor to demonstrate rationally that the Creator has no need of the ritual precepts and commandments grows constantly greater. The important thing, they maintain, is only that man "understand God and comprehend the wisdom of His creation," for it is certainly of no interest to Him "whether the body is clean or unclean, whether one is sated or afflicts himself with fasts." They wander lost on crooked ways and proudly proclaim their reason as the sole sure guide. Waste and void do they make souls that yearn for commandments and good deeds. They extinguish the flame of longing hearts. They wish to destroy the immortal spirit.[53]

49. Naḥmanides and Jonah Gerondi were cousins.
50. *Ginzei Nistarot*, IV (1872).
51. *Iggerot Kenaot* (Leipzig edition, 1859), p. 5a.
52. *Kitab al Rasa'il*, pp. 10 and 14.
53. *Iggerot Kenaot*, p. 6b.

Between the Maimunists and their antagonists, we see, the ancient dispute which a thousand years before had divided into hostile camps the sages of the Mishnah and the Gnostics was revived. The chief principle of the Gnostics was "And thou shalt know the Lord"—knowledge, inquiry. The sages of the Mishnah, however, emphasized that "everything is according to the work," that man's actions are primary. Rabbi Simeon ben Rabban Gamaliel declares, "Not study is the chief thing, but deed." It is not "interpretation," seeking allegorical allusions in the Torah, that is of ultimate significance, but observing the commandments and precepts. "Everyone whose deeds are greater than his wisdom," says Rabbi Ḥanina ben Dosa, "his wisdom will endure; and everyone whose wisdom is greater than his deeds, his wisdom will not endure" (*Pirkei Avot*, 3:10).

Abulafia gladly admits that the merits of Maimonides are very great. He calls him "the man of God" who opened the eyes of all with his *Mishneh Torah.* On the other hand, he very sharply assails his *Guide for the Perplexed.* "Page after page," writes Abulafia, "I diligently studied this book, and I became convinced that he wishes, indeed, to strengthen the roots of faith but in reality cuts off its branches. He does, indeed, try to mend all the splits and holes, but thereby destroys all restraints. This book contains death and life together."[54] On the other hand, Abulafia speaks with great respect of Solomon of Montpellier because the latter had the courage to step forth publicly and point out the danger which, in his opinion, continued to grow.

In the meantime the controversy flared up ever stronger, and in some places came to the point of intense conflict and even fisticuffs. There is no doubt, however, that in this intensified struggle a definite role was played by social and economic rivalries, as well as by purely ideological motives. We have already noted that the "scholars of Béziers" brought into the conflict purely personal motives and sought, through a false accusation, to discredit the Gerondi family to which Jonah, the disciple of Solomon of Montpellier, and Naḥmanides belonged. Of considerable significance is a letter of Naḥmanides which is to be found, unfortunately only in extracts,[55] in the above mentioned packet of letters published by

54. *Ibid.* It is interesting that the same view of Maimonides' *Guide* was expressed by an Arabic scholar of that time. Abdul al-Latif relates in his autobiography, "I read this book [the *Guide*] and found that it is a harmful book, for it is more suited to destroy the very foundations of the faith which it wishes to confirm" (see *Literaturblatt des Orients,* 1846, p. 355).

55. See Kobak's *Jeschurun,* VII, 120–24. The first to note the true significance of this letter was Yitzḥak Baer in *Devir, II* (1924), 316–17.

Halberstam. In this letter the court Jews of Saragossa, Baḥya and Solomon Alconstantini, are spoken of with great anger. Baḥya was court physician to the king of Aragon, James I, and also his secretary and interpreter in the negotiations with the Arabs at the time of the wars that James waged against Morocco and Valencia. Baḥya and his brother Solomon were very influential at court and occupied important financial posts. By royal decree Solomon was appointed prince and chief judge over all the Jewish communities of Aragon. It appears that the brothers Alconstantini conducted their office high-handedly and exploited their influence at court for self-aggrandizement. This went so far that the communities of Aragon considered it necessary to complain to the king about their "princes" and "judges." Naḥmanides himself personally appeared before the king with very grievous charges against the "wretches" and "men of ugly deeds," as he calls the brothers Alconstantini in the abovementioned letter. With great indignation and disgust he speaks of these "court Jews" who cast off all the commandments of the Torah, do not pray, do not say grace, take no care in drinking and eating, do not observe the Sabbath, and conduct themselves like Moslems. "Where has it ever been heard," Naḥmanides cries out, "that a complete ignoramus and boor should become a 'master and ruler, a prince and noble' who reigns over the community?"

In the camp of the Maimunists and rationalists there was, in fact, quite a large representation of court Jews, bankers, and financiers who, in their manner of life, were "like Moslems" and had a strong desire to liberate themselves from what they considered the heavy yoke of the commandments. It is therefore not surprising that in the intensified struggle against Solomon of Montpellier and his followers the Alconstantinis took a very active part.

The Alconstantinis, together with ten other members of the community, excommunicated Solomon of Montpellier and his collaborators, and immediately thereafter (July 1232) addressed a summons to all the communities of Aragon "to rise to the aid of Moses [Maimonides] and his sacred doctrine," to champion the great man "who drew us out of the swamp of barbarism and superstition." They proposed that other communities should give their consent and place under the ban "these three disturbers of the peace and corrupters."[56] To this summons four communities of Aragon[57] promptly replied. They agreed that the "little foxes," the "three sinners in Israel," the "vile" Solomon and his disciples, who permitted themselves to blaspheme the "light of the exile, Rabbi Moses ben Maimon," must be excommunicated.

56. *Iggerot Kenaot*, p. 5.
57. Huesca, Monzon, Lerida, and Calatayud.

At that moment, in the heat of the conflict, Naḥmanides stepped forth once again. A man of noble character, he set aside all external motives, overlooked the personal insults he had received, and sought a compromise that would bring peace between the two sides. Given his world outlook, Naḥmanides had to be completely opposed to the rationalists who followed Maimonides' system. He had profound respect for Maimonides as the author of the *Mishneh Torah,* as one of the greatest scholars in the realm of Talmud, but the philosophical world of ideas of the *Guide* was alien and objectionable to him. A man with a dreaming, enthusiastic nature, Naḥmanides, as we shall later see, was one of the founders of the mystical doctrine, the "Torah of the heart," which regarded philosophical rationalism as its mortal enemy.

To still the conflict, Naḥmanides addressed a long epistle to the rabbis of France.[58] Restrainedly and calmly he points out to the pious French rabbis how grievously they erred when they accused such a great scholar as Maimonides of heresy. With their prohibition against reading Maimonides' work and their ban against the study of philosophy, they will accomplish nothing. They will only intensify the controversy, for the authority of Maimonides is too great and the cultural conditions under which the Jews in Spain and in France live are too disparate. Naḥmanides notes the important place that the Spanish Jews assign to the "external wisdoms" or secular sciences and Greek philosophy. The Spanish communities will thus take no account of the ban, and it will not be carried out. "With peace and love must you, the shepherds of Israel, pasture your flock." "You cannot force all Jews," Naḥmanides insists, "to be pious and ascetic."

Naḥmanides speaks with great respect of Solomon of Montpellier, with whom he even had an exchange of correspondence,[59] but he indicates that he cannot decide which of the adversaries is right. He only begs the rabbis of France to seek peace and try to still the conflict, and he proposes that they make the following compromise: a removal of the ban against Maimonides' *Sefer Ha-Madda,* in exchange for prohibiting the dissemination among broad strata of the people of his *Guide for the Perplexed.*

This compromise, however, could satisfy neither side. Naḥmanides' letter had an effect only in one particular: the rabbis of France completely withdrew and took no further part in the conflict. In the end they could, as far as their own communities were concerned, be quite at ease. The French Jews never saw the

58. *Iggerot Kenaot,* pp. 8–10.
59. See *Letterbode* (1887), p. 1.

*Guide*, and the problems so sharply posed in it did not interest them at all.

In Provence, however, the battle became all the more intense at that time. The Maimunists dispatched the aged Rabbi David Kimḥi to Spain to propagandize for them in the most important communities. "The Maimunists," complains Solomon of Montpellier in his previously quoted letter,

> sent a special emissary to intensify the conflict and to incite your communities against us. They spread false rumors and accuse us of having dishonored the memory of Maimonides. God is my witness that I have never allowed myself to touch the honor of the great scholar and his doctrine with an evil word, for his words are highly esteemed and precious to me and I always mention his decisions and conclusions with great respect. . . . I believe that the man with the long beard [i.e., David Kimḥi] will do the same thing among you that his comrades permitted themselves to do among us. They gave a false account of my call to the rabbis of France and accused me of having proposed that all of Maimonides' followers be put under the ban.

Kimḥi's propaganda tour had very slight success. In many communities he was received quite coldly, because the French rabbis had sharply attacked his rationalist interpretation of "the work of creation" (*maaseh bereshit*) and "the work of the chariot or throne" (*maaseh merkavah*). In the city of Burgos, Kimḥi was received with such hostility that he had to leave immediately. One of the prominent leaders of this community, Joseph ben Todros Ha-Levi, immediately thereafter issued a proclamation to the communities of Provence. This proclamation is particularly interesting because its author did not belong to either of the rival parties.[60] Joseph ben Todros was an impartial witness who looked at the historic controversy from the sidelines. Hence his words have a special value. "Very sad things are now happening in God's holy camp," he complains.

> The elders set the fire and the children throw on more material for burning, and constantly greater grows the flame which envelops the foundations of the ancient faith, and its firm walls are destroyed. . . . Men have appeared who violate the restraints of the Torah. . . . Everyone comes forth with his own notions and thinks only of how to throw off all prohibitions, how to free himself from all restraints. . . . All the words of the Torah, all that we have by way of tradition from our fathers, become for them merely a parable and allegory. The

60. See *Ginzei Nistarot*, IV, 6. The proclamation is printed *ibid.*, III, 149–75.

miracles and wonders mentioned in the Torah become a mockery and scorn. They make of day, night, and of darkness, light. They scorn the words of our sages . . . and even have the gall to rely in this on a great authority; they declare themselves disciples and followers of one of our foremost scholars whose like has not been seen since Rabina and Rav Ashi. Rabbi Moses ben Maimon, the light of the exile, they make their protector; they always invoke his name. They refuse to understand that our great teacher created his *Guide for the Perplexed* only for the elect few, for those who have penetrated into the mysteries of Greek philosophy. For these the *Guide* became the firm support, the true pointer of the way which taught them how to hold fast to the eternal truths of our Torah against the profundities of philosophical thought and not stumble or stray from the right path. But even for the chosen few, the great scholar gave mere hints, nothing more than allusions. Indeed, he admonished that his work should not be placed in the hands of those not suited for it. The master's will, however, was not fulfilled. Men with very slight knowledge came and began to give Maimonides' philosophical book into the hands of the "mixed multitude," of plain ignoramuses. They disseminated Ibn Tibbon's translation, and even the translation of Alḥarizi, which often corrupted the author's thought[61] and put into his mouth words he never uttered. Every ignoramus considers himself an expert in the profound work of Rabbi Moses ben Maimon. Everyone handles it with his gross hands. Every fool considers himself a full-fledged philosopher, criticizes all things in heaven and on earth. They know everything that God intends and thinks, all mysteries are revealed to them. There are no "holy things." Everything is common and profane. To pray, to put on *tefillin*—they consider such things foolishness and laugh at them.[62] Though Maimonides gave his book the title *Guide for the Perplexed*, it has now become "the perplexity of the rebels."

It is interesting to note that Joseph ben Todros divides the rationalists of his era into two groups: (1) the class of flatterers and hypocrites, who desecrate the words of the Torah and cover their lusts with the mantle of knowledge, and who now commit publicly the sins which they formerly did in secret; and (2) the

61. In the literature of that era one frequently encounters hostile references to Alḥarizi's translation of the *Guide*. Maimonides' son Abraham insists in his *Milḥamot Adonai* that "when Rabbi Jehudah Alḥarizi translated it . . . his translation was faulty and spoiled" (*meshubeshet u-mekulkelet*). The well-known Jewish scholar of the thirteenth century, Shemtov Falaquera, also complains in his open letter on the controversy against Maimonides that "the second [Alḥarizi's] translation was filled with errors, and what was right in it did not escape crookedness."

62. *Ginzei Nistarot*, III, 165.

class of the rich, who have become fat from the sweat of the poor, and who wish to enjoy all the pleasures of the world and are delighted that, through rationalism, one can liberate himself from religious commandments and duties.[63]

"No," declares Joseph Ha-Levi, "the values of faith are not weighed on the scales of cold reason. In this way the Torah loses all its fragrance and odor, and you arrive at very false conclusions."[64] He exhorts the leaders of the Provençal communities to take measures against the growing danger as quickly as possible.

Do not console yourself that your land is still a hostel of Torah. You are versed in all aspects of Jewish knowledge, and before you all the ways of God's statutes are open. But remember the future. Behold, the days come when you will no longer be among the living, and your children will arrive and their hearts will be eaten through with the poison of this new heresy which is far more dangerous than that which the schism of the Karaites brought, because they [the Karaites] deny only a part of our doctrine and accept the other part. These, however, cast off everything and wish to recognize nothing.[65]

Despite his slight success, David Kimḥi did not lose courage. The major goal of his propaganda tour was Toledo. He was certain that if he succeeded in receiving from this largest Jewish community assent to the excommunication of Solomon of Montpellier, it would be a great victory for his party. Not far from Toledo, however, the aged Kimḥi was taken ill and had to stop in the city of Avila. From there he sent a letter to the head of the Jewish community in Toledo, the learned physician Jehudah ben Joseph Ibn Alfachar. Kimḥi, however, once again committed an error in judgment. He was certain that Alfachar would agree with him. In the end, however, the latter came forward as his most determined adversary. The epistolary disputation[66] between Kimḥi and Alfachar best demonstrates how one-sided is the view that the anti-Maimunists were merely "foolish ignoramuses" with the gross concepts of

63. *Ibid.*, p. 172. We shall speak of the role of the rich court Jews in the Maimunist camp in the fourth part of this work.
64. *Ibid.*, p. 160.
65. *Ibid.*, p. 156.
66. The first four letters of this interesting correspondence were printed in *Iggerot Kenaot* in incorrect chronological order. As reply to Kimḥi's first letter, which begins with the words "Lo, I went out," Alfachar wrote his reply, which begins with "Who is like the sage" (printed in the fourth place in *Iggerot Kenaot*), and to Kimḥi's second letter "Jehudah, thee shall they praise," Alfachar replied with a letter beginning "The Lord rebuke thee, Satan," which is printed in the second place.

idolaters. Alfachar was not only very competent in Talmudic literature but stood at the highest cultural level of that age. In addition, he was blessed with a keen, analytic mind which enabled him to expose all the weak aspects of Maimonides' philosophical system, despite the fact that he greatly esteemed Maimonides as a powerful thinker and first-rate Talmudic scholar.

In his first reply to Kimḥi's letter, Alfachar declares categorically that he agrees with Solomon of Montpellier. "You ask me," he writes to Kimḥi,

> to persuade the leaders of our community to give their assent to the ban which you have issued against the pious Solomon and his faithful disciples. God forbid that I should do such a thing against this righteous man, who deserves the greatest praise for the fact that he, with his disciples, had the courage to come forth for the sake of God's name against those who violate the precepts of the Torah and destroy the foundations of the faith.

At the end Alfachar adds, "As far as your question concerning my opinion of Maimonides' *Guide* is concerned, it is best to hold to the ancient proverb, 'Speech is silver but silence is gold.' "

Alfachar, however, did not hold to the proverb. In one of his later letters to Kimḥi he declares quite openly that it is his firm conviction that in Maimonides' rationalism inheres a great danger, especially in the conclusions which the mediocre and shallow followers of the author of the *Guide* draw from it. In a rich and pungent style Alfachar endeavors to show that Maimonides' basic error consists in wishing to reconcile two world outlooks that have no relationship to each other and are essentially incompatible.

> Maimonides always desires to pair the Torah with Greek philosophy. He endeavors to show that they are of one cast and similar to one another, like twins. The whole effort, however, is in vain. There can be no peace between them. They are too disparate and will never become twin sisters. A deep abyss separates them. They are two completely different worlds, and each of them argues, like the women in King Solomon's judgment, "My son is the living one, and yours the dead." One may not and must not speak of peace where there is no peace. Maimonides considers nothing of this. He always wishes to reconcile the foundations of our faith and the conclusions of Greek philosophy. He has himself admitted, in speaking of the "eternity of the world," that if he should find in Aristotle convincing logical proofs that matter was not created and has existed from eternity, he would know how to interpret the relevant verses in the Book of Genesis so that they should not contradict Aristotle's conclusion.[67]

67. *Iggerot Kenaot*, p. 1.

"For Maimonides," Alfachar further says,

> the highest authority is the syllogism, the intellectual discoveries of Greek philosophy. He forgets, however, that the logical demonstrations on which the philosophers rely are not free of the defect that bears in Greek the name "sophistry," which consists in artificiality, in dazzling with clever tricks and notions which only lead one astray and bring him to completely false opinions.

"It is true," Alfachar writes further,

> we are all obliged to treat with great respect the memory of Rabbi Moses ben Maimon, the incomparable author of the *Mishneh Torah*, which itself has no peer. I realize very well that only a powerful and acute thinker could have created such a work as the *Guide for the Perplexed*. I also know, however, what danger lies in this book. He has kindled an alien fire on God's altar. He brings hateful ideas into the Torah of Moses, and the danger becomes even greater through those who call themselves his disciples and speak in his name. The number of supposedly educated and half-educated people who declare themselves Maimonides' followers and, in reliance on his *Guide* and the false conclusions they reach from his words which they do not properly understand, spurn God's word grows constantly greater. The *Guide* has become the armor of all apostates and heretics. Basing themselves on the *Guide*, they deny all the miracles and signs and wonders in the Torah. Everything for them is merely a parable and an alllegory. The verses and doctrines, precious as gold and pearls, they have sold to the Greeks and clothed in alien and unseemly garments.

Alfachar realizes very well that among the Maimunists there are also men of comprehensive knowledge, and it is precisely to these that he turns with the question:

> Since when does the Torah shine forth from Egypt[68] and not from Zion, and does God's word no longer come forth from Jerusalem? . . . Among you the *Guide* has become a new Torah. You declare, "This is the doctrine that Moses[69] commanded us." You wish to place him [Maimonides] above the prophets. Know, then, that God is not with you. Bethink yourselves while it is not yet too late. Remove from your tents the strange gods and purify your hearts. . . . Remember that you are destroying your support with your own hands, yourselves breaking down the foundations of your faith. Days of trial, dreadful, dark days, will come. Your own children will turn away from you, will exchange their faith, will forget the old doctrine for the sake of

68. A reference to Maimonides' place of residence.
69. I.e., Moses Maimonides.

the new. And you who, on the authority of the *Guide*, seduce the children of the people and bring apostasy into the holy camp will then want to turn back, but it will be too late. You will wish to row back to shore, but the waves will cover you and around yourselves you will hear only the cold laughter of the indifferent and the proud mockery of those who have become alien.

Alfachar's entire letter is permeated with the conviction that the faith of the people, with its customs and traditions firmly established for generations, is a solid instrument of unity for the national community. The rationalist principle, however, which regards as the highest authority human reason, the thought of the individual, of the intelligent and highly developed personality, destroys this bond. The national unity, the integrity of the community, is thereby brought into jeopardy.

All the polemical letters which the antagonists dispatched to each other are written in rhymed prose,[70] adorned with Oriental rhetorical flourishes and spiced with the *musiv* style. Besides polemical tracts, the contenders in the heat of the conflict also employed a sharper weapon—the caustic epigram. The Maimunists made the most use of this. Some eighty epigrams of that time have come down to us,[71] and we here present a few of them.

The poet Meshullam Dapiera addresses Maimonides' *Guide* with the following: "Be silent, you *Guide for the Perplexed!* Lock your lips! Never have such words been heard! All who say that the word of the Torah is a parable and the revelation of the prophet a dream are sinners" (*Moreh Mekom Ha-Moreh*, 16).

This epigram enraged the Maimunists and from all sides they fired their own against the fanatical poet. We quote only a few of them:

They, the rebellious ones, dare to declare war against the *Guide*. They curse and shame the bearer of light. Fragrant incense they wish to brand as poison![72]

Consider the *Guide* well, learn to appreciate its value, for only then

70. The custom of writing letters in rhymed prose was also very popular among the Arabs.
71. Steinschneider gathered a considerable part of these epigrams in his *Moreh Mekom Ha-Moreh* (in *Kovetz Al Yad*, I, 1–32; II, 1–6). See also *ZHB*, VI, 93–94, where a polemic composition of the Maimunists which found its way into the Romanian *Maḥzor* is given. The writer of these lines also found in an old manuscript several other epigrams still not published (see *infra*).
72. We found this epigram, together with three others unknown till now, in a manuscript of the first Firkovich Collection (No. 479) written in the year 1333 by the scribe Ḥabib ben Eliakam.

will you understand that its tent stretches to the heavens. The pointer of the way for men of understanding, it shatters the rebellious with its glory. Whoever has understanding perceives and comprehends that among all the books of the great scholars it has no peer.

Accept, O *Guide for the Perplexed,* my greeting and the greeting of all who long for knowledge. Close quickly the insolent mouth of foolishness. The man of understanding knows how to value the pearls of the *Guide for the Perplexed.* But you, stubborn and rebellious one, withdraw, do not dare approach it![73]

You fool, with the bridle of a horse close the mouth of your folly. Take off your shoes, you knave, and dare not set your foot here. You cannot understand in what a parable consists; how, then, can you distinguish what is a dream and what revelation?

(The *Guide for the Perplexed* speaks of itself here): I am the burning serpent that Moses raised on high to heal all who had been bitten. I enlighten the eyes and endow men with immortality; therefore is my name *A Guide for the Perplexed.*

Another poet, Jacob ben Ezra Gabbai, declares: "The best doctrine is *A Guide for the Perplexed,* but not for stopped-up hearts and dull minds. These will not understand it until the Messiah comes. Let the corrupt withdraw from it. Only righteous and understanding men know how to appreciate it."

Just at that time was written the poem (which we discovered in an old manuscript) in which is recounted with great enthusiasm that when Maimonides died and his soul rose to the heavens, God Himself called out to the angels: "Lo, here comes the faithful steward of My house. Blessed is the people that merited this!" And from the ends of the earth, from east and west, all, great and small, wept and lamented the great loss.

There is no doubt that the Maimunists, among whom were men of high social position, were much more aggressive than their opponents. The condition of Solomon of Montpellier and his followers therefore became extremely precarious. The rabbis of France became detached observers. Looking at them, others also withdrew. Solomon realized that he was now without support and that his antagonists and enemies were storming him from all sides with a terrible weapon—the ban of excommunication. Then, in his plight, Solomon committed a crime which covered his name with shame for all generations.

Immediately after his bloody settling of accounts with the Albigenses, the fanatical Pope Innocent III cast suspicion on the great Aristotle and saw in his works the source of heresy and free-

73. *Moreh Mekom Ha-Moreh,* p. 17.

thinking. In the year 1209 the University of Paris had proscribed as "heretical" and "Aristotelian" a large number of books—among them, the philosophical work *De Causis*, which was widely known in the Middle Ages, as well as the composition of Avicebron, i.e., the *Fons Vitae* of Solomon Ibn Gabirol. At the command of Innocent III it was forbidden to study Aristotle's *Physics* and *Metaphysics*. At the order of Pope Gregory IX in 1231 a prohibition was also issued against Aristotle's works on natural science until a strict censor should have removed all suspect passages from them. Two years later, at the command of the same pope, the Inquisition, which had been created to root out the remnants of the Albigensian heresy, became a permanent juridical establishment instead of a temporary one. A division of this establishment was located in Montpellier in the monastery of the Dominicans. It was to these grim battlers against heresy and free thought that Solomon of Montpellier applied for aid in his struggle with the Maimunists. Unfortunately we know of Solomon's foolhardy step only from sources that are very hostile to him, the reports of his Maimunist opponents. According to these not very trustworthy sources,[74] Solomon came with his followers to the Franciscans and Dominicans, set before them Maimonides' *Sefer Ha-Madda* and *Guide for the Perplexed*, and declared: "You are always rummaging about for heresy. You destroy your heretics. Know, then, that among us also are heretical books, the books of Moses of Egypt, the *Sefer Ha-Madda* and the *Guide*. These are very dangerous works. Destroy them also."

The Dominicans, following the command of the Pope, were just then conducting a campaign against works translated from Arabic in which there was some suspicion of Aristotelian rationalism. Precisely at that time, in the 1230's, Maimonides' ideas began to penetrate into the Christian world also, and at the court of the pope's chief enemy, Frederick II, a group of scholars translated the *Guide* into Latin. It is therefore not surprising that the Dominicans rejoiced at obtaining an opportunity to avenge themselves on Maimonides' heretical books. The local Inquisition promptly agreed to burn Maimonides' two works. A house-to-house search was conducted and all copies of the *Sefer Ha-Madda* and the *Guide* were confiscated and burned on pyres. Solomon's fellow-battler, Jonah Gerondi, brought it about that in Paris also many copies of Maimonides' philosophical works were burned in a public square.

74. The summons of the brothers Ibn Ḥasdai to the communities in Castile and Aragon (*Ginzei Nistarot*, III, 177) and Kimḥi's third letter to Alfachar (*Iggerot Kenaot*, p. 4).

A popular legend relates that the pyre was lit from a candle taken from the altar of the cathedral of Notre Dame.[75]

The public burning of Maimonides' works created a considerable sensation. The young Samuel ben Abraham Saporta wrote a long letter[76] to the rabbis of France and begged them to champion the desecrated books of the great scholar, and, with their powerful authority, publicly to declare that Maimonides' works are free of heresy. An anonymous poet lamented the books destroyed in the fire in a lovely elegy:

> How foolish are they who believe that with fire
> One can destroy books precious as fine gold.
> These books are themselves consuming fire;
> How, then, can they perish in flames?
> Know, you who have brought about
> And helped this dreadful deed occur:
> Like Elijah, they rose in flames;
> On wings of angels they flew to the heavens.[77]

Only two men had the courage to champion Solomon of Montpellier after his denunciation. These were Jehudah Alfachar and Joseph ben Todros Ha-Levi. "To this," wrote Jehudah Alfachar to David Kimḥi, "you have brought him with your persecutions. It is not permitted to drive any man to the last boundary of despair. Now you are receiving your recompense for your deeds."[78] "True," writes Joseph Ha-Levi,

> to hand over our treasures to our enemies is a great crime, but in this matter all of you are guilty, in that you have persecuted him so. You threw him under the ban. You oppressed him and made his life miserable, never giving him a moment's rest. . . . But what has happened has happened. At least now make an end of the controversy. Do not push Rabbi Solomon away with both hands.[79]

But the flame of controversy was already too strong to be extinguished with calm words. We have seen that, according to Kimḥi's report, Solomon's denunciation was directed not only against heretical books but also against heretics. In Kimḥi's ac-

75. See the letter of Hillel of Verona in *Taam Zekenim,* p. 71.
76. *Ginzei Nistarot,* IV, 36–67.
77. *Moreh Mekom Ha-Moreh,* p. 15. There is a tradition that this poem was written by Maimonides' son Abraham.
78. *Iggerot Kenaot,* p. 4.
79. *Ginzei Nistarot,* III, 171 and 174.

count, Solomon declared to the Dominicans: "Know that in our community the number of heretics who deny God has greatly increased. They have been led astray by the doctrine of Moses ben Maimon of Egypt who wrote heretical books."

The Inquisition began to search for Jewish freethinkers, and there is no doubt that many Maimunists were in great jeopardy. It must not be overlooked that at this time, under the reign of Louis IX, "the Saint," the Inquisitor of France, Robert, in the course of the six years from 1234 to 1239 sentenced 222 persons who had the presumption to profess "opinions" of their own to be burned at the stake.

The Maimunists, among whom were persons who occupied very important social positions, however, managed to show that the accusation was ungrounded, and the informers were then handed over to the court as false witnesses.[80] The verdict of the court was that the executioner should cut out their tongues. And the hatred between the parties was so intense that the victims had to listen, even under the executioner's hand, to the mockery and laughter of their opponents. One of the Maimunists (very likely the talented translator of *Ben Ha-Melech Veha-Nazir,* Abraham Ibn Ḥasdai) wrote the following lines:

> The dark, accursed leaders determined
> To destroy the *Guide*, the teacher of light.
> Therefore God poured out His wrath upon them.
> Ruin after ruin befell them.
> Against the heavens they raised their mouths,
> Now their tongues are trodden in the dust.[81]

It is almost certain that the condemned included the chief of the anti-Maimunists, Solomon ben Abraham of Montpellier,[82] because from that moment on there is complete silence about him. After the ringleaders of one party were condemned, the controversy was for a brief time stilled. A few years later the famous disputation against the Talmud took place in Paris, and in the place where, not

80. It seems likely that the largest part in the handing-over of the informers to the court was taken by the abovementioned Baḥya Alconstantini, who was very prominent in the court of the king of Aragon, James I, under whose dominion the city of Montpellier then was.
81. The epigram is given in the summons of Abraham Jehudah Ibn Ḥasdai (*Ginzei Nistarot,* III, 19) and in *Milḥamot Adonai* of Maimonides' son Abraham.
82. Some basis for this may be found in the fact that several medieval scholars mention his name with the epithet Ha-Kadosh, the "saint" or "martyr."

long before, Maimonides' works had been burned entire wagon-loads of tractates of the Talmud were now put to the torch. Many saw in this a punishment for the fact that, in the heat of controversy, the books of the great scholar had been handed over to the Catholic clergy for burning. One of Solomon ben Abraham's most energetic collaborators, Jonah Gerondi, then repented. He imposed upon himself a heavy penance for the grievous sin he had committed against Maimonides,[83] and afterwards wrote a book on the value of repentance, *Sefer Shaarei Teshuvah.*[84]

The controversy, however, was not stilled for long. It *had* to flare up anew, because it was not dependent on the evil will of various "rebels against the light." Here deeper and more powerful causes were operative. The controversy drew nourishment from life itself, from profound psychological as well as social roots. Against Aristotelian rationalism, the proud "sovereignty of reason," rose the "Torah of the heart," mystical feeling and enthusiasm. Maimonides had set forth his epoch-making slogan "freedom of human thought." And the men of the Kabbalah came forward with their slogan about the world-liberating role of the human personality.

The controversy continued for many generations. Indeed, it endures to the present day. But before we proceed to the further stages of the historic conflict we must turn our attention to an important Jewish cultural center in which, precisely at the time when the battle over Maimonides' system first erupted, his ideas began to gain growing numbers of followers and his philosophical work became the guide of the Jewish intelligentsia. This center was located under the blue skies of Italy, where the first harbingers of the new era, the era of the Renaissance, then began to appear.

83. Gerondi's pupil, Hillel of Verona, tells of this at length in his above-mentioned letter.

84. Typical of the penitent Jonah Gerondi are the following lines from his *Sefer Shaarei Teshuvah:* "And there is a sin of which the soul cannot cleanse itself and for which it is not forgiven until death separates it from the body that committed it, just as there is a sickness from which the body cannot be cured all its days. And this is the sin of desecrating God's name" (Warsaw edition [1848], p. 39). Gerondi became particularly renowned through another book of ethical instruction, *Sefer Ha-Yirah,* which was also translated into Yiddish.

# THE JEWISH COMMUNITY OF MEDIEVAL ITALY

# CHAPTER ONE

## *The Four Elders;* SHABBETAI DONNOLO; *JOSIPPON*

IN ITALY, the birthplace of the modern European political order, industrial capitalism developed earlier than in the other countries of Europe. As a result of Italy's favorable geographical location and the traditions of the ancient Roman era, still not altogether vanished, large-scale commerce flourished in the Italian cities in the early Middle Ages, and their harbors supplied all of Europe with precious goods from the lands of the East. Italy, however, exercised a middleman's function not only in relation to goods for material use but in the realms of literature and science as well. It was the meeting point at which the most varied cultures, among them the Arabic and Byzantine, came together.[1]

In this mediating enterprise Jews played no small role in Italy. They contributed much to the fact that the lands of western Europe became familiar with the treasures of the Graeco-Roman civilization which then lay buried in half-rotted and completely forgotten manuscripts. The Italian Jews also played a very significant mediating role in regard to Judaic knowledge among the Jewries of Babylonia, Palestine, north Africa, and western Europe. There is an old legend about four Talmudic scholars from Babylonia who were taken captive on a journey to Europe and who brought it about that the center of Jewish cultural life changed its

1. One must take into account that Sicily for a long time was in the hands of the Arabs, and the regions of Apulia and Calabria passed in the course of the ninth and tenth centuries from the Greeks to the Arabs and then again to the Greeks.

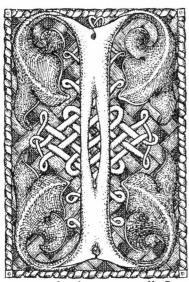

locale and moved from anterior Asia to north Africa and western Europe.[2] In the legend the following particular is significant: the four elders were captured when they set out on ship from the Italian city of Bari.

Even if we take the tale of the captivity of the four elders merely as legend, it is still beyond doubt that the migration of Jewish scholars from anterior Asia to Europe, as well as their role as culture-bearers, are genuine historical facts. Moreover, it is possible that in this story, as is the way with popular legends, a long and gradual process is concentrated into a definite moment and depicted as the conscious, willed act of an individual or individuals. In the story of the four elders the mediating function of the Italian Jewish communities is noted. Thanks to the *Megillat Yuḥasin* of the Italian Aḥimaaz ben Paltiel,[3] we now know that a hundred years before the four elders of Babylonia, according to the legend, visited Bari, a scholar from Baghdad, Abu Aharon, came in the 860's to Italy, and that, as a result of his activity, the communities of the old south Italian cities of Oria and Bari became centers of Jewish culture and Torah study. It is therefore hardly surprising that the first Jewish scholar in Europe whose name has come down to us was a native of Oria. This was the physician Shabbetai ben Abraham Donnolo.

From the preface to Donnolo's major work, *Ḥakemani*,[4] we know that he was born in the year 913. When he was twelve years old, the Arabs who then ruled Sicily sacked Oria and took many of its inhabitants captive, among them the young Donnolo. The neighboring Jewish communities, however, were very devoted to the traditional commandment prescribing redemption of captives, and Donnolo was promptly ransomed. Highly talented and with a great thirst for knowledge, Donnolo, after much effort, managed to study medicine, astronomy, and astrology thoroughly, and his reputation became so great that the viceroy of the Byzantine emperor made him his house physician. Donnolo's account of the trials he had to undergo in his youth to quench his thirst for knowledge has a certain cultural-historical value and is worth quoting here.

2. The legend is first given in Rabbi Abraham Ibn Daud's *Sefer Ha-Kabbalah*.
3. Published by A. Neubauer in *Seder Ha-Ḥachamim Ve-Korot Ha-Yamim*, II, 110–32.
4. The preface to the *Ḥakemani* was first published by Abraham Geiger in his *Melo Chofnajim*, pp. 29–32. It was reprinted in *Kerem Ḥemed*, VII. The entire work was published by David Castelli in 1880.

"I had a very great desire," he relates in the preface to his *Ḥakemani*,

> to study medicine and astronomy. To this end I copied many old Hebrew manuscripts. I did not, however, find in the whole land men of such knowledge that they could understand these and explain them to me properly. Among the Jewish scholars there were even some so ignorant that they assured me that the old Jewish books dealing with such realms of knowledge as astronomy and astrology have no real value, since the truly scientific works in this field were written by gentile scholars, who are not at all in agreement with the opinions expressed in the Hebrew books. I then decided to become acquainted with, and thoroughly investigate, the science of the Greeks and Arabs, as well as the wisdom of Babylonia and India. I did not rest until I had copied numerous works in their original languages with the appropriate commentaries and studied all of them through. Then I became convinced that everything they write about astronomy and astrology agrees completely with the views of our sages. . . . To perfect myself in these sciences I travelled from land to land, everywhere seeking astronomers from whom I might learn more about this science. I became acquainted with a scholar from Babylonia named Bagdash. With his remarkably extensive knowledge of astronomy and astrology, with his amazing mathematical calculations, he had no peer. . . . When I became convinced of the great knowledge of this scholar, I managed, in exchange for much money, to have him reveal to me the qualities of the stars and planets, their hidden ways and the mysterious powers which arise and rule at the convergence of various planets at a definite moment. . . . All this knowledge which I accumulated, I decided to set down in a work entitled *Ḥakemani.*[5]

Donnolo's work is divided into two parts. The first and briefer part deals with the philosophical-theological problem of God's "glory" (*Kavod*), i.e., the Creator's emanation in its various manifestations. Donnolo here develops at considerable length the idea, already widespread in antiquity, that the human body is a faithful mirror image of the structure of the universe. Man and the world, says the author, are very similar to each other. Man's head is like the heavens, his skull like the heavenly firmament, his eyes like the sun and the moon, etc.[6] "Hence," he concludes, "whoever kills a man, it is as if he had destroyed a whole world."

The second part of Donnolo's work is a commentary to the *Sefer Yetzirah*. The most interesting aspect of this commentary is

5. *Ḥakemani*, pp. 4–5; see also *Melo Chofnajim*, p. 29; *Kerem Ḥemed*, VII, pp. 97–100.
6. *Ḥakemani*, pp. 19–25.

his attempt to demonstrate experimentally, i.e., with proofs from natural science, the truth of the theological-cosmological ideas expressed in the *Sefer Yetzirah.* Since the sciences at that time, particularly in Christian Europe, were still in their infancy, it is quite natural that Donnolo's experiments are very childish and naive, and have merely historical interest. In order, for example, to demonstrate the truth of the principle set forth in the *Sefer Yetzirah* that fire comes from water, Donnolo proposes the following:[7] If on a bright summer day you set a transparent glass vessel filled with water in the sun and then hold at a certain distance from the vessel, in the direction of the rays of the sun, a piece of tow or a chip of rotted wood, it will soon become ignited; "thus we see that fire comes from water." The *Sefer Yetzirah* also teaches that through the power of fire one can produce the element of earth from water. Everyone, Donnolo asserts, can easily prove this to himself: Let him take a copper vessel, fill it with river water, heat it over fire, and each time the water boils over pour fresh water on it. If one does this for quite a long time and then cuts the vessel in half, he can see that inside the vessel a rather thick layer of earth has formed. To one who does not wish to spend a great deal of time Donnolo gives the following advice: Let him buy an old, used copper jug, called a *miliarum,* in which servants among the nobility and officials constantly boil water in order to have hot water ready at all times to mix with strong wine when their lord requests drink; if one cuts such a vessel in which water has been boiled for many years in half, he will notice that inside a thick layer of earth, hard as stone, has formed. "We thus clearly see," explains Donnolo, "how earth, sand, and stone are formed out of water through the power of fire."[8]

In this naive way the tenth-century Italian Jewish scholar attempts to prove experimentally the truth of scientific theories. At the same time he introduces into his book many long tables with fantastic "combinations of letters." Donnolo does not consider it at all necessary to demonstrate the significance of these; no one of that age doubted their mystical power. Everyone at that time also believed in the great scientific value of astrology, and Donnolo describes precisely at what time and under what conditions each star rules man's fate.[9]

Properly to appreciate the importance of this Jewish scholar, one must remember that, however slight the scientific knowledge

7. *Ibid.*, p. 28.
8. *Ibid.*, p. 29.
9. *Ibid.*, p. 71 ff.

of the Italian Jews still was in those days, their cultural level was considerably above that of the surrounding Christian populace. Interesting in this respect is a story[10] recounted in the biography of Donnolo's contemporary, the abbot Nilus the Younger, born around 910. Donnolo, who had known Nilus from childhood on, learned that the friend of his youth was very ill. He came to see him and, as a skilled physician,[11] determined that the illness came from long self-mortification and constant fasting. He proposed various remedies, but the pious monk categorically rejected Donnolo's aid. He explained, "If I make use of your remedies, it will give you occasion to boast that a Jew has cured me, and this can make a very bad impression on pious Christians."[12]

Donnolo's *Ḥakemani* is the only Hebrew book from that period in Italy of which we know definitely who its author was and where he lived. At that time other Hebrew books were written in Italy. Several of these were, in fact, extremely popular among Jewish readers, but all lack title pages. It is not known who their authors were, and only from certain signs can one conjecture that their birthplace was Italy.

About the time[13] that Donnolo wrote his *Ḥakemani* a Hebrew book appeared in Italy which enjoyed great success in later ages and became one of the most popular books for the ordinary reader. It was translated into numerous languages, and since the invention of printing it has been published in a large number of editions. Nevertheless, a great mystery surrounds this work. Not only is the name of its author unknown; we do not even know for certain the

10. The story is given in the second volume of Güdemann's *Ha-Torah Veha-Ḥayyim.*
11. Donnolo also composed a medical work in Hebrew, *Sefer Ha-Yakar.* Fragments of the book were published by Steinschneider (1867).
12. The extent of the ignorance at that time, even among the representatives of the only educated class of the Christian populace, the clergy, can be estimated from the following fact: In the middle of the eleventh century, at a council of the highest clergy in Rome, the decision was taken that it would be extremely desirable that every priest should at least have the most elementary knowledge of school learning and some notion of the text of sacred Scripture. Even among the popes of that time there was so ignorant a man as Benedict X (1058–69), who could not understand a single verse in the Psalms (see Dresdner, *Kultur und Sitten: Geschichte der italienischer Geistlichkeit im X und XI Jahrhundert,* p. 178; quoted in Vogelstein and Rieger, *Geschichte der Juden in Rom,* I, 351).
13. If not earlier, for D. Chwolson's conjecture (*Kovetz Al Yad,* VII, "Sarid U-Palit," p. 5) that *Josippon* was written as early as the end of the ninth century is very plausible.

correct title of the book itself, though it is universally known as *Josippon.*[14] Only one detail can be regarded as assured: the author of the book was from Italy[15] and spent some time in Rome.[16]

An excellent stylist with a thorough knowledge of Latin and Greek sources, the author set himself the comprehensive task of presenting the history of the Jewish people during the whole period from the Babylonian exile to the destruction of the Second Temple against the background of world history. He considers it necessary to stress that a historian must first of all employ only completely certain and reliable sources. "Truth," he declares, "is more important than anything else; it is the foundation of the world." At that time, however, it was no simple matter to obtain historical truth. At the beginning of the Middle Ages history as a science did not yet exist, and fantastic legends and popular tales were considered strictly historical. In this respect *Josippon* is a typical product of its age, and it is not at all surprising that its author himself often violates, without intent, the "foundation of the world" of which he speaks so eloquently. *Josippon* begins with Adam's times, and it is quite understandable that the medieval author endeavors to bring the beginnings of the history of the ancient peoples into harmony with what is recounted in the first chapters of the Book of Genesis. However, he demonstrates geographical knowledge which is quite astonishing, when it is taken into consideration that one has to do here with a man of the tenth century. The author then proceeds to the legendary period of ancient Rome, and forges the old Roman legends together with Hebraic ones: Esau's nephew, Zaphan ben Eliphaz, makes the Romans tremble before his power, and Romulus, the Roman hero, encircles Rome with a strong wall out of fear of King David and his mighty men.[17]

Into the history of Babylonia the author ingeniously weaves the story of Daniel and Zerubbabel. After this, Cyrus and his war with the Scythians and the emperors of Persia and their wars are de-

14. It may be that the work was originally entitled *Divrei Yerushalayim.* Testimony to this is given by the closing sentence in the first edition: "Ad henah ketz Divrei Yerushalayim" (Here ends *Divrei Yerushalayim*).
15. See Zunz, *Gottesdienstlichen Vorträge,* second edition, pp. 158–59; Vogelstein and Rieger, *op. cit.,* 192–93.
16. According to the conjecture of the French historian Basnage (*Histoire des Juifs,* VII, 89), the description of the coronation in *Josippon* (Chapter 77) is a faithful portrayal of a man who himself witnessed the coronation ceremony of the emperor Otto the Great in Rome in 962. This description, however, is lacking in the older Mantua edition. It is likely that the entire chapter is a later addition.
17. *Josippon,* Chapters 2 and 3.

scribed. The author devotes a special section of his work[18] to the supreme hero of antiquity, Alexander of Macedon, and his exploits.

The "Alexander book" included in *Josippon* has considerable cultural-literary interest because it is closely bound up with the Alexander romances, well known in world literature, which tell of the great deeds of the Macedonian hero. The author of *Josippon* indicates in his account of Alexander's life and triumphs that he took these from an old Alexander book which the "magicians of Egypt" wrote in their day.[19]

The "Alexander book" in *Josippon* is really a reworked translation of the oldest Alexander romance, which an ancient legend associates with the name of Aristotle's pupil Kallisthenes, who accompanied Alexander on his campaigns. In point of fact this romance was composed considerably later, around the beginning of the third century of the Christian era. Already in the Talmud (both Babylonian and Palestinian) and in the Midrashim various episodes from this romance, together with numerous details taken from other sources,[20] are introduced. Alexander's appearance in the fortress of Zion and in the court of the Temple in Jerusalem made a great impression on the popular imagination, and in time a whole garland of Hebrew folk legends concerning the hero who conquered half the world was formed. The legends, created in an alien environment, wrenched themselves completely away from historical ground, from the Greek way of life and Greek mythology. This Jewish-Oriental version of the Alexander romance has come down to us in several manuscripts.[21] But the Egyptian-Greek romance, which was erroneously attributed to Kallisthenes,[22] was also extremely popular among the Jews in the Middle Ages. The Greek text of this romance was brought from Constantinople to

18. In the Constantinople edition (1510), according to the text version of which all later editions, both Hebrew and Yiddish, were printed, *Josippon* is divided into six parts.
19. *Josippon*, beginning of Chapter 6. We quote according to the Yiddish edition of Amsterdam, 1781.
20. See I. G. Orshanski, "Talmudicheskiya Skazaniya ob Alexandrye Makedonskom" (*Sbornik Statyei*, 1867); Harkavy, *Nyeizdannaya Vyersia* . . . (1892), p. 78.
21. One manuscript (incomplete) which derives from anterior Asia is to be found in Leningrad in the library of the Society for the Dissemination of Enlightenment Among Jews (Harkavy Collection). The same version was published, according to the Oxford manuscript, by Y. Levy in the collection *Tehillah Le-Mosheh*, pp. 142–63, and Harkavy wrote his abovementioned work, *Nyeizdannaya Vyersia*, on it.
22. The romance is known as *Pseudokallisthenes*.

Italy in the tenth century by a Catholic priest, Leo, who reworked it into Latin under the title *Historia de prelis.* This Latin version served as the model for the numerous Alexander romances which soon appeared in most European literatures. There is no doubt whatever that in the Alexander narrative contained in our *Josippon* the same source is employed—apparently, however, not the Latin text but the Arabic translation of it which was very widespread among the Jews and was even several times translated into Hebrew.[23] One of the translators was Samuel Ibn Tibbon,[24] familiar to us as the translator of Maimonides' *Guide for the Perplexed.* Apparently the Alexander narrative was only later inserted into *Josippon* by one of its copiers and reworkers, for the author of *Josippon* was a contemporary of the presbyter Leo, and it is hard to believe that an Arabic translation of his Latin *Historia de prelis* already existed at that time.[25]

*Josippon* dwells very little on Alexander's successors and proceeds immediately again to Jewish history, especially to the war of the Hasmoneans with Antiochus. Here the author employs as his major sources the Books of the Maccabees in the Apocrypha. The later chapters (27 to 55), dealing with the period from Simon the Maccabee's death to the reconstruction of the Temple by Herod, are put together following Flavius Josephus' *Jewish Antiquities.* In the last forty-two chapters, which conclude with the destruction of the Second Temple, the author mainly used Josephus' other work, *The Jewish Wars*—not in the Greek original, however, but in the Latin reworking known as *Hegesippus.*[26] For this last part of the Hebrew work the author apparently had a special name, *Josippon* or *Sefer ben Gorion.* Because in the Latin *Hegesippus* only Joseph ben Gorion, the prefect of Jerusalem at the time of the war against Rome, is mentioned, the Hebrew author confused him with the famous historian Joseph ben Mattathias, or Flavius Josephus, who served as commander-in-chief in Galilee during the war.[27]

23. A Hebrew translation direct from the Latin text, *Historia de Prelis,* was first completed in the fourteenth century by Immanuel Bonfils of Tarascon, the author of the well-known book *Shesh Kenafayim.*
24. The translation is to be found in manuscript in London. Another translation, following a Paris manuscript, was published by Y. Levy in *Kovetz Al Yad,* II (1886).
25. For a complete bibliography on the Alexander literature see Steinschneider, *Die hebräischen Übersetzungen des Mittelalters und die Juden als Dolmetscher,* pp. 894–904, and "Zur Alexander-Sage," *Hebräische Bibliographie,* IX, 13–19 and 44–53.
26. Derived from the name Josephus.
27. It is characteristic that at the end of an old *Josippon* manuscript is a statement of the copyist: "And Joseph ben Gorion Ha-Kohen the son

This erroneous identification of two completely different persons created vast confusion and brought it about that scholars obtained an altogether false notion of *Josippon*'s talented author. The Christian scholar Franz Delitszch, when dwelling in his *Zur Geschichte der jüdischen Poesie* on *Josippon*, praises the literary skill of the anonymous author but calls him an "insolent liar" and a "base deceiver" who had the gall to mislead his readers and give himself out as the famous "Greek-Jewish historian."[28] These epithets are quite unmerited and derive from the fact that both Delitszch and Zunz were familiar only with the common *Josippon* text which Tam Ibn Yaḥya published in 1510 in Constantinople and did not compare it with the older version of the Mantua edition.[29] In reality it never entered the mind of the author of *Josippon* to deceive the reader, to present his work as an ancient book written by the great historian of the first century. He is not to blame for the fact that in all of medieval Hebrew literature it is difficult to find another book with such a sad fate as *Josippon*, which numerous copiers and compilers appropriated as their own. Each of these reworked it and inserted into it his own views and quotations from other sources as the spirit moved him.[30]

As early as the middle of the twelfth century a skillful compiler, Yeraḥmiel ben Solomon,[31] introduced into his copy of *Josippon*

---

of Mattathias was his name, and his surname was Gorion; this is the Joseph ben Mattathias Ha-Kohen who composed many books" (see A. Neubauer, *Seder Ha-Ḥachamim Ve-Korot Ha-Yamim*, I, 190–91). In this way one person was made of two different Josephs.

28. P. 37: "Der rätselhafte Fabulant . . . der seiner Autorschaft die Nebel und Schellenkoppe überzogen hat, und sich mit übergreiflicher Dreistigkeit und lügnerischer Frivolität zum Doppelgänger des griechisch-jüdischen Geschichtschreiber, Joseph ben Matatja, macht." See also Zunz, *Gottesdienstlichen Vorträge*.

29. *Josippon* has come down to us in two versions. The first and older one was published by the well-known printer Abraham Conat in Mantua, 1477–80. This edition is extremely rare. It was, however, reprinted *verbatim* by the Orientalist Baron David Günzburg, 1896–1913. The second and considerably larger version was published in Constantinople in 1510 and was, as has already been indicated, many times reprinted.

30. The first person who, with his critical sensitivity, noticed that the *Josippon* text was eventually filled with numerous errors and changes was the famous scholar Azariah dei Rossi (see his *Meor Enayim*, Vilna edition [1865], pp. 114–18, 124–25).

31. On Yeraḥmiel ben Solomon and his compilations, see A. Neubauer, *Seder Ha-Ḥachamim*, I, 70–174; *MGWJ*, 1887, pp. 505–8; *JQR*, 1899, pp. 364–84, where Yeraḥmiel's poems are published. Yeraḥmiel himself relates how he "remade" *Josippon:* "And I, Yeraḥmiel ben Solomon, extracted things from the book of ben Gorion and from the books of other writers who wrote the history of our ancestors, and I gathered them together in one scroll."

numerous episodes out of what he called the "great *Josippon*," i.e., Flavius Josephus' *The Jewish Wars.* Thus, among later copiers and compilers the conviction grew that our work, i.e., the "small *Josippon*," was written especially for Jews by the author of the "great *Josippon*"—"Joseph ben Gorion who was called by the Greeks Josephus and by the Romans Hegesippus." Accordingly, subsequent copiers and compilers inserted into the text still other remarks and explanations[32] which only strengthened among later generations the false view that *Josippon* is a very ancient book, written by Joseph ben Gorion in the period of the destruction of the Second Temple.

A very interesting report which gives us a clear idea of its many versions and the numerous changes that were made in the *Josippon* text has been preserved. This is the preface which a scholar of the fourteenth century, Jehudah Leon ben Moses Mosconi, wrote to the exemplar of *Josippon* which he copied with his own hand.[33] The preface has considerable cultural-historical value, for from it we obtain a clear picture of the transformations which especially popular works had to undergo in the Middle Ages and in still earlier times. Mosconi relates that he had before him no less than five different versions of *Josippon.* One of these was written by the author of the *Sefer Ha-Kabbalah*, Abraham Ibn Daud (Ravad), another by the famous Samuel Ha-Nagid. These two versions and two others, Mosconi reports, were not divided into books or chapters, and he conjectures that these versions were "not complete ones" because "many stories and details that were included in one were lacking in the other."[34] The fifth version, Mosconi asserts, was "the most complete." It is this version, he adds, "which from beginning to end was written in person by the author himself, Joseph ben Gorion," i.e., the whole narrative is related in the name of Joseph ben Gorion.[35] Precisely for this reason Mosconi considered this the most accurate version and made his copy from it. This version was already divided into books, and Mosconi further divided each of the six books into chapters.

There is no doubt that it was precisely the version written down by Mosconi that was employed by Tam Ibn Yaḥya when he published *Josippon* in Constantinople in 1510. Along with it, Ibn Yaḥya appropriated a considerable part of Mosconi's preface, simply reprinting it in his introduction to the book. Only when one compares page after page of this edition of 1510 with the older

32. E.g., in Chapter 55 (Menaḥem Mann's translation, Amsterdam, 1781).
33. The preface was published in *Otzar Tov,* 1878, pp. 17–23.
34. *Ibid.*, p. 23.
35. *Ibid.*, p. 21.

Mantua edition, which was printed around 1480, according to a shorter, "incomplete" version, as Mosconi calls it, does it become clear how little the author of *Josippon* deserves to be considered a swindler and deceiver. The shorter version according to which the Mantua edition is printed is a considerably older one, and doubtless also much closer to the original, lost *Josippon* text than the later Constantinople edition. While in the Mantua edition Joseph ben Gorion is never mentioned *in the first person*, the Constantinople edition constantly reminds the reader that this work was written by the same Joseph ben Gorion who wrote the "great" *Josippon* "for the Romans." But all of these are *later additions*, a kind of "commentary" to the text which copyists and compilers added. Thus, for example, in the Mantua edition (page 50) where the emperor Cyrus is discussed, the author adds that "the rest of his deeds are written in the chronicles of the kings of Persia and Media and of the kings of Rome." But in the Constantinople edition, after the words "of the kings of Persia and Media" and before the closing words "and of the kings of Rome," the following is inserted: "and in my book which I, Joseph Ha-Kohen ben Gorion, wrote for the Romans and called *Josephus*, and I am the same Joseph ben Gorion whom Titus and Vespasian exiled from Jerusalem." Furthermore, in the Mantua edition *Josippon* proceeds immediately, without any interruption, from King Hyrcanus, the son of Simon the Hasmonean, to the history of Alexander of Macedon.[36] In the version which Tam Ibn Yaḥya printed in Constantinople, however, after the story of Hyrcanus there is an interruption with the following concluding sentence: "Herewith ends the first book of Joseph ben Gorion the priest." Then the second book, with the Alexander romance, begins, but at the outset is the following introduction: "Thus says Joseph ben Gorion to him who here looks at his books. . . . [The author has] undertaken to relate a little about his birth, etc." In the Mantua edition (page 204), after the account of the death of Queen Alexandra appear the words quoted above, to the effect that a historian must introduce only correct and reliable information; thereafter the author proceeds immediately without interruption to the events in Rome. In the Constantinople edition the fourth book ends with Alexandra's death, and the fifth begins again with the statement: "Thus said Joseph the priest, the son of Gorion the priest, who recounts the events of Israel and its sufferings, that they may be a lesson for those who come after him, that they may read his books and through them see God's grace." The same thing is repeated in many other places. Where in the

36. Pp. 64–65.

Mantua edition (pages 218, 222, and 223) Joseph ben Gorion's name is not even mentioned, in the Constantinople edition in the corresponding passages is indicated "and this Joseph the priest said." At the end of the fifth book and the beginning of the sixth in the Constantinople edition, Joseph ben Gorion again speaks in his own name: "I, Joseph ben Gorion the priest, who am also called Josephus, have written all this in my book which I composed in the time of Julius Caesar." In the Mantua edition, however, the entire sentence is lacking and Joseph ben Gorion's name is not even mentioned. In the last part of the work, where the siege of Jerusalem is described, Joseph ben Gorion is, in the Mantua edition, everywhere mentioned in the third person; in the Constantinople edition, however, in the first: "I, Joseph ben Gorion."

When one compares the two versions it becomes apparent how much the literary value of *Josippon*, its style and power of portrayal, have suffered from all these additions and "improvements" on the part of copyists and compilers. The sculptured and beautifully brief description in the older, and therefore less corrupted, version of how the chains of the captured Joseph are taken off,[37] or the powerful closing scenes, filled with dramatic expressiveness, in which the heroic death of Eliezer together with several thousand Jewish warriors is recounted, are, in the later version, watered down and blurred through many additions and "commentaries" of the unasked-for "improvers." In the Mantua edition the profound lyricism of Joseph's prayer in the cave (page 414) and the pathos of his lament when he sees the horrible deeds taking place in the beleaguered city make a powerful impression. In the later version these two examples of religious lyric suffer greatly from the diffuse rhetoric of the subsequent interpolators.

Despite the fact that the original text was so ruthlessly distorted and corrupted by foreign hands, *Josippon* even in its present form clearly bears evidence of considerable literary talent. Its author was a genuine artist who knew the secret of portraying living, colorful, tragic feelings, the violent outbreak of passion, the intoxication of battle and victory, the abysses of sorrow and woe. His efforts are often highly successful. *Josippon* does not relate but pictures in vivid colors how the young Hyrcanus, the son of Simon the Hasmonean, lays siege to the city in which the murderer of his father has locked himself and in which his mother and sister are now held captive. The two women are displayed on the walls and horribly tortured in Hyrcanus' sight, while the murderer threatens to destroy them if he does not withdraw from the city

37. Mantua edition, p. 428.

with his army. But the proud Hasmonean mother, despite her sufferings, cries out from the wall words in which contradictory feelings struggle: "Bethink you, my son, you did not come here to show mercy but to take revenge! Not of us must your thought now be but how to avenge yourself on the deceitful enemy, the murderer of your father!" And the author compels the reader to live through the profound drama of the young Hasmonean in whom antithetical feelings, thirst for avenging the blood of his father and love for his mother and sister, wrangle so intensely.[38]

The Roman general managed to break through the walls of Jerusalem as a result of the bitter struggle which the two Hasmonean brothers waged with each other at that time. The Roman soldiers, drunk with blood, entered the sanctuary while the divine service was being conducted and the priests were occupied with the sacrifice. *Josippon* gives us a fearful picture of how the soldiers keep advancing and kill one priest after another while the service continues in the customary way. Not a single priest trembled before the swords and spears of the enemy. Calmly, "as in a peaceful valley," the servants of God step over the still-writhing bodies of their brethren and perform their task. If one fell at the enemy's hand, another immediately took his place at the altar. "We must die at our watch," they said.[39]

Such dramatic scenes, with descriptions of heroic battles to the death, are very numerous in *Josippon*—for example, the tragic death of the Zealot Simon and his whole family,[40] or the destruction of the priest Amittai and his three sons,[41] or the terrible battle in the narrow forecourt of the Temple between the Roman and Jewish soldiers—the Romans drunk with victory, the Jews embittered by hatred and despair.

> The exit was cut off, one soldier was pressed against another, the enemy surrounded them in their last battle. The wounded, the stabbed, those still living and fighting—all fell, one on top of the other, in a bloody heap, and in a mighty clamor were poured together all the voices, all the sounds, the groans and gasps of the dying, the victory shout of the conquerors, the clang of swords, the striking of armor, and the scraping and squeaking of human bones and skulls under the edge of the sword and axe.[42]

The well-known story in the Talmud about the rich Jewess Miriam who, out of unbearable hunger in the besieged city of

38. *Ibid.*, p. 169; in the Constantinople edition, Chapter 27.
39. In the Mantua edition, p. 221; in the Constantinople edition, Chapter 39.
40. Constantinople edition, end of Chapter 64.
41. *Ibid.*, Chapter 89; in the Mantua edition, pp. 491–92.
42. *Ibid.*, Chapter 91; in the Mantua edition, pp. 504–5.

Jerusalem, slaughtered her only child is told in *Josippon* in particularly vivid colors. The reader literally feels the dread which seizes the stony-hearted Zealots when they come running from the streets at the odor of roasted flesh. The miserable mother, crazed with agony, begins to praise the savory roast of her own child's "little feet and hands."[43] With a few brief strokes the author also engraves in the memory of the reader the picture of Joseph the priest's eighty-five-year-old mother who learns that her son has fallen, wounded by the stone of an enemy, and is in mortal danger. The old woman, with her snow-white hair let down, runs around the wall of the city and shrieks, "Joseph, my son, the light of my eyes!"[44]

Even the modern reader peruses with arrested attention the masterfully portrayed scene between the cruel, pathologically suspicious Herod and his son Antipater. Through skillful intrigues the deceitful Antipater has succeeded in making his two elder brothers suspect in the eyes of his father. The latter has killed both of them, and Antipater remains the only heir of his father's crown. Herod, however, has learned of Antipater's secret plans. He suspects that Antipater wishes to take the throne away from him and he summons him home from Rome, where he has been staying. Antipater has had to come immediately at his father's command; the stern father greets him with an angry speech of accusation. Antipater sees that all is lost, his hidden plans are revealed; and with the courage of despair the clever intriguer tries to cleanse himself of guilt before the eyes of his cruel father. He knows that his life hangs in the balance. This gives his words, his entire bearing, a special pathos and extraordinary power of persuasion, and the reader is borne along with it. He listens to Antipater's speech of defense with arrested attention. "Father," Antipater exclaims in the middle of his speech,

> see, you have called me and I have come at once, I stand here before you . . . I bring before you three witnesses who know of no bribery, whose eyes cannot be blinded, and who cannot be bought for any amount. Let them give testimony before God and before you. The heaven, the earth, the sea—these are my witnesses, and they will not have mercy on one who has plotted to shed his own father's blood. See, I have travelled to you. Why did the heavens not hurl their thunder at me on the way, why did they not shatter me with a lightning stroke from their depths, if I am really guilty before you? I travelled over the sea, and it did not swallow me like Jonah when he wished to flee from

43. *Ibid.*, Chapter 93; in the Mantua edition, pp. 519–23.
44. *Ibid.*, Chapter 90; in the Mantua edition, p. 494.

God's command. I travelled over the earth. Why did not the earth crack under my feet and swallow me up like Dathan and Abiram who rose against Moses, who was a merciful father and guardian to the people? . . . But if my fate is already determined, I beg only one thing, my father. Give me not into strange hands; let me have death through your own fatherly hand. Open my heart, cut up all its hidden little chambers, and become convinced for yourself whether my heart has ever devised evil against you. Say not, "How can I raise my hand against my own son, against my own flesh and blood?" Can he who had in mind to lift his murderous hand against you be your flesh and blood?[45]

With no less mastery the highly dramatic scene in which the last remnant of the Jewish army, led by Joseph ben Gorion, hid in a cave which the Roman soldiers promptly encircled is portrayed. The Jewish warriors decided that it would be better to die at their own hands than at the enemy's. The cold-blooded and wily Joseph agreed. But he managed, through clever talk and trickery, to be the last survivor and thus save his life.[46]

A lovely closing chord at the end of *Josippon* is the elegy of Joseph ben Gorion over the ruins of Jerusalem:

Oh, how forsaken is the proud, royal city now! By the feet of the unclean are you now trodden, you whom holy princes defended. The heavens battled for you, the planets went forth from their orbits to come to your aid and shatter your enemies. Now you lie in dust and ruins, a cemetery have you become. . . . Awake, now, you patriarchs, Abraham, Isaac, and Jacob, rise and see: the whole earth is covered with the corpses of your children! Rise up, Moses and Aaron, awake from your sleep! See, your Torah is burned together with the priests and Levites. Rise up and see, fulfilled are your prophetic words: like water is blood poured around Jerusalem! Woe to us who have survived that we must look upon the frightful destruction! Better for us to have lost our eyes than to see how God's sanctuary lies in the dust and His palace burns in flame! Fallen is the crown of our head. Woe to us for our great sin![47]

It is no wonder that *Josippon* quickly became extremely popular, not only in Italy but throughout the Jewish world. As early as the eleventh century an Arabic Jew, Zechariah ben Said al-

45. *Ibid.*, Chapter 60; in the Mantua edition, p. 343.
46. *Ibid.*, Chapters 71–72; in the Mantua edition, pp. 406–15.
47. In the Mantua edition, pp. 532–33. In the later version, which Ibn Yaḥya published, this elegy is lacking. In its place is another rhymed poem. Both the poem and the closing lines following it, however, are doubtless a later addition of one of the copyists and interpolators.

Yemini al-Yisraeli, translated *Josippon* into Arabic,[48] and as soon as printing was invented, it was rendered into various European languages[49] and published either in its entirety or in many reworkings and condensations.

48. Printed in 1872 under the title *Ta'rikh Yosippus al-Yahudi* in Beirut. From Arabic *Josippon* was also translated into Ethiopic.
49. Into Latin by Sebastian Muenster and Friedrich Breithaupt; into English by Peter Morvyn; into Yiddish by Michael Adam and others. All the translations, except the Latin, were made from the later version printed in Constantinople.

# CHAPTER TWO

# *The Beginnings of Liturgical Poetry in Italy;* THE *SEFER YUḤASIN*

JOSIPPON, the fascinating historical work of an anonymous author, also contains pages from a different genre—religious poetry. Many of the persons in the book address prayers to God or pour out their hearts in lamentations and supplications at certain critical moments in their lives. Franz Delitszch[1] was mistaken, however, when he believed that the supplications and elegies in *Josippon* are the oldest religious poems among the Jews in Italy. Thanks to the *Megillat Yuḥasin*, or *Sefer Yuḥasin*, which was published after his day, we know that in the ninth century there lived in the city of Oria the *paytan* or liturgical poet Shephatyah who, until modern times, was virtually a legendary figure and of whose life no scholar was able to provide any details.[2] It has now been established that he was a disciple of Abu Aharon, the disseminator of Jewish culture in south Italy. Abu Aharon, relates the *Sefer Yuḥasin*, inducted Shephatyah into all the mysteries of the "hidden wisdom." He became renowned not only as a religious poet but also as a miracle-worker.[3]

1. Delitszch, *Zur Geschichte der jüdischen Poesie*, p. 40.
2. See, e.g., Zunz, *Die synagogale Poesie des Mittelalters*, p. 170.
3. Shephatyah is supposed to have performed his miracles with the aid of the mystical book *Sefer Merkavah*, which, as we have noted, is also known under the titles *Hechal Rabbati* and *Pirkei De-Rabbi Ishmael* (see *Sefer Yuḥasin*, Neubauer's edition, p. 125).

Shephatyah was venerated and his name surrounded with numerous popular legends. One of these associates him with a famous enemy of the Jews, the Byzantine emperor Basil I. The "master of miracles" is alleged to have cured the emperor's daughter, an only child who was mentally ill, with the aid of miraculous incantations. For this, the legend further relates, when all the other communities in the Byzantine empire were forced to conversion, Shephatyah in 868 received as reward from the emperor a sealed letter of privilege in which the community of Oria[4] was granted the right to observe all the customs and commandments of Judaism freely and without hindrance.[5]

The dreadful persecutions of the emperor Basil, the "vile murderer steeped in blood" as he is called by the author of *Sefer Yuḥasin,* find an echo in Shephatyah's prayer "Yisrael Nosha Ba-Adonai," which is still read on the days when *seliḥot* (supplicatory or penitential prayers) are included in the synagogue service.

Israel is saved forever by God. Help us now, too, O Lord who art in the heavens! Thou art the God of great compassion and mercy. Like the poorest beggars they knock on Thy gates; accept, Thou exalted One, their petition. . . . There is no affliction which does not affright them, by countless enemies are they oppressed and mocked. Forsake them not, Thou God of their fathers! . . . In the day of punishment and terror aid them with Thy grace, send Thy help and redemption in their great need. . . . Liberate us openly before all the peoples; let the wicked no longer rule over us. Destroy the dominion of Seir,[6] and let the redeemed ascend to Zion. . . . Hear, O God, their cries of woe, let their prayer reach Thy heavens! For thou art the God of great compassion and mercy.

According to *Sefer Yuḥasin,* Shephatyah died several days after the emperor Basil's death, on September 3, 886.[7] His literary gift was inherited by his son, the well-known liturgical poet Amittai.

4. The city of Oria, like all southern Italy, was at that time under the dominion of the Byzantine empire.
5. *Sefer Yuḥasin,* pp. 115–17; D. Kaufmann, *Die Chronik des Aḥimaaz von Oria,* pp. 14–16. The oldest Jewish author known to us from the Slavic lands, Abraham ben Azriel of Bohemia, also tells us of this legend in his commentary to the *Maḥzor, Arugat Ha-Bosem* (D. Kaufmann, *MGWJ,* 1882, p. 421). A similar report was found by Samuel David Luzzatto in a manuscript collection of *seliḥot* (see *Iggerot Shadal,* p. 1148). In the collection of *seliḥot* printed in Amsterdam in 1785 there is a note reporting the same legend before the *seliḥah* entitled "Yisrael Nosha Ba-Adonai," p. 132.
6. Seir is the Byzantine empire. Because of the censorship, in numerous editions of *seliḥot* printed in Czarist Russia the words "destroy Seir" were changed to "destroy the evil."
7. The emperor Basil died in a hunting accident on August 29, 886.

The author of *Sefer Yuḥasin* relates that Amittai wrote all types of poems for his friends and acquaintances: odes, hymns, wedding songs, etc. When a prominent member of the community died, Amittai would mourn him in an elegy. He accepted no payment for his poems because he was a man of wealth and owned a large vineyard outside the city. All the occasional songs written by Amittai have been lost. Only a few of his religious poems survived in prayer books,[8] and the pious Jew at midnight, as well as on Yom Kippur at the Neilah service when the sun is setting, still chants with a tender, melancholy melody the ancient poet's lovely and touching verses:

Lord, Lord, merciful and gracious God! Thou God of grace, of truth and of great righteousness. . . . When I remember, O God, my heart mourns within me. I see every city rooted firmly in its ground, but God's holy city is degraded to the lowest abyss. Yet we think of God alone, our entire hope is only in God! . . . Cover us with thy wings, thou attribute of mercy! Raise to the Eternal our petition, beg mercy for thy people! See how all hearts are grieved and every spirit is filled with despair! . . . I put my hope in Thy divine word, I trust that the gates of mercy will not be closed before the streams of our tears. Therefore I pour out my plaint before Thee, to whom all hearts are revealed. Thou wilt not forsake us because of the merit of the fathers. . . . Thou who dost accept every sob and cry, in Thy vessel receive our tears. Save us from all cruel decrees. Thou alone art our hope and consolation.

Shephatyah and his son Amittai wrote their liturgical poems in simple, easily comprehensible Hebrew. Like that of *Josippon*, their style is very close to the Biblical. In their works only a few expressions taken from the post-Biblical era are to be found. Their images and similes are clear and sharp, enlivened by the breath of poetic inspiration. However, they created no school of their own and had very few successors in Italy. Shortly after them, in the tenth century, the influence of Eleazar Kallir becomes increasingly discernible among the Italian liturgical poets. Kallir came to be regarded as an ancient and holy Tanna, and his difficult, cumbersome hymns were considered supreme models and classical masterpieces. The less comprehensible they were, the more pro-

8. Zunz (*Literaturgeschichte*, pp. 166–68 and 286) lists about twenty of Amittai's liturgical poems and supplications. There is no doubt, however, that there were two religious poets, both named Amittai. The second lived around two hundred years after the first, as may easily be conjectured from the following words in one of the later poet's prayers: "Why have all our neighbors rebuilt their ruins, while I weep for the two destructions more than a thousand years?" (see *Iggerot Shadal*, p. 898).

fundity was sought in them, and every religious poet felt obliged to imitate Kallir's work.

More industrious than all others in this respect was the most gifted *paytan* of that era, Solomon ben Jehudah Ha-Bavli. His penitential prayers and hymns such as "Or Yesha Meusharim," "El Nissa," "Aḥashvah Ladaat," and many others, with their heavy style and antiquated expressions, are strongly reminiscent of Kallir's poems. But Solomon was a man with a poetic gift, and through the stiff garment of the difficult, clumsy language the flame of genuine inspiration occasionally appears. We quote here one of his poems, the *seliḥah* "Av Leraḥem," which is read on the eve of Rosh Hashanah:

Father of mercy and vast grace, Thou hast not shamed us, the children of the holy covenant! We wander in exile, but Thou art with us. Forgive our sins, pardon our guilt, grant us redemption! Wash us clean from the bloody stain, erase from our foreheads the mark of sin, brighten our hearts with the ray of forgiveness. Let Thy verdict be heard: forgiven is the last remnant.

We are steeped in sin, like crawling things covered with dirt. Let Thy pure spring refresh our souls—for Thou art the God of love and forgiveness!

We are cast away because of our sins. The holy waters which might wash us clean are not. For Thy name's sake, O great God, forgive Thy people for their grievous sin.

There is no limit to Thy grace. Thou hast ever forgiven Thy rebellious people. Forgive their great guilt now, too.

Spread over us Thy holy mantle. Awaken our hearts to new life. Teach us to be pure and clean. Judge us not strictly, O God of compassion! . . .

From our degradation raise us, O God; calm and quiet our anguished hearts. Let the days of shame and destruction come to an end. Be our protector, have compassion upon us.

An insignificant remnant are we. Who beside Thee will have compassion on us? Our only protection is Thy grace. Hear us, O God! Accept us, O God! Forgive us and help us. . . .

To Thee all human hearts are open. There are no hidden secrets before Thee. Thou knowest how our hearts languish under the burden of sin. Thus we have come to Thee to beg consolation and help, to Thee, the God of compassion, grace and kindness. . . .

Along with religious poetry, exemplars of the unique didactic-narrative type of Midrash literature also appeared in Italy in that period. Here we must pause first on an interesting work associated with the name of the favorite hero of popular Jewish legendry, the prophet Elijah. This is the well-known Midrash *Tanna De-Be*

*Eliahu Rabba*.[9] The name of its author and the place of his birth are veiled in mystery. Even when he lived is not quite certain. In a few places in the Midrash itself, e.g., in the last, the thirty-first, chapter, it is expressly stated that "nine hundred years have passed since the destruction of the Second Temple." Nevertheless, several scholars, e.g., W. Markon,[10] have attempted to show that these are later additions and that the Midrash is an ancient work written as early as the Talmudic age. The majority of investigators, however, believe that the Midrash was composed in the tenth century.[11] Some, like S. J. Rapoport, express the view that the anonymous author lived in Babylonia. We are more inclined to the opinion of Graetz and Güdemann that *Tanna De-Be Eliahu Rabba* was written in Italy and that its author came from Rome, which in medieval Hebrew literature is frequently called Babylon. But it is very likely that the anonymous author employed to a certain extent an older work deriving from Palestine. Apparently the author travelled a great deal over the world,[12] visited the great Jewish communities of Babylonia, and also spent time in Rome, which he calls "the great world-city." His scientific knowledge was quite limited and, in this respect, he was not superior to most of the contemporary Jewish scholars of Italy. His numerous journeys, however, broadened his outlook, and in his ethical instruction is discernible a man of liberal views with a tolerant attitude toward alien religious ideas.

To be sure, the pious author complains that the Italian Jews of his age adopt the customs of their Christian neighbors, eat with them, and even at times intermarry with them.[13] There is no people that does not persecute Jews, the author suggests, and this is because "Abraham our father" made a covenant with an idolater, Abimelech (Chapter 7). A Jew must take care not to eat at the same table with an idolater, *Tanna De-Be Eliahu* admonishes, for he who does so is as one who himself practices idolatry.[14] The

9. The second part, *Eliahu Zuta*, was apparently composed later.
10. *Mi-Sifrutenu Ha-Atikah* (1910), pp. 26–46. Markon's arguments are hardly convincing.
11. See Zunz, *Gottesdienstlichen Vorträge*, second edition, pp. 119–24; Vogelstein and Rieger, *Geschichte der Juden in Rom*, pp. 200–203. Of interest in connection with the still unclear problem of the sources of *Tanna De-Be Eliahu* is the *genizah* fragment *Pirkei Teshuvah Ve-Gehinnom* published by L. Ginzberg in *Ginzei Schechter*, Vol. I (1928).
12. Many of his stories begin with the remark: "Once I was passing from place to place" (see, e.g., Chapters 14, 18, 20, and 23).
13. One must here take into consideration that in that era many Italian Jews were occupied in agriculture and the cultivation of vineyards.
14. *Tanna De-Be Eliahu*, Chapter 8 (at the beginning and at the end), Chapter 12, etc. In some editions "idolaters" is indicated by the term

author further relates the story of a maiden who threw herself from a roof and was killed because her father, an ignorant man, wanted to marry her to a gentile with whom he had associated.[15] But the author, who takes the position that the Jews must be a "people that dwelleth alone," separated from other nations, is convinced that every man is made in the image of God and demonstrates a tolerance that was not at all common in that benighted age. "I call heaven and earth to witness," he declares, "whether it be a Jew or a gentile, a man or a woman, a manservant or a maidservant—on each the holy spirit rests according to his deeds."[16] In another chapter we read, "I said to him: My son, it is written in the Torah, 'Thou shalt not oppress thy neighbor or rob him.' 'Thy neighbor'—this is the Canaanite, the one who believes differently. He must be like your brother." From this it is concluded that to rob or cheat a gentile is a grievous sin.[17] The pious author naturally values study of Torah highly. Even when a man, he says, has a hundred houses of his own, a hundred vineyards and a hundred fields, he must leave them and go to the house of study to study Torah. But that knowledge which a man has obtained, he must not hide for himself; he is obliged to employ it for the general good. Even if a man is as wise as Moses our teacher, as pious as Aaron the priest, he may not say, "It is well with me; I will dwell in peace in my own house." No, he must go into the community and share its troubles and sorrows.[18]

This social motif is very sharply expressed throughout the book. Characteristic is the following passage:

> Do you know why, in the days of the Judges, seventy thousand persons perished in the Valley of Benjamin? Because the leaders of the people were duty-bound to tuck their skirts above their knees, gird up their loins with iron bands, and go through the Jewish cities—one day in Lachish, one day in Beth-El, one day in Hebron, one day in Jerusalem, so in all the Jewish communities—and there teach the people proper conduct, how to hallow and exalt the name of God, blessed be He, over all the worlds. But they did not do so. As soon as they came into the land, each devoted himself to his own field and vineyard, was concerned only with his own peace and well-being, and did not think at all of the general welfare.[19]

"worshippers of the stars," in others, by "Chaldeans." We quote according to the Warsaw edition of 1880.

15. *Ibid.*, Chapter 21.
16. *Ibid.*, beginning of Chapter 9.
17. *Ibid.*, Chapter 15.
18. *Ibid.*, Chapter 20.
19. *Ibid.*, Chapter 11.

Highly as the study of Torah is regarded in *Tanna De-Be Eliahu,* it is nevertheless indicated that there is something even higher and more important—man himself. A pupil is reported to have said: "Rabbi, there are two things in the world which I love with all the flame of my heart, the Torah and the people of Israel. But I do not know which of them is preferable." The answer given is: "The majority think that the Torah is preferable, but I say to you, Israel is more important."[20]

*Tanna De-Be Eliahu* does not approve of asceticism and self-mortification and considers it a "bad sign" when someone does not care for the present world and the pleasures of life.[21]

The entire book is written in a sincere and tender style. The author frequently concludes his instruction with a prayer to the "Father in heaven."[22] And the "Father in heaven," he is convinced, is pure loving-kindness and graciousness. "We must," he constantly reiterates, "thank and love the Holy One, Blessed be He, for His great mercies." The secrets of "the hidden wisdom," of the Kabbalah, interest him very slightly. He looks at the world with believing but sober and clear eyes. Hence, his style is also plain and simple, without allusions or enigmas, without "combinations of letters" and *gematria.*

Written in an altogether different fashion is another Midrash of that era, whose birthplace was also undoubtedly Italy. This little Midrash is called *Sefer Zerubbabel* and is composed in the style of the Biblical Book of Daniel.[23] Zerubbabel, "a shoot of the stock of Jesse," a scion of the royal house of David, wished to learn what would happen "in the last days," when the "end" would come and the Messiah would arrive. Thereupon a wind lifted him up, carried him between heaven and earth, and brought him to the "city of blood," sinful Rome. He came to the marketplace of shame and there met a man whose appearance was extremely disgusting. This ugly man explained to Zerubbabel that he was the Messiah of the house of David whom the dispersed people of Israel so longingly await. With shudders of terror Zerubbabel looked at the disgusting man, and suddenly the man was transformed; his face became beautiful and bright. And Zerubbabel recognized him as the redeemer. For such is the will of the Creator of all worlds, the great God of Israel: that in chains and terrible afflictions shall the Mes-

20. *Ibid.*, Chapter 14, p. 267.
21. *Ibid.*, p. 258.
22. See, e.g., the end of Chapter 19.
23. Printed for the first time in Constantinople in 1519; reprinted at the end of the *Sefer Malkiel* in 1819, and also in A. Jellinek's *Bet Ha-Midrash*, II.

siah, the redeemer of the world, languish in the "city of blood" until the appointed time arrives and God remembers His exiled people. Then his chains will fall away, and he will appear in all his splendor and beauty.

Suddenly another figure presents himself to Zerubbabel—the six-winged angel Metatron, the "prince of the presence" (*sar ha-panim*). This emissary of God reveals to him the great secret: Already in the days of Nebuchadnezzar, immediately after the destruction of the First Temple, the Messiah was born, and a wind sent by God carried him to the world-city of Rome and concealed him there until the day of redemption should arrive. Further and further Metatron unrolls before Zerubbabel the divine scroll containing the profound mysteries of the future that lie hidden in the womb of "the end of days." Metatron informs him that the redeemer whom he sees is Menaḥem ben Amiel. But before the time comes when the Messiah must reveal himself, his forerunner, Messiah ben Joseph, whose name is Neḥemiah ben Ḥushiel, will appear. The latter will gather the exiles to Jerusalem, and there all the people will offer their sacrifices three months in succession. And Metatron shows Zerubbabel the stone statue of a woman and tells him that through the union of Satan with this stony woman the monster Armilus will be born. The appearance of this son of Satan and the woman of stone will be frightful: he will be entirely covered with red hair, his height will be twelve cubits, and his hands will reach to his ankles. His glance will spread poison and terror.[24] Armilus will conquer the whole world; no one will be able to resist him. He will kill Messiah ben Joseph and again scatter the Jewish people throughout the world. After Messiah ben Joseph has been slain, his staff will pass at God's command into the hands of Ḥephzibah, the mother of Menaḥem ben Amiel (Messiah ben David). This staff is the miraculous one that was in the hands of Moses and Aaron when they came to Pharaoh. It is the staff that was held by King David, and stems from the days of Adam and Seth. It was this staff that Elijah ben Eliezer hid in a cave near Tiberias, and from there Messiah ben Joseph obtained it.

24. The legend about Armilus, the son of Satan and the woman of stone, is also found in several other Midrashim, such as *Tefillot Rabbi Shimeon ben Yoḥai* (*Bet Ha-Midrash*, IV, 124), *Midrash Otiot Ha-Mashiah* (*ibid.*, II, 60), and *Midrash Va-Yosha*. In *Midrash Otiot Ha-Mashiaḥ* it is noted that Armilus is "the one whom the peoples of the world call the anti-Christ." This indicates that this legend passed into the Jewish Midrashim from Christian sources. On the connection of the Armilus legend with the ancient legend that the poet Virgil created a remarkably beautiful statue of a woman, see Güdemann, *Ha-Torah Veha-Ḥayyim*, II, *Beilage* IV.

With this miraculous staff Ḥephzibah will appear. All the stars and planets will fight for her and she will overcome two powerful kings, the greatest enemies of Zion. And when nine hundred and ninety years since Jerusalem was destroyed will have passed (i.e., in 1058 C.E.) the courageous woman will hand over the staff of Aaron to her son Menaḥem ben Amiel. And the redeemer will reveal himself in the Valley of Arbel. At first the leaders of Israel will be suspicious of him. Then he will shine forth in all his glory and beauty; at his summons the prophet Elijah will appear and Messiah ben Joseph will rise from his grave. And the three of them —the redeemer with his two messengers—will march into the gates of the holy city of Jerusalem. From the depths of the sea all the martyrs who perished for the sanctification of God's name will rise. The earth will tremble and her abysses shake. Joyously the redeemed children of Israel will assemble from all corners of the world. With the blast of his breath Messiah ben David will slay the wicked monster Armilus. Once again, as in ancient days, the Temple will rise above the five peaks of Zion, and Israel will inherit its land forever.

*Sefer Zerubbabel* relates what will happen "in the end of days." Around the time it was written, another book was composed in Italy which relates what had already occurred in past generations. This is the chronicle to which we have previously referred, *Sefer Yuḥasin.* Only one copy of this interesting work has come down to us. It was discovered in Spain in the library of the cathedral of Toledo, and published by Neubauer at the end of the nineteenth century.[25]

The author indicates at the end of his work not only his name but also the city and year in which he wrote his chronicle. "I, Aḥimaaz bar Paltiel bar Samuel," he reports, "have in the city of my residence, Oria, in the year 4814 since the creation of the world [1054 C.E.], compiled this book of my genealogy."[26] Aḥimaaz had no intention of writing a historical work; he wished, as we see, merely to write "the book of his genealogy." A descendant of the *paytanim* Shephatyah and Amittai, he set himself the modest task of recording the chronicle of his own family in the course of the preceding two hundred years (from the middle of

25. In *Seder Ha-Ḥachamim Ve-Korot Ha-Yamim,* II, 111–32.
26. Aḥimaaz ben Paltiel was born in 1017. He wrote his work when he was thirty-seven years old. Apparently the *Sefer Zerubbabel* was known to him, because at the end of his *Sefer Yuḥasin,* where he expresses the hope that the Messiah may come in the lifetime of his two children, he emphasizes: "And may the redeemers, Menaḥem ben Amiel and Neḥemiah ben Ḥushiel, sprout forth."

the ninth to the middle of the eleventh centuries), of reporting everything known to him of the life of his grandparents and great-grandparents. But, in describing the history of his family, which produced several significant personalities, the author incidentally touches on numerous interesting historical events and acquaints us with characteristic details of the cultural life style of the Jews in Italy in that ancient period which is separated from us by a millennium.

We have already alluded to the historical value of Aḥimaaz' chronicle. Now we shall consider it exclusively as a cultural and literary memorial of the Middle Ages. It is by no means a matter of accident that the wars which the Arabs waged in Apulia and Calabria are frequently mentioned in the *Sefer Yuḥasin*. Arabic influence at that time was very considerable in south Italy, and it is also discernible in the style of Aḥimaaz' chronicle. The *Sefer Yuḥasin* is written in the manner of the Arabic *makama*. Into the rhymed prose are woven, though to be sure only in rare instances, poems, e.g., Ḥananel's prayer "El Adon Al Kol Ha-Olam," and the elegy "Eten Tzedek Le-Eli" in memory of the astronomer and minister Paltiel. The influence of the Arabic language is also noticeable in numerous expressions.[27] But Aḥimaaz' style does not by any means attain to the mastery which the later Hebrew *makama* poets, Alḥarizi, Zabara, and others, displayed. His expressions are crude and stilted in places. It is also evident how limited grammatical knowledge still was in that era among the Italian Jews. Yet Aḥimaaz' language is quite rich, and he demonstrates considerable knowledge of Biblical and post-Biblical literature.

Like the author of *Josippon*, Aḥimaaz ben Paltiel makes no distinction between solidly established historical facts and simple folk legends. Fantastic tales do not arouse the least suspicion in our author, and he reports them as actual historical events. But it is precisely these legends and miracle tales, related with such naive simplicity, that are extremely interesting, for in them the cultural situation of that time is reflected most clearly.

Most of the legends introduced into the *Sefer Yuḥasin* are associated with the names of Abu Aharon and the *paytan* Shephatyah. Rabbi Eleazar of Worms asserts in his *Rokeaḥ* that Abu Aharon's father was "Samuel the prince [*nasi*] of Babylonia." In the *Sefer Yuḥasin*, however, Abu Aharon figures as the son of a wealthy miller of Baghdad. The chronicle relates that the father once left his son to look after his mill. The young Abu Aharon, however, became engrossed in his studies, and a lion ate up the donkey which

27. On this see D. Kaufmann, *Die Chronik des Aḥimaaz von Oria*, p. 39.

set the millstones in motion. The youthful Kabbalist did not hesitate long but, with incantations and magical "names," forced the lion into harness in place of the consumed donkey. Soon the father arrived and saw with astonishment and fright how the king of the beasts was working with bowed back like a common donkey. The miller of Baghdad regarded this as a kind of rebellion against the order of the world: What—to take a king who was created to rule, put him in harness, and make him work like a beast of burden? The father decreed as punishment for his son's arrogance that he must go into exile for three years and only then return home. The young Abu Aharon then proceeded to Jaffa and there boarded a ship that was about to set sail. In place of payment he gave the captain a guarantee that his vessel would sail in peace and no misfortune would befall him on the way. Abu Aharon arrived with the ship at the port of Gaeta in Italy and there at once commenced to perform miracles.

Since it was the eve of the Sabbath, he stopped with a certain Jew to spend the Sabbath. He quickly noticed that, despite the holy day, the man was in a very melancholy mood. His host explained that a great tragedy had befallen him: his little boy, an only child, had been lost. Immediately after Havdalah, the ceremony marking the closing of the Sabbath, Abu Aharon proposed to the Jew that he go with him on the route the little boy always followed on his walks. This way soon led them to a cave where an old witch lived. The woman at first denied everything; Abu Aharon, however, was not deceived. Near the cave stood a donkey tied with a rope. Abu Aharon immediately perceived that this was the lost child whom the witch had put under a spell in order to use him for hard labor. Abu Aharon did not engage in long arguments. He took the donkey away from the witch, broke the spell with incantations, and the happy father saw before him his only son.[28]

No less a miracle was performed by Abu Aharon in the city of Benevento. The community there welcomed him and invited him to the synagogue on the Sabbath to hear a young cantor who was renowned for his remarkably beautiful voice. As soon as the cantor began to conduct the service, Abu Aharon realized that this was not a living man but a ghost who had been wandering for a long time in "the world of the lost." He immediately stopped the cantor (after all, it is explicitly stated in Scripture: "The dead do not praise the Lord") and conducted an investigation. The cantor admitted the truth and, weeping, related his sad tale: A wealthy and pious Jew by the name of Ahimaaz had once lived in Italy.

28. *Sefer Yuḥasin*, in *Seder Ha-Ḥachamim Ve-Korot Ha-Yamim*, pp. 112–13.

This man would frequently go as a pilgrim to Jerusalem and there distribute large sums in alms. It was there that he once met the young man with the remarkable voice. He requested the young man's mother to let her son go with him for a while to Italy and swore by his own children that he would return him to her healthy and well. The mother consented, and the young cantor left for Italy with Aḥimaaz. Immediately after their arrival Aḥimaaz arranged a great banquet and invited many prominent guests, including the head of the Talmudic academy with his pupils. At the banquet the young cantor charmed everyone with his singing. The rejoicing was great, but it was suddenly interrupted by an old man who had been invited to the banquet. He listened to the cantor singing and all at once broke into a loud cry. He wept because he had just learned that in the "court on high" a decree had been issued that the young cantor must soon die. When Aḥimaaz heard this, he was terribly frightened. "I swore by my children to his mother; I cannot violate my oath." To help Aḥimaaz out of his plight, a holy "name" was written on a parchment amulet, the young man's flesh incised above the elbow, and the amulet inserted there. When the angel of death appeared, he lost his power over the young man. The latter's death warrant, however, had already been issued; he was thus erased from the book of life, and yet was not dead either. He returned to his mother and roamed from that time on over the world, a dead man among the living, wandering without rest, unable either to live or to die. Now that his secret had been revealed, he begged them to make an end to his eternal wandering and give rest to his body and soul. So they took a white bedsheet and laid him down on it. The rabbi then cut the man's arm open, removed the amulet with the "name," and the corpse at once dissolved into dust and ashes.

Abu Aharon's disciple, the *paytan* Shephatyah, was also a great miracle-worker. With the help of "names" and "combinations of letters" he used to employ the secret of *kefitzat ha-derech* (miraculous shortening of the way) and in a moment traverse the longest distance. He also, as has been noted, expelled with incantations the *dybbuk*, or demon, from the emperor Basil's only daughter.[29] Once, relates the *Sefer Yuḥasin*, Shephatyah passed the home of one of his acquaintances at night and heard a child's cry. He looked around and saw two women standing near the house. "Sister," said one of them to the other, "take the child; we shall both sate ourselves with it." Shephatyah at once understood that he had to do with witches. He took the child away from them and brought it

29. *Ibid.*, pp. 115–17.

home, where he and his wife recognized it as their neighbor's child. At the neighbor's, however, there was much wailing and weeping. In the morning, when they rose, they had found the child dead in its cradle. Soon Shephatyah came to his neighbor, and when he learned that the child had already been buried, he said in astonishment: "I do not understand. Whom did you bury? Your child is still living." They went to the cemetery, opened the fresh grave, and there, in the place of a child, lay a broom. Shephatyah led his neighbors directly from the cemetery to his house, and with great joy they saw their child hale and hearty.[30]

Miracles were also performed with the aid of "the ineffable name" of God by Shephatyah's brother Ḥananel and his great-grandsons, Shabbetai and Papuleon. These two young men boarded a ship and explained to the captain that they knew the secret of *kefitzat ha-derech* and that in one night the ship would reach the shores of Africa. They wrote a "name" on parchment and threw it into the water near the ship. Like an arrow out of a bow, the ship shot over the sea. However, a great catastrophe occurred. The young miracle-workers had strictly admonished the sailors not to let them sleep, even for a moment. But the sailors, as a result of the work of Satan, paid no attention, and Shabbetai and his brother drowsed. The ship then flew with such force that all the people were thrown from the deck into the sea. It was carried further and further on the waves until it finally struck some sharp rocks and split in half.[31]

We find, however, in the *Sefer Yuḥasin* not only legends such as the foregoing but authentic portrayals that have a certain cultural-historical interest, e.g., the long narrative concerning the brilliant career which the stargazer Paltiel had at the court of the famous Al-Mu'izz, the conqueror of Egypt, thanks to his astronomical knowledge.[32] Interesting also are several genre pictures in the *Sefer Yuḥasin.* One of these tells us of a happy buffoon, a *paytan* of the ninth century, Silano of Venosa.

A prominent scholar once came from Palestine to Venosa. The Jerusalemite was extremely popular among the local Jews, who begged him to remain with them as a preacher. Every Sabbath day the scholar used to give a sermon. He would always begin with a Midrash, and on the basis of the Midrashic text build his sermon. He used to speak in the Hebrew-Aramaic dialect, and since most of his listeners did not understand this dialect, an interpreter, the

30. *Ibid.*, p. 122.
31. *Ibid.*, pp. 113–14.
32. *Ibid.*, pp. 125–30.

local *paytan* Silano, stood by and explained every sentence of the preacher in the vernacular. Once, on a market day, many villagers came to Venosa, and a quarrel broke out between them and the local residents. The quarrel, in fact, promptly became a pitched battle, in which the women also took part with their weapons—pokers, brooms, and the like. For a whole week the whole town seethed with the incident. Men and women kept on talking about the battle. On Friday Silano the interpreter, who was a great wag, stealthily took the Jerusalemite's parchment Midrash. He knew quite well what passage the preacher would employ the next day for his sermon, and so he scratched out several lines and in the empty space described in a poem the entire battle in all its details, not omitting the women with their weapons. On the Sabbath the preacher opened his Midrash, read the text aloud, and the interpreter Silano stood by and translated earnestly and calmly, word by word. The community was astounded at God's miracles: in the Jerusalemite's Midrash is described with all particulars the battle that had just taken place in their own town! To the preacher the matter was also very puzzling—but there it was in the Midrash. He soon surmised, however, that this must be Silano's prank. This greatly angered the people, and the community decided to drive Silano out of Venosa. Who knows how long Silano would have had to wander in exile if the same pious Aḥimaaz of whom we have previously heard had not taken pity on him. On the way from Jerusalem Aḥimaaz stopped in Venosa on the Ten Days of Penitence. The community requested the honored guest to lead the synagogue service. At that time in Italy there was still no firmly fixed order of supplications or penitential prayers (*seliḥot*), and every precentor or cantor could read the poems and supplications which pleased him most. Not infrequently the precentor himself was also a poet, and he would then present his own compositions. Aḥimaaz with a heartfelt melody chanted a remarkably beautiful supplication which touched the people greatly and called forth tears from many of them. After the service people asked Aḥimaaz who the author of the lovely supplication which had moved everyone so was. "This is the work of your own townsman Silano who is now unfortunately a wanderer," Aḥimaaz replied. The community regretted its banishment of Silano, and the latter soon received notice that he might return to Venosa.[33]

33. *Ibid.*, pp. 113–15.

# CHAPTER THREE

## *Italian Jewry Comes of Age;* ANATOLI'S *MALMAD HA-TALMIDIM*

WE HAVE observed that the old Italian cities were the first centers of Jewish culture in Europe. There the initial pages of European Jewish literature were written. Before either the Spanish or the French Jews entered the realm of cultural creativity there were already in Italy such gifted poets as Shephatyah and Amittai and such brilliant stylists as the author of *Josippon*. Even in the twelfth century the Spanish grammarian Solomon Parḥon, on coming to Italy, admitted that, as far as Hebrew prose is concerned, the Jews of "Edom"[1] are greater masters than their brethren in Arabic Spain. "I strongly beg," writes Parḥon at the end of his *Maḥberet He-Aruch*,

> that if my readers find in my work inappropriate and unsuccessful expressions, they judge me in the scale of merit. In our country [Spain] people are not so proficient in Hebrew, for in all the Moslem lands one language is prevalent, and wherever our Spanish Jews come, their language is understood and they can easily converse with their

1. Edom signifies Christian Europe, especially Italy.

brethren. It is otherwise, however, in the Christian lands; in every country a different tongue is spoken, and when a Jew comes from one country to another, his language is not understood and he cannot converse with his brethren there except in the holy tongue. As a result, they are more accustomed to think and speak in Hebrew.

We have noted that the foundations of Judaic culture and Talmudic knowledge were obtained by the Jews of the Rhine provinces from Italy. As early as the ninth century the old cities of south Italy—Oria, Bari, and Otranto—were famed for their Talmudic academies. At that time the slogan "For the Torah shall go forth from Bari and the word of the Lord from Otranto" was widespread. But the "Torah" that stemmed from the Italian cities was deficient in one thing: the stamp of originality, the living breath of creative inspiration. The scholars of Italy lacked the broad education and comprehensive knowledge of their Spanish brethren, as well as the simple originality of the French scholars. For a long time the Italian scholars did not rise above the level of mere middlemen. They did not enrich the Talmudic knowledge they had received from Asia with new ideas or creative energies. Talmudic investigation was conducted among them along the ancient lines, as ordained in the academies of Sura and Pumbeditha. They lacked the courage to seek new ways. Hebrew philology and Biblical exegesis were still in their infancy among them, as may easily be observed not only in the liturgical poets of the type of Solomon Ha-Bavli but also in the authors of *Josippon* and the *Sefer Yuḥasin.*

Only at the threshold of the twelfth century did Italian Jewry produce for the first time a scientific work which, though still not characterized by original creative thought, is undoubtedly a significant monument of medieval Jewish culture. This is the great Talmudic dictionary *Aruch*, which Nathan bar Yeḥiel[2] completed in Rome in the year 1101. The *Aruch* is not only an etymological dictionary in which the meaning of every word is given; in a certain sense, it is also an encyclopedia, in which the significance of all the subjects mentioned is described and explained. The account of various customs as well as the meaning of numerous words were taken by Rabbi Nathan mainly from the Geonim of Babylonia.[3] Some of the works which the author of the *Aruch*

2. Rabbi Nathan bar Yeḥiel lived in Rome all his life (1035–1106). His father was a *paytan* who wrote numerous liturgical poems. Nathan's teacher was Moses Ha-Darshan of Narbonne.
3. For a time Rabbi Nathan studied with Rabbi Hai Gaon's disciple Rabbi Matzliaḥ, who familiarized him with the literature of the Geonim of Babylonia.

quotes were eventually lost, and we now know of them only because of him. As a result, the *Aruch* obtains considerable bibliographical value; it is the only source for many decisions and ordinances of the Geonim and for numerous texts of important but lost Midrashim.[4] The *Aruch*, to be sure, is merely a compiled work, gathered with great industry from external sources. The author himself notes this in his poem placed before the introduction in which he thanks "the Holy One who has enlightened my mind and led me in the good and proper way, so that I might write down in order everything that I have seen, heard and learned." This, however, does not diminish the great value of Rabbi Nathan's work, which became one of the most significant guides in the realm of Talmudic study and the most important foundation for all later lexicographers. Nathan bar Yeḥiel lived in a transitional period, when the sun of Jewish Babylonia inclined toward its setting. The *yeshivot* located there ceased to be the major centers of Jewish scholarship, and the hegemony of Jewish culture passed to the European countries. It was precisely at that time that the Italian rabbi diligently assembled whole treasuries of the scientific and cultural heritage which the Jews of the Orient had produced over the centuries. Much of this heritage was in fact preserved for later generations only because of the assiduous and modest compiler. It is therefore not surprising that as early as the first half of the twelfth century the *Aruch* was highly regarded not only in Italy but also in France among the Tosafists and Bible exegetes of Rashi's school.[5]

At the same time in Italy once again, as in the case of Abu Aharon of Babylonia in the ninth century, a scholar appeared from abroad. He came, however, not from the east but from the west. This figure, who with his enlightening activity contributed greatly to the further cultural development of Italian Jewry, was the famous Abraham Ibn Ezra, who came to Italy around 1140. Not all the Italian communities welcomed the Spanish scholar with the respect he deserved. There has come down to us a poem of Ibn Ezra's, "Nedod Hesir Oni," in which he speaks with bitter indignation of the community in Salerno where some half-educated

4. On this see M. Steinschneider, *MGWJ*, 1898, pp. 121–22.
5. The *Aruch* was first published in 1477. The best scientific edition is that produced by A. Kohut, who employed not only the older editions but seven manuscripts. Kohut's edition appeared in eight volumes, 1878–92. On Nathan bar Yeḥiel see S. J. Rapoport, *Toledot*, I, 127; II, 143–60; I. H. Weiss, *Dor Dor Ve-Doreshav*, IV, 272–74; Kohut, preface and supplements to the *Aruch;* Vogelstein and Rieger, *Geschichte der Juden in Rom*, I, 357–66.

"scholar" from Byzantium (Greece) was welcomed with far more respect than he, the world-famous savant. "In Edom [Italy]," Ibn Ezra complains, "they understand very little how to appreciate the scholars who come to them from Arabic lands; but if some little man from Byzantium arrives, they are carried into transports by him and he crawls over the heads of all." Not everywhere, however, was he so coldly received, and Ibn Ezra in fact remained in Italy quite a long time. He visited Lucca, Mantua, Rome, and other cities. Young and old were attracted to the very learned and much-travelled Spanish scholar. He was the first to teach the Italian Jews the elements of exact Hebrew grammar. In the lexicon *Even Boḥan,* which Menaḥem ben Solomon of Rome completed in 1143,[6] the author still relies on the obsolete views of Menaḥem ben Saruk. *Even Boḥan* was soon recognized as dated, for just then Ibn Ezra came to Italy, there translated into Hebrew the epoch-making grammatical work of Ḥayyuj, and then wrote his own grammatical work *Moznayim,* in which he presents a general historical overview of the development of scientific philology among the Jews. Ibn Ezra also endeavored to arouse interest in poetry and art among the Jews of Italy. Since in the realm of liturgical poetry at that time, as we have observed, the ancient *paytan* Eleazar Kallir was regarded as the foremost authority, Ibn Ezra attacked him in a sharp critique in which he asserts that Kallir had a very slight understanding of the spirit and inner laws of the Hebrew language, and therefore, the form and style of his poems are old-fashioned and dull.[7]

Ibn Ezra's enlightenment activity was continued by his pupil, Solomon ben Abraham Parḥon of Aragon, who lived for a period of time in Salerno. He, too, set himself the task of acquainting the Italian Jews with the Hebrew philologists who had written their works in Arabic, and to this end composed his lexicon, *Maḥberet He-Aruch,* completed in Salerno in 1160.

External factors also contributed significantly to strengthening interest in secular culture and general science among the Italian Jews of that era. We have noted that the cultural level of the Italian Jews at first was not especially high but nevertheless considerably above that of the people in their environment. The Crusades, however, effected a complete revolution in the material as well as cultural life of the urban population of Italy. The old Roman civilization had naturally left deepest roots in the land of

6. On the Italian scholar Menaḥem ben Solomon and his philological work see Steinschneider, *ZHB,* XVII, 38–41, 131–34; W. Bacher in *Graetz-Jubelschrift,* pp. 94–115.

7. See Ibn Ezra's commentary to Ecclesiastes 5:1.

its birth, and even the darkness and barbarism of the Middle Ages could not annihilate the remnants of this civilization. The Italian cities never suffered the same total destruction as the cities in other Christian lands. Thanks to their extensive trade with Byzantium and the Arabic countries, their economic condition was at a high level, and even at the time when feudalism was most powerfully prevalent, the urban population in Italy did not lose its independence and lived according to its own autonomous way.

As a result of the Crusades, the Italian cities attained an even more flourishing condition. The seaports of Italy were gathering points for the knights who participated in the Crusades, and the major arteries through which the riches of the Moslem East streamed into Christian lands. They were, however, not only the channels through which treasures of gold flowed but also the gate through which fresh air and rays of light broke in upon the stifling, dark night of medieval Europe. "From Asia," writes the French historian Michelet,

> from the land which the Christian Europeans intended to destroy, began to shine the marvelous light whose rays broke through the darkness in which Europe was enveloped. A world of wealth and extraordinary beauty, a wondrous world which medieval barbarism and ignorance wanted to spit on in its hatred, rushed triumphantly into the lands of the West, overcame her conquerors, vanquished her enemy, seduced and dazzled him with her riches, her way of life, her intoxicating pleasures. All were enchanted, all fell in love with this wonderful new world. Everyone desired only what came from Asia. And Asia was extremely generous; she came forward with overflowing hands. The most precious tapestries, fabrics, furnishings and carpets—soft, colorful, with marvelous grace and harmonious beauty; weapons from the best, hardened steel, inlaid with gold, ivory and the loveliest gems—all these attested how backward Europe was. This, however, was still not enough. Precisely the "accursed" lands where infidel "idolaters" live and where Satan himself sits proudly on his throne are blessed of heaven. There nature provides its best gifts. There the richest juices of life spurt and bubble. There the noblest of plants, coffee, and the most beautiful of beasts, the Arabian horse, grow. There is a wonderland of immense treasures: silks, sugar, the best drugs and medicinal herbs which strengthen hearts, bring comfort and healing to the body.[8]

All these streamed into Europe through the Italian seaports. This greatly enhanced trade and money exchange, and in the cities of Italy a strong and wealthy merchant class which felt capable of overcoming the power of the feudal nobility was formed. Grad-

8. Michelet, *La Sorcière*, Part I, Chapter VIII.

ually most of the Italian cities became free and independent republics.

In the wealthy urban population, which thus became so powerful, Jews performed an important function. As in Provence at that time, so in Italy the general populace was quite friendly and the Jews were not oppressed, as they were in other Christian lands. They lived in freedom, and a major community such as that in Rome was even exempt from all special taxes. With the rise of the money economy which the Crusades called forth, the happiest time for the Jewish merchant class in Italy began. The more varied and richer economic life in the commercial cities of Italy became and the more their needs increased, the greater became the necessity for credit institutions. Since, however, Christianity prohibited the lending of money at interest and considered such an occupation sinful, it is not surprising that credit enterprises were almost entirely in the hands of the Jews. The urban governments and even the state itself leased their banks to Jews, and the Jews of that era thus became the monopolists of credit, the first founders of great banking institutions in Christian Europe.

But spiritual and intellectual culture developed apace with material culture. The intimate contact with the unique civilization of the Orient, and the new forms of communal life which intensified social conflicts, provoked new strivings and demands. To be sure, the mind of the terrified man of the Middle Ages was still unable to liberate itself from the scholastic web in which it was entangled. But its sleep was already disturbed. The frightened spirit became restless and, wandering about, began to seek a way out, to free itself from the doubts that robbed it of peace. The first shoots of communist heresy, which attacked above all the most powerful representative of might and wealth, the Roman pontiff, began to appear. Already in the middle of the twelfth century a priest, Arnold of Brescia (a pupil of the famous thinker Abelard), preached fiery sermons in Rome against papal power. He argued that the pope was not a faithful servant of God because he did not live as Jesus and his disciples ordained. The pope pursues secular power, wishes to rule over all, and loves the pleasures of the world, while the Gospel teaches that one must be humble, withdrawn from the world, not commanding and ruling but lowly and small, as befits God's true servant. This dissatisfaction with papal power as the major cause of social injustice produced a number of heretical sects, such as the Cathari, the Waldensians, and others. These democratically minded sects manifested a special interest in what they called the "Old Testament," because it is dominated by a democratic spirit and a strong protest against the powerful and rich is discernible in it.[9] As a result of this, many prominent leaders of the sects were in close and friendly relations with Jews and even frequently took over from them certain customs and ordinances.[10]

These intimate relations with Christian heretical sects also aroused free thought in the Jewish milieu. To be sure, the friendship between the sectarians and Jews had some very painful consequences for the latter. Pope Innocent III, a man of iron will and stony heart, after managing to drown the Albigensian movement in blood, promptly undertook to settle accounts with the hated Jews. It is difficult to determine whether Innocent III really believed that the Jews influenced the heretical Albigensians, or whether this was merely a pretext on his part to make the sects despised in the eyes of the Christian populace. In any case, he endeavored to represent the Albigensians as followers and disciples of the rabbis. Innocent III was the first pope for whom persecution of Jews was a planned, systematic undertaking. Jews have him to thank for the fact that the Fourth Lateran Council in Rome (1215) ordained, among other restrictions, that Jews were to wear a special badge on their garments. Jews in other Christian lands suffered especially from Innocent's persecutions, but he had no power over the Jews of Italy. It is noteworthy that the mighty popes, before whom kings and emperors trembled, were themselves powerless in their own land. Precisely there they had very slight authority, and it happened not infrequently that the very pope for whom it was a simple matter to depose powerful kings from their thrones had to flee in shame from his own capital out of fear of the mob's wrath.[11]

At the same time as the great monastic orders of the Franciscans and Dominicans, who waged relentless war against free critical thought, were established in Italy, the foundations of new universities in which all branches of science flourished were also laid.

9. It is interesting that the activist social character of the Old Testament was later especially emphasized by Martin Luther, who was politically very conservative. In his tract *Wider die räuberischen und mörderischen Rotten der Bauern* (Against the Robbing and Murderous Hordes of Peasants) Luther says: "Es hilft auch den Bauern nicht, dass sie fürgeben, Genesis 1 und 2 sein alle Dinge frei und gemein geschafen, und dass wir alle gleich sind. Denn in neuen Testament halt und gilt Moses nicht; sondern da steht unser Meister Jesus Christus und wirf uns mit Leib und Gut unter den Kaiser und das weltliche Recht."

10. It is told, for example, of the "Poor of Lyon" (*Pauvres de Lyon*) that they used to observe the Sabbath, circumcize their children, etc.

11. Giesebrecht, *Deutsche Kaiserzeit*, III, 550; Vogelstein and Rieger, *op. cit.*, I, 227; Em. Gebhardt, *L'Italie mystique*, Chapter 1.

This occurred mainly in south Italy, where the more enlightened Christian populace came into close contact with the Saracens and their civilization. In the development of the sciences in the Italian universities Jews participated prominently. In the first half of the thirteenth century medicine was already the favorite occupation of the Jewish scholars of Italy. Indeed, Jewish doctors were responsible for the fame obtained by the medical schools of Naples, particularly that of Salerno, to which students streamed from all of western Europe. In south Italy, where the most varied civilizations came into close contact, the spirit of free thought emerged earlier than anywhere else in Christian Europe.

"The states of south Italy, especially Sicily," rightly observes F. A. Lange in his excellent work *Geschichte des Materialismus*, "precisely where blind superstition and barbarous fanaticism now rule, were, at that time, the birthplace of free thought, the cradle of tolerance and humanism." And the Jews played a very significant role in this. They were the industrious awakeners, the indefatigable popularizers of philosophical thought. This enlightening role of theirs was properly appreciated by the emperor Frederick II (1194–1250), who was himself proficient in the natural sciences. This remarkable man,[12] "the first European," as Nietzsche[13] describes him, in whom light and dark threads were so strangely interwoven, supported Jewish scholars and endeavored to attract them to the university which he founded in Naples.[14] The versatile and cultured emperor was rightly renowned as a great heretic and the most dangerous enemy of the papacy. It is even related how once, with a mocking smile, he spoke of "the three impostors" (*de tribus ympostoribus*), Moses, Jesus, and Mohammed. In Frederick's court a scientific center at which representatives of various faiths came together in friendship was formed.[15] Among the Arabic[16] and Christian scholars there, the

12. On Frederick II see Höfler, *Kaiser Friedrich II;* Gebhardt, *op. cit.*, Chapter 4.
13. *Jenseits von Gut und Böse* (1899), pp. 131–32.
14. Frederick was not only the Holy Roman Emperor but King of Naples and Sicily.
15. This phenomenon also found an echo in the *novella* literature of that period. In the group of stories and tales that were produced in the environs of Frederick's court and were later included in the well-known collection entitled *Novelino* there is (*Novella* 61) the legend of the three rings related by the Jewish merchant to the Sultan Saladin—a legend which became so familiar because of Lessing.
16. According to some (to be sure, not altogether reliable) sources, both sons of the famous Arabic thinker Averroes spent some time at Frederick's court.

Jewish translators who, at the emperor's command, translated Arabic philosophic works into Latin and Hebrew played an important role. The learned Jewish astronomer Jehudah ben Solomon Ha-Kohen Ibn Matkah of Toledo (born in 1215),[17] with whom Frederick conducted a learned correspondence even before he knew him personally, lived for a time at the emperor's court.[18] There also Jacob ben Abba Mari Anatoli, the first Aristotelian in Italy, with whom Frederick used to carry on long discussions about Maimonides' philosophy and to whom he even proposed his own explanations of some difficult passages in *A Guide for the Perplexed*, spent a period of time.[19]

Jacob Anatoli occupies an honored place in the history of Jewish culture in Italy. A thoroughgoing rationalist and ardent admirer of Maimonides' ideas, he energetically prepared the way for these ideas in Italy and popularized them in Jewish intellectual circles which, until then, had generally a very limited notion of the philosopher and his significance. Born in Provence in the city of Narbonne,[20] he was inducted by his father-in-law, Samuel Ibn Tibbon, the translator of *A Guide for the Perplexed*, into Maimonides' philosophy. It became for him the "pillar of fire," the star that

17. Ibn Matkah composed an encyclopedic work in Arabic and himself translated it into Hebrew under the title *Midrash Ha-Ḥochmah.* Two manuscripts of this work are in the Bodleian Library at Oxford. In Christian literature the work is known as *Inquisitio Sapientiae.* In S. Sachs' catalog of Baron Günzburg's collection of manuscripts the following work is noted (under No. 234): "*Sod Ha-Galgalim* by Rabbi Jehudah ben Solomon Ha-Kohen ben Matkah." The Kabbalist Isaiah ben Joseph, who lived in the thirteenth century, quotes Ibn Matkah's work *Sefer Ha-Shamayim.*
18. See *Otzar Neḥmad,* II, 234.
19. See Anatoli, *Malmad Ha-Talmidim,* p. 53b. In the same work, in "Parashat Parah," in which the "red heifer" of the Bible is discussed, Anatoli again indicates that Frederick provided an explanation for the heifer. This reference to Frederick is missing in the printed edition of *Malmad Ha-Talmidim* but is in the manuscript copy in the Firkovich Collection, No. 48, p. 49. See also Steinschneider, *ZHB,* VII, 62–65, and XX, 24, where it is related that Frederick used to carry on scientific discourses with the poet Jehudah Alḥarizi.
20. Neither the year of Anatoli's birth nor the year of his death has been definitely established. In one source (*Journal Asiatique,* XIV, 34) it is indicated that Anatoli lived c. 1194–1256. However, we are somewhat dubious about these dates. Anatoli himself indicates (*Malmad Ha-Talmidim,* p. 186) that when he wrote this work he was fifty-five years old. However, in the previously mentioned manuscript copy of *Malmad Ha-Talmidim* which we employed, the following remark is to be found at the end of "Parashat Ishah Ki Tazria": "the eighth day of the month of Av in the year 5025 from creation." Thus it appears that Anatoli was still alive in the year 1266.

guided him throughout his life. "*A Guide for the Perplexed,*" Anatoli declares with great enthusiasm, "makes the blind see, and it also liberated my eyes from blindness." He speaks with intense indignation of Maimonides' opponents. He is certain that their battle against the great scholar merely demonstrates their evil and foolishness, and that they would have attacked King David himself had he lived in their time.[21]

The reputation of the young scholar reached Frederick II, who invited him to come to Naples.[22] At the court of the enlightened monarch Anatoli became friendly with the Christian savant Michael Scotus, whom he mentions frequently with gratitude.[23] This scholar aided Anatoli considerably in his fruitful scientific enterprise—the familiarization of the European West with the scientific knowledge the Arabs had accumulated. After Anatoli had translated several astronomical works,[24] he, the first among European scholars, undertook to translate the philosophic writings of the major Arabic Aristotelian, Averroes. With this a new period in the historical development of Aristotle's ideas in Christian Europe was inaugurated.[25]

Anatoli completed his translations around the year 1235. His subsequent scholarly activity is closely associated with Maimonides' philosophical work. Maimonides, as we have noted, was his authoritative teacher and guide. As a loyal disciple of his father-in-law, Samuel Ibn Tibbon, Anatoli employed the rationalist–allegorical method in the broadest manner. In the miracles of the Bible, and

21. *Malmad Ha-Talmidim,* p. 52.
22. At the end of his translation of Averroes' commentary to Aristotle, Anatoli relates that he was receiving a stipend from the emperor, "who greatly loves science and those who engage in it" (see Munk, *Mélanges de la philosophie juive et arabe,* p. 355; *ZHB*, XII, 127).
23. Anatoli notes in the preface to *Malmad Ha-Talmidim,* "which I heard from the mouth of the great scholar Michael with whom I associated." In *Malmad Ha-Talmidim* itself he quotes his Christian friend seventeen times: pp. 2b, 5b, 9b, 38a, 45b, 47a, 48a, 53b (twice), 54b, 83a, 122b, 136b, 154b, 170a, 170b, and 177b.
24. Anatoli translated from the Arabic *Ḥibbur Ha-Gadol Ha-Nikra Al-Magesti* (The *Almagest* of Ptolemy); *Kitzur Al-Magesti* (Compendium of the *Almagest*); and *Yesodot Ha-Techunah* (The Elements of Astronomy).
25. Anatoli translated the first five books of Averroes' "intermediate" commentary on Aristotle's *Logic*, consisting of the Introduction of Porphyry and the four books of Aristotle on the Categories, Interpretation, Syllogism, and Demonstration. A parchment manuscript of this translation is included in the first Firkovich Collection, Nos. 380–84. From the preface it may be conjectured that Anatoli began this translation while still living in Provence, fulfilling the request of his friends in Narbonne and Béziers.

in all its narratives and proverbs as well, Anatoli saw only philosophical allegories and allusions. While still living in Provence, he had attempted to disseminate his ideas among the general public. On Sabbaths and festivals he would preach in the synagogues, and in his sermons explain the meaning of the Biblical text in a rationalist-allegorical fashion. This aroused fierce indignation among the orthodox elements of the community. The same thing recurred when he attempted to preach in Italy. Anatoli finally realized that the pulpit was not an appropriate forum for propagating his free-thinking conceptions. He therefore decided to spread Maimonides' ideas not orally but through writing. Together with his Christian friend Michael Scotus, he translated *A Guide for the Perplexed* into Latin,[26] and the ideas that he had earlier expressed orally from the pulpit he assembled in a book entitled *Malmad Ha-Talmidim*, which he divided into forty-eight chapters, according to the weekly *sidrot* or synagogal readings of the Torah.[27] This work is a fascinating cultural document in which the virtues as well as the defects of Maimonidean rationalism are most clearly reflected. Hence, it is worthwhile to pause at some length on it.

In the introduction to *Malmad Ha-Talmidim* Anatoli explains that the most important of all sciences is metaphysics, delving into the *maaseh merkavah* (the lore of the divine chariot or throne). "All the sciences are merely auxiliary" to this greatest science. The "discussions of Abbaye and Rava," i.e., Talmudic study, however, are not essential. One can be content merely with the Mishnah and with one of the codifiers. "Unfortunately," Anatoli adds in this connection,

> among our present-day rabbis, the chief thing is to occupy oneself with the Talmud, to raise difficult questions and seek solutions for them. But of philosophy, of "divine wisdom," they have an altogether slight notion and consider it not only a secondary but, indeed, a very pernicious and dangerous thing.

Through his work, Anatoli explains, he aims to demonstrate how the true meaning of the Biblical text can be attained. He wishes "to remove the outer shell in order to uncover the pearl hidden beneath it" and to reveal the word of the Torah in all its glory and

26. As many point out, the translation was made at the command of Frederick II (see Steinschneider, *Hebräische Bibliographie,* VI, 31 and 62–66).
27. When Anatoli completed his work he was fifty-five years old (see *Malmad Ha-Talmidim,* p. 186b). *Malmad Ha-Talmidim* was first published by the Mekitzei Nirdamim Society in 1886.

beauty.[28] "Every story related in the Torah has a special meaning: either it teaches us how to conduct ourselves in matters of state or its purpose is to strengthen faith in us."[29] It is clear, the author further observes, that all the narratives of the Torah are merely parables and allegories. The Torah is written in this way in order to be comprehensible to all Israel. In every simple story, however, inheres a deeper, concealed meaning which only the elect few understand. "The multitude cannot comprehend the true significance of all the events described in the Torah. They take everything literally, just as it is related, but the philosophically enlightened understand the hidden secret." This, Anatoli insists, is the case not merely in regard to the Pentateuch. As Maimonides already pointed out,[30] even in the Book of Proverbs every verse has a double meaning, one that is plain and comprehensible to all, and another, esoteric meaning.[31] The same, Anatoli adds, is true of the prophets and sages. Every expression of theirs has a twofold import, one for those who can grasp only the meaning of the words, and another, profounder significance which only certain individuals can attain.[32] Many deep mysteries, the author of *Malmad Ha-Talmidim* insists, are hidden in the sacred books and in the Talmud, mysteries of whose existence most of our scholars had not even begun to suspect anything until the great Maimonides appeared and revealed that which was deeply concealed. To be sure, Maimonides did not in his *Guide for the Perplexed* disclose every mystery; he did, however, open the eyes of all and taught how one can attain that which before was veiled for us blind men. You must know, says Anatoli, that for everything I reveal to you in this book I am indebted to our great guide, in whose path we go and whose precepts we follow.[33]

To provide some notion of the philosophical-allegorical method according to which Anatoli expounded the text of the Bible, it may suffice to cite the following examples. Noah's ark, with its three divisions, is, in Anatoli's interpretation, a parable of the three divisions of science: metaphysics, physics, and mathematics.[34] The narrative of the burning bush that was not consumed is an allusion to lowly matter which "is burned up in the fire of destruction."[35]

28. *Malmad Ha-Talmidim*, p. 8a.
29. *Ibid.*, p. 31a.
30. *Moreh Nevuchim*, I, Chapter 17; III, Chapter 8.
31. *Malmad Ha-Talmidim*, pp. 56b and 124b.
32. *Ibid.*, p. 116b.
33. *Ibid.*, pp. 119b and 122a.
34. *Ibid.*, p. 12a.
35. *Ibid.*, p. 45b.

By the Garden of Eden, in Anatoli's view, the sages understood the focal point of all the sciences.[36] The candelabrum with its seven branches is an allusion to the seven planets.[37] By the Canaanite who is so frequently mentioned in the Torah is meant the "evil inclination."[38] The harlot of whom the prophet Hosea speaks is again lowly matter.[39] The "little sister" mentioned in the Song of Songs is the "acquired intellect," the high level of understanding which man obtains through philosophical inquiry and thought.

The reader should bear in mind what we noted previously, that the allegorical method of explaining the Bible was at that time extremely popular among Christian theologians as well. Moreover, among the latter, the parables and allegories did not bear a rational character, as they did with the Maimunist Anatoli, but a scholastic-theological cast. The Christian theologians of that age not only perceived in Queen Esther an allusion to the "mother of God," in Isaac to "God the Father," in Jacob to the savior Jesus, in Cain to Judaism, and in Abel to Christianity; even the poets of pagan antiquity, such as Virgil, Ovid, and others, took on among them a Christian dress, and their works, through allegorical interpretation, received a completely Christian theological character. Nature, with its pulsating life, was also transformed by them into a profound allegory in which a wealth of instruction about morality and right conduct is concealed. At that time, in the heyday of scholasticism, appeared various works under such strange designations as "bestiary," "lapidary," and the like, in which there is an intensive search for the meaning and allusion supposed to inhere in every stone, every creature. Each entity, each living being, is only a symbol, a parable: "it must teach us something."

In Anatoli all this bore a purely rationalist aspect. Everything for him was merely a garment for philosophical thought and intellectual argumentation. With his consistent rationalism Anatoli was a categorical opponent of superstition and fantastic old wives' tales. In that era, when the entire atmosphere was filled with all kinds of destroyers, afflictions, and evil spirits, the author of *Malmad Ha-Talmidim* had the courage publicly to proclaim that he did not believe in witches or demons or rebellious angels who were transformed into evil spirits. Anatoli was firmly convinced that this "foolish superstition" was adopted by the Jews from other peoples. In his view it is a great error to think that the Hebrew Bible and the Gemara also contain tales of demons and evil spirits;

36. *Ibid.*, p. 142a.
37. *Ibid.*, p. 134b.
38. *Ibid.*, p. 134a.
39. *Ibid.*, p. 115a.

this is simply a misunderstanding of their true meaning. For him it is clear that when Satan or Samael is mentioned, this is merely a symbol of man's evil inclination which leads him away from the right path.[40] Anatoli also reminds his readers constantly that they ought to value the secular sciences highly. In that era of fanaticism and hatred, he also endeavored to promote the consciousness that all men are equal, that all are brothers. He insists that one must value the human person above all, irrespective of the people or nation to which he belongs. All men, Anatoli writes, are created in God's image, and it is absurd to think that only Jews have a divine soul and other peoples do not. We must not imitate those who say that Jews have no soul; this they do out of ignorance and foolish pride. Every gentile who engages in the study appropriate to him, Anatoli repeats, is far worthier than the Jew who does not occupy himself with what is suitable for him.[41]

But, along with this, the darker, more negative side of Anatoli's world outlook is clearly revealed. His free critical thought rises above the medieval boundaries and restraints, but he also creates new ones of his own. He teaches men to value the human person, not taking account of national and religious distinctions, but regarding only the cultured person who understands philosophy. Anatoli's rationalism is permeated with intellectual aristocratism, with contempt for the multitude, the "foolish ignoramuses." An ardent disciple of Maimonides, Anatoli disdains speaking half-words; he poses every problem sharply and clearly. He has the courage frequently to emphasize the anti-democratic character of Maimonidean rationalism, and his *Malmad Ha-Talmidim* therefore obtains a special historical-literary interest.

Three powers, says Anatoli, rule in man: the power of growth, the power of life and movement, and the power of speech and thought.[42] Man shares the first power together with all growing things and plants; the second, in common with all living beasts; the third, however, only in common with the angels. According to these three powers, men are divided into three classes. The first provides everything necessary for the first power, i.e., for normal growth and sustenance—food, drink, dress, and the like. This class is the largest in number. To it belong, first of all, tillers of the soil, then merchants, artisans, and also practitioners of such practical sciences as medicine. This class is obviously a very useful and

40. *Ibid.*, pp. 182b, 183b, and 184a.
41. *Ibid.*, p. 25b.
42. *Ibid.*, p. 143b.

necessary one, but its members are not ordained to play a leading role in social life as moral educators, and especially not as teachers and guides in the realm of philosophy and science. It is not in this class that man's greatness is manifest, because it provides only for the same requirements that simple growing things and plants do. The second class, smaller in size, provides for all social needs, pays attention to order, and conducts the entire program of the government. This class is definitely superior to the first, but again man does not attain his supreme level in it. For we know that certain species of living things, such as apes and the like, and even simple insects, also carry on a social life and manifest much political wisdom and skill. Only the third class, the smallest numerically, is the bearer of man's highest perfection—the power of speech and thought. These are the thinkers and philosophers, who reveal the profoundest mysteries and disclose the way of truth. They are the worthiest of all men, the crown of the human species. And just as in a fruit tree all its parts—the roots, the sap, the leaves—aim at one definite goal, namely, to ripen the fruit, so both the first two classes aim with their entire existence at one purpose: to create the opportunity for the third group, the smallest in number and highest in quality and value, to flourish and endure. But even in the third, chosen class all are not equal. He who penetrates most deeply into philosophical truth is superior to his comrades, and the whole third class ought to obey him. The second class must fulfill the will of the third, and the first of the second. Only in such a way, Anatoli asserts, can man attain the acme of perfection.[43]

Precisely herein, Anatoli insists, consists the great error of those who argue that all men are equal and think: I am like everyone else. This is utter foolishness.[44] Anatoli is convinced that not all men bear the "image of God," the divine impress, but only the philosophically thinking person, the man of scientific education. It is written by the prophet, Anatoli declares, that "the earth shall be full of knowledge, as the waters cover the sea" and that God "will pour out His spirit upon all flesh." The term "all flesh" means, according to him, every *living* creature, i.e., every creature with an understanding heart. "For it is ridiculous to think," he adds,

> that God pours out His spirit over ignorant fools also. May God keep us from believing in such folly which has unfortunately at present become prevalent among the people. The multitude is even persuaded that the most pious and best of our generation believe in this nonsense.

43. *Ibid.*
44. *Ibid.*, p. 144.

They believe that thereby they extol and exalt God's name. In truth, however, they blaspheme Him with this.[45]

Anatoli has no doubt that this great error was taken over by the Jews from the peoples of the world.

This "great error," the belief that God's *Shechinah* (divine presence) rests on all creatures and that all men are equal was, in fact, widespread among the communist sects which appeared in Italy at that time. This explains the hatred with which Anatoli speaks of the sects, whose followers he calls "evil heretics."[46] Anatoli admonishes,

One must keep as far away as possible from these harmful, restless men who, with their lies, seduce innocent people. The leaders of these rebellious societies at first speak soft words: "Let us live in peace; let us lead a pure, moral life; let all the money go into charity boxes to aid the needy; let one purse be for all of us." This, however, they say only externally. Their hidden intention is to incite men against the honest leaders . . . and to shed blood.[47]

Thus, all at once, the rationalist and freethinker reveals his social stance, his blind fear of the rebellious "mob."

45. *Ibid.*, p. 150a.
46. *Ibid.*, p. 115a.
47. *Ibid.*, p. 142b.

# CHAPTER FOUR

# *Scholars and Poets in Italy*

SPECULATION on philosophical questions became popular in enlightened Jewish circles thanks to Jacob Anatoli, who created an entire Italian school. In these circles Anatoli's favorite thinker, Maimonides, aroused great interest. Many persons studied his *Guide for the Perplexed*, lectures were given on it, and a number of commentaries to it were written.

Shortly after Anatoli's death we encounter in Italy an interesting figure, the philosopher and physician Moses ben Solomon of Salerno, who composed a commentary on the *Guide*. Of his life we know only that he was a pupil of the son of the author of *Malmad Ha-Talmidim*, who is known by his father's family name, Anatolio, as well as Anatolino ben Jacob.[1] With his thorough knowledge of Latin, Moses of Salerno assiduously studied not only the philosophic literature but the Christian theological writings of his time. Like Jacob Anatoli, who, in his scientific work, employed the aid of the Christian scholar Michael Scotus, so Moses ben Solomon studied

1. In Moses ben Solomon's commentary to Maimonides' *Moreh Nevuchim* we encounter quite frequently such expressions as "my teacher Rabbi Anatoli, may his memory be for a blessing" (I, Chapter 30, p. 13); "the sage Rabbi Anatoli ben Rabbi Jacob, may his memory be for a blessing" (I, Chapter 31, p. 14); "and when I asked the sage Anatolio about this, he told me" (I, Chapter 21, p. 7); etc. Moses, however, never calls the author of *Malmad Ha-Talmidim*, whom he quotes very often, Anatoli, but refers to him as "Rabbi Jacob ben Abba Mari" or says simply "Rabbi Jacob, in his work *Malmad Ha-Talmidim*" (see I, Chapter 19, p. 5; II, Chapter 26, p. 170; etc.).

*A Guide for the Perplexed* in the Latin translation[2] with the Christian theologian Nicolaus de Palea.[3] He was also acquainted with many other Christian theologians and in his work several times mentions the bishop Mazzeo and a priest named Philip of Tuscany.

Moses of Salerno was an ardent disciple of Maimonides, whom he calls "our perfect master, the great teacher," and for many years worked on a large commentary to the *Guide*[4] which remained unfinished.[5] He was thoroughly persuaded that in the Torah numerous allegories and allusions to profound philosophical matters are concealed, and indicates that the Greek philosophers, such as Plato and others, also frequently employed allegories and allusions.[6] Quite in the spirit of Maimonides' system, Moses declares the view of Saadiah Gaon that men are more worthy than angels false.[7]

Characteristic of the cultural situation of that era in Italy is the fact that this Jewish scholar had occasion to carry on sharp religious disputations with prominent Catholic priests and, in these, felt quite free to criticize the dogmas of Christianity. Basing himself on Maimonides' view, Moses, in his commentary to the *Guide*, berates the rabbis who permit themselves to portray God anthropomorphically;[8] but he attacks even more sharply, in his polemic works *Maamar Ha-Emunah* and *Taanot*,[9] the chief dogmas of the

2. Moses ben Solomon very frequently quotes the Latin translation of Maimonides' *Guide* in his commentary, referring to "the Christian translation" or "the Christian translator."
3. Moses refers on numerous occasions in his commentary to "the Christian scholar with whom I associated," and in one passage (II, Chapter 74, p. 105) indicates, "And this the Christian scholar Pietro de Bereah explained to me."
4. Steinschneider believes that Moses ben Solomon wrote his commentary in the years 1240–50 (see *Hebräische Bibliographie*, XV, 86), but we consider these dates incorrect. In the commentary the author of *Malmad Ha-Talmidim* is always mentioned as deceased. Very likely Moses reworked his commentary only at the end of the 1260's.
5. In all the manuscript copies (the work has not been printed) the commentary is only to the first two parts of the *Guide*. We employed the manuscript in the first Firkovich Collection, No. 482. This manuscript is a large, thick volume of 181 pages, paper mixed with parchment (the first pages are missing).
6. See his *Commentary*, I, Chapter 16, p. 3.
7. *Ibid.*, II, Chapter 11.
8. See Perles, *MGWJ*, 1875, p. 23.
9. Moses ben Solomon's work *Maamar Ha-Emunah* was eventually lost, and is known only from the quotations he himself introduces in his commentary to the *Guide*. A manuscript copy of his *Taanot* is found in the library of the Jewish Theological Seminary in Breslau. For a discussion of Moses' work, see the article by Perles on the Latin translation

Christian faith—the Trinity and the incarnation of God in human form.

Gradually, toward the second half of the thirteenth century, Jewish scholars began to play a prominent cultural role in Italy.[10] The court of the enlightened King Charles of Anjou (1266–88) in Naples was the gathering place of Jewish scholars from Provence, Spain, and Italy who industriously translated Arabic philosophical and medical works. Medicine became the most popular occupation among the Italian Jews,[11] but they also participated extensively in other scientific realms as well. Many young Jews travelled from Italy to Provence and Spain to study philosophy and natural science with Jewish and Arabic scholars. Returning home, they endeavored to acquaint Christian society also with the scientific treasures of Arabic civilization. An entire library of medicine, philosophy, and astronomy could be assembled merely out of the books which Italian Jews translated in the course of the thirteenth century. The most significant Arabic thinker, Averroes, was not lost to the Christian world only because of the Jewish scholars in Italy who carefully translated his works.[12]

At the head of Italian Jewry was the wealthy community of Rome. The traveller Benjamin of Tudela, who visited Rome in the 1170's, speaks very enthusiastically of the flourishing state of the Jewish community, which then consisted of over two hundred families. A century later, the situation of the community had become even more favorable. Among the members of the Roman community in that period were numerous wealthy financiers, as well as scholars, doctors, literary men, and the like. In Rome at that time lived the Talmudist Zedekiah ben Abraham Anaw,[13] the author of the well-known collection of laws and customs entitled

of the *Moreh* (*MGWJ*, 1875). See also Güdemann, *Ha-Torah Veha-Ḥayyim*, II, and Vogelstein and Rieger, *Geschichte der Juden in Rom*, I, 269–70.

10. It is characteristic that only in the thirteenth century, with the cultural flowering of Italian Jewry, did the first significant scholar in the realm of Talmudic study also appear. This was Isaiah di Trani (the Elder), who, because of his great knowledge and keen critical sense, became one of the recognized authorities among Talmudic scholars. On Isaiah di Trani see Güdemann, *op. cit.*, II, Index; Zunz, *Zur Geschichte und Literatur*, Index; Weiss, *Dor Dor Ve-Doreshav*, IV, 274–76; and especially the monograph of Gross in *ZHB*, XIII, 46–58, 87–92, and 118–23.

11. On Jewish doctors in Italy in the thirteenth century, see Güdemann, *op. cit.*, II, 128–33; Vogelstein and Rieger, *op. cit.*, I, 276; Eiger, "Yevreyskie Vrachi V Italii" (*Yevreyskaya Lyetopis*, III [1924], 8–23).

12. See Steinschneider, *Otzar Neḥmad*, II, 230, and *Sifrut Yisrael*, p. 138.

13. Anaw, a prominent and cultured family in Rome.

*Shibbolei Ha-Leket.*[14] A century earlier, the Spanish Abraham Ibn Ezra had been the first to have the courage to fight (in his commentary to Ecclesiastes) against the authority of the famous *paytan* Eleazar Kallir; now, in the thirteenth century, this native Italian deemed it proper to include in his *Shibbolei Ha-Leket* Ibn Ezra's sharp critique, in order to show that Kallir's poems, which had been so widely accepted by the community, are not at all suitable as prayers and occupy an honored place in the synagogue liturgy without good reason, since no one can understand their strange, difficult, erroneous, and corrupt language.[15]

At the same time as the author of *Shibbolei Ha-Leket,* there also lived in Rome two other prominent members of the gifted Anaw family: Zedekiah's brother, the poet Benjamin ben Abraham, and their relative Yeḥiel ben Yekutiel, a translator from Arabic and author of the finest book of ethical instruction to appear in Italy, *Maalot Ha-Middot.*

Benjamin ben Abraham is one of the most interesting personalities of the Roman community of that age. Besides Italian, he knew Latin, Greek, and Arabic thoroughly. Proficient in the Talmud,[16] he had, as demonstrated by his scientific works, an extensive knowledge of philology, astronomy, and mathematics as well. His true vocation, however, was poetry. Of his numerous poems and supplications, the best known are two[17] which apparently were composed after the defection from Judaism of the apostate Nicholas Donin, through whose denunciation hundreds of copies of the Talmud were publicly burned. Permeated with pain and indignation is his prayer *El Mi Anusah Le-Ezrah,* in which he addresses God the protector: "To whom shall I flee for help, of whom shall I seek protection, when the vile enemy arrogantly issues forth and

14. A complete, critically edited text of this work was published by S. Buber in 1886.

15. It is interesting that this criticism, which takes up four entire columns, is lacking even in Buber's complete edition, despite the fact that he employed several old manuscripts of *Shibbolei Ha-Leket.* Apparently most copyists, out of their great respect for the famed *paytan,* simply threw out the critique directed against him. Only in one old parchment manuscript of *Shibbolei Ha-Leket,* which very probably was written in the author's own lifetime and is now in Leningrad in the Library of the Society for the Dissemination of Enlightenment Among Jews, have we found this critique in complete form.

16. Some of his legal decisions are even introduced into *Shibbolei Ha-Leket,* in which the author refers frequently, as to an authority, to "my brother Benjamin."

17. These are printed in *Kovetz Al Yad,* IV (1888), 6–8, 15–17. On his other liturgical poems, see Landshuth, *Ammudei Ha-Avodah,* p. 51; Zunz, *Literaturgeschichte,* p. 332.

wounds so terribly with his poisonous denunciation and false slanders?" And when the "vile enemy" triumphed and, as a result of his "poisonous denunciation," the sacred books were burned on pyres, the poet in his elegy *Oḥilah Kirot Libi* expressed his profound sorrow that "the fiery pages given us by God have been robbed by the traitor who blasphemes his Creator."

The poet's true gift, however, is revealed not in his religious poems but in his secular satires. We have alluded to the flourishing condition of the Roman community at that time. The Jewish financial aristocracy played a prominent role in the old world-city. Jewish bankers and merchants had occasion to come into intimate and frequent contact with the religious and secular princes and officials. And they attempted to lead the same kind of life as these, to indulge their love of luxury, to dazzle men with their glory and wealth. Among the Jewish magnates and bankers were also many parvenus whom blind accident had, all of a sudden, raised to great fortunes. These parvenus regarded with contempt and arrogance those whose economic position was lower than their own and sought to show off their wealth. The *jeunesse dorée*, the children of these financiers and magnates, imbibed eagerly of the pleasures of life. They were the arbiters of fashion; their clothes and their chariots had to be the best and richest; their banquets, balls, and parties were carried on with great excitement and clamor, so that all should see and gape. This materialistic side of life in the wealthy Roman community was attacked by our poet in his masterly *Massa Ge Ḥizzayon*,[18] one of the loveliest satires in Hebrew literature. The most successful translation cannot render the unique stylistic qualities of this work in which Biblical phrases and expressions are employed with the mastery which Benjamin's successor, the brilliant poet Immanuel of Rome, later made so famous.

"Neither truth nor right prevails among us today," complains Benjamin ben Abraham Anaw.

The desire of the eyes is the only law; jealousy and lust rule without restraint. The greedy eye reigns over human hearts. In honor and glory are held now only the golden calves; those who possess wealth, they and their servants, presently rule over everything and their power is boundless. With arrogance and laughter they openly declare: "Why not sin when sin is sweet? Rich are the gifts of life; let him who can enjoy them and draw with full hands." Newly risen, petty men sit on high and look with pride and contempt on men of knowledge and wisdom, for the latter are poor and have no bread. "These learned

18. First printed in Riva di Trento in 1560, reprinted in Lemberg in 1860. We have employed both editions.

ones," they say with mockery, "glory in their wisdom, but we can buy them with their whole Torah for a piece of bread, a cup of wine. For who can resist the clang of gold and silver? Everything can be purchased with these—the richest luxuries and the most beautiful women. Money is everything! What gold destroys no one can build up again; what it builds up can no longer be destroyed; and the chains forged by gold cannot be broken by anyone. Gold is the greatest aristocrat; no one can be compared to it. And wise is the old proverb, "Silver purifies bastards."

"The parvenu rules our generation," the author further says. "These newly risen men are the model for everyone. All emulate them, and stand humbly before them while they lie stretched out in their palaces, mock the learned, and glory in their power and wealth." The satirist portrays how these people, accidentally chosen by fate, exult before each other, one with his rich dress, another with his horses and chariots, still another with his estates or elegantly ornamented weapons. "And woe to him," he declares, "who does not bow low before them and declines to acknowledge their greatness. Their power is vast because of their bags of money. And the officials are also on their side and allow them to do unhindered whatever their heart desires."

Benjamin gives us an interesting genre portrait when he describes how one of the "gilded youth" appears in his "pomp" on a stroll. The satirist renders the smallest detail of the dandy's dress, not forgetting even the rings on his fingers or the fringes hanging from the ingeniously adorned hat which covers only half his head. Apparently at that time it was the height of fashion to wear long hair hanging down in waves over the shoulders. Benjamin ironizes over the "thick forest which no comb can go through and no sharp scissors can overcome." "If I did not know," he sarcastically remarks, "how they love the cup and the kind of life they lead, I would have thought they had all become penitents and taken vows as Nazirites."[19]

Later[20] comes a portrait reminiscent of the style of the "visions" in the Book of Daniel. In a dream, a monstrous creature appears before the author. Its head is of gold, its ribs of silver, its loins of copper, its ankles of iron, and the soles of its feet of lime dipped in dirt. "And by these feet of the monster the luckless poor are trodden like the dust in the streets."[21] As he regards the monster with astonishment and terror, an emissary from heaven appears. He ex-

19. A Nazirite, as is known, would not drink wine nor cut his hair.
20. *Massa Ge Ḥizzayon*, pp. 6–10 (we quote according to the first edition).
21. *Ibid.*, p. 10a.

plains to the author the significance of the terrible figure standing before him and consoles him that this idol with the golden head and iron feet will not reign forever. The great day of judgment will come. "Go then," the emissary commands,

> assemble the entire community, men and women, young and old. Tell all what you have seen and heard. Let them know, let it be for a memorial for future generations. Let them remember that God's righteous judgment rules the world. . . . Call out loudly so that all may hear: "Woe to the lost fools who blunder on crooked ways, on the ways of deceit and baseness, in order to attain wealth and fortune, and thereby forget the day of judgment, the day of recompense."[22]

Then the author turns to his generation. He calls all, great and small alike, "to the banks of the river called Love" and preaches to them in Biblical fashion about justice and righteousness, about the vanity of the petty lusts which fill daily life to overflowing, and about the nobility of the human ideal. He demands of them that they "cast away the idols of gold and silver," and abandon the way of pride and sin, for it leads to shame and degradation. There is another way, the poet declares, the way of morality and knowledge, and only in it can one find rest, true joy, and the consciousness of inner spiritual freedom.[23]

This theme of his ethical preaching was later reworked by Benjamin ben Abraham into a didactic poem, *Shaarei Etz Ḥayyim.* The poem consists of 63 four-line stanzas, according to the order of the alphabet. Each stanza ends with the word *ḥayyim* (life) and deals with one of the virtues or corresponding vices.[24]

Benjamin ben Abraham's poem served as a model for his younger relative, Yeḥiel ben Yekutiel, the author of the ethical book *Maalot Ha-Middot.*[25] In the twenty-four chapters of his work the author considers the major principles of virtue in accordance with which every decent and morally upright man should conduct himself in life. Like the author of *Massa Ge Ḥizzayon,* Yeḥiel ben Yekutiel also complains strongly of his generation, which he calls "a generation of sinful men, with knife-sharp teeth, who oppress the poor and tread upon the needy, a rebellious and stubborn genera-

22. *Ibid.*, pp. 12a–13.
23. *Ibid.*, p. 20b (in the second edition, p. 53).
24. The poem was printed in Prague in 1598, reprinted in *Kovetz Al Yad,* I, 71–74.
25. Yeḥiel ben Yekutiel is also the author of the collection of ritual laws entitled *Tanya* or *Minhag Avot. Maalot Ha-Middot* was completed by the author in 1287 (see Steinschneider, *Catalogus Librorum Hebraeorum in Bibliotheca Bodleiana,* 1277).

tion that knows nothing of morality and justice, of ethics and right conduct, but blindly follows the lusts of the heart."[26]

The author explains that he composed his work mainly for the young; these, the "young men and students," he wishes to teach "piety and right conduct." And Yeḥiel ben Yekutiel in fact had the capacities required for this. The book is written in clear, easily comprehensible language, and the tone is sincere and tender. "My children" is the customary way in which the author addresses his readers. "My children," he writes at the beginning of his work, "come hither. I will teach you to follow God's way. Not out of pride do I do this, nor because I wish to become renowned or parade my wisdom. I only desire to familiarize you with what our fathers taught us with their wise words, their sincere instruction."

Like the *Sefer Ḥasidim*, so *Maalot Ha-Middot* sees the foundation of morality in love for the Creator and His creatures. "Hatred is a deep sorrow and a great grief," teaches the wise old book *Kalilah Ve-Dimnah*. Of this the pious Rabbi Yeḥiel of Rome is equally persuaded. "There is nothing in the world so evil," we read in *Maalot Ha-Middot*, "as hatred between men, and it is all one whether the hatred is in the hearts of worthy or base men."[27] "He who truly loves cannot hate. One may not bear hatred toward anyone, for everyone carries the impress of the Creator. Love must be given freely and generously to all, whether good or bad. It is written, 'And thou shalt love thy neighbor as thyself.'" *Tanna De-Be Eliahu*, Yeḥiel ben Yekutiel remarks in this connection, construes quite correctly that by "thy neighbor" here is to be understood *every man:* "and thy neighbor must be like thy brother." It is not permitted to deceive anyone, either one's own or a stranger, because whoever acts falsely, whoever accustoms himself to lying, falls away from God and denies Him, for God is Himself truth.[28] The Jewish people is the chosen people because God out of great love endowed it with the gift of compassion.[29] "It is written in the Torah, 'Thou shalt not take vengeance or bear any grudge,' for vengeance is generated by the terrible quality of cruelty, and this quality is proper only for wild beasts in the forest."[30]

Many proverbs and maxims in *Maalot Ha-Middot* are reminiscent of the *Sefer Ḥasidim*. It is quite obvious, however, that *Maalot Ha-Middot* was produced not in the stifling, benighted

26. *Maalot Ha-Middot*, Preface (we quote according to the Zolkiev edition of 1806).
27. *Ibid.*, p. 14a.
28. *Ibid.*, p. 51b.
29. *Ibid.*, p. 54b.
30. *Ibid.*, p. 56a.

period of the Crusades but under the mild, blue skies of Italy. It breathes a lighter air and has more vivid colors. One does not feel in it the leaden wings of terror that pressed so heavily on the authors of the *Sefer Ḥasidim.* The Roman Jewish community (aside from some isolated instances) lived generally in amicable relations with its neighbors, and the author of *Maalot Ha-Middot* even deems it necessary to admonish his readers not to spend time in taverns and not to eat and drink with Christians.[31] Since the wealthy Jews of Rome, as we have observed, were exceedingly fond of the pleasures of the world, Yeḥiel ben Yekutiel admonishes, "Know, my children, that it is a disgrace for a man to be a glutton and a drunkard, to yield to the desire of carousing and overeating; this is the way of those who are thoroughly evil."[32]

The author of *Maalot Ha-Middot* also dwells on those negative aspects of the social life of the Roman Jewish community which Benjamin ben Abraham attacked so powerfully in his satire. "There are not a few among our rich men," he laments,

> who wish to rule the community only on the basis of their money. They desire to be greater than all. They consider themselves higher and worthier than the wisest and finest men merely because they are wealthy; but they are really worthless, for they are without wisdom, without Torah, without good deeds, without piety. These arrogant, crude parvenus think that gold is the chief thing, that wealth alone gives them the right to be leaders. All other qualities have no value in their eyes. He who has money also has wisdom, pedigree, Torah, and knowledge. Filled with arrogance and pride, they consider themselves cleverer than all. I warn you, my children: know that this is the way of the wicked.[33]

Yeḥiel, however, does not have an eye only for the negative aspects of the life of his society, and he does not consider all rich men alike. As we shall see further on, there were in the Roman community at that time some very prominent, cultivated philanthropists who generously supported scholars and artists and themselves had a strong interest in cultural matters. These Jewish patrons also occupied a prominent place in Christian society and thereby contributed not a little to the high state of the entire community. This phenomenon also finds an echo in *Maalot Ha-Middot*. "See how great is the power of wealth," Yeḥiel ben Yekutiel notes. "All knock on the door of the rich man, all come to his house and seek rest under his roof. If there are wise men, they are at the homes of the wealthy. Masters of the Mishnah, masters

31. *Ibid.*, p. 83a.
32. *Ibid.*, p. 84a.
33. *Ibid.*, pp. 76–77.

of the Talmud, scholars and writers—all come to the rich man. Every needy person is there constantly."[34]

"Wealth obtained in a proper way," *Maalot Ha-Middot* insists, "is a great gift." It gives one the opportunity to do good and manifest kindness, "and this is the greatest joy of the heart."[35] Besides, the author naively adds, money is the effective instrument with the aid of which one can obtain honor and attention among the officials and the ruling power.[36]

"A wise man was once asked why scholars always knock on the gates of the rich, while the rich do not consider it necessary to visit the homes of scholars. The sage replied: 'Because scholars know how to appreciate the value of wealth; the rich, however, do not understand how highly one must esteem knowledge and wisdom.'" "Therefore, my children," Yeḥiel ben Yekutiel adds, "know how to esteem the rich who do not glory in their gold but understand that wealth was given them not for the sake of pride and dominion over others but that they might have the opportunity to do good and give aid."[37]

One other detail in this work is noteworthy. The author quotes not only Jewish sources but gentile scholars and philosophers, such as Aristotle and others, and himself indicates in the preface that he does this intentionally, "in order to attract the hearts of the young."[38] This explanation reflects the intellectual tendencies and interests of the Jewish youth of that era. The Roman community was then the center to which scholars from Provence and Spain migrated in the hope of finding an audience as well as patrons who would support them. The young who desired knowledge would gather around these men, and the latter would give lectures on philosophy and other sciences before them.[39] Even those who were occupied with earning a living by day delved into philosophic works at night.[40]

34. *Ibid.*, p. 76a.
35. *Ibid.*, p. 85a.
36. *Ibid.*, p. 76b.
37. *Ibid.*, p. 76a.
38. *Ibid.*, p. 2a.
39. One of these foreign scholars who at that time settled in Rome divides the sciences which every educated man ought to know into two groups —mathematical and philosophical. To the first belong arithmetic, geometry, music, and astronomy. To the second, the natural sciences, metaphysics, and political science (see Zeraḥyah ben Shealtiel's commentary to Job 9).
40. Interesting in this respect is the letter of Yeḥiel ben Joab to Shabbetai ben Solomon which was published in Berliner's *Magazin*, XVII (1890), 37–40.

As in Provence, so in Rome at that time the most popular scholar was Maimonides. The educated and enlightened youth literally idolized him. Lectures were given on his *Guide for the Perplexed*, and the Roman community considered it imperative to dispatch one of its teachers, Rabbi Simḥah, to Spain in 1296 on a special mission: to obtain a copy of Maimonides' commentary to the Mishnah.[41] In the famous poet of that era, Immanuel of Rome, we find an interesting story that gives us a clear picture of the profound interest in scientific works which the young Jews of Italy at that time had. A Spanish Jew named Aaron, on his way to Rome, met the young Immanuel and his friends in Peruggia. The Spaniard carried with him his library, packed in tightly closed chests. Becoming acquainted with them, he decided to leave the chests with them until he returned from Rome. Aaron also left with them the catalogue of his collection. When the young people read the catalogue and saw what fascinating works were contained in the library, they could not resist their temptation. They broke open the chests, and before the Spaniard returned, Immanuel and his friends had copied a considerable part of his manuscripts.[42]

As a result of the great thirst for knowledge which at that time could be stilled only through the handwritten book, a special institute or society of copyists flourished in Rome. Men of extensive knowledge, often themselves authors of learned works, devotedly undertook to copy scientific books because they recognized this as an important instrument for disseminating knowledge and culture.[43] The Roman community also included not a few cultured patrons who generously supported scholars and gave them the opportunity to engage in scientific study. Among these maecenases the most important were the philosophically educated physician Isaac ben Mordecai[44] and Rabbi Shabbetai bar Solomon, an ardent disciple of Maimonides who used to read lectures on philosophy. At the request of Isaac ben Mordecai, Nathan Ha-Meati (Cento), who was crowned with the title "the father of translators," in the 1280's translated numerous medical, philosophical, and astronomical works.[45] At the same time another expert translator, the Spanish philosopher and physician Zeraḥyah ben Isaac ben Shealtiel Ḥen,

41. See Vogelstein and Rieger, *op. cit.*, I, 263, 420.
42. See Immanuel's *Maḥberot, Makama* 8.
43. See Vogelstein and Rieger, *op. cit.*, I, 277, where about twenty such learned copyists are listed by name.
44. Isaac ben Mordecai (known by the Italian name Majestro Gajo) was court physician to Pope Nicholas IV.
45. There is a splendid manuscript copy of Nathan Cento's translation of Averroes' "Canon" in the Asiatic Museum in Leningrad.

translated for Rabbi Shabbetai bar Solomon a whole series of works by Aristotle, Averroes, Al-Farabi, and others.[46]

Zeraḥyah Ḥen is an extremely interesting figure. He received his philosophical education[47] in Spain, and Maimonides was the greatest authority for him. "Everything that came from Maimonides' pen," he declares, "is pure truth; all the ideas expressed by him are free of the slightest contradiction."[48] His favorite book was the *Guide for the Perplexed.* He read lectures[49] on it and wrote a commentary to it, in order, as he explains in the introduction,[50] to make Maimonides' work comprehensible to those who are mere novices in philosophy. This man of the thirteenth century frequently declared reason the only authority. Faith, the tradition of the fathers—these must undergo the test of critical thought and *prove* that they do not contradict common sense. Everything associated with mysticism, the hidden, and the incomprehensible is merely child's play. Zeraḥyan Ḥen speaks contemptuously not only of the Kabbalists of his time, but also of the ancient Pythagoras and his followers.[51] The Bible[52] also, and all the miracles related in it, he explains in a purely rationalist way. The story of Jacob wrestling in the night with the angel is interpreted by Zeraḥyah as the struggle of the earthly, material powers with the human intellect.[53] The stories of Abraham binding Isaac and of the three angels who come to visit Abraham are explained by Zeraḥyah as merely dreams which the patriarch saw in his sleep. The narratives of Lot and his daughters, and of Balaam's ass that spoke like a man, are interpreted as parables.[54] Zeraḥyah further has no doubt that the story of the prophet Jonah "can only be accepted as true by the common multitude, but every understanding person at once perceives that

46. On Zeraḥyah Ḥen, see Kirchheim in *Otzar Neḥmad,* II, 117–23; Steinschneider, *ibid.,* 229–43; Carmoly, *ibid.,* III, 110–11; Vogelstein and Rieger, *op. cit.,* I, Index; Graetz, *Geschichte der Juden,* VII, Index; Güdemann, *op. cit.,* II, Index.
47. "From childhood on," Zeraḥyah Ḥen proudly declares, "wisdom [i.e., science] raised me like a mother" (*Otzar Neḥmad,* II, 126).
48. *Ibid.,* p. 133.
49. *Ibid.,* p. 123.
50. *Ibid.,* III, 111.
51. See his commentary to Proverbs (*Ha-Shaḥar,* II, 67): "All the loss or damage of those days came first from Pythagoras and his party." Steinschneider concludes that this is a mistake, that it should read not Pythagoras, but Epicurus (see *Hebräische Bibliographie,* XII, 46).
52. Zeraḥyah himself indicates (*Otzar Neḥmad,* II, 123 and 137) that he composed a commentary to the Pentateuch. This commentary apparently was lost.
53. See his letter to Hillel of Verona in *ibid.,* pp. 129 and 131.
54. *Ibid.,* pp. 129 and 138.

the whole story from beginning to end is merely a dream which the prophet saw in sleep." Zeraḥyah also speaks mockingly of the view, accepted at that time everywhere in learned circles, that the first language which mankind spoke was Hebrew, and that Adam, as soon as he was created, spoke the holy tongue.[55] In Rome, where he lived until his old age,[56] Zeraḥyah, in an altogether free, rationalist spirit, used to read before a group of intellectually curious young people lectures on Biblical books, especially on Job and Proverbs.[57] The commentaries on these two books[58] which the Spanish freethinker composed have come down to us in full and are fascinating cultural documents of that era.

Like Maimonides and Jacob Anatoli, Zeraḥyah was persuaded that the literal meaning of the Book of Proverbs is merely for "ignorant fools" whose limited minds cannot grasp profound allusions and parables and who "therefore run away from them as one runs from the bite of a poisonous snake." In Proverbs another, deeper meaning is hidden, and this only the elect few can understand. "Our great teacher, the light of the exile, Rabbi Moses ben Maimon," Zeraḥyah declares, "was the first who pointed out the proper way to understand the true meaning of Proverbs. He explained that this work teaches us how we must not let ourselves be led astray by matter, which in Proverbs bears the veiled name 'woman.' "[59]

In Zeraḥyah's commentary the Biblical book of wisdom obtains an extremely odd appearance. It is no longer a popular book, but a purely philosophic, rationalist work. A well-known passage in Proverbs reads, "Wisdom has built her house; she has hewn out her seven pillars" (9:1). For Zeraḥyah it is clear that the seven pillars are the seven scientific disciplines, and he lists them by name. It is written further in Proverbs, "She has sent out her maidens." For our commentator there is no doubt that by "maidens" are meant the auxiliary sciences, e.g., logic and the like. Typical is the following. On the verse "A false witness speaks lies and sows con-

55. *Ibid.*, pp. 135–36.
56. In his first letter to Hillel of Verona, written in 1290, he reports that he is preparing to return home "in order to lie with his fathers" (see *Otzar Neḥmad*, II, 124).
57. In his commentary to Job, Zeraḥyah Ḥen indicates that he read lectures "in the company of the delightful youths in the community of Rome."
58. The commentary to Proverbs under the title *Imrei Daat* was written by Zeraḥyah in 1284, and reworked and edited in Rome in 1288–89. It was published by I. Schwartz in *Ha-Shahar*, II (it also appeared separately). The commentary to Job, entitled *Tikvat Enosh*, was composed in 1290 and published by Y. Schwartz in 1868.
59. See *Ha-Shaḥar*, II, 67.

flict among brethren" (6:19), Zeraḥyah comments: "This is said of those who stir up conflict and hatred between men of the same faith who have one Torah and the same morality." As an example he cites the schism between the Jews and the Karaites, "the animosity between whom is so great that it is not to be believed that their faith is from one source; they do not even intermarry with each other, so great is their mutual enmity." This terrible hatred and ferocious struggle broke out, in Zeraḥyah's opinion, only because of personal motives, greed for honor and thirst for power and sovereignty.

> Indeed, this accursed desire for dominion, this pursuit of honor leads man away from the right path. . . . It is the real reason why various faiths have multiplied among men and there are so many ways of serving God. The Creator, however, set the world on another order: all men on earth ought to have one faith, and all alike, like true brothers, ought to serve Him.[60]

Zeraḥyah recognizes clearly that such talk smacks of extreme heresy. "I know," he says, "that these words will greatly enrage many, but I have no fear. Let my thought remain alien to hundreds who do not understand, as long as the single chosen one will appreciate it."[61] It is characteristic of the intellectual tendencies in the Jewish circles of that time in Rome that a man with such radical ideas achieved great success and found numerous adherents who eagerly imbibed his words.[62]

But Zeraḥyah was suddenly attacked by an antagonist, not from the "hundreds who do not understand" but from one of his own camp. His extreme rationalistic views occasioned a long controversy with an old friend who was also a devoted follower of Maimonides. This adversary was the philosopher and physician Hillel ben Samuel of Verona.[63]

60. See *ibid.*, p. 213.
61. *Ibid.*
62. Zeraḥyah himself frequently emphasizes this. In his second letter to Hillel of Verona he proudly declares: "For the scholars of my generation who have heard my words and seen what I have written and what I have expounded have all said: 'Here is one through whom the spirit of God speaks, and its word is upon his tongue' " (*Otzar Neḥmad*, II, 126).
63. On Hillel of Verona, see Steinschneider, Preface to *Tagmulei Ha-Nefesh;* Edelmann, in the Preface to *Ḥemdah Genuzah;* Vogelstein and Rieger, *op. cit.*, I, 400–409 and 415–18; Weiss, *Dor Dor Ve-Doreshav*, IV, 103–6; Bernfeld, *Daat Elohim*, pp. 406–16; Güdemann, *op. cit.*, II, Index; Graetz, *op. cit.*, Index. We have not had the opportunity to see the monograph of M. Geier, *Hillels aus Verona Tagmulei Ha-Nefesh,* which appeared in 1912.

Like many other young people in Italy with an intense desire for knowledge, Hillel ben Samuel went in his youth to Spain. In Barcelona he studied natural sciences for three years.[64] At the same time, he was a student in the *yeshivah* of the Talmudist Jonah Gerondi.[65] Later Hillel studied medicine in Montpellier and returned home a trained physician. He spent some years in Rome where he made acquaintances in the philosophically enlightened circles. Later Hillel went to Capua, where he gave systematic lectures on philosophy. In his old age he settled in the city of Forli as a practicing physician, occupying himself also with pure science. Proficient in Arabic and Latin, Hillel translated numerous philosophical and medical works.[66] His favorite thinker was Maimonides. He wrote a commentary to the famous twenty-five philosophical theses with which the second part of *A Guide for the Perplexed* begins and proudly asserted that "at present among Jews there is no one who understands Maimonides' *Guide* better and more profoundly than I."[67] Hillel attacked Naḥmanides because the latter permitted himself to assert that some of Maimonides' ideas contradict certain views of the Talmud and Midrashim. He found Naḥmanides' arguments "superficial, tasteless, without seasoning." And in the 1280's, at the beginning of the anti-Maimunist movement headed by Solomon Petit, who came for propaganda purposes from anterior Asia to Italy, Hillel addressed the prominent patron Isaac ben Mordecai in Rome and begged him to employ all means to prevent Solomon's propaganda from succeeding.[68] He also wrote to Maimonides' grandson Rabbi David and to the foremost rabbis of Egypt and Babylonia, requesting them to calm the German and French rabbis who were waging war against Mai-

64. See *Tagmulei Ha-Nefesh*, p. 18a.
65. In his letter to the patron Isaac ben Mordecai, Hillel notes that "in his youth" he studied three years with Rabbi Jonah, who immediately thereafter went to Toledo, where he died a year later (*Taam Zekenim*, p. 72a). From his well-preserved tombstone it is known that Jonah Gerondi died in Heshvan 1263, and so Hillel ben Samuel studied with him in the period 1259–62. From this it is clear that Graetz is mistaken when he suggests that Hillel was born in the year 1220. We see that at the beginning of the 1260's he was still in "his youth." Thus he was born no earlier than the end of the 1230's.
66. On his translations, see Steinschneider's preface to *Tagmulei Ha-Nefesh*. See also Vogelstein and Rieger, *op. cit.*, I, 403.
67. See *Taam Zekenim*, p. 72a.
68. Two of his letters to Majestro Gajo (Isaac ben Mordecai) have been preserved. Especially interesting is the first (printed in *Ḥemdah Genuzah*, *Taam Zekenim*, and also in *Iggerot Kenaot*), for it contains some very important details relating to the first battle against Maimonides and his works.

monides' works. He proposed that they convene a conference of the most respected rabbis, listen to the arguments of both sides, and then have the conference reach a definite decision that would be final and valid for all.[69]

Quite in the spirit of Maimonides, Hillel interprets many passages in the Bible in a rationalist manner, and declares that the legend of the rebellious angels who fell and were changed into evil spirits and destroyers is "a foolish, fabricated superstition."[70] Nevertheless, the old Italian traditions were not entirely stifled in the rationalist Hillel, and he did not always concur with the views of his "great teacher," as he calls Maimonides. Jacob Anatoli's arid, logically consistent rationalism found no echo in Hillel's soul, which unconsciously longed for the ancient traditions and for mystical religious experiences. The poetic world of the tales stemming from Babylonia and Palestine, the naive legends of old Italy from the time of Abu Aharon and Shephatyah the miracle-worker and liturgical poet, were not forgotten and still found a welcome response in dreaming spirits. Hillel was a genuinely fervent admirer of Maimonides, but he could not believe that thought and reason alone are essential, and that the heart, with its world of feelings and dreams, is merely secondary. Maimonides' *Guide* was, to be sure, the profoundest of books for him, but he could not assent to the view that man's happiness as well as his value must be measured only according to the acuteness of his thought and the subtlety of his philosophical conceptions. He therefore decided to write a work on the human soul, to investigate its nature and essence, to analyze its experiences, and to throw light on the question of its further existence after it frees itself from earthly matter and leaves the body. He completed this work, which he entitled *Tagmulei Ha-Nefesh*, in Forli in 1291.[71]

The book is written in a cumbersome, wooden style. In places the author lacks suitable words and invents his own rather unsuccessful ones, explaining them in Italian, so that the reader may understand what he means. Nevertheless, the hidden fire of an inner conflict, the pathos of a searching, restless spirit, is evident in this work, and the book with its difficult, clumsy language draws the attention of the reader against his will.[72]

69. See *Taam Zekenim*, p. 72b.
70. See Supplements to *Tagmulei Ha-Nefesh*, p. 54.
71. Published by the Mekitzei Nirdamim Society under the editorship of S. J. Halberstam in 1874.
72. The author himself proudly notes that he is the first both among Jews and Christians to attempt to illuminate such problems philosophically (see *Ḥemdah Genuzah*, p. 22; *Tagmulei Ha-Nefesh*, p. 7b).

*Tagmulei Ha-Nefesh* is divided into two parts. In the first the nature of the soul is considered. The second part deals with the question of "the rewards of the soul," the kind of recompense and punishment that await it. After extensive logical and philosophical discussion, the author comes to the conclusion that the essence of the soul is a purely spiritual one, free of the least material addition, and that it is immortal. Hillel then confronts the difficult question: what is the nature of this immortality? Does the soul survive by itself as a separate, independent ego, or is the view of Averroes and his disciples correct, that denies the individual survival of the soul and maintains that after man's death it no longer exists separately but rather as a part of the so-called active intellect which is incorporated in mankind as a whole? Hillel admits that Averroes' theory is undoubtedly based on solid logical foundations which recommend themselves strongly to the mind.[73] But it is obvious to him that once there is no immortality of the soul for the individual, there can be no talk of reward or punishment.[74] Hillel considers the ancient foundations too precious to be content with such a conclusion. He seeks means of escaping from the dilemma, and he believes he has found a solution in which "the peace between reason and faith is not destroyed."[75]

Like all the thinkers of his age, Hillel emphasizes the great distinction between immortal form and transient matter. The "world spirit" (the *sechel ha-poel* or active intellect, as it is called in medieval Hebrew literature) as general or universal spiritual form is the source of countless separate, independent forms, "just as from one central point many lines are drawn in all directions."[76] These separate, independent forms that emanate from the world spirit or active intellect are the human souls. How is the immortality of these souls realized? First the author explains at length, proceeding from Aristotle's view, how man's inborn intellectual potentiality (*ha-sechel ha-efshari*) develops in him to the degree that it becomes a part of the active intellect. Hillel further follows Aristotle's system when he divides human reason into three levels —the technical (*melachuti*), the practical (*maasi*), and the theoretical-speculative (*iyyuni*).[77] Later, however, Hillel abandons both Aristotle and his Jewish interpreter, Maimonides. Taking the position that in the perfect man all the qualities of his spirit must be

73. *Tagmulei Ha-Nefesh*, p. 10a.
74. *Ibid.*, p. 14b.
75. *Ibid.*, p. 10a.
76. *Ibid.*, p. 8b.
77. *Ibid.*, p. 21b.

harmoniously developed, he cannot agree that only man's rational part (*ha-ḥelek ha-sichli*), i.e., only the intellect, is deathless. I wish to demonstrate, he insists, that man's feeling and moral striving are also immortal.[78] Do not think, he further says, that man can attain the summit of perfection only through the development of reason, not caring about the moral demands of the soul. Our sages have remarked that to him who only hones his mind, who gathers knowledge alone and does not think of good deeds, the phrase "a golden ring in the nose of a pig" applies.[79] One must also remember the other two powers of the soul, feeling and will (*koaḥ ha-margish ve-koaḥ ha-meorer*). Only through their aid can man actually demonstrate his perfection, his immortal spirit.[80] Hillel reiterates that with thought and keenness of intellect alone man cannot attain the acme of perfection; besides knowledge, ethical behavior is also necessary. A man must show through deeds that he fulfills God's commandments; he must demonstrate that not only in his thought but also in his feeling and will is he devoted to the divine and holy.[81] And let no one dare, Hillel further admonishes, to interpret the commandments and ordinances of the Torah merely as allegories and parables. Let him not say: As long as I understand the reason and meaning of a given commandment, why must I also fulfill it? He who speaks thus is a "heretic." He actually denies the Torah of Moses.[82] Only he whose intellect, harmoniously connected with his will and feeling (*ha-koḥot ha-maskilot veha-margishot*), is directed to one high, divine goal is the righteous man of the generation, the elect and perfect man.

Precisely in this, the author of *Tagmulei Ha-Nefesh* maintains, lies the profound mystery: to what end must the immortal soul wander in the garment of earthly matter? Because this is the way of perfection, because thereby the soul attains a more exalted level. For it is clear that the soul, when it separates from the body, is more perfect than before it pilgrimaged through man's life on earth. It is on a far higher level than even the ministering angels, for an angel or a spirit which has never been associated with a human body has no will or desire. Angels are bright and pure according to their spiritual nature; they have not the power to be otherwise. They do not even know that one can be different—impure, unclean. It is quite otherwise, however, with the soul that is connected with sinful matter. Through arduous struggle,

78. *Ibid.*, p. 9b.
79. *Ibid.*, p. 22a.
80. *Ibid.*
81. *Ibid.*, p. 22b.
82. *Ibid.*, p. 25a.

through constant and strenuous exertion of the will, it succeeds in overcoming the desires of the body and in exalting and sanctifying it. Such a soul, which has triumphed over the sinful and the low through the hard way of strenuous battle and remained pure, has thereby raised itself to a much loftier level and come closer to the divine source of light than before it wandered over the terrestrial world and fought through its human life. And the privilege of attaining such a high level—this is its "world to come," its paradise.[83] The soul, however, which has not passed the test of the sinful body and has desecrated itself is thereby thrust away from the source of light and purity. It gropes in darkness, and this pain and affliction is its punishment. In eternal wondering and longing consists the punishment of hell.[84]

Hillel repeatedly maintains that it is not merely the rational part of man's soul that is immortal, as Aristotle and Maimonides think, but also the emotional, which is bound up with the moral sentiment.[85] Along with this, however, he does not forget the doctrine of Maimonides' *Guide for the Perplexed* and insists that reward and punishment in the next world are to be understood in a purely spiritual sense.[86] To be sure, Hillel must admit that in the Talmud and Midrashim corporeal reward and punishment in the world to come are frequently spoken of. And if in some places this may be interpreted as parable and allegory, there is no doubt that in many passages the text must be understood literally. This, explains Hillel, is because our sages and Tannaim, when they spoke to the multitude, "the he-goats in the form of men," were compelled to speak in language their listeners would be able to comprehend. The multitude was so ignorant that it could understand reward and punishment only in corporeal forms.[87]

It is not difficult to see that our Italian rationalist did not always succeed "in making peace between faith and philosophy." Not everything in his religious-philosophical structure is consistent and well fitted together. Internal contradictions are noticeable in it because different aspirations conflict in the author himself. This rationalist and disciple of Maimonides and Averroes had such reverence for the ancient traditions that he even regarded the fantastic tales of Ḥoni Ha-Meagel and Naḥum Ish Gimzo as pure truth.[88] Not without effect did Hillel grow up in Italy, the home

83. *Ibid.*, pp. 23–24.
84. *Ibid.*, p. 24b.
85. *Ibid.*, p. 23a.
86. *Ibid.*, p. 24a.
87. *Ibid.*, pp. 27a–28a.
88. *Ibid.*, p. 26a.

of the mystical tendencies imported from anterior Asia which later played such a significant role in the culture of European Jewry.

It is not surprising, therefore, that so consistent and obdurate a rationalist as the Spaniard Zeraḥyah Ḥen, to whom any kind of compromise was alien, could not be at all satisfied with Hillel's philosophy. It seemed to him vague and full of contradictions. When Hillel in 1290 addressed a letter to Zeraḥyah, as an old acquaintance,[89] with an inquiry regarding the correct meaning of several obscure passages in *A Guide for the Perplexed*, a heated controversy between these two very different disciples of Maimonides promptly flared up. Zeraḥyah immediately defines the issue. He declares that there can be no talk of "making peace between faith and philosophy." "When you concern yourself with philosophical problems," he writes to Hillel, "do not try to compare them with the opinions of the sages of the Talmud, for these opinions are not consonant with the views of the philosophers. This can only create great confusion, as indeed happened with many of our scholars, among them Naḥmanides in his commentary to the Torah."[90]

Zeraḥyah is particularly unable to pardon the Italian Maimunist for his attitude toward the miracles related in the Bible and Talmud. "In regard to this question," Zeraḥyah writes in his letter to Hillel, "you are like the Ashkenazim, the German rabbis who dwell in darkness and have never seen a ray of light."[91] Zeraḥyah knows that Hillel considers Naḥmanides a very slight authority in philosophical matters. For this reason he points out sarcastically that Hillel himself is no greater expert than Naḥmanides in this area. "Why," he asks mockingly, "do you concern yourself with such exalted matters? Better turn to the traditions of the fathers, wrap yourself in a prayer shawl, immerse yourself in long devotions, read the *Sefer Yetzirah* and the Book of Ben Sira, investigate the *Shiur Ha-Komah* and the *Sefer Ha-Razim*,[92] and leave philosophy and natural science alone."[93]

It is worth noting that the philosophical circles sided with Zeraḥyah in this dispute. The most important personality of Italian Jewry of that era—the young poet Immanuel of Rome, the fresh, laughing spirit of the newly awakened Renaissance springtime—also issued forth against Hillel of Verona.

89. Zeraḥyah declares in his second letter to Hillel: "I have loved you for a long time" (*Otzar Neḥmad*, II, 126). It appears that they first met in Zeraḥyah's birthplace, Barcelona, when Hillel studied there.

90. *Otzar Neḥmad*, II, 125.

91. *Ibid.*, 137.

92. The *Shiur Ha-Komah* and the *Sefer Ha-Razim* are Kabbalist books.

93. *Otzar Neḥmad*, II, 142.

# CHAPTER FIVE

## *Immanuel of Rome*

FREDERICK II's court was not only a center of scientific knowledge. To a degree, it was also the cradle of the newborn Italian national literature. Here the *gaja scianza* blossomed. Frederick's court was a place of refuge for the troubadours who fled Provence after the Albigensian war, as well as for the Italian poets, who initially wrote their poetry in the Provençal dialect. Around the enlightened and versatile emperor, who himself composed love songs, also gathered the first Italian poets who attempted to write verse in their own dialect. At first these took as their models the Provençal poets, but the old-fashioned, knightly tones of Provençal poetry were soon displaced by new forms produced by new ways of life. The republics of Tuscany and Lombardy in the thirteenth century attained the peak of their splendor. The larger cities of northern Italy—Venice, Milan, Genoa, and others—flourished, and their economic and cultural advance proceeded at a remarkably rapid rate. Social life was extremely dynamic, and the greater the political and cultural role of the democratic urban elements grew, the more the popular dialect, the speech of the masses, displaced Latin, which, until late in the Middle Ages, was the language of the higher, educated classes. Gradually the Tuscan dialect, which, thanks to the learned stylist Guido Cavalcanti, was enriched with many new forms, obtained dominance and the genius of Dante all at once raised it to the level of a national literary language.

As a result of the dynamic and intense life in the cities and republics, the constant struggle between political parties, and the frequent change of political forms and ways of life, the medieval barriers between different classes and social circles were least noticeable in Italy. The individual here felt much more free, and enjoyed the opportunity to express his own will without restraint. The ascetic world view of the Middle Ages, with its contempt for "sinful" secular concerns and constant fear of the "evil inclination," could no longer satisfy the urban Italian citizen, who had awakened to new, conscious life. Ever sharper and clearer became the awareness that "this world" is not sinful, that not only heaven, "the other world," but also the real human world, with all its yearnings and desires, is of great value and significance. These new tendencies first found a strong echo in the budding Italian national literature. This literature was the harbinger of the humanist movement; in it were first heard the triumphant notes of the new poetry, the powerful song of the sweet earth. The joyous secular lyric, filled with love of life, appeared. The poet Guittone d'Arezzo introduced the sonnet into Italian literature, and this ingenious form was promptly utilized by Italian poetry. The dim, melancholy atmosphere of medieval scholasticism was sundered by laughter, and the sharp arrows of happy humor and mockery glittered.

These new moods were powerfully echoed in Jewish intellectual circles, especially in the wealthy Roman community which, at the end of the thirteenth century, attained the zenith of its cultural and economic advance. Numerous documents of that era have a great deal to say about the carefree life, dazzling luxury, banquets with the finest food and drink, and elegant clothing and ornamentation in the Roman community.[1] Of the spiritual tendencies, the impetuous drive for knowledge and free inquiry that dominated the intellectual circles of the Jewish community of Rome, we have spoken in the previous chapter. It was in this milieu that the lusty song of Immanuel of Rome with its loud laughter arose and flourished.

Of the life of this oldest significant Jewish poet of the Italian Renaissance era we have only the scanty information to be found in his own work. Immanuel was born in Rome around the year 1265. His father Solomon ben Yekutiel was a scion of the wealthy and prominent Cipróni family which had settled in Rome in dim

1. On this subject see Vogelstein and Rieger, *Geschichte der Juden in Rom*, pp. 237–38, 280–85. See also the previously mentioned satires, *Massa Ge Ḥizzayon* and *Masechat Purim* of Kalonymos ben Kalonymos.

antiquity.[2] The young Immanuel received an excellent education. He studied Talmud with the foremost rabbis and also devoted much attention to the natural sciences, especially medicine. The rationalist Zeraḥyah Ḥen taught him Greek-Arabic philosophy. All this, however, did not hinder his enjoyment of the pleasures of life. He himself relates how in his younger years, together with a bosom friend, he used to spend his time in the company of beautiful women, and describes how the two friends greatly angered the community guardians of piety with their way of life. The pious elders and leaders of the city shook their heads indignantly over the two "profligate youths" who violated the Jewish religion because they looked into "improper books" and studied Greek philosophy, which is more poisonous than the "vineyards of Sodom."[3] This mode of life did not, however, stifle Immanuel's thirst for knowledge. Proudly he notes, "I have spent more money on lamp oil than others have on wine."[4]

Extremely industrious and splendidly gifted, Immanuel acquired encyclopedic knowledge. His favorite occupation and true love, however, was poetry. Proficient in both Arabic and Latin, he found the poetry of the Moslem as well as the Christian worlds readily accessible. The Italian language and literature were so precious to him that he considered himself a true Italian. "My home," he proudly notes, "is Rome, and my people the Italians."[5] Immanuel also participated in the new Italian national poetry and, through his excellent Italian sonnets, became prominent in literary and learned circles. "The happily laughing soul" (*la mente tua, che gia ridea*) the Jewish poet is called by Dante's friend Bosone. Thanks to the now published sonnets which Bosone and Immanuel exchanged after Dante's death and those which Bosone exchanged with the poet Cino of Pistoja,[6] there is no longer any doubt that Immanuel was acquainted with Italy's great genius, the immortal creator of the *Divine Comedy*. It is still not clear where the two poets first met. Some believe it was in Rome, others in Verona at the court of the prince Can Grande della Scala. This princely

2. According to an old legend the Ciproni family settled in Rome in the days of Titus.
3. *Maḥberot, Makama* 9.
4. *Ibid.*, p. 10. We quote following the Lemberg edition of 1870, because it is the most easily obtainable. The text here, however, is much more erroneous than in the two oldest editions, that of Italy and of Constantinople.
5. *Ibid.*, p. 14.
6. These sonnets were first printed by Philip Mercury in 1853; reprinted in the Russian-Jewish journal *Voskhod*, I (1906), 114–17.

court, at which brilliant balls and banquets were constantly being held, was a gathering place for scholars, artists, and poets from all over Italy.[7] Dante spent three years (1316–19) there. Immanuel was also a frequent guest, as attested by his Italian poem[8] in which he celebrates the glory of Verona's prince. "How happy," the poet concludes his paean, "must this prince, whose praise is spread over land and sea, be in his great might."[9]

In the Roman Jewish community Immanuel occupied an honored office. He conducted its official correspondence and was also required on certain ceremonial occasions to give public addresses. In his old age, however, fortune suddenly turned away from him and he had to suffer many trials. With his cutting sallies, his mockery and pointed epigrams, he had acquired many secret enemies. Immanuel promptly experienced their animosity when a misfortune befell him: through serving as guarantor to help a needy friend,[10] he lost his entire fortune. Then his foes began to persecute the poet as a "godless" and "profligate" man. Immanuel was compelled to flee from Rome and become a wanderer, bent, as he puts it, "under the double burden of old age and poverty." He laments his sorrows in two poems, "Ereh Zemani" and "Havirkat Ha-Zeman."

"O time, bitter time," laments the poet,

> in twain has it torn my robe of honor, and I stand naked and uncovered. . . . Bitter time has pierced my ear like a slave's—as token of eternal servitude. Everything is forgotten! They pursue me, they pour gall and mockery over me, like the most wretched of men. But yesterday I was the pride of the community; today, the sinful outcast of the people. . . . Who could have believed it: he who only yesterday, with his wisdom and spirit, aroused amazement and reverence, is today made by every fool and good-for-nothing the butt of his dull-minded wit. Who could have believed that over the depths of his knowledge every lame and blind man would arrogantly tread and every petty ignoramus impudently declare, "This man blasphemed God; he is a debauched and immoral person." . . . Before whom shall I lament,

7. See Jacob Burckhardt, *Die Kultur des Renaissance in Italien*, I (1908), 9.
8. Published by Leonello Modona in *Il Vesillo Israelitico*, XXXIII (1884), 380–86.
9. *Ibid.*, p. 386:

   Et questo è'l Signore
   Di tanto valore
   Ch'el suo grande honore
   Va per terra et per mare.

10. The poet himself indicates: "I was guarantor for my friend and gave my hand to a stranger" (*Maḥberot*, p. 3).

before whom pour out my woe? I am forsaken by all—fatherless, motherless, brotherless, friendless. No one will hear my cries. Barred before me are the paths of life, and the gates of death opened wide.

Fortunately for Hebrew poetry, the wandering poet did not remain "forsaken by all." Immanuel found a savior, a rich patron in Fermo, in the Marca D'Ancona, who greatly admired his talent. In his home the aged and persecuted poet found refuge and rest. Suddenly and unexpectedly a new and fruitful period of creativity began for the spiritually broken Immanuel. Life in the home of the Jewish magnate, which the poet portrays in the most vivid colors, revived his love of life. This maecenas (he calls him "the prince") suggested to Immanuel that he collect all his poems into one work. The poet replied that "it is easier to bring together the Jews scattered over the entire world" than to make a single thing out of his dispersed poems, but he followed his "prince's" suggestion. In his patron's home Immanuel around 1328 reworked his poems and novellas into twenty-seven *makama*s, in which the chief person is played by himself and the role of the second person is taken by the "prince."

It is no accident that Immanuel gave his work the *makama* form. Of all the earlier Jewish poets, it was Jehudah Alḥarizi, the famous *makama* poet and author of *Taḥkemoni*, who had the profoundest influence on him. Immanuel himself admits this. To his patron's question whether Alḥarizi's songs are known to him, the poet answers enthusiastically: "Know, my lord, that with Alḥarizi's pearls I adorn my neck. They are our loveliest ornament, for in poetry he has no peer."[11]

Immanuel, however, surpassed his teacher. To be sure, the much-travelled Alharizi saw more of the world than Immanuel, who spent all his life in Italy, and his *makama*s therefore move in a much broader arena than Immanuel's. On the other hand, the Italian poet is deeper and more versatile. Immanuel is doubtless one of the most interesting and original Jewish figures of the Middle Ages. In his person as well as his work the influences of two different civilizations, two great spiritual movements, were harmoniously blended: the Judeo-Arabic of the Spanish era and the Italian of Dante's time, the dawn of the Renaissance era.

In philosophy the greatest authority for Immanuel, as for his teacher Zeraḥyah Ḥen, was Maimonides. To the question of the "prince" as to which books he had read most eagerly in his youth,

11. *Maḥberot*, beginning of the ninth *makama*. For a discussion of Alḥarizi's influence on Immanuel's poetry, see Z. Hayyut in *Ha-Kedem*, 1906, p. 49, and Sabato Morais, *Italian Hebrew Literature* (1926), pp. 9–10.

the poet replies fervently: "The books of our teacher, Moses ben Maimon. He is the surest guide on the paths of knowledge. He is the light that illuminates everything deep and hidden. . . . His books are queens; all others are merely concubines."[12]

The "articles of faith," in which Maimonides made the first attempt to formulate the essence of Judaism in thirteen principles, produced such a strong impression on Immanuel that he composed a religious-philosophical poem, "Eftaḥ Be-Chinor Al Alamot Shir,"[13] in which he celebrates with great feeling the "thirteen foundations of the Jewish religion." There is even a slight possibility that the well-known prayer "Yigdal Elohim Ḥai," which is similar in spirit and content to the poem just mentioned, was also written by Immanuel.[14]

As a faithful disciple of Maimonides, Immanuel also believed that man can approach the divine only by way of inquiry, by delving into philosophical problems and penetrating through searching thought into the essence of the God concept. "Wisdom," says the poet, "is a ladder whose feet rest on the earth and whose top reaches the heavens; and the higher man ascends the ladder of knowledge, the closer he comes to God."[15] Both in his poetic and prose[16] works, Immanuel constantly emphasizes the extreme importance of scientific investigation. When his friends asked him how he had obtained so much knowledge, he answered, "Because I have subordinated all things to my spirit and have not allowed the things to rule over my spirit."[17] In his poem *Ha-Tofet Veha-Eden*

12. *Maḥberot, Makama* 9, p. 85.
13. Published by Hirschfeld in *JQR*, V, 534–36.
14. *Ibid.*, p. 529; *ibid.*, XI, 86–88.
15. *Maḥberot*, p. 224.
16. Immanuel composed numerous philological and exegetical works. Besides his handbook on Jewish hermeneutics, *Even Boḥan* (on this interesting work, which is still in manuscript, see Bacher in *MGWJ*, 1885, pp. 241–57), Immanuel wrote a commentary to most of the books of the Bible. In his explanations he is faithful to Zeraḥyah Ḥen's way and employs the rationalist-allegorical method. Only his commentary on Proverbs, which was very popular at that time, was printed (1486). In modern times the Italian scholars De Rossi and Abbé Perreau published several fragments of his commentary to Psalms and the Pentateuch. Of the remainder of his prose works some were lost and others are in the manuscript collections of the Parma, Vatican, and other libraries. Immanuel's commentary to the Song of Songs was printed in 1908 from a manuscript in Munich. Hectographed copies of his commentary to Psalms and the Scroll of Esther are to be found in Leningrad in the library of the Society for Dissemination of Enlightenment Among Jews.
17. *Maḥberot*, p. 10.

he points out a special corner in hell for those who are concerned only with corporeal pleasures and do not think of knowledge and spiritual perfection. Also detained in hell for terrible sufferings, he believes, are those who "considered the study of science foolishness." There also are those who "know how to appreciate the value of knowledge but do not follow its precepts" and who keep to themselves the knowledge they have obtained "and are unwilling to disseminate it among others." As a disciple of Zeraḥyah Ḥen, Immanuel was convinced that the way leading to true knowledge of God lies in the realm of philosophical investigation rather than within the established boundaries of dogmatic religion. Hence he makes no distinction between men of various faiths. In one of his Italian sonnets which has come down to us, he frankly admits, "I am not a good Jew, but also no Moslem, and I do not follow the doctrine of the Christians."[18]

Here is revealed most clearly the profound difference in the world view and in the cultural ambience distinguishing Immanuel from his brilliant friend Dante Alighieri. The author of the *Divine Comedy* with his master pen drew up the great summation, the final account, of the Christian Middle Ages. To be sure, in producing his synthesis of the past, Dante was also the harbinger of a new era. But his stern, melancholy gaze is always directed to the past, to the medieval Christian world. His guiding star over the narrow pathways of life remains the Catholic Church with the pope as its spiritual leader. The "present world" is still for him the sinful world. Earthly life is the "thick forest" in which he was lost, and only the emissary of heaven, the angelically pure Beatrice, shows him the way "to the heights, to the stars." Thus, it is no surprise that Dante does not allow into heaven a single person of a different faith who did not have the privilege of being "sanctified" through Christian baptism.

Quite different is the attitude of the Jewish poet Immanuel, the disciple of the rationalist Zeraḥyah Ḥen and ardent admirer of the great battler for freedom of thought, Maimonides. Immanuel opens the gates of heaven wide for all who believe in different religions but have faith in one God, in a single "cause" that created the world, and also expresses[19] liberal ideas that must have appeared truly heretical at that time. He relates how he met in heaven certain unknown persons whose "glory dazzles the sun and the stars." Astonished, he asks his guide, Daniel Ish Ḥamudot, who these persons are, and receives the reply:

18. Mal judeo so, e no saracino
Ver cristiani no drezo la proda.

19. In *Ha-Tofet Veha-Eden.*

These are the righteous of the peoples of the world who rose to the highest levels of knowledge and wisdom. . . . With their reason they inquired who their creator and the author of the world is and to what end they were created. . . . They investigated all faiths and became convinced that each considers itself the only true one and all others false. But they were not satisfied with this. They did not say, "Let us cleave to our faith which we have inherited from our fathers," but out of all religions they chose the true opinions which men of knowledge do not deny, and to these they held fast. . . . With regard to the question of God they came to the following conclusion: every people calls Him by a different name, but we say, whatever name He may have, we believe in the first creative power which exists throughout all eternity and which created the world and leads it in wisdom. Hidden and incomprehensible because of His greatness, He reveals Himself to us in His wisdom and grace which He pours out on all creatures and then calls them back to Himself and illuminates them with His glory.[20]

Immanuel of Rome, however, is not only a follower of Maimonides and under the influence of Spanish-Arabic culture; he is also a typical representative of the newly awakened Italian Renaissance. In him the aspirations that had just been aroused in Italian society, the movements to throw off the yoke of the ascetic world view of the Middle Ages, to be rid of all the eternal worries about the next world, to overcome the constant fear of sin and let the thirst for earthly happiness and joy in life, the feeling for beauty, and the pleasures of love and passion flourish freely—all find the clearest resonance.

Properly to appreciate Immanuel's significance, we must remember that as a lyric poet, he was a predecessor of Petrarch and, as a satirist, of Boccaccio. Petrarch, the "first man of the modern age," suffered terribly from inner spiritual conflict, from a deep "rent in his heart" from which he could never liberate himself. He set forth the great slogan "Freedom of thought," but the medieval view of the world still dominated him. His desire for earthly glory and pleasure was powerful, but at the same time he was also a great "penitent," constantly reciting *mea culpa* for his sins, wishing to forget the present world, and prepared to declare the love sonnets that immortalized him "empty little songs" (*cantiuncule inanes*). Until his death, in his heart "took place a painful struggle between heaven and earth, between the thirst for earthly happiness and longing for the other world, between the Madonna and the beloved Laura, between Cicero and Christ."[21]

20. *Maḥberot,* p. 230.
21. M. Gershenson, *Petrarka,* p. 31 (Russian).

Immanuel, who was older than Petrarch, was in this respect much more fortunate. He also, as we shall see, was not altogether free of doubts. He, too, was not infrequently assailed by melancholy thoughts, but he did not know of any conflict, of any "rent in the heart." Immanuel did not obtain freedom of thought through difficult, painful struggle, as did Petrarch; he inherited it from his teacher Zeraḥyah Ḥen and from Maimonides' *Guide for the Perplexed.* And the ascetic ideal of renouncing the world, mortifying the sinful body, and overcoming the "evil inclination"—all this could have very little attraction for one raised on Alḥarizi's *Taḥkemoni.* A harbinger of the dawning Renaissance era, Immanuel became the poet of desire and passion, the prophet and preacher of earthly love with all its joys and sorrows, triumphs and regrets. If knowledge and inquiry are the way bringing man closer to God, love—Immanuel was convinced—is the most important dynamic power in man's life on earth.

Love, he writes in his commentary to the Song of Songs, is the central point of the whole Torah.[22] In one of his Italian sonnets he declares,

> Love does not care to know of laws or statutes. It is deaf and blind. It does not wish to know of hindrances. Boundless is its power, not to be turned aside are its wishes. Love rules the whole world; the earth is filled with its mighty demands. Unconquerable is love; powerless against it are "Our Father" and other prayers, and all incantations and amulets can be of no avail. Its pride can be broken by no one; none can oppose its will. No one can avoid the nets which lusty Amor[23] spreads, and to all my arguments and pleas I hear ever the same answer: "I wish it so!"[24]

In one of his Hebrew songs the poet confesses, "If I were not ashamed before God and did not fear the holy people of Israel, I would build altars to the goddess of love; I would fall on my knees before beautiful women and kiss the dust before their feet."[25]

Immanuel in fact was not "ashamed" and did not have any "fear." In eloquent poems he celebrates the sweet, irresistible power of desire and passion, and "builds sinful altars" to the magic of

22. A much older poet, Moses Ibn Ezra, declares in one of his religious poems that the earth "is cradled in the bands of God's love."
23. The pagan god of love.
24. "Ma sempre mi sa dir: pur cosi voglio!" This sonnet was published by Th. Paur in *Jahrbuch der deutschen Dantegesellschaft,* IV, 67, and reprinted in *Voskhod,* III (1906), 82.
25. *Maḥberot, Makama* 8, p. 58.

feminine beauty, the charm of the female body.[26] Entire *makamas* in Immanuel's collection are paeans to earthly love. In the third *makama*, in which he mockingly relates how he tried to win the heart of a stern young beauty who had taken a vow to lead a solitary life and strictly avoid the company of men, the healthy, defiant laughter of the youthful Renaissance is heard. The poet dispatches to the proud beauty one love song after another and always receives an angry refusal. But he will not desist; ever stormier becomes his song, ever more powerfully sound the passionate chords of love which rise higher and higher until they pour themselves out in flaming, wondrously lovely stanzas.[27] And the poet's songs finally triumph; the proud lady surrenders.

In his love songs, which are among the finest exemplars of medieval Hebrew lyric, Immanuel was the first Jewish poet to make use of the sonnet. This form, which had just been introduced into Italian poetry, he mastered with great artistry. In one of his sonnets he addresses his beloved "young Ophrah":[28]

Who could have believed such a miracle? In the heavens shine your eyes, and the splendor of the stars I behold in the bright day when I regard your radiant face. My beloved, my whole life hangs captivated on the curve of your polished ear. The loveliest treasures from the farthest Orient cannot be compared with it! I am dazzled when you open your eyes! I am enchanted by the magic pearls guarding your carmine lips. O tell me, my dear one, are your wondrous eyes stars from heaven which you capture at dawn and which wander freely in the heavens only through the nights? Or are these stars given to us to illuminate the earth, so that the radiance of your face may remind us of the heavens and the most beautiful of the world know that their charm and grace are, in comparison with your splendor, like a little dust trodden on the ground?[29]

Naturally a prose translation cannot reflect the artistic grace of this sonnet. Nor is it possible to render the beauty of the love scene in which the poet relates how in a blooming garden he meets a lovely lady with whom he falls in love at first glance and how he succeeds in winning her heart. Especially typical of the youthful Renaissance era are the sixteenth and seventeenth *makamas*. The heroine of the sixteenth *makama*, a young lady with a weak, good-

26. His biographers emphasize a characteristic point. Immanuel had a very happy and peaceful family life. From his works we know that he enthusiastically praised the virtues of his wife (*Mahberot*, p. 10), as well as of his father-in-law Samuel and his mother-in-law Brunetta (according to certain manuscripts her name was Beruria).
27. *Mahberot*, p. 24.
28. *Ophrah* means a gazelle or hind in Hebrew.
29. The sonnet "Mi He'emin Ophrah Asher Enayich," *Makama* 16.

for-nothing husband, is convinced that "the woman who dies a virgin is doomed; she loses her share in the world to come."[30] A daughter of her time, she throws off the veil of modesty and in erotic sonnets pours out her indignation and pain over the fact that two years after her wedding she has still not enjoyed the embrace of love. "Ah," she calls out, "how much happier is my friend; in thirty months she has already buried her third husband, but I was born under such an unlucky constellation and am still not quit of my good-for-nothing." Even more characteristic is the seventeenth *makama.* Three gallants, the poet among them, are in love with the same woman, and so they make a wager: they will sing love poems to the beloved, and to the one whose song she prefers she will give her love. It is typical of the poet that this unique tournament takes place in the presence of the woman's oafish husband, and the songs that are sung know of no modesty or bashful allusions. Everything is free and naked. The eroticism of the youthful Renaissance is not hypocritically concealed; it expresses itself openly with triumphant impudence. And Immanuel is the first important poet of this new era, the forerunner of the erotic, lusty tendency which eventually found its classic expression in Boccaccio's *Decameron.*

Immanuel rightly called himself the "master of love and passion," and expressed his conviction that if a crown were given for the most successful erotic poems, he would be the first to receive it.[31] It must, in fact, be admitted that he took no account of the rules of modesty and the prohibition against vulgarity. Such erotic, cynical poems as his "Al Titmah Dod,"[32] "Ech E'etzar Koaḥ,"[33] "Naval Asher Tishal,"[34] "Ophrat Ḥen,"[35] and several others have no analogue in all of Hebrew literature.

Closely connected with Immanuel's erotic poems are his wine songs. Mockingly the poet assures us that he has learned by way of tradition from his grandfathers that he who does not drink wine loses his share in the world to come.[36] An entire *makama* is devoted to wine. Filled with bright, triumphant joy, the impudent poem declares that the power of wine is boundless; it conquers all, intoxicates all, rules over all.[37] Here we encounter the most char-

30. *Maḥberot,* p. 117.
31. *Ibid.,* p. 31.
32. *Ibid., Makama* 7, p. 54.
33. *Ibid.*
34. *Ibid., Makama* 20, p. 156.
35. *Ibid., Makama* 17, p. 129.
36. *Ibid.,* p. 198.
37. *Ibid.,* pp. 199–200.

acteristic feature of the poet's talent—its laughter. Into the stern and gloomy temple of Hebrew poetry, Immanuel's healthy, cheerful laughter rushed defiantly and loudly. And this laughter has no respect for anyone. Immanuel laughs at frivolous young women and explains with a pious mien "in the name of all the rabbis" that "the best guardian of a woman's chastity is an ugly face."[38] He also pokes fun at faded beauties who try to make themselves look young, and mocks himself, who still plays at love in old age and only makes himself ridiculous. Nor does his wit spare young girls who affect too much delicacy,[39] pedantic, dry-as-parchment scholars, miserly rich men, charlatan doctors, talentless rhymesters. More than all, however, he mocks cuckolded husbands whose wives put horns on their heads. Here the poet often passes beyond the bounds of decency, but in this he was merely reflecting the spirit of his age.

Full of wit and laughter is the second *makama*, where a comparison is drawn between two women, the dazzlingly beautiful Tamar and the appallingly ugly Beriah. When Tamar lifts her eyes to the heavens, all the stars laugh with joy toward her. When she turns her glance to the earth, the dead in their graves immediately awaken. But Beriah with her glance kills the most venomous snakes; Satan himself runs away in terror when he sees her face. The human tongue cannot describe Tamar's beauty; if angels saw her, they would recognize their sister in her. Beriah is very useful for ripened vineyards; her frightful visage can drive away birds and beasts, etc.[40]

Filled with impudent laughter also is Immanuel's account of the proud, pedantic grammarian who leaves no one alone but immediately launches into learned disputations to display his scholarship. The dry-as-dust pedant, however, has a beautiful young wife, and the poet therefore gladly enters into a learned discussion with him. The philologist is overjoyed; it is so easy for him to score over the poet in a philological tournament. The poet, however, is also quite content; at the same time as the pedant demonstrates his cleverness in grammar and expertise in the Bible, the poet achieves a conquest of the young woman's heart. In the twenty-second *makama* the poet sets forth a whole gallery of such foolish, pedantic philologists and Bible exegetes. Each of them comes forward with a silly question, one clumsier than the other. And their

38. *Ibid.*, p. 14.
39. Typical is the account in which Immanuel describes how he, as a physician, visits a young woman and she refuses to open her hand so that he may take her pulse (*Makama* 11, pp. 81–82).
40. *Maḥberot, Makama* 7, pp. 55–57.

faces are so serious and stern, their eyes glazed, their foreheads wrinkled. This masterly parody which is impossible to translate—one must read it in the original—can make even the gloomiest hypochondriac laugh. To the same genre belongs Immanuel's parody on preachers with their eulogies. The mocking poet himself becomes a preacher and stands before his own open grave pronouncing a eulogy over himself.[41]

Even for heaven our poet has little respect, and he hurls his sharp witticisms at it. He finds hell much more interesting than heaven. It is so dreadfully boring to be in heaven with the dried-out, bent, pious old ladies with warts on their noses. What have I to do in heaven, complains the poet, when only freaks and monsters are gathered there?[42] Immanuel has much greater desire for hell. There sin is so sweet and beautiful. There the most beautiful women are assembled, their eyes burning with love, their voices demanding and calling. With them hell becomes heaven; without them heaven is really hell.[43]

Immanuel, however, is not always so frivolously happy. Under the loud, healthy laughter very different tones are heard at times. Typical in this respect is the fifteenth *makama*. We have before us here a very interesting novella of the early Renaissance before the period of the *Decameron*. The poet, together with his patron, walks the streets on a wager. Whomever the two meet they ask whether he would wish to exchange his fate for another's. In the framework of the narrative the poet sets forth a kaleidoscope of people of all classes. Typical is the whore who refuses under any

41. *Ibid.*, pp. 173–74.
42. *Ibid.*, p. 116.
43. This passage in Immanuel is of special interest. It shows that not only the Italian but also the Jewish poets were under the influence of Provençal poetry. The joking about boring heaven and desirable, lively hell shows clearly that Immanuel was acquainted with the Provençal or Old French version of the well-known story of the two lovers Aucassin and Nicolette. When Aucassin is threatened with hell if Nicolette becomes his lover, he answers quite calmly: "What need have I of heaven? I have no desire whatever to go there. My desire is only Nicolette, my precious, beautiful one whom I love so dearly." "After all, to heaven," he further says, "come only a dirty troop of old priests who day and night wander around the altars and all the raggle-taggle cripples who go barefoot and naked. All these hasten to heaven, but I have nothing to do there." He much prefers hell. "There," he says, "come the cheerful scholars, the proud knights who died in tournaments and on the battlefield. There also come the delicate, lovely women who have two or three lovers besides their own husbands. There everything shimmers in gold and silver, clad in loveliest garments and decorated with the most precious sables. I wish to be with them!"

circumstances to exchange either with a queen or with princesses. These must yearn silently, for they are surrounded by guards and eunuchs. Every step of theirs is watched, and they cannot fulfull their desires. But the whore openly and freely enjoys the pleasures of love. She has no need to dissemble; she can embrace whomever she wishes and without hindrance give herself to him. Further on, however, the tone becomes more serious. The madman also refuses to exchange his lot. He has constructed for himself an imaginary world far more beautiful than the normal world in which settled, sober people live. Our heroes later encounter two blind men, one of whom had had his eyes put out at the verdict of the court. Neither of the blind men wishes to see the world any more; both are content with their fate. Their inner world, they say, is far more interesting. This ironic, melancholy smile plays quite frequently on the lips of the life-loving children of the Renaissance era.

We have observed that our Jewish poet did not know of any such inner conflict as Petrarch. Nevertheless, he too experienced moments of profound doubt and painful spiritual questioning. The nostalgic, romantic tendency which found such a clear echo in the hearts of the Renaissance age is discernible in his work as well. In the midst of silly mockery, the smile of romantic irony, the dreamy tremble of longing emotion, suddenly appears. Immanuel, the ardent disciple of the rationalist Maimonides, was also deeply interested in the mystical, the secrets of the Kabbalah. The erotic poet, the laughing "master of love and passion" cannot, after all, forget how frivolous and transient love is. To its sad and inevitable end Immanuel frequently turns in his poems. In moments of doubt and soul-searching he feels the pettiness and vanity of earthly love and comes to the sorrowful reflection that "the soul and passion are enemies between whom there can never be any compromise." Then he regrets having "crowned passion queen of his songs." "It is time, my friend," the poet sadly declares, "to cut off our youthful locks, time to free the spirit which has so long been enslaved to earthly lusts. For our youth is now long past, and our soul is still in exile, forsaken. The sickness of passion is over, and there is nothing with which to heal its wounds."[44]

Written in such elegiac tones are not only Immanuel's religious poems[45] but also a number of secular ones in which the cry of inconsolable despair occasionally breaks through. "Were it not for the fear of God," we read in one poem, "I would make an end of

44. *Mahberot*, p. 59.

45. Some of these, such as *Elohim Naflu Fanai* and others, are printed in the Mahzorim according to the Roman Rite. See Zunz, *Die synagogale Poesie des Mittelalters*, p. 311.

myself, for life is without value when the wells of knowledge are dried up, when wisdom and understanding are degraded, and baseness and hypocrisy are on high."[46] Permeated with tender sadness are the poet's lovely elegies in which he mourns the death of dear ones—his son,[47] his brother, his father-in-law.[48] The gentle, elegiac tones, however, at times pass over into monitions of punishment. Quiet sorrow is drowned by sounds of pain and indignation. We encounter such poems already in the first *makama* of Immanuel's *Maḥberot*, in which the poet tells of the injustices committed against him in his old age when he had to flee his home. Here he displays the full power of his literary gift. His joyous, carefree laughter is often transformed into caustic satire and reproof.

Characteristic in this respect is the poem *Ha-Tofet Veha-Eden*, which the poet wrote in his old age around 1330.[49] To be sure, even here Immanuel's laughter is heard at times. Full of humor is the poet's description of how he comes to heaven and, as soon as the patriarchs and prophets see him from afar, they give him a great welcome and all joyfully call out: "Immanuel is coming; we shall have much laughter." With a sincere, pious mien, under which the sarcastic smile of the freethinking wit is artfully hidden, the poet lists the "sins" for which such famous thinkers and scholars as Plato, Aristotle, Galen, and others were sentenced to hell.[50] The fundamental tone of Immanuel's poem, however, is not mocking but admonitory. Not carefree laughter but the lash of satire is heard here.

In the deepest abysses of hell the poet meets a "band of blind persons" whom he recognizes at once. In the terrestrial world these passed as "heads of the thousands of Israel," the recognized leaders of the people. "Great is the sin of these men, for they had eyes and refused to see, and at noonday groped in darkness." They must suffer the direst punishments because they declined to recognize the value of knowledge and wisdom, and ridiculed those who engage in the sciences and devote themselves to philosophy.[51] In the lowest chambers of hell the poet also locks up the hypocrites who defrauded the people, were pious and God-fearing on the outside

46. *Maḥberot*, p. 108.
47. *Ibid.*, end of the twenty-first *makama*, p. 174.
48. Immanuel's father-in-law Samuel was a prominent community leader and perished in a tragic death in 1322. See Vogelstein and Rieger, *op. cit.*, I, 308.
49. For a comparison of Immanuel's poem with Dante's brilliant work, which served the Jewish poet as pattern, see Franz Delitzsch, "Zwei kleine Dantestudien," in *Zeitschrift für Kirchliche Wissenschaft*, 1886, p. 51.
50. *Maḥberot*, p. 221.
51. *Ibid.*, pp. 223 and 224.

and passed as great men of the generation while in stealth they did the vilest deeds.[52] Among them he also finds many community leaders who rose to power and honor through all kinds of deceit, oppressed the people, and hated the poor "like Moslems hate swine and Nazirites despise beautiful women."

The poet glories in the consciousness that he is the "rod of anger," that the reproving power of the poetic art is great. He trusts that the whip of his satire will attain its goal, that "deep in men's hearts will his words be inscribed and he will not be a singer to the dead or a preacher for statues of stone."[53]

Both in the content and the form of Immanuel's poetry the influence of two different cultures is discernible. Arabic *ghazals* with their unique rhymes stand here in proximity to sonnets with their ingeniously constructed lines. In his *makamas*, which are built according to the Arabic pattern, are woven tales strongly reminiscent of the favorite literary form of the Renaissance era, the novella, which reached its peak shortly after Immanuel in Boccaccio's *Decameron.* As master of poetic prose, Immanuel has no peer in all of medieval Hebrew literature, and with him the *musiv* style attains the highest degree of perfection. Many of his witticisms and aphorisms entered the treasury of popular speech and became the property of the people.[54]

Immanuel himself proudly underscores the significance of his poetic work. He declares himself "prince of the poets" (*sar ha-meshorerim*) before whom "all the singers bow low and those who dream of art do obeisance," for he "possesses the great secret of poetic art and creates miracles never seen or heard."[55] In him lives the fond hope that future generations will remember him and that the brilliance of his songs will shine for entire peoples.[56] Immanuel is certain that "he will die, but his works will not,"[57] that "whomever he curses will be cursed, and he whom he blesses will be blessed."[58]

The poet's hope, however, was not entirely fulfilled. To be sure, "his works did not die," but his *Mahberot*, which occupy such an

52. *Ibid.*, pp. 225 and 226.
53. *Ibid.*, p. 234.
54. For example, the well-known proverb *Ahare mot kedoshim emor* (After death one is called a saint) is also a witticism of Immanuel's, one in which he cleverly employs the names of the three weekly *sidrot* or synagogal readings from the Pentateuch that follow one another in the summertime.
55. *Mahberot*, p. 18.
56. *Ibid.*, *Makama* 18, p. 138.
57. *Ibid.*, p. 9.
58. *Ibid.*, pp. 172 and 179.

important place in medieval Hebrew poetry, had very slight influence on later ages. As the atmosphere in the Jewish quarter became ever darker and more melancholy, Immanuel's frivolous, laughing Muse came to appear alien and impudently profligate. At the end of the fourteenth century the cultured rabbi and poet Moses Rieti declared Immanuel's poetry indecent,[59] and the author of the *Shulḥan Aruch*, the famous codifier Joseph Karo, ruled that it is forbidden to read Immanuel's poems, either on the Sabbath or on weekdays, because of the prohibition against "sitting in the seat of scorners."[60] The ban of the *Shulḥan Aruch* was authoritative for centuries, and it was regarded as sinful to take Immanuel's *Maḥberot* into one's hands. Before Joseph Karo issued his prohibition Immanuel's poems were printed twice, but even then so enlightened a publisher as Gershom Soncino[61] deemed it necessary to strike out certain lines in Immanuel's work which seemed to him overly heretical. In one of the two copies of Soncino's very rare edition, which are located in the Asiatic Museum in Leningrad, someone of that time wrote in (apparently from a manuscript copy) several such lines which the pious printer had thrown out. In the fourth *makama*, for example, the "prince," charmed by Immanuel's artistry, calls out, "Your songs are like the songs that were sung in the Temple; those of others are merely the songs of the idol Baal."

After the Constantinople edition (1535), Immanuel's *Maḥberot*, banned by the *Shulḥan Aruch*, was not reprinted until the end of the eighteenth century,[62] when the Haskalah movement, with its new tendencies, revived interest in the gay poet of the Renaissance era. An exception was made only for Immanuel's last work, *Ha-Tofet Veha-Eden*. This was printed several times and also rendered into Yiddish[63] as a moral tale in which the happy "master of love and passion" is transformed into the "righteous and godly man–Rabbi Immanuel, the son of Rabbi Ishmael the high priest."[64]

59. In his *Mikdash Meat*, p. 106a.
60. *Oraḥ Ḥayyim*, *Hilchot Shabbat*, Chapter 307, sec. 16.
61. On the famous publishing family Soncino, see Daniel Chwolson, *Staropechatnyya Yevreyskiya Knigi* (1897), pp. 8–11; also Freimann in *ZHB*, IX, 22.
62. In Berlin in 1796. All editions suffer from the same defect: the text is very erroneous. In 1926 H. Brody undertook a critical edition of Immanuel's *Maḥberot*, employing not only the older printed versions but two manuscripts as well. At present only the first eight *makama*s have appeared (Berlin, 1926). Unfortunately we have not had the opportunity to see this edition.
63. *Gan Eden Ve-Gehinnom*. We have seen the edition of 1782. There are many others besides.
64. For a discussion of this moral tale, see our article in the third volume of *Filologishe Shriften*.

CHAPTER SIX

# *The Roman Poets;*

## KALONYMOS BAR KALONYMOS

BY NO means was Immanuel the only Hebrew poet of his time in Italy. He himself often mentions the *meshorerei ha-zeman* (poets of the time), the *melitzei Romi* (Roman singers or rhetors), and the *shirei ḥachmei Romi* (poems by Roman scholars).[1] The most important of these contemporary poets, apparently, was Jehudah Siciliano. Immanuel, who gloried in his own talent, was so enchanted by young Siciliano's poems that he publicly declared that he could not compare with his colleague and surrendered his birthright to him.[2] As Jehudah Halevi and Moses Ibn Ezra had corresponded with one another through poems, so the two Italians, Immanuel and Jehudah Siciliano, wrote letters in verse to each other. Of this correspondence, however, only four poems[3] sent by Immanuel to his friend have survived.

According to Immanuel, Siciliano lived in dire poverty. His livelihood was derived from teaching young people the technique of writing verses.[4] He was also commissioned to compose poems celebrating certain ceremonial occasions for a fee. Of everything the indigent poet wrote, however, only a dictionary of rhymes, *Aremat Ha-Ḥittim*,[5] has been preserved. Siciliano was not blessed with Immanuel's good fortune. He did not find a patron for his

1. *Maḥberot*, beginning of *Makama* 6, and elsewhere.
2. *Ibid.*, *Makama* 13.
3. *Ibid.*
4. *Maḥberot*, p. 101.
5. It is to be found in manuscript in the library of Oxford University.

poetic work, and all the songs he wrote and sold for trifling sums simply to keep body and soul together were lost, leaving no memory behind.

Another poet of that era had better luck. This was Joab, a member of a prominent Roman family. It is probable that this younger contemporary of Immanuel is the Joab ben Yeḥiel many of whose liturgical poems are to be found in the *Maḥzor Minhag Roma* (Roman Rite Prayer Book).[6] Joab bore himself arrogantly in his personal conduct and thereby enraged Immanuel. The latter, therefore, attacked him with all his keen sarcasm. It may be that Immanuel is justified when he reproaches Joab with ignorance of the natural and other sciences. One thing, however, is certain. Joab was a gifted poet who experienced nature as a colorful, living, fragrant revelation of the divine, a disclosure of God's power and splendor. A prose translation naturally can give only a slight notion of the beauty of his well-known religious poem "Yom Yom Yeḥidati":

Every day, my only one,[7] tremble and pray! Every morning pour out thy cry before Him whom radiance, power and glory veil like a mantle. His wondrous deeds astonish me. All boundaries and worlds are filled with Him, as a cloud is pregnant with the blessed rain which fructifies the womb of the earth and covers the wilderness with a colorful carpet of heavy, golden stalks of wheat. He bestows balsam on the deepest wounds; He heals the greatest woes and makes them forgotten.

He commands and all the stars quickly adorn the vault of heaven, like delicate flowers blooming on the meadows, like a frightened band of migratory birds twittering on the fields. Wanderers by night, they are awakened with fright by the first ray of the sun, and humbly they bow before Him who spans the heavens and the earth, who tears the celestial vaults like a spiderweb and makes the deepest abysses quake in the storm.

Himself uncreated and the Creator of all, Himself without fear, He makes the strongest tremble. Where is the might and power that can fight against Thee? Where is the way that is hidden from Thee? I stand before Thee in my sorrowful mood. I beg mercy from Thee. Forgive my guilt, pardon my misery, my shame, my sinful deeds. Rejoice my heart with the tidings: forgiven is thy sin! Thou great, omnipotent One, who punishes and forgives and mercifully transforms the day of sorrow into the day of joy.

Even more gifted than Joab was another poet who, it is conjectured, lived in the same period, a poet who is almost completely

6. See Zunz, *Die Literaturgeschichte der synagogalen Poesie*, p. 501.
7. I.e., the soul.

unknown. We have no details of his life, who he was or in what country he lived. Only his name, Naḥum, is known—and this thanks to his poems into which his name is woven. M. Sachs considers him one of the Spanish poets; others discern in his songs the breath of the Renaissance era. We agree with the latter, and therefore mention him among the *melitzei Romi,* Immanuel's contemporaries.[8] Naḥum's poetic legacy is very slender; only six compositions bearing his name have come down to us.[9] Yet these few songs testify that he was a genuine poet with a powerful, vibrant talent. A prose rendering of his poems is obviously incapable of giving a clear notion of the unique beauty of his delicate, modestly gracious Muse:

I

Winter is over; with it sorrow also is past. The trees are covered with blossoms; with joy does my heart also bloom. How fragrant their spices, how intoxicating their odor! My blooming garden laughs and rejoices; filled are all hearts with joy and gladness.

My love, my beautiful one, you have forsaken me. Enough have you wandered; return to my home. Overflowing is my cup; my sap and my wine await you.

Quickly do woe and grief pass when the green beds adorn the myrtle with their fragrant wreath. Before the enchanted play of the splendid colors, sorrow and pain disappear.

Towers of fragrant branches and blossoms drip spices on me. I am caught in green captivity. The thick branches of the nut tree have encompassed me. And everywhere, from all the trees, fragrance and odorous shade breathe. On the left acacia trees shimmer, on the right aloes bloom.

How beautifully polished is every petal, the cup of flowers. And the cup is full; it sparkles and glistens with enchanting liquid. In it will I drown my sorrow, the sadness that gnaws at my heart.

Where is my beloved who rested on my breasts? He has left my tent and wanders in alien forests. Oh, return to your beloved. You will rest in her arms, lulled by her songs.

My desired one, my love! Like a flaming torch light up my way! My anointed cherub! In my deep darkness be my morning star, my bright dawn![10]

8. Very probably Naḥum was older than Immanuel, for in the Sarajevo manuscript Haggadah, which is renowned for its artistic miniatures and was written not later than the first half of the fourteenth century, two compositions of our poet are already to be found.
9. Zunz, *Literaturgeschichte,* p. 492.
10. The poem "Ha-Setav Araḥ, Araḥ Maatzavi."

## II

Spikenard and crocus bloom in my garden. The thorns are faded, and where the silvery brook flows the bright green myrtle shimmers.

The trees have cast off their cloak of mourning and joyously laugh in their fragrant garments. How jubilant everything all around is! The turtle dove sings and the lark chirps, each in its way—one with soft, quiet tones, the other with loud trilling. All are blended together in one chorus, one great song of praise and gratitude to the almighty Creator.

Behold, the rose beds have adorned themselves in crimson; the dogwood trees bloom with their rose-white petals. And the laughter rejoices all human hearts, finds an echo in those who watch cheerfully as well as those who dream in sweet slumber.

Now has the little twilight wind given a cry, and from all the shrubs, all the trees, drips dew—dew that refreshes like balsam those who are weary of labor, that makes misery and affliction forgotten.

There, the edge of the eastern sky becomes light and clear; the sun has sent forth its first rays. In my garden new shoots have appeared, and in my ears resound the tidings: David's shoot[11] also begins to bloom. My Friend has seen how great are my sorrows, He has shown compassion to His forsaken dwelling. The day of redemption is at hand. It brings liberation for those who have languished in captivity and ever hoped and waited.[12]

A special place among the *melitzei Romi* of Immanuel's generation is occupied by Kalonymos bar Kalonymos, known to the Christian world under the name Maestro Calo. He was not an Italian by birth but came from the Provençal city of Arles. He was the scion of a very prominent family that traced its descent from the Kalonymos family which, in the time of Charles the Bald, migrated from the Italian city of Lucca to the Rhine cities. The young Kalonymos[13] received a broad and thorough education.

11. The "shoot of David" is the Messiah.

12. A poem for Shemini Atzeret entitled "Nerd Ve-Charkom Tzatz Be-Gani."

13. Kalonymos was born in 1286, as may easily be conjectured from some of his remarks. At the end of one of his translations, which he completed on April 1, 1308, Kalonymos indicates that he is now in his twenty-second year (see Steinschneider, *Hebräischen Übersetzungen*, p. 653; Renan-Neubauer, *Les Écrivains juifs français*, p. 419). In Firkovich's first collection, No. 424, there is a manuscript of Averroes' work *Biur Ha-Shema Ha-Tivii* in Kalonymos' translation which the latter completed in Arles in 1316 and in which he indicates that he was then thirty years old (on this see also *ZHB*, XII, 152). From the polemic work in which Kalonymos attacked Joseph Ibn Kaspi (published by Perles in 1879) we learn that the young Kalonymos was educated in Salonika and his teachers were Moses of Beaucaire and Senior Astruc de Noves.

Besides Talmudic literature, he studied medicine and philosophy, and became completely familiar with Arabic and Latin. His scholarly activity began in his twentieth year. Kalonymos' goal was to introduce Christians and Jews to the scientific achievements of Arabic civilization. In the course of twenty years he translated numerous Arabic scientific works into Hebrew and Latin with tireless diligence. In Avignon, where he settled in 1314, he made the acquaintance of the intellectually inquiring King Charles of Anjou. The latter sent him to Rome on a scientific mission. There he soon became a popular member of the local philosophical circles and a friend of Immanuel. The poet celebrates in eloquent verses the virtues of his Provençal friend, declaring Kalonymos "king among translators" and the greatest stylist of his time.[14] When Kalonymos, because of family matters, was compelled to leave Rome and return home, Immanuel sent the head of the community in Arles a letter in which he expressed, in his own name as well as that of the Jews of Rome, their profound regret at parting with a man of such vast knowledge and remarkably noble character.[15]

The years Kalonymos spent in Rome had a considerable influence on all his work. Highly gifted and full of bubbling wit, Kalonymos took a prominent part not only in the intellectual activity of the Roman Jewish community but also in its exciting daily life. This is attested by his excellent Purim parody *Masechat Purim*. Earlier, when he still lived in Provence, in a controversy with Joseph Ibn Kaspi he reproached the latter as behaving sinfully for allowing himself to mention one of the matriarchs, Rebecca, with insufficient respect. Now, however, after spending some time in "sinful" Rome, he permitted himself to write a clever parody in the style of the sacred books of the Talmud and Midrashim. Many sharp arrows and sarcastic remarks are directed in Kalonymos' satire against certain members of the Roman community,[16] but louder than all these is the joyous laughter of the happy scoffer with his witty imagination. The spirit of the youthful Italian Renaissance is strongly discernible in this parody, in which the most precise information is provided about festival banquets and rich meals with the finest food and costliest wines.[17]

14. *Mahberot, Makama* 18, p. 184.
15. *Ibid.*, pp. 184–85.
16. The largest part is directed against one of the *parnassim* and his wife, whom he calls by the ambiguous name Kardinalit.
17. The gay satire of Kalonymos in later times elicited considerable dissatisfaction among the pious rabbis because the style of the Talmud is parodied in it. The ill-tempered zealot Samuel Aboab in his *Responsa* (No. 193) expressed the desire that this "babbling" book be destroyed, and his wish was in a certain sense fulfilled. Many copies of Kalonymos'

During the years that Kalonymos lived in Rome[18] he wrote the major part of his social satire *Even Boḥan.* The section composed there is written in rhymed prose, and the influence of Immanuel's poems is clearly reflected in it. In the style of his older friend, Kalonymos mockingly confesses his "grievous" sins. The heart, the satirist laments, is guilty in all things and leads to all transgressions. He is, after all, a common mortal and therefore has failed to overcome the "evil inclination," enjoyed all good things, eaten the finest foods and drunk the best wines, dressed in the richest clothing, and devoted himself to love of women. He also complains to God for having created him a man instead of a woman. "Cursed be he," he calls out,

> who told my father the news: a son is born to you. Woe to him whose children are males. What a grievous yoke awaits them! Whole armies of prohibitions and commandments lie in wait for them—all the 613 commandments, positive and negative. Who can fulfill all these? No man, no matter how diligent he may be. Who can withstand whole regiments? It is impossible to save oneself. One remains a sinner and lawbreaker. . . . But how well it would have been for me had I been born a maiden. I should have sat quietly without worries at the spinning wheel or crocheting with my friends. We would have entertained ourselves by the light of the moon or in the dusk of twilight, told pleasant stories, discussed all the events that had happened in the city. Ah, what an expert I would have been at crocheting! People would have been astonished at the artistic patterns I would sew and embroider with the loveliest silks of the most splendid colors. . . . And later when the time came to be married, what a lovely youth would have fallen to my lot, how he would have loved me, caressed me. He would have adorned me with gold and diamonds; he would have carried me on his hands, embraced and kissed me. . . . But my bitter fate has been to be born a man. So God willed, and it is now too late; I shall not be changed from a man into a woman. I must accept it in love, and thank the Holy One, blessed be He, with a pious mien: "Blessed art thou, Lord, who has not made me a woman."[19]

Later on, the tone of the work becomes more somber. The poet becomes a man of admonitions, a moral preacher. The reproving speeches of Kalonymos ben Kalonymos have a considerable ethno-

---

*Masechat Purim* were burned, and copies of the first edition (1552) are now of extreme rarity. We have employed a manuscript copy located in the Asiatic Museum in Leningrad. The work of Kalonymos served as pattern for numerous other parodies which appeared in neo-Hebrew literature.

18. 1318–22.

19. *Even Boḥan,* 15–18.

graphic-cultural value, for in them the contemporary way of life is sharply mirrored. We learn from them how the Italian Jews in the era of Immanuel and Kalonymos celebrated their festivals, how people used to greet each other with witticisms on the eve of Rosh Hashanah,[20] how gay young blades conducted themselves during the Ten Days of Penitence which occur just at the time when the newly matured wine is poured out,[21] and how men used to wrangle and bargain at the parceling-out of *aliyyot* (the honor of being called to the reading of the Torah) on Yom Kippur.[22] *Even Boḥan,* incidentally, also acquaints us with the festival meals, the richly ornamented *sukkot,*[23] the happy games and entertainments during the intermediate days of the festivals,[24] the celebrations on Hanukah,[25] the noisy, colorful carnivals at Purim when people were carried away by wine and liquor,[26] the extensive preparations for the Passover seder night,[27] the tasty foods at the dairy meal on Shavuot.[28] All these Kalonymos portrays for us in his own manner—gaily, vividly, in bright, loud colors.

Like Immanuel, Kalonymos also mocks charlatan doctors,[29] dry-as-dust, pedantic philologists,[30] untalented rhymesters,[31] arrogant rich men, and proud and foolish men of pedigree.[32] But along with this he reproves with the rod of the satirist social evils and injustices. Kalonymos speaks indignantly of hypocritical communal leaders.

> I know them well, these hypocrites with glazed eyes, who are supposedly entirely separated from the present world and constantly pray to God, but in secret do the most shameful deeds. They hang their doors with *mezuzot,* and the thresholds of their houses are filled with blood and sin. They bind the thongs of the *tefillin* around their arms, and their hands are stained with the innocent blood of poor people.[33]

In Rome, as well as in other important urban centers of Italy and Provence, Jewish bankers and financiers frequently played an

20. *Ibid.*, 25.
21. *Ibid.*, 26.
22. *Ibid.*, 27.
23. *Ibid.*
24. *Ibid.*, 28.
25. *Ibid.*
26. *Ibid.*, 29–30.
27. *Ibid.*, 31–32.
28. *Ibid.*, 33.
29. *Ibid.*, 44–48.
30. *Ibid.*, 52–53.
31. *Ibid.*, 54.
32. *Ibid.*, 36.
33. *Ibid.*, 40–41.

influential role at the courts of the rulers. These "worthies," to be sure, often did favors for their brethren and interceded on behalf of the community with the lord of the city. At times, however, such court Jews also exploited their influence for nefarious purposes, to terrify their opponents and to cast fear on the community so that all should show them deference. It is these that Kalonymos attacks with his angry words: "They boast of their importance and glory in the fact that they find favor in the sight of the Christian princes; they frighten everyone, saying, 'We are accepted at court, we can take vengeance.' "[34]

Kalonymos also speaks with much bitterness of the rabbis and rabbinic judges of his time:

> They carry on constant controversies among themselves. Each tries to bring the other down. If one permits something, the other at once forbids it. Their learning is only for the sake of glory. How many of them nowadays take bribes, judge falsely, teach and render legal decisions only for payment, demand recompense for every word, every step. Everything is valued by them only in terms of money.[35]

Kalonymos left Rome when his *Even Boḥan* was still incomplete and wrote the conclusion in Provence at the end of 1322 or in January 1323.[36] This concluding part is sharply distinguished, both in form and content, from the first, larger section written in Italy. No longer here do we have the *makama* style with its rhymed prose. Kalonymos abandoned laughter as soon as he left gay Rome. In his home in Provence at that time (1320–22) the Jews had just experienced the terrors of the bloodthirsty bands of Pastoureaux and "leprous ones" who poured out their hatred on the unprotected Jewish communities. In Kalonymos, shattered by their terrible

34. *Ibid.*, 59.
35. *Ibid.*, 56–57 (we quote according to the Lemberg edition of 1865).
36. When Kalonymos mentions the expulsion of the Jews from Provence, which occurred in 1306, he emphasizes that this took place "seventeen years ago" (*Even Boḥan*, 102). In the closing lines of *Even Boḥan*, in which the author indicates the date when he completed his work, is to be found the conspicuous statement "I am eighty-three years old." His biographers have concluded from this that Kalonymos was already a man of eighty-three when he completed his *Even Boḥan*. But Zunz pointed out (*Gesammelte Schriften*, III, 150–51) that the text has been corrupted by copyists and that the allusion here is to the eighty-third year of the sixth millennium according to the traditional Jewish mode of reckoning time, i.e., the year 5083 (1323 C.E.). At that time Kalonymos was only thirty-eight years old. According to the report of S. Munk (*ZHB*, XIII, 123), Kalonymos ended his work with the following words: "I completed this composition in the tenth month, i.e., the month of Tebet of the year 5083, I, the poor . . ."

deeds, new moods, moods of sorrow and pious submission, were aroused. The erstwhile scoffer and satirist becomes a penitent. Humbly he praises God and accepts His punishment in love. With quiet sorrow he speaks of the vanity of man's life; like a shadow all his joys, all his power and greatness, pass away. In a sincere, tender tone Kalonymos speaks of the intense sufferings which the Provençal Jews had experienced in the preceding two years, and the conclusion of the work, in which he addresses a prayer to God begging help and protection for his brethren, resounds with humble chords.

*Masechat Purim* and *Even Boḥan* are not Kalonymos' only literary works. Not without reason is he called by Immanuel "the prince among translators." We know that, at the request of King Charles of Anjou, Kalonymos translated numerous Arabic scientific works.[37] Of all these, however, only his *Iggeret Baalei Ḥayyim* is of distinguished literary quality. The Arabic religious-philosophical order of the Pure Brethren had created a complete encyclopedia which exercised considerable influence on the spiritual and intellectual life of that era.[38] From this monumental work Kalonymos took one chapter, made of it an independent work, a kind of epic of beasts and birds which is reminiscent in places of *Kalilah Ve-Dimnah*,[39] and gave it the title *Iggeret Baalei Ḥayyim.* Kalonymos' work, which is written in a simple, easily comprehensible style, was very warmly received among Jews. It was published numerous times, and in order that the common people and women might also be able to read it, it was translated into Yiddish. *Iggeret Baalei Ḥayyim* truly deserved to become a folk classic. Full of wit and humor, spiced with moral instruction and ethical maxims, and interwoven with an ingenious web of simple tales of birds and beasts, it has a genuinely popular character.

The epic begins with a description of how the beasts sent a delegation to the king of spirits to accuse men who have enslaved them and forced them into hard labor. The king of the spirits, Birsef, was a gracious and kindly monarch. He summoned all his counselors and commanded that representatives of all the nations and also of all species of beasts, birds, insects, reptiles, and creeping things come to an assize. The king would listen to their arguments,

37. For the complete roster of Kalonymos' translations see Zunz, *Gesammelte Schriften,* III, 153–54; Steinschneider, *op. cit.,* Index; and especially Renan-Neubauer, *op. cit.,* pp. 424–41, where thirty works that Kalonymos translated are described at length.
38. On this encyclopedia see *Hebräische Bibliographie,* XIII, 16–18, 29–37.
39. One of these two jackals, Kalilah, figures incidentally also in the *Iggeret Baalei Ḥayyim.*

take counsel with his advisors, and then issue a verdict. However, no verdict was actually reached, because neither the Pure Brethren nor their Jewish translator were really interested in this. The important thing was the arguments themselves, the way of speaking and the attitude of the contending parties and their representatives assembled at the hearings.

With fine irony the fear that descends on men when the beasts rebel and go to the king to complain is portrayed. "What does this mean?" the frightened humans cry out. "How can one do without beasts and cattle? How can one get along without meat and milk, without wool and skins?" And they begin to guess and predict what the king will decide, whether he will order the beasts to be freed without any compensation, or whether the liberated animals will at least have to pay their former owners.[40] Some propose bribing the king's deputy, the eldest among the counsellors, for "a gift in secret makes the wisest eyes not to see."[41] In vivid colors is portrayed the election—how all the beasts and creeping things that live on the dry land and in the waters, from the lion and the shark to the smallest fly, participate in choosing representatives for the assembly that is to gather at the king's command. Here is demonstrated especially clearly how familiar the Pure Brethren were with the way of life of all creatures. Lovingly and attentively they dwell on the unique qualities by which one species of creature is distinguished from another, as they describe the manner of life of the bees,[42] ants,[43] locusts,[44] spiders,[45] and the like.

The judgment begins. The men keep arguing that such is the order of the world: "we are the masters and the beasts are our slaves." That Providence itself has arranged it so is obvious from the very structure of the body: men have straight backs and their eyes are turned to the heavens, while beasts look down to the earth. Men also, in their wisdom, have created marvelous technical instruments and organized the wisest political institutions, as a result of which a complex social life is conducted with greatest orderliness. The representatives of the beasts and birds, however, refute these arguments. The structure of the body, they point out, is dependent on the manner in which every creature seeks and obtains nourishment, and it is not only men who turn their gaze to the heavens; birds and insects likewise do so. And who does not know

40. *Iggeret Baalei Ḥayyim,* Chapter 3.
41. *Ibid.*
42. *Ibid.*, 49.
43. *Ibid.*, 52.
44. *Ibid.*, 53.
45. *Ibid.* (We quote according to the Warsaw edition of 1877.)

that in very small bodies are frequently found great and noble souls?[46] Men boast so much of their technology, of their social order, but the little bees and the still smaller ants are not inferior technologists than they, and their social order is also not inferior to men's.

Then the Jew from Palestine steps forth together with the Moslem from Arabia. They point out that only men, who are the crown of all creatures, have been endowed with sacred laws and statutes, and have been given specific days for festivals and fasts. On these days men gather in houses of prayer, repent, pray to God, and purify themselves of sin. True, the representatives of the birds reply to this, you humans must fast and repent and wash yourselves clean, for you are steeped in sin. Your hands are defiled with robbery and murder, for you despoil the weak and poor. You have been given laws because only these can restrain you from your evil deeds. You must always bathe and cleanse your bodies, because you lead an impure life filled with unchastity and sin. You glory in your houses of prayer and synagogues, and in your festivals; but for us the whole world is a house of prayer, and not only on certain days. Every day is for us a festival, every day we sing and praise our Creator.[47]

Then the men issue forth in the name of mercy and compassion. They cannot abide the killings that take place among the beasts. The stronger, with their sharp nails and teeth, consume the weaker, drink their blood, eat their flesh, and the shrieks and cries ascend to the heavens. Here there is a great tumult among the beasts. What —cries out the jackal, beside himself with rage—you men dare to speak of mercy? You reproach us for cruelty and shedding blood —you who kill not only animals but even your own kind, cut off their hands and feet, and inflict the greatest sufferings on them? You torture, plunder, kill without mercy. The wild beasts first learned from you what cruelty is; they are your pupils. But how can they attain your level? They always remain backward. The best among you, the truly gracious and tenderhearted, when they can no longer look upon your killings, flee to the desert to the beasts and live with them as with brothers, for the wildest animals are better than you.[48]

Then the humans attempt to invoke the merit of their fathers. Among them, after all, are great saints, profound thinkers, and brilliant poets and artists. That is true—replies the representative

46. *Ibid.*, 73.
47. *Ibid.*, 58.
48. *Ibid.*, Part IV, Chapters 8 and 9.

of the birds, the popinjay—these righteous men of the generation, however, are lost among the many thousands and tens of thousands of thieves, robbers, liars, informers, hypocrites, drunkards, barbaric outcasts, base and shameful men, sullied with scandal and sin.[49] And have you, with your slavish souls, still the impudence to treat us as slaves? We deserve to be free far more than you! You glory so in your inspired poets. We also have gifted poets and singers, but you cannot understand their language.[50]

Then the men come forth with their final argument. They are the majority. Men are of one kind, while all other creatures are divided into so many genera and species.[51] This argument also does not remain without reply. Infinite, answer the birds, is the number of the creatures who swarm on the dry land and in the waters. The human species cannot be compared with them. To be sure, men are of one species; the form of their bodies is identical. How various, however, are their souls, their opinions. They are divided into so many religions, sects, and classes, and each hates and persecutes the other. With us, however, there is one faith; we all believe in the one and only Creator, and we praise Him day and night.[52]

Here one of the king's wise counselors intervenes in the controversy. Yes, he says, great is the number of men in the world. Infinitely numerous creatures cover the earth and fill the waters. If, however, you could see and count the millions upon millions of spirits that fill all the hollows and farthest spaces of all the worlds and planets, you would understand how small and petty you are and how ridiculous is your desire to rule over all other creatures. No, all of us, all without distinction, are merely God's servants. We are His creatures and do His will, but He alone deserves praise and glory.[53]

We have noted how significant were the merits of Kalonymos ben Kalonymos as a scientific translator, but in this respect another of Immanuel's young friends, Jehudah Leon ben Moses Romano, known in the Christian world by the title *philosophus divinus* (the divine philosopher) acquired even greater fame. A man of encyclopedic knowledge, Romano even in his early years was renowned as a distinguished scholar. From all regions of Italy young people eager for knowledge came to Rome to study under the direction of the young Jewish savant. Like Kalonymos, Romano also spent some time at the court of the king of Anjou, who studied Hebrew

49. *Ibid.*, Part V, Chapter 1.
50. *Ibid.*, Chapter 3.
51. *Ibid.*, Chapter 9.
52. *Ibid.*
53. *Ibid.*, Chapter 10.

with him.[54] Considerably younger than his friend and relative Immanuel,[55] Romano had a great influence on the intellectually curious poet. The latter frankly admits, "From Romano's thoughts I have gathered pearls and placed them in my work . . . let the whole world know that without the profound wisdom assembled in Romano's works, it would never have seen mine."[56]

Jehudah Romano himself indicates that he assumed the task of demonstrating to his co-religionists, who were so proud of their extensive knowledge, that other peoples, especially the Christians, were also not lacking in wisdom and scientific treasures. And, indeed, he contributed not a little to introducing Jewish learned circles to the work of Christian scholars. He translated the works of Albertus Magnus, Thomas Aquinas, and Boethius, as well as the philosophical book *De causis,* which was very highly regarded in the Middle Ages. He also translated Averroes' commentary on Aristotle, himself produced commentaries on the Hebrew Bible, composed a work on prophecy, and wrote a commentary on Maimonides' *Sefer Ha-Madda* under the title *Ben Porat.*[57]

"The sea of ignorance he dried up, the eyes of the exiled children he illuminated," says Immanuel of Jehudah Romano. He also accords him, as "the crown of his time," one of the most honored places in heaven.[58] "You anointed angel," Immanuel enthusiastically exclaims in one of his sonnets,

> raise high your burning word. Let those who are bitten by our time be healed by the sight of you. You are our fortress! O proud eagle, in your mighty wings do we find our protection. Sweeter than honey is your name, and all distances are illuminated by your light. Rise, O pride of Jacob! Your companions cannot tell your praise to the world. Let God's anointed himself appear in the chariot of his splendor, and over our vale of sorrow let the proclamation of the glorious tidings resound.[59]

At the threshold of the fourteenth century Italian Jewry attained the highest level of cultural flowering. Rationalist philo-

54. See Rieti, *Mikdash Meat,* p. 106a.
55. Immanuel indicates that when he completed his *Maḥberot* (in 1328) Romano was thirty-six years old. Thus Romano was born in 1292. That Romano was related to Immanuel is indicated by Immanuel's words, "bone of my bone and flesh of my flesh" (*Maḥberot,* p. 90). Rieti relates that Romano was a cousin of Immanuel's.
56. *Maḥberot,* pp. 90–91.
57. A complete list of Romano's work is given by Zunz, *Gesammelte Schriften,* III, 159–61.
58. *Maḥberot,* p. 230.
59. *Ibid., Makama* 20, p. 168.

sophic ideas found ever larger numbers of adherents among the Jewish intelligentsia. But signs of new tendencies already began to appear. Moods hostile to Maimonidean Aristotelianism manifested themselves from two different sides, from the external world and from the Jewish milieu itself. In Italy the first rays of the Renaissance era appeared. Italian humanism, which adopted an attitude of hostility toward medieval scholasticism, endeavored to liberate men from the authority of Aristotle, for the Greek philosopher was the idol of the Christian scholars and clergy who braided his system so closely together with orthodox Christian dogmatics. One observes from the fourteenth century on in humanistic circles, as a protest against Aristotle's philosophy, a special interest in Plato and neo-Platonism. These new tendencies found a certain echo among the Jewish intelligentsia. But within Jewish cultural life also an enemy, filled with lust for battle, came forth against the teaching of Aristotle in its Maimonidean interpretation. This militant adversary of rationalist philosophy was the mysterious doctrine of the *ḥochmat ha-nistar* (hidden wisdom), the mystical *Torah shebalev* (Torah in the heart). This struggle, however, broke out not in Italy but in the neighboring lands, Provence and Spain. The struggle of these two tendencies, philosophic rationalism and the fervent *Torah shebalev*, the long, obdurate struggle which erupted in the thirteenth century and brought, toward the end of the fifteenth century, victory for the Kabbalah over Maimonides' philosophy, was intimately associated with the entire social and cultural life of the Jewish community in Provence and Spain. In the various stages of this historic struggle all the great changes which took place in Jewish life when Christian civilization obtained dominance over the Arabs in Spain were very clearly reflected. Of these we shall speak in the next volume.

# BIBLIOGRAPHICAL NOTES

# *French and German Jewry in the Early Middle Ages*

CHAPTER ONE

## BIBLICAL EXEGESIS IN FRANCE; RASHI AND THE TOSAFISTS

On the early history and culture of the Franco-German Jewish community, see H. Graetz, *Geschichte der Juden* (Leipzig, 1853–76); S. W. Baron, *A Social and Religious History of the Jews*, rev. ed. (Philadelphia, 1952–); R. Anchel, *Les Juifs de France* (Paris, 1946); L. Berman, *Histoire des Juifs de France* (Paris, 1937); H. Gross, *Gallia Judaica* (Paris, 1897); L. Kahn, *Les Juifs à Paris depuis le VIe siècle* (Paris, 1889); I. Elbogen, *Geschichte der Juden in Deutschland* (Berlin, 1935); M. Lowenthal, *The Jews of Germany* (Philadelphia, 1936); A. Berliner, *Aus dem inneren Leben der deutschen Juden in Mittelalter*, 2nd ed. (Berlin, 1900); O. Stobbe, *Die Juden in Deutschland während des Mittelalters in politischer, sozialer und rechtlicher Beziehung*, 3rd impression (Berlin, 1923); I. Abrahams, *Jewish Life in the Middle Ages*, 2nd ed. (London, 1932); L. Finkelstein, *Jewish Self-Government in the Middle Ages* (New York, 1924); and I. Agus, *Rabbi Meir of Rothenburg* (Philadelphia, 1947).

On Rabbenu Gershom, see Naftali ben Samuel (Simḥoni), "Rabbenu Gershom Meor Ha-Golah," *Ha-Shiloaḥ*, XXVIII (1913), 14–22, 119–28, 201–12; A. Epstein, "Der Gershom Meir Ha-Golah zugeschriebene Talmud-Commentar," in *Festschrift zum achtzigsten Geburtstag Moritz Steinschneiders* (Leipzig, 1896), pp. 115–43; Z. W. Falk, *Tikkunim Be-Dinei Ha-Mishpaḥah Be-Yahadut Ashkenaz Ve-Tzarefat* (Jerusalem, 1958); A. Marx, "Rabbenu Gershom, Light of the Exile," in his *Essays in Jewish Biography* (Philadelphia, 1947), pp. 39–60. Rabbenu Gershom's *Selihot U-Pizmonim* was edited by A. M. Habermann (Jerusalem, 1943).

On the early Jewish Bible commentators of France, see W. Bacher, "Die jüdische Bibelexegese vom Anfange des zehnten bis zum Ende des fünfzehnten Jahrhunderts," in J. Winter and A. Wünsche, *Die jüdische Literatur*, II (Trier, 1894–96), 237–339; M. H. Segal, *Parshanut Ha-Mikra* (Jerusalem, 1952); and B. Smalley, *The Study of the Bible in the Middle Ages*, 2nd ed. (Oxford, 1952).

On Rashi, see American Academy for Jewish Research, *Rashi Anniversary Volume* (New York, 1941); H. Hailperin, *Rashi and the Christian Scholars* (Pittsburgh, 1963); E. M. Lipschütz, *Rabbi Shelomo Yitzḥaki* (Warsaw, 1912); J. L. Maimon (ed.), *Sefer Rashi* (Jerusalem, 1955–56); M. Liber, *Rashi* (Philadelphia, 1906); S. M. Blumenfeld, *Master of Troyes: A Study of Rashi the Educator* (New York, 1946); A. Marx, "Rashi," in his *Essays in Jewish Biography* (Philadelphia, 1947), pp. 61–86; R. Levy, "Rashi's Contribution to the French Language," *JQR*, XXXII (1941); S. Zeitlin, "Rashi and the Rabbinate," *JQR*, XXXI (1940), 1–58; N. Kronberg, *Raschi Als Exeget* (Halle, 1882); A. Geiger, *Parshandata: Die nordfranzösische Exegetenschule* (Leipzig, 1855); Joseph Pereira-Mendoza, *Rashi as Philologist* (Manchester, 1940). The Pentateuch with Rashi's commentary was translated into English and annotated by M. Rosenbaum and A. M. Silbermann, 5 vols. (London, 1929–34).

An important work on the Tosafists is E. A. Urbach, *Baalei Ha-Tosafot: Toledoteihem Ḥibbureihem Ve-Shitatam* (Jerusalem, 1955). See also D. Rosin's *Rabbi Samuel ben Meir* (Breslau, 1880).

CHAPTER TWO

## SUPPLICATIONS AND LAMENTATIONS IN THE PERIOD OF THE CRUSADES

On the Crusades and their effect on the Jews of Europe, see S. Runciman, *A History of the Crusades*, 3 vols. (Cambridge, 1951–54); N. Golb, "New Light on the Persecution of French Jews at the Time of the First Crusade," *PAAJR*, XXXIV (1966), 1–63; J. Katz, *Exclusiveness and Tolerance: Studies in Jewish-Gentile Relations in Medieval and Modern Times* (London, 1961); and S. Landau, *Christian-Jewish Relations: A New Era in Germany as the Result of the First Crusade* (New York, 1960).

*Quellen zur Geschichte der Juden in Deutschland*, published by Die historische Kommission für die Geschichte der Juden in Deutschland, 3 vols. (Berlin, 1888–98), contains *Hebräische Berichte über die Judenverfolgungen während der Kreuzzüge*, edited by A. Neubauer and M. Stern, with a German translation by S. Baer (Vol. II), and *Das Martyrologium des Nürnberger Memorbuches*, edited by S. Salfeld (Vol. III). A collection of sources on the persecution of Jews is also to be found in S. Bernfeld's *Sefer Ha-Demaot*, 3 vols. (Berlin, 1924–26). For penitential poems, elegies, and laments of the era of the Crusades, see A. M. Habermann, *Sefer Gezerot Ashkenaz Ve-Tzarefat* (Jerusalem, 1946).

CHAPTER THREE

## THE *SEFER ḤASIDIM*

On the *Sefer Ḥasidim* and Hasidism in medieval Germany, see J. Freimann's introduction to the second edition of J. Wistenetzki's edition of the *Sefer Ḥasidim* (Frankfurt-am-Main, 1924); G. Scholem, *Major Trends in Jewish Mysticism*, rev. ed. (New York, 1946), pp. 80–118; *idem*, "Reste neuplatonischer Spekulation bei den deutschen Chassidim," *MGWJ*, LXXV (1931), 172–91; A. Epstein, "Rabbi Shemuel Ḥasid," *Ha-Goren*, IV (1904), 81–101; M. Güdemann, *Die Geschichte des Erziehungswesen und der Kultur der Juden in Frankreich und Deutschland*, I (Vienna, 1880), Chs. 5–8; J. Kamelhar, *Ḥasidim Ha-Rishonim* (Waitzen, 1917); I. N. Simhoni, "Ha-Ḥasidut Ha-Ashkenazit Be-Yemei Ha-Beinayim," in *Ha-Tzefirah* (1917); J. Trachtenberg, *Jewish Magic and Superstition* (New York, 1939); Y. Baer, "Ha-Megammah Ha-Datit-Ḥevratit Shel Sefer Ḥasidim," *Tziyyon*, III (1938), 1–50; A. Cronbach, "Social Thinking in the *Sefer Ḥasidim*," *Hebrew Union College Annual*, XXII (1949), 1–147; M. Harris, "The Concept of Love in *Sepher Ḥassidim*," *JQR*, L (1959), 13–44; and S. G. Kramer, *God and Man in the Sefer Ḥasidim* (New York, 1966). A new English translation of the *Sefer Ḥasidim* appears in S. A. Singer, *Medieval Jewish Mysticism: The Book of the Pious* (Northbrook, Ill., 1972).

CHAPTER FOUR

## JEWISH MYSTICISM; ELEAZAR OF WORMS

On the development of the Kabbalah and Jewish mysticism generally, see G. Scholem, *Major Trends in Jewish Mysticism*, rev. ed. (New York, 1946); *idem*, *Jewish Gnosticism, Merkabah Mysticism, and Talmudic Tradition* (New York, 1960); *idem*, *On the*

*Kabbalah and Its Symbolism* (New York, 1965); *idem*, *Ursprung und Anfänge der Kabbala* (Berlin, 1962); *idem*, *Von der mystischen Gestalt der Gottheit: Studien zu Grundbegriffen der Kabbala* (Zurich, 1962); *idem*, *Bibliographia Kabbalistica* (Leipzig, 1927); *idem*, "Kabbala," in *Encyclopedia Judaica*, Vol. IX (Berlin, 1932); J. Abelson, *Jewish Mysticism* (London, 1913); A. Franck, *The Kabbalah: The Religious Philosophy of the Hebrews* (New Hyde Park, N.Y., 1967); A. E. Waite, *The Holy Kabbalah: A Study of the Secret Tradition in Israel* (New Hyde Park, N.Y., 1960).

The *Sefer Yetzirah* was translated into English by K. Stenring under the title *The Book of Formation* (London, 1923) and into German by L. Goldschmidt under the title *Das Buch der Schöpfung* (Frankfurt-am-Main, 1894). On the *Sefer Yetzirah*, see G. Scholem's works listed above; A. Epstein, *Recherches sur le Sefer Yeçira* (Versailles, 1894); L. Baeck, "Zum Sepher Jezira," *MGWJ*, LXX (1926), 371–76; *idem*, "Die zehn Sephiroth im Sepher Jezira," *MGWJ*, LXXVIII (1934), 448–55; and L. Ginzberg, "Yezirah, Sefer," in *Jewish Encyclopedia*, Vol. XII (New York, 1906).

On Merkavah mysticism, see the works of G. Scholem listed above; P. Bloch, "Die Yordei Merkavah, die Mystiker der Gaonenzeit, und ihr Einfluss auf die Liturgie," *MGWJ*, XXXVII (1893), 18–25, 69–74, 257–66, 305–11; A. Aptowitzer, "Bet Ha-Mikdash She-Lemaalah Al Pi Ha-Aggadah," *Tarbitz*, II (1931), 137–53, 257–87; and H. Odeberg, *III Enoch or the Hebrew Book of Enoch*, edited and translated with introduction, commentary, and critical notes (Cambridge, 1928)

On Eleazar of Worms, see I. Kamelhar, *Rabbenu Eleazar Mi-Germaiza Baal Ha-Rokeaḥ* (1930); E. A. Urbach, *Baalei Ha-Tosafot: Toledoteihem Ḥibbureihem Ve-Shitatum* (Jerusalem, 1955), pp. 321–41; and J. Dan, "Safrut Ha-Yiḥud Shel Ḥasidei Ashkenaz," *Kiryat Sefer*, XLI (1965–66), 533–44.

CHAPTER FIVE

## THE KIMḤIS, TIBBONIDES, AND OTHER PROVENÇAL SCHOLARS

For historical background on the Jewish community of Provence, see R. Emery, *The Jews of Perpignan in the Thirteenth Century* (New York, 1959), and B. Z. Benedict, "Le-Toledotav Shel Merkaz Ha-Torah Be-Provans," *Tarbitz*, XXII (1951), 85–109.

The *Massaot* of Benjamin ben Jonah of Tudela was translated into English under the title *The Itinerary of Benjamin of Tudela,* together with a critical edition of the Hebrew text and a commentary, by M. N. Adler (London, 1907).

Abraham bar Ḥiyya's *Hegyon Ha-Nefesh* was edited by J. Freimann (Leipzig, 1860) and translated into English by G. Wigoder under the title *Meditation of the Sad Soul* (New York, 1969). His *Megillat Ha-Megalleh* was edited by A. S. Poznanski, with an introduction by Julius Guttmann (Berlin, 1924). On his philosophy, see G. Vajda, "Les Idées théologiques et philosophiques d'Abraham ben Ḥiyya," *Archives d'histoire doctrinale et littéraire du moyen âge,* XV (1946), and L. D. Stitskin, *Judaism as a Philosophy: The Philosophy of Abraham bar Ḥiyya* (New York, 1961). On Abraham bar Ḥiyya's scientific influence, see S. Gandz, "Studies in Hebrew Mathematics and Astronomy," *PAAJR,* IX (1939), 5–55.

Joseph Kimḥi's *Shekel Ha-Kodesh* was edited, with an English translation, introduction, and notes, by H. Gollancz (Oxford, 1919). Excerpts from his *Sefer Ha-Berit* are reprinted in J. D. Eisenstein's *Otzar Vikkuḥim* (New York, 1928). On his work, see A. Geiger, *Nachgelassene Schriften* (Breslau, 1877), and L. I. Newman, "Joseph ben Isaac Kimḥi as a Religious Controversialist," in *Jewish Studies in Memory of Israel Abrahams* (New York, 1927).

David Kimḥi's *Perush Al Ha-Torah* (Commentary on the Pentateuch) is printed in numerous editions of the Hebrew Bible. Critical editions of his commentaries to other books of the Bible include *The Commentary of David Kimḥi on Isaiah (1–39),* edited, with Kimḥi's allegorical commentary on Genesis, by L. Finkelstein (New York, 1926); *The Commentary of Rabbi David Kimḥi on Hosea,* ed. H. Cohen (New York, 1929); *The Commentary of Rabbi Kimḥi on Psalms (42–72),* ed. S. Esterson (Cincinnati, 1935); *Der Kommentar des David Qimchi zum Propheten Nahum,* ed. W. Windfuhr (Giessen, 1927); *Perush Radak al Tehillim (107–150),* ed. J. Bosniak (New York, 1954). On Kimḥi's apologetic works, see F. Talmage, "R. David Kimḥi as Polemicist," *Hebrew Union College Annual,* XXXVIII (1967), 213–35.

I. Abrahams (ed.), *Hebrew Ethical Wills,* 2 vols. (Philadelphia, 1926), contains the Hebrew text and an English translation of Jehudah Ibn Tibbon's *Tzevaah* (I, 51–93), as well as many other interesting "testaments" of Jewish figures.

On Samuel Ibn Tibbon, see G. Vajda, "An Analysis of the *Ma'amar Yiqqawu Ha-Mayyim* by Samuel ben Judah ibn Tibbon," *Journal of Jewish Studies,* X (1959), 137–51.

On the Hebrew poets of Provence, see L. Zunz, "Die jüdischen Dichter der Provence," in his *Zur Geschichte und Literatur* (Berlin, 1845), pp. 459–83; E. Renan and A. Neubauer, *Les Rabbins français du commencement du XIVe siècle* (Paris, 1877); *idem, Les Écrivains juifs français du XIVe siècle.*

Joseph Ezobi's *Kaarat Kesef* was edited, with introduction and notes, by M. Steinschneider in his *Musar Ha-Sechel* (Berlin, 1860), and translated into English by J. Freedman, *JQR,* VIII (1896), 534–40.

On Abraham Bedersi, see T. Kroner, *De Abraham Bedaressii vitae e operibus* (Breslau, 1868), and Renan-Neubauer, *Les Rabbins français,* pp. 707–19. See also J. Schirmann, "Iyyunim Be-Kovetz Ha-Shirim Veha-Melitzot Shel Avraham Bedersi," in *Sefer Yovel Le-Yitzḥak Baer* (Jerusalem, 1951), 154–73.

On Isaac Gorni, see Renan and Neubauer, *Les Rabbins français,* pp. 719–23, and J. Schirmann, "Isaac Gorni, poète hebreu de Provence," *Lettres Romanes,* III (Louvain, 1949), 175–200.

CHAPTER SIX

## THE BEGINNING OF THE WAR AGAINST RATIONALISM

An excellent treatment of the controversy revolving around the works of Maimonides at the end of the twelfth and in the first half of the thirteenth centuries is to be found in D. J. Silver, *Maimonidean Criticism and the Maimonidean Controversy 1180–1240* (Leiden, 1965), which also contains an exhaustive bibliography. An older account is J. Sarachek, *Faith and Reason: The Conflict over the Rationalism of Maimonides* (Williamsport, Pa., 1935). The controversy is also discussed in Y. Baer, *A History of the Jews in Christian Spain,* 2 vols. (Philadelphia, 1960, 1966).

On Maimonides' first significant critic, Rabbi Abraham ben David, see I. Twersky's fine study, *Rabad of Posquières: A Twelfth Century Talmudist* (Cambridge, 1962), with its full bibliography.

For the work of Meir Abulafia, see H. Brody, *Shirim U-Michtavim Mi-Rabbi Meir Halevi Abulafia,* in *Yediot Ha-Machon Le-Ḥeker Ha-Shirah Ha-Ivrit,* II (1936), 1–90. Abulafia's poems and letters are here annotated by Brody. For a study of Abulafia's literary work, see I. Ta-Shmah, "Yetzirato Ha-Safrutit Shel Rabbi Meir Ha-Levi Abulafia," *Kiryat Sefer,* XLIII (1967–68), 569–76; XLIV (1968–69), 429–35; XLV (1969–70), 119–26.

The poems of Meshullam ben Solomon Dapiera were published by H. Brody in *Yediot Ha-Machon Le-Ḥeker Ha-Shirah Ha-Ivrit,* IV (1938), 1–117.

# *The Jewish Community of Medieval Italy*

CHAPTER ONE

## THE FOUR ELDERS; SHABBETAI DONNOLO; *JOSIPPON*

For a bibliography of older works on the Jews and Jewish history and culture in Italy, see G. Gabrieli, *Italia Judaica* (Rome, 1924). More recent works include P. Orano, *Gli ebrei in Italia* (Rome, 1938); G. Bedarida, *Ebrei d'Italia* (Livorno, 1950); C. Roth, *A History of the Jews in Italy* (Philadelphia, 1946); *idem, The Jews in the Renaissance* (Philadelphia, 1959); and M. Shulvass, *Ḥayyei Ha-Yehudim Be-Italyah Be-Tekufat Ha-Renaissance* (New York, 1955). See also A. Milano, *Storia degli ebrei in Italia* (Turin, 1963).

Shabbetai Donnolo's *Ḥakemani* was published by D. Castelli under the title *Il Commento di Sabbetai Donnolo sul libro della Creazione* (Florence, 1880). For his medical writings, see S. Munter, *Kitvei Ha-Refuah Le-Rabbi Shabbetai Donnolo* (Jerusalem, 1949). On Donnolo's work, see H. Friedenwald, *The Jews and Medicine* (Baltimore, 1944); S. Munter, "Shabbetai Donnolo Ha-Rofe," *Ha-Rofe Ha-Ivri*, XIII (1946), 86–97; *idem, Rabbi Shabbetai Donnolo* (Jerusalem, 1949); and G. Nebbia, *Donnolo: Medico e Sapiente Ebreo di Oria* (Rome, 1963).

Recent studies on *Josippon* include Y. Baer, "Sefer Yosippon Ha-Ivri," in *Sefer Dinaburg* (Jerusalem, 1949), pp. 178–205, and D. Flusser, "Meḥabber Sefer Yosippon: Demuto U-Tekufato," *Tziyyon* (1953), pp. 89–103.

CHAPTER TWO

## THE BEGINNINGS OF LITURGICAL POETRY IN ITALY; THE *SEFER YUḤASIN*

For the liturgical poems of Shephatyah and Amittai, see B. Klar (ed.), *Megillat Aḥimaatz* (Jerusalem, 1944–46).

For the liturgical poems of Solomon Ha-Bavli, see D. Goldschmidt, "Mi-Piyyutov Shel Rabbi Shelomoh Ha-Bavli," *Tarbitz*, XXIII (1952), 203–9.

For recent studies on the *Tanna De-Be Eliahu*, see E. A. Urbach, "Le-Sheelat Leshono U-Mekorotav Shel Sefer Seder Eliahu," *Leshonenu*, XXI (1957), 35–49, and M. Margaliot, "Le-Beayat Kadmuto Shel Seder Eliahu," in *Sefer Asaf* (Jerusalem, 1953), pp. 370–90.

The Midrash Sefer Zerubbabel is included in *Midreshei Geulah*, ed. J. Ibn Shemuel (Kaufman) with introduction and notes (Jerusalem, 1944). On the legend of Armilus, see M. Buttenwieser, *Outline of the Neo-Hebraic Apocalyptic Literature* (Cincinnati, 1901), and M. Friedlaender, *Der Antichrist in den vorchristlichen jüdischen Quellen* (Göttingen, 1901).

The Sefer Yuḥasin is reprinted, with introduction and notes, in B. Klar (ed.), *Megillat Aḥimaatz* (Jerusalem, 1944–46). For studies of this work, see D. Kaufmann, "Die Chronik des Achimaaz von Oria," in his *Gesammelte Schriften*, III (Frankfurt-am-Main, 1915), 1–55; M. Salzman, *The Chronicle of Aḥimaaz* (New York, 1924); and J. Marcus, "Studies in the Chronicle of Aḥimaaz," *PAAJR*, V (1933–34), 85–93.

CHAPTER THREE

## ITALIAN JEWRY COMES OF AGE; ANATOLI'S *MALMAD HA-TALMIDIM*

On Nathan bar Yeḥiel and his work, see A. Kohut, *Aruch Completum*, 8 vols. (Vienna and New York, 1878–92), Introduction and Supplements; A. Geiger, *Nachgelassene Schriften*, III (Breslau, 1877), 267–74; H. Vogelstein and P. Rieger, *Geschichte der Juden in Rom*, I (Berlin, 1896), 357–66; and "Nathan ben Jeḥiel," in *Jewish Encyclopedia*, IX (New York, 1905).

On the development of Jewish cultural life in Italy, see C. Roth, *A History of the Jews in Italy* (Philadelphia, 1946).

On Jacob Anatoli and his work, see I. Bettan, "The Sermons of Jacob Anatoli," *Hebrew Union College Annual*, XI (1936), 391–424; E. Renan and A. Neubauer, *Les Rabbins français du commencement du quatorzième siècle* (Paris, 1877), pp. 580–89; C. Roth, *The Jews in the Renaissance* (Philadelphia, 1959); and M. Steinschneider, *Die hebräischen Übersetzungen des Mittelalters und die Juden als Dolmetescher* (Berlin, 1893), 57–62.

CHAPTER FOUR

## SCHOLARS AND POETS IN ITALY

On Moses ben Solomon of Salerno and his polemics against Christianity, see S. Simon, *Mose ben Salomo von Salerno und seine philosophischen Auseinandersetzungen mit den Lehren des Christentums* (Ohlau, 1932).

On the Jewish community of Rome, see H. Vogelstein and P. Rieger, *Geschichte der Juden in Rom*, 2 vols. (Berlin, 1895–96); A. Berliner, *Geschichte der Juden in Rom*, 2 vols. (Frankfurt-am-Main, 1893); and C. Roth, *A History of the Jews in Italy* (Philadelphia, 1946).

On the members of Anaw family and their work, see Vogelstein and Rieger, *op. cit.*, Vol. I; Berliner, *op. cit.*, Vol. II; M. Güdemann, *Geschichte des Erziehungswesen und der Kultur der Juden in Italien* (Berlin, 1884); and S. K. Mirsky, *Shibbolei Ha-Leket Ha-Shalem* (New York, 1966), Introduction.

On Hillel ben Samuel of Verona, see I. Elbogen, *Annuario di studi ebraici*, II (1935–37), 99–105; I. B. Sermoneta, *World Congress of Jewish Studies: Synopses of Lectures*, IV (1961); I. Husik, *A History of Medieval Jewish Philosophy* (Philadelphia, 1916), pp. 312–27; and J. Guttman, *Philosophies of Judaism* (Philadelphia, 1964), pp. 197–200.

CHAPTER FIVE

## IMMANUEL OF ROME

The *Maḥberot* of Immanuel of Rome were issued in annotated editions by A. M. Habermann (Tel Aviv, 1950) and by D. Jarden (Jerusalem, 1957). Both editions also contain Immanuel's Italian poems. The poet's *Tophet and Eden* (*Hell and Paradise*) was translated into English, with introduction and notes, by H. Gollancz (London, 1921).

There is a fairly extensive literature on Immanuel. Among the more significant items are A. Geiger, "Der Dichter Immanuel, der Freund Dantes," *Jüdische Zeitschrift*, V (1867), 286–301; M. Güdemann, *Geschichte des Erziehungswesen und der Kultur der Juden in Italien* (Berlin, 1884), pp. 108–47; 314–16; W. Bacher, "Immanuel ben Salomos Eben Bochan," *MGWJ*, XXXIV (1885), 241–57; J. Chotzner, "Immanuel di Romi, a Thirteenth Century

Hebrew Poet and Novelist," *JQR*, IV (1892), 64–89; S. Bernfeld, "Rabbi Immanuel Romi U-Maḥberotav," *Aḥiasaf*, IV (1896), 19–43; D. Kaufmann, "Manoello et Dante," *REJ*, XXXVII (1898), 252–58; L. Modona, *Vita e opera di Immanuele Romano* (Florence, 1904); D. Kaufmann, *Gesammelte Schriften*, I (Berlin, 1908), 151–60; U. Cassuto, "Dante und Manoello," *Jahrbuch des Vereins für jüdische Geschichte und Literatur*, XXIV (1921–22), 90–121; M. Steinschneider, *Gesammelte Schriften*, I (Berlin, 1925), 271–308, 322–26; S. Morais, *Italian Hebrew Literature* (New York, 1926), pp. 9–51; I. Sonne, "Safrut Ha-Musar Veha-Pilosofia Be-Shirei Immanuel Ha-Romi," *Tarbitz*, V (1934), 324–40; S. H. Lewis, "Immanuel of Rome," *PAAJR*, VI (1935), 277–308; D. Jarden, "Iyyunei Lashon U-Melitzah Be-Maḥberot Immanuel," *Leshonenu*, XVII (1950–51), 12–28, 145–72; C. Roth, "New Light on Dante's Circle," *Modern Language Review*, XLVIII (January, 1953), 26–32; and *idem*, *The Jews in the Renaissance* (Philadelphia, 1950).

CHAPTER SIX

## THE ROMAN POETS; KALONYMOS BAR KALONYMOS

On the Roman poets Jehudah Siciliano and Joab, see L. Zunz, *Gesammelte Schriften*, Vol. III (Berlin, 1876), and H. Vogelstein and P. Rieger, *Geschichte der Juden in Rom*, Vol. I (Berlin, 1896).

On Naḥum, see M. Sachs, *Die religiöse Poesie der Juden in Spanien*, 2nd ed. (Berlin, 1901), and L. Zunz, *Literaturgeschichte der synagogalen Poesie* (Berlin, 1865). For texts of his poems, see H. Brody and M. Wiener, *Mivḥar Ha-Shirah Ha-Ivrit* (Leipzig, 1922), and J. Schirmann, *Ha-Shirah Ha-Ivrit Be-Sefarad Ube-Provans* (Jerusalem, 1956).

Kalonymos bar Kalonymos' *Even Boḥan* was edited by A. M. Habermann (Tel Aviv, 1956), and his *Iggeret Baalei Ḥayyim* by Y. Toforovsky (Tel Aviv, 1949).

On Kalonymos, see M. Steinschneider, *Gesammelte Schriften*, I (Berlin, 1925), 196–215; E. Renan and A. Neubauer, *Les Ècrivains juifs français du XIVe siècle* (Paris, 1893), pp. 417–60; J. Chotzner, "Kalonymos ben Kalonymos, a Thirteenth Century Satirist," *JQR*, XIII (1901), 128–46; I. Davidson, *Parody in Jewish Literature* (New York, 1907); and I. Sonne, "Iggeret Ha-Musar Le-Kalonymos ben Kalonymos," *Kovetz Al Yad*, new series, I (1936), 91–110.

On Jehudah Romano, see L. Zunz, *Gesammelte Schriften*, III (Berlin, 1876), 155–61.

# *Glossary of Hebrew Terms*

**Amora** (pl. **Amoraim**): The title given to the Jewish scholars of Palestine and especially of Babylonia in the third to the sixth centuries whose work and thought is recorded in the Gemara of the Talmud.

***atzilut***: Literally, "emanation." The term is used in Kabbalist literature to designate the emanation or radiation of the Divine through the *sefirot* (see ***sefirah***).

**Bet Ha-Midrash**: In the Talmudic age, a school for higher rabbinic learning where students assembled for study and discussion as well as prayer. In the post-Talmudic age most synagogues had a Bet Ha-Midrash or were themselves called by the term, insofar as they were places of study.

***derush***: Homiletical interpretation of Scripture.

**Gemara**: The second basic strand of the Talmud, consisting of a commentary on, and supplement to, the Mishnah.

***gematria***: A system of exegesis based on the interpretation of a word or words according to the numerical value of the constituent letters in the Hebrew alphabet.

***kinah***: In Biblical and Talmudic times, a dirge over the dead. Later the term came to be applied to a liturgical composition for the Ninth of Av dealing with the destruction of the Temple as well as with contemporary persecutions.

***kuntras***: Medieval Hebrew term for a notebook. In France the term was used for collected commentaries and, especially by the Tosafists, for Rashi's commentary to the Talmud.

***maaseh bereshit***: Literally, "work of creation." The term refers to the first chapter of Genesis, the exposition of which was one of the primary concerns of early Jewish mysticism.

***maaseh merkavah*:** Literally, "work of the chariot." The term refers to the first chapter of Ezekiel, the exposition of which constituted the second basic concern of early Jewish mysticism.

***mezuzah*:** A parchment scroll placed in a container and affixed to the doorposts of rooms occupied by Jews, in fulfillment of an injunction in the sixth chapter of Deuteronomy.

***musar*:** Traditional Jewish moral literature.

**Neilah**: The closing service of the Day of Atonement at sunset when, according to tradition, the gates of the Temple were closed and the heavenly "gates of judgment" are sealed.

***notarikon*:** A method of abbreviating Hebrew words and phrases by writing only single letters, usually the initials.

***paytan*:** A liturgical poet (see ***piyyut***).

***peshat*:** The plain, literal meaning of Scripture.

***pilpul*:** In Talmudic and rabbinic literature a clarification of a difficult point. Later the term came to denote a sharp dialectical distinction or, more generally, a certain type of Talmudic study emphasizing dialectical distinctions and introduced into the Talmudic academies of Poland by Jacob Pollak in the sixteenth century. Pejoratively, the term means hairsplitting.

***piyyut*** (pl. ***piyyutim***): A Hebrew liturgical poem. The practice of writing such poems began in Palestine, probably around the fifth century C.E., and continued throughout the ages, enriching the Jewish Prayer Book. Perhaps the greatest of the medieval writers of *piyyutim* were Solomon Ibn Gabirol and Moses Ibn Ezra.

***sefirah*** (pl. ***sefirot***): A technical term in Kabbalah, employed from the twelfth century on, to denote the ten potencies or emanations through which the Divine manifests itself.

***seliḥah*** (pl. ***seliḥot***): A special type of *piyyut* begging mercy and pardon for sin.

***takkanah*:** A regulation supplementing the law of the Torah.

**Talmud**: The title applied to the two great compilations, distinguished as the Babylonian Talmud and the Palestinian Talmud, in which the records of academic discussion and of judicial administration of post-Biblical Jewish law are assembled. Both Talmuds also contain Aggadah or non-legal material.

**Tanna** (pl. **Tannaim**): A teacher mentioned in the Mishnah, or in literature contemporaneous with the Mishnah, and living during the first two centuries C.E.

***tefillin***: Two black leather boxes fastened to leather straps worn on the arm and head by an adult male Jew, especially during the weekday morning prayer. The boxes contain four portions of the Pentateuch written on parchment.

**Targum** (pl. **Targumim**): The Aramaic translation of the Bible. There are three Targumim to the Pentateuch: Targum Onkelos, Targum Jonathan, and Targum Yerushalmi.

**Torah**: In its narrowest meaning, the Pentateuch. Torah is also known in Judaism as the Written Law. In its broader meaning, Torah comprises as well the Oral Law, the traditional exposition of the Pentateuch and its commandments developed in the late Biblical and post-Biblical ages. In its widest meaning Torah signifies every exposition of both the Written and the Oral Law, including all of Talmudic literature and its commentaries. The term is sometimes used also to designate the scroll of the Pentateuch read in the synagogue service.

***tzitzit:*** Threads intertwined with blue cords, the wearing of which on the corners of garments is ordained by Biblical law (Numbers 15:37–41).

***yeshivah*** (pl. ***yeshivot***): A traditional Jewish school devoted primarily to the study of the Talmud and rabbinic literature.

**Zohar**: The chief work of the Spanish Kabbalah, traditionally ascribed to the Tanna Simeon ben Yoḥai (second century) but probably written by the Spanish Kabbalist Moses de Leon at the end of the thirteenth century.

# Index


Aaron, 108, 156, 158
Aaron ben Meshullam, 79, 92, 104, 105
Abdul al-Latif, 118n
Abel, 177
Abelard, Peter, 108, 170
Aboab, Samuel, 223n
Abraham, 60, 63, 88n, 192
Abraham bar Ḥiyya Ha-Nasi, 80–82
Abraham ben Azriel, 152n
Abraham ben David of Posquières, 79n, 100, 101, 103
Abraham ben Moses ben Maimon, 112, 122n, 130n
Abu Aharon ben Samuel Ha-Nasi, 65, 136, 151, 160, 161, 162, 167, 196
Abulafia, Meir, 104, 105, 117–18
Abulafia, Todros, 96n, 104
Adam, Michael, 150n
Afendopolo, Caleb, 85
Aḥimaaz ben Paltiel, 6, 136, 152, 159ff
Albertus Magnus, 231
Albigenses, 77, 78, 111, 127, 128, 171, 201
Alconstantini, Baḥya, 83, 119, 130n
Alconstantini, Solomon, 119
Alexander of Macedon, 141
Alexander romances, 141–42
Alexandra, Queen, 145
Al-Farabi, 192
Alfasi, Isaac, 100
Alfonsi, Peter (Moses the Spaniard), 84, 85
Alḥarizi, Jehudah, 90n, 94, 97, 100n, 111, 115, 122, 160, 173n, 205, 209
*Al-Magesti, Ḥibbur Ha-Gadol Ha-Nikra*, 174n
Al-Mu'izz, 163
Amittai, 152, 153, 159, 165
*Ammudei Ha-Avodah*, 8n, 28n, 71n, 83n, 100n, 184n
Amram, 108
Anatoli, Jacob ben Abba Mari, 94, 173–80, 181, 193, 196
Anatolio (Anatolino ben Jacob), 181
Anaw, Benjamin ben Abraham, 184–87, 189
Anaw, Zedekiah ben Abraham, 183, 184
Antiochus, 142
Antipater, 148
Aquinas, Thomas, 231
*Aremat Ha-Ḥittim*, 219
Aristobulus, 107
Aristotelianism, 105, 106, 111, 124, 127, 128, 131, 141, 174, 190, 192, 197, 199, 215, 231, 232
Armilus, 158–59
Arnold of Brescia, 170
*Aruch* (Nathan bar Yeḥiel), 166–67
*Arugat Ha-Bosem*, 152n
Astruc de Noves, Senior, 222n
Augustine, Saint, 85, 108
Averroes (Ibn Roshd), 94, 105, 106, 172n, 174, 183, 191n, 192, 197, 199, 222n, 231
Avicebron. *See* Solomon Ibn Gabirol
Azriel, 115

Bacher, Wilhelm, 168n
Baer, Yitzḥak (Fritz), 8n, 118n
*Bahir, Sefer Ha-*, 66
Baḥur, Elijah (Elijah Levita), 74n, 87
*Baruch Mi-Magentzah*, 36n
Basil I, 152, 162
Basnage, Jacques Christian, 140n
Bechor Shor, Joseph ben Isaac, 19n, 108
Bede, Saint, 108
Bedersi, Abraham, 96–98
Benedict X, Pope, 139n
Beneveniste, Sheshet bar Isaac, 104, 105n

*Ben Ha-Melech Veha-Nazir*, 130
Benjamin of Tudela, 78, 89, 183
*Ben Porat*, 231
Ben Sira, Book of, 200
*Berit, Sefer Ha-*, 84
Berliner, A., 15n, 17n
Bernfeld, Simon, 27n, 35n, 194n
*Bet Ha-Midrash*, 62n, 63n, 64n, 67n, 157n
*Bet Talmud*, 13n, 14n
*Bibliotheca Hebraea*, 95n
Biseliches, M., 109n
*Biur Ha-Shema Ha-Tivii*, 222n
Blanche of Castile, 112
Boccaccio, Giovanni, 208, 211, 216
Boethius, 231
Bonfils, Immanuel, 142n
Bosone, 203
Breithaupt, Friedrich, 150n
Brody, H., 217n
Brüll, N., 38n, 58n
Bruna, Israel, 76n
Buber, Solomon, 17n, 184n
Burckhardt, Jacob, 204n
Buxtorf, Johannes (the Elder), 4n

Cain, 177
Calo, Maestro. *See* Kalonymos bar Kalonymos
Can Grande della Scala, 203
Cardenal, Peire, 96
Carmoly, Eliakim, 6n, 192n
Castelli, David, 136n
*Catalogus Librorum Hebraeorum in Bibliotheca Bodleiana*, 6n, 187n
Cathari, 170
Cavalcanti, Guido, 201
Cento (Nathan Ha-Meati), 191
Charlemagne, 3, 6
Charles II (the Bald), 6, 222
Charles of Anjou, King, 183, 223, 227
Chronicles, Book of, 88n
*Chronik des Ahimaaz von Oria, Die*, 152n, 160n
Chwolson, Daniel, 139n, 217n
Cino of Pistoja, 203
*Commentaire sur le Sefer Jezira*, 59n
Conat, Abraham, 143n
Corinthians, First Letter to the, 108n
Cyrus, 140, 145

*Daat Elohim*, 194n
Daniel, Book of, 82, 157, 186
Dante Alighieri, 77, 201, 203, 204, 207, 215n
Dapiera, Meshullam ben Solomon, 115, 126
David, King, 50, 108, 140, 158, 174
David ben Meshullam, 25
David ben Saul, 113
*Decameron*, 211, 213, 216
*De Causis*, 128, 231
Delitszch, Franz, 143, 151, 215n
*Demaot, Sefer Ha-*, 27n, 35n
De Rossi, Giovanni Bernardo, 206n
*Deutsche Kaiserzeit*, 171n
*Dialogi* (Peter Alfonsi), 84
*Disciplina clericalis*, 84
*Divine Comedy*, 203, 207
*Divrei Ḥachamim*, 115n
Dominicans, 128, 171
Donin, Nicholas, 115, 184
Donnolo, Shabbetai ben Abraham, 38n, 60, 73n, 74n, 136–39
*Dor Dor Ve-Doreshav*, 6n, 13n, 18n, 58n, 103n, 167n, 183n, 194n
Dukes, Leopold, 9n, 83n
Dunash ben Labrat, 10, 20
Duran, Profiat, 107n

Ecclesiastes, Book of, 184
*Écrivains juifs français, Les*, 222n
Eleazar bar Nathan, 29, 35
Eleazar of Worms, 6, 37, 38, 38n, 46n, 60, 65, 66, 70–74, 160
*Eliahu Zuta*, 155n
Elijah, 88n, 154, 159
Elijah, Gaon of Vilna, 60
*Emek Ha-Bacha*, 6n
*Emunot, Sefer Ha-*, 59n, 66n
*Emunot Veha-Deot, Sefer Ha-*, 90
Ephraim bar Isaac, 28
Ephraim ben Jacob, 23n, 27n, 29
Epicurus, 192n
Epstein, A., 9n, 18n, 38n, 59n, 69n, 71n, 79n
Essenes, 58
Esther, Queen, 177
Esther, Scroll of, 206n
Eusebius, 108
*Even Boḥan* (Kalonymos bar Kalonymos), 224ff
*Even Boḥan* (Menaḥem ben Solomon), 168

*Even Ha-Ezer,* 29
Ezekiel, Book of, 58
Ezobi, Joseph, 95
Ezra (Biblical), 110
Ezra (Spanish mystic), 115
Ezra, Book of, 87

Falaquera, Shemtov, 93n, 122n
Filipowski, Herschell, 20n, 80n
Finkelstein, L., 8n
Folquet de Marseille, 96
*Fons Vitae,* 128
Franciscans, 128, 171
Francis of Assisi, Saint, 66
Frederick I, 24n
Frederick II, 24n, 128, 172–73, 174, 175n, 201
Freimann, J., 80n, 217n

Gabbai, Jacob ben Ezra, 127
Galatians, Letter to the, 108n
Galen, 215
*Galui, Sefer Ha-,* 83
Gebhardt, Em., 171n, 172n
Geier, M., 194n
Geiger, Abraham, 4n, 9n, 11, 15n, 83n, 136n
Genesis, Book of, 88n, 108, 140
Gerondi, Jonah ben Abraham, 113, 114, 117, 118, 128, 131, 195
Gerondi, Zeraḥyah Ha-Halevi (Zeraḥyah Ha-Levi), 100, 101
Gershenson, M., 208n
Gershom, Rabbenu, 6–8, 11, 12, 17, 79n
Gershom of Damascus, Rabbi, 66
*Geschichte die Erziehungswesen und der Kultur der abendländischen Juden, Die,* 37n, 43n
*Geschichte der Juden, Die,* 78n, 111n, 192n
*Geschichte der Juden in Rom, Die,* 139n, 155n, 167n, 183n, 202n
*Geschichte des Alten Testaments in die christlichen Kirche, Die,* 108n
*Geschichte des Materialismus, Die,* 172
Ghirondi, M., 6n
Ginzberg, L., 155n
*Ginzei Nistarot,* 128n, 129n, 130n
*Ginzei Schechter,* 155n
Gnostics, 58, 59, 118
Godfrey of Bouillon, 15, 16
Goldenthal, J., 80n
Gollancz, H., 83n
Gorni, Isaac ben Abraham, 97–100
*Gottesdienstlichen Vorträge der Juden, Die,* 140n, 143n, 155n
Gracian. *See* Ḥen, Zeraḥyah
Graetz, Heinrich, 35, 74n, 78n, 111n, 155, 192n, 194n, 195n
*Graetz-Jubelschrift,* 168n
Gregory IX, Pope, 128
Gross, H., 100n, 101n, 105n, 183n
Grünbaum, A., 58n
Güdemann, Moritz, 37, 43n, 139n, 155, 158n, 183n, 192n, 194n
*Guide for the Perplexed, A (Moreh Nevuchim),* 45n, 88n, 93, 94, 105, 109, 111, 112, 113, 114, 115, 116, 118, 120, 121, 122, 124, 125, 126, 127, 128, 142, 173, 174, 175, 176, 181, 182, 191, 192, 195, 196, 199, 200, 209
Guittone d'Arezzo, 202
Günzburg, Baron David, 143n, 173n

*Hachraah, Sefer Ha-,* 20
*Ḥadashim Gam Yeshanim,* 73n
Hadassi, Jehudah ben Elijah, 73n
Hai, Gaon, 166n
*Ḥakemani,* 38n, 73n, 74n, 136–39
*Halachot Gedolot,* 51
Halberstam, S. J., 112n, 114, 119, 196n
Halevi, Jehudah, 60n, 90, 96, 219
Ḥananiah ben Teradyon, Rabbi, 40
Ḥanina ben Dosa, Rabbi, 118
Harkavy, Abraham Elijah, 73n, 141n
*Hassagot,* 79n, 100, 101, 103n
Hatch, E., 108n
*Ḥayyei Ha-Nefesh,* 64
Ḥayyuj, Jehudah ben David, 10, 13, 82, 168
Hayyut, Z., 205n
*Hebräische Berichte über die Judenverfolgungen während der Kreuzzüge,* 23n, 29n, 30n
*Hebräischen Übersetzungen des Mittelalters und die Juden als Dolmetscher, Die,* 142n, 222n
*Hechal Rabbati (Sefer Merkavah, Pirkei De-Rabbi Ishmael),* 151n
*Hechalot Rabbati,* 62, 63n

*Hegesippus*, 142
*Hegyon Ha-Nefesh, Sefer*, 81
*Ḥemdah Genuzah*, 194n, 196n
Ḥen, Zeraḥyah ben Isaac ben Shealtiel (Gracian), 190n, 191–94, 200, 203, 205, 206, 207, 209
Herod, 142, 148
Hillel ben Jacob, 27
Hillel ben Samuel of Verona, 129n, 131n, 192n, 193n, 194–200
*Hillels aus Verona Tagmulei Ha-Nefesh*, 194n
*Histoire des Juifs* (Basnage), 140n
*Historia de prelis*, 142
*Ḥochmat Ha-Nefesh*, 74n
*Ḥofes Matmonim*, 15n
Homer, 77, 106, 107
*Ḥoni Ha-Meagel*, 199
Hosea, 177
*Ḥotam Tochnit*, 96n
*Ḥovot Ha-Levavot*, 83, 89, 90
Hyrcanus, King, 145, 146

*Ibbur, Sefer Ha-*, 80n, 81
Ibn Aknin, Joseph, 105
Ibn Alfachar, Jehudah ben Joseph, 123, 124, 125, 126, 128n, 129
Ibn Daud, Abraham, 15, 20, 136n, 144
Ibn Ezra, Abraham, 14n, 15, 20, 82, 83, 87, 167, 168, 184
Ibn Ezra, Moses, 209n, 219
Ibn Gabir, Joseph, 93n
Ibn Gabirol, Solomon (Avicebron), 60, 83, 89, 90, 128
Ibn Ḥasdai, Abraham, 104, 130, 130n
Ibn Jannaḥ, Jonah, 10, 13, 90
Ibn Kaspi, Joseph, 22n, 223
Ibn Matkah, Jehudah ben Solomon Ha-Kohen, 173
Ibn Pakuda, Baḥya ben Joseph, 89
Ibn Roshd. *See* Averroes
Ibn Saruk, Menaḥem, 10, 20, 168
Ibn Tibbon, Jehudah ben Saul, 79, 89, 90, 91, 92, 95
Ibn Tibbon, Samuel, 88n, 90, 92, 93, 109, 111, 113n, 122, 142, 173, 174
Ibn Yaḥya, Tam, 143, 144, 145, 149n
*Iggeret Baalei Ḥayyim*, 227ff
*Iggerot Kenaot*, 92n, 104n, 115n, 117n, 120n, 123n, 124n, 128n, 129n, 195n
*Iggerot Shadal*, 74n, 152n, 153n
*Iliad*, 106
Immanuel of Rome, 185, 191, 200, 201–17
*Imrei Daat*, 193n
*Influence of Greek Ideas and Usages on the Christian Church, The*, 108n
Innocent III, Pope, 84, 127, 128, 171
*Inquisitio Sapientiae*, 173n
Isaac, 177, 192
Isaac bar Samuel, 58
Isaac bar Sheshet (Ribash), 19n
Isaac ben Asher, 18
Isaac ben Jacob, 66
Isaac ben Jehudah, 12
Isaac ben Mordecai (Majestro Gajo), 191, 195
Isaac ben Shalom, 26
Isaiah ben Joseph, 64, 173n
Isaiah ben Samuel Devash (Muel), 97n, 98
Ishmael, Rabbi, 91n
Isidore of Seville, 108
*Italian Hebrew Literature*, 205n
*Italie mystique, L'*, 171n

Jacob, 108, 177
Jacob ben Reuben, 85
Jacob ben Yakir, 12
James I, 119, 130n
Jehudah bar Kalonymos, 65, 70n
Jehudah ben Meir Ha-Kohen (Sir Leontin), 6
Jehudah Ḥasid (Jehudah the Pious), Rabbi, 37, 38, 46n, 57, 58, 59n, 64, 65, 66, 69, 70, 71, 72n, 73n, 74n, 75, 110
Jellinek, A., 59n, 62n, 63n, 83n, 157n
*Jenseits von Gut und Böse*, 172n
Jerome, Saint, 85
Jesus, 107, 108, 172, 177
*Jewish Antiquities*, 142
*Jewish Wars, The*, 142, 144
Joab (Joab ben Yeḥiel?), 220
Job, Book of, 87, 193
Jonah, 192
Jonathan Ha-Kohen, 93, 94
*Josef Bechor Shor der letzter nordfranzösischer Bibel-Exeget*, 19n
Joseph ben Gorion, 142, 144, 145, 146, 149
Joseph ben Todros Ha-Levi, 121, 122, 123, 129

Joseph Ha-Kohen, 6n
Josephus, Flavius, 142, 144, 146
*Josippon,* 139–50, 151, 153, 160, 165, 166
*Juden in Deutschland während des Mittelalters, Die,* 4n
*Jüdisch-deutsche Chrestomathie,* 58n
Julius Caesar, 146
Juspa Shamash, 57n

*Kaarat Kesef,* 95
*Kabbalah, Sefer Ha-* (Abraham Ibn Daud), 15, 20, 136n, 144
*Kaiser Friedrich II,* 172n
*Kalilah Ve-Dimnah,* 188, 227
Kallir, Eleazar, 25, 153, 154, 168, 184
Kallisthenes, 141
Kalonymos bar Kalonymos, 202n, 222ff
Kalonymos ben Jehudah, 26
Kalonymos ben Meir, 96n
Kara, Joseph ben Shimeon, 4n, 9, 10–11, 14, 18
Kara, Shimeon, 9
Karaites, 73n, 85, 123, 194
Karo, Joseph, 217
Kaufmann, David, 4n, 18n, 94n, 105n, 152n, 160n
*Kavod, Sefer Ha-,* 69, 73n
*Kelimmat Ha-Goyyim,* 107n
*Ketav Tamin,* 25n, 69n, 72n, 73n, 75, 76n
Kimḥi, David, 70n, 88, 121, 123, 124, 128n, 129
Kimḥi, Joseph ben Isaac, 83, 84, 85, 87, 89, 90
Kimḥi, Moses, 87, 88
Kisch, A., 115n
*Kitab al-Rasa'il* (*Sefer Iggerot*), 104n, 105n, 117n
Kohut, A., 167n
*Kovetz Teshuvot Ha-Rambam,* 110n
*Kultur des Renaissance in Italien, Die,* 204n
*Kultur und Sitten: Geschichte der italienischer Geistlichkeit im X und XI Jahrhundert,* 139n
*Kuzari,* 60n, 90

Lambert, M., 59n
Landauer, Meyer, 69n
Landshuth, L., 8n, 28n, 29n, 71n, 83n, 100n, 184n
Lange, F. A., 172
Lattes, Isaac, 13n
Leo (author of *Historia de prelis*), 142
Leonardo of Pisa, 80
Lessing, Gotthold Ephraim, 172n
Levita, Elijah (Elijah Baḥur), 74n, 87
Levy, Y., 141n, 142n
*Likkutim Mi-Rav Hai Gaon,* 75n
Lipschütz, E. M., 9n, 15n
*Literaturgeschichte der synagogalen Poesie, Die,* 6n, 28n, 29n, 69n, 153n, 184n, 220n, 221n
Littmann, M., 4n
*Logic* (Aristotle), 174n
Louis IX (Saint Louis), 112, 130
Luria, Solomon, 6n, 65n
Luther, Martin, 15, 171n
Luzzatto, Samuel David, 11, 74n, 152n

*Maalot Ha-Middot,* 184, 187–90
*Maamar Ha-Emunah,* 182
*Maamar Teḥiat Ha-Metim,* 103, 104
*Maarechet Elohim,* 60n
*Maasei Nissim,* 16n, 57n
Maccabees, Books of, 142
*Madda, Sefer Ha-,* 113, 115, 116, 120, 128, 231
Maestro Gajo (Isaac ben Mordecai), 191, 195
*Mahalach Shevilei Ha-Daat,* 87
*Maḥberet He-Aruch,* 165, 168
*Maḥberot* (Immanuel of Rome), 191n, 201–17
*Maḥzor Minhag Roma,* 220
Maimonides (Moses ben Maimon), 45, 57n, 69, 75, 80n, 88, 88n, 92, 93, 94, 103, 104, 105, 106, 109, 110n, 111, 112, 113n, 114n, 115, 116, 118, 119, 120, 121, 122, 124, 125, 126, 127, 128, 130, 142, 173, 174, 175, 176, 178, 181, 182, 191, 192, 193, 194, 195, 196, 197, 199, 205, 206, 207, 208, 209, 214, 231
*Malkiel, Sefer,* 157n
*Malmad Ha-Talmidim,* 173n, 174n, 175–80, 181

Mann, Jacob, 68n
Mann, Menaḥem, 144n
*Maor, Sefer Ha-*, 101
Markon, W., 155
Marx, Alexander, 83n
*Masechat Purim*, 202n, 223, 224n, 227
*Maskiyyot Kesef*, 96n
*Masoret Seyag La-Torah*, 104n
*Massa Ge Ḥizzayon*, 185–87, 202n
Matthew, Gospel according to, 107n
*Matzref Le-Ḥochmah*, 6n, 65
*Megillat Ha-Megalleh*, 82
*Megillat Setarim*, 38n
*Megillat Yuḥasin*. See *Yuḥasin, Sefer*
Meir, Rabbi, 91n
Meir ben Samuel, 18
*Mélanges de la philosophie juive et arabe*, 174n
*Melo Chofnajim*, 136n, 137n
Menaḥem bar Ḥelbo, 4n, 9, 10, 14, 18
Menaḥem ben Amiel (Messiah ben David), 158–59
Menaḥem ben Jacob, 26n
Menaḥem ben Solomon, 168
Menaḥem ben Zeraḥ, 7n
Mendelssohn, Moses, 109n
*Meor Enayim*, 143n
Mercury, Philip, 203n
*Merkavah, Sefer* (*Hechal Rabbati, Pirkei De-Rabbi Ishmael*), 151n
*Meshichah Veha-Tishboret, Ḥibbur Ha-*, 80
Meshullam ben Jacob, 89
Messiah ben David (Menaḥem ben Amiel), 158–59
Messiah ben Joseph (Neḥemiah ben Ḥushiel), 158–59
*Metaphysics* (Aristotle), 128
Metatron, 158
Michael Scotus, 174, 175, 181
Michelet, Jules, 169
*Michlol*, 88
*Midrash Alfa Beta De-Rabbi Akiba* (*Otiot De-Rabbi Akiba*), 62n
*Midrash Ha-Ḥochmah*, 173n
Midrashim, 9, 14, 18, 51, 67, 116, 141, 154, 155, 157, 163, 164, 167, 195, 199, 223
*Midrash Otiot Ha-Mashiaḥ*, 158n
*Midrash Rabbi Simeon ben Yoḥai*, 67
*Midrash Va-Yosha*, 158n
*Mikdash Meat*, 217n, 231n
*Milḥamot Adonai* (Abraham ben Moses ben Maimon), 112, 122n, 130n
*Milḥamot Ha-Shem* (*Sefer Ha-Teshuvot*, Jacob ben Reuben), 85
*Milḥemet Ḥovah*, 84n, 85n, 89n
*Minhag Avot* (*Tanya*), 187n
Mishnah, 17, 94, 118, 175
*Mishneh Torah*, 80n, 93, 103, 105, 110n, 113n, 118, 120, 125
*Mi-Sifrutenu Ha-Atikah*, 155n
*Mitzvot Gadol, Sefer* (*Semag*), 110n, 111n
*Mivḥar Ha-Peninim*, 83, 84n, 90
Modona, Leonello, 204n
Mohammed, 172
Morais, Sabato, 205n
*Moreh Ha-Moreh*, 93n
*Moreh Mekom Ha-Moreh*, 115n, 126, 126n, 127n, 129n
*Moreh Nevuchim*. See *Guide for the Perplexed, A*
Morvyn, Peter, 150n
Mosconi, Jehudah Leon ben Moses, 144, 145
Moses, 11, 20n, 38n, 107, 108, 110, 110n, 156, 158, 172
Moses bar Kalonymos, 5–6, 8, 65
Moses ben Jacob of Coucy, 110–11
Moses ben Naḥman. *See* Naḥmanides
Moses ben Solomon of Salerno, 181, 182
Moses Ha-Darshan, 79n, 166n
*Moses Ha-Darshan aus Narbonne*, 79n
Moses of Beaucaire, 222n
Moses the Spaniard (Peter Alfonsi), 84, 85
*Moznayim*, 168
Muel (Isaiah ben Samuel Devash), 97, 98
Muenster, Sebastian, 81, 87, 88, 150n
Munk, S., 174n, 226n
*Musiv*, 126, 216

Nahavendi, Benjamin, 73n
Naḥmanides (Moses ben Naḥman), 60, 114n, 115, 117, 118, 119, 120, 195, 200
Naḥum, 221
Naḥum Ish Gimzo, 199
Nathan bar Yeḥiel, 166–67
Nathan Ha-Meati (Cento), 191
Nebuchadnezzar, 158
Nehemiah, Book of, 87
Neḥemiah ben Ḥushiel (Messiah ben Joseph), 158–59
Neo-Platonism, 60, 232
Neubauer, A., 6n, 29n, 65n, 136n, 143n, 151n, 159
Nicholas IV, Pope, 191n
Nicholas de Lyra, 15
Nietzsche, Friedrich, 172
Nilus the Younger, 139
Nissan bar Moses of Marseilles, 110n
Nissim ben Jacob, 38n
*Novelino*, 172n

*Odyssey*, 106
Oesterreicher, Joseph, 84n
Origen, 108
Orshanski, I. G., 141n
*Otiot De-Rabbi Akiba* (*Midrash Alfa Beta De-Rabbi Akiba*), 62n
Otto the Great, 140n
*Otzrot Ḥayyim*, 85n
Ovid, 177

*Pardes*, 14n
Parḥon, Solomon ben Abraham, 165, 168
*Parschandatha*, 4n, 9n
Paul, Saint, 107, 108
Paur, T., 209n
*Pauvres de Lyon*, 171n
Pentateuch, 11, 13, 14, 18, 107, 108, 176, 206n
Perles, F., 182n, 222n
Perreau, Pietro, 206n
Peter Alfonsi (Moses the Spaniard), 84, 85
Petrarch, 77, 208, 209, 214
*Petrarka*, 208n
Philo of Alexandria, 59n, 73n, 107
*Physics* (Aristotle), 128
*Pirkei Avot*, 83, 118
*Pirkei De-Rabbi Ishmael* (*Hechal Rabbati, Sefer Merkavah*), 151n
Plato, 182, 215, 232
Plato of Tivoli, 80
Porges, N., 19n
Porphyry, 174n
Potebnya, A. A., 43n
Poznanski, S., 9n
*Practicia Geometriae*, 80
Proverbs, Book of, 83, 87, 176, 192n, 193, 206n
Provinciali, Jacob, 100n
Psalms, Book of, 88n, 206n
Pseudokallisthenes, 141n
Pure Brethren, 227, 228
Pythagoras, 192

*Quellen zur Geschichte der Juden in Deutschland*, 27n, 35n

*Rabbins français du commencement du quatôrzième siècle, Les*, 96n, 97n, 100n
*Rabbi Shelomoh Yitzḥaki*, 9n, 15n
*Rabbi Shimeon Kara Veha-Yalkut Shimeoni*, 9n
Rabinowich, M., 100n
Rapoport, Solomon Judah, 9n, 80n, 116n, 155, 167n
Rashbam (Samuel ben Meir), 18, 19
Rashi (Rabbi Shelomoh ben Yitzḥak), 4n, 7n, 10, 11–16, 17, 18, 70n, 167
*Rashis Einfluss auf Nicolaus de Lyra und Luther*, 15n
Raymond of Toulouse, Count, 78, 80, 112
*Razayya, Sefer*, 74n
*Raziel, Sefer* (*Sodei Razayya*), 74, 75
*Razim, Sefer Ha-*, 200
Reifmann, Jacob, 69n, 101n
Renan, Ernest, 96n, 100n, 222n, 227n
Reuchlin, Johannes, 88, 95
Ribash (Isaac bar Sheshet), 19n
Rieger, P., 139n, 140n, 155n, 167n, 171n, 183n, 191n, 192n, 194n, 195n, 202n, 215n
Rieti, Moses, 217, 231n
*Rikmah, Sefer Ha-*, 90
Robert, Inquisitor of France, 130
*Rokeaḥ*, 71n, 72, 74, 75, 160

Romano, Jehudah Leon ben Moses, 230–31
Romans, Epistle to the, 108
Romulus, 140
Rosin, D., 18n, 19n
Rossi, Azariah dei, 143n
Rüdiger of Speyer, 4

Saadiah Gaon, 38n, 60, 90, 182
Sachs, Michael, 221
Sachs, S., 173n
*Safah Berurah,* 14n
Saladin, 172n
Samael, 178
Samson, 50
Samson of Sens, 105
Samuel, Book of, 10, 11
Samuel ben Kalonymos, 47, 69n
Samuel ben Meir (Rashbam), 18, 19
Samuel Ha-Kohen, 27
Samuel Ha-Nagid, 10, 144
Samuel Ḥasid, Rabbi, 57–58, 69n
Saporta, Samuel ben Abraham, 116n, 129
Satan, 108, 158, 163, 178
Schlosser, Friedrich Christoph, 77
Schulman, Eliezer, 108n
Schwartz, Y., 87n, 193n
*Seder Ha-Ḥachamim Ve-Korot Ha-Yamim,* 136n, 143n, 159n, 161n
*Sefer Ḥasidim,* 3n, 4n, 24n, 35–56
*Sefer Ha-Teshuvot (Milḥamot Ha-Shem),* 85
*Sefer Ha-Yovel Le-Naḥum Sokolow,* 9n, 108n
*Sefer Iggerot (Kitab al-Rasa'il),* 104n, 105n, 117n
*Sefer Shaashuim,* 105n
*Semag (Sefer Mitzvot Gadol),* 110n, 111n
*Shaarei Teshuvah,* 113n, 114n, 131
*Shaarei Tziyyon,* 13n
Shabbetai bar Solomon, 190n, 191, 192
*Shalshelet Ha-Kabbalah,* 20n, 38n, 57n
*Shamayim, Sefer Ha-,* 173n
*Shekel Ha-Kodesh,* 83, 84
Shelomoh ben Yitzḥak, Rabbi. *See* Rashi
*Sheloshah Baalei Ha-Massaot,* 80n
Shemtov Ibn Shemtov, 59n, 66n
Shephatyah, 151–52, 153, 159, 160, 162, 163, 165, 196
*Shesh Kenafayim,* 142n
*Shibbolei Ha-Leket,* 17n, 184
*Shiur Ha-Komah,* 200
*Shorashim, Sefer Ha-,* 88n, 90
*Shulḥan Aruch,* 217
Siciliano, Jehudah, 219
Siegfried, K., 15n
*Sifrut Yisrael,* 183n
Silano of Venosa, 163, 164
Simeon ben Rabban Gamaliel, Rabbi, 118
Simeon Ha-Pakoli, Rabbi, 65
Simon the Maccabee, 142, 145, 146
Sir Leontin (Jehudah ben Meir Ha-Kohen), 6
*Sodei Razayya (Sefer Raziel),* 74, 75
*Sod Ha-Galgalim,* 173n
*Sod Sechel,* 65
Sokolow, M., 84n
Solomon bar Abraham of Montpellier, 113ff
Solomon ben Jehudah Ha-Bavli, 154, 166
Solomon ben Samson, 29, 31
Solomon Petit, 195
Soncino, Gershom, 217
Song of Songs, 117, 206n, 209
*Sorcière, La,* 169n
Steinschneider, Moritz, 66n, 80n, 85n, 91n, 100n, 114n, 126n, 139n, 142n, 167n, 168n, 173n, 175n, 182n, 183n, 187n, 192n, 194n, 195n, 222n, 227n
Stobbe, Otto, 4n
*Synagogale Poesie des Mittelalters, Die,* 24n, 35n, 151n

*Taam Zekenim,* 92n, 93n, 104n, 129n, 195n, 196n
*Taanot,* 182
*Tagmulei Ha-Nefesh,* 194n, 195n, 196–98
*Taḥkemoni,* 90n, 94n, 205, 209
Taku, Moses, 25n, 69n, 72n, 73n, 75, 76
Talmud, 7, 8, 11, 12, 13, 14, 17, 19, 20, 26, 46, 51, 58, 83, 84, 91n, 103, 107, 116, 120, 124, 130, 141, 167, 175, 176, 184, 195, 199, 200, 223

Tam, Rabbenu Jacob, 18, 19, 20, 23, 38n, 58
Tamah, Mordecai, 96n
*Tanna De-Be Eliahu*, 154–55, 157
*Tanya* (*Minhag Avot*), 187n
*Ta'rikh Yosippus al-Yahudi*, 150n
*Tefillot Rabbi Shimeon ben Yoḥai*, 158n
*Tehillah Le-Mosheh*, 141n
Tertullian, 108
*Teshuvah, Sefer*, 38n
*Teshuvot Ḥachmei Tzarefat Ve-Lutir*, 5n, 7n
*Teshuvot Ha-Ramban*, 92n, 93n, 94n, 111n
*Teshuvot La-Notzrim*, 89n
*Tikkun Middot Ha-Nefesh*, 89
*Tikvat Enosh*, 87n, 193n
Titus, 145
*Tofet Veha-Eden, Ha-*, 206, 207n, 215, 217
*Toledot Gedolei Yisrael*, 6n
*Torah Veha-Ḥayyim, Ha-*, 139n, 158n, 183n
Tosafists, 17ff, 36, 46, 167
Trani, Isaiah di (the Elder), 183n
Tschernichowsky, Saul, 36n
*Tzava, Sefer Ha-*, 101n
*Tzedah La-Derech*, 7n
*Tzevaah* (Jehudah Ibn Tibbon), 90–92
*Tzurat Ha-Aretz*, 81

*Verzeichnis der hebräischen Handschriften der königlichen Bibliothek zu Berlin*, 66n
Vespasian, 145
*Vikkuaḥ*, 89n
*Vikkuaḥ Ha-Ramban*, 85n
Virgil, 158n, 177
Vogelstein, H., 139n, 140n, 155n, 167n, 171n, 183n, 191n, 192n, 194n, 195n, 202n, 215n

Waldenses, 78, 170
Walter, N., 19n
Weiss, I. H., 6n, 13n, 14n, 18n, 103n, 167n, 183n, 194n
*Weltgeschichte für das deutsche Volk*, 77
*Wider die rauberischen und mörderischen Rotten der Bauern*, 171n
Wiener, M., 76n
Wiener, S., 87n
William of Auvergne, 111n
Wistinetzki, Jehudah, 36n, 37
Wolf, Johann Christoph, 95n
Wolfram of Eschenbach, 5
*Wormser Minhag-bücher, Die*, 71n

*Yad Ramah*, 104
*Yakar, Sefer Ha-*, 139n
*Yalkut Shimeoni*, 9
Yeḥiel ben Joseph, 114
Yeḥiel ben Yekutiel, 184, 187–90
Yeraḥmiel ben Solomon, 143
*Yesodot Ha-Techunah*, 174n
*Yetzirah, Sefer*, 59, 60, 61, 73, 74n, 137, 138, 200
*Yikkavu Ha-Mayyim*, 109
*Yirah, Sefer Ha-*, 83, 113n, 131n
Yordei Merkavah, 62, 63, 64
*Yuḥasin, Sefer* (*Megillat Yuḥasin*), 6, 136, 151, 152, 153, 159–64, 166

Zabara, Joseph, 105n, 160
Zechariah ben Said al-Yemini al-Yisraeli, 149–50
Zeraḥyah Ha-Levi (Gerondi, Zeraḥyah Ha-Levi), 100, 101
Zerubbabel, 140
*Zerubbabel, Sefer*, 157–59
*Zikkaron, Sefer*, 83
Zunz, L., 6n, 17n, 19n, 24, 28n, 29n, 35n, 69n, 70n, 76n, 95, 100n, 140n, 143n, 151n, 153n, 155n, 183n, 184n, 220n, 221n, 226n, 227n, 231n
*Zur Geschichte der jüdischen Poesie*, 143, 151n
*Zur Geschichte und Literatur*, 17n, 19n, 95, 100n, 183n

This book was set in eleven point Janson, it was composed, printed and bound by Kingsport Press, Kingsport, Tennessee, the paper is 'Lock Haven' Offset, manufactured by the Hammermill Paper Company. The design is by Edgar J. Frank. Initial design is by Edward F. Zink.

Date Due